T0340311

THE FUTURE OF THE LIBERAL ORDER

This book brings together some of the finest minds of social science to answer the great questions about the future of the liberal order.

With contributions from the world of economics, sociology, political science, management, international relations, and the humanities, this book provides a unique series of insights. Chapters explore the great questions of our time as they relate to the future of the liberal international and domestic order. Contemporary issues such as populism, authoritarianism, trust and social cohesion, the future of global governance, finance, religion, and citizenship are addressed along with geopolitical implications and with a balance between expert authority and open-minded critique.

It will be essential reading for students, scholars, and reflective practitioners across the human and social sciences.

Helmut K. Anheier is Professor of Sociology and past president at the Hertie School, Germany, and on the faculty of the Luskin School of Public Affairs, University of California, Los Angeles, USA.

THE FUTURE OF THE LIBERAL ORDER

The Key Questions

Edited by Helmut K. Anheier

Routledge
Taylor & Francis Group

LONDON AND NEW YORK

Cover image: Emilia Birlo is an artist who splits her time between
Berlin and Los Angeles. www.atelier-birlo.com

First published 2022
by Routledge
4 Park Square, Milton Park, Abingdon, Oxon OX14 4RN

and by Routledge
605 Third Avenue, New York, NY 10158

Routledge is an imprint of the Taylor & Francis Group, an informa business

British Library Cataloguing-in-Publication Data
A catalogue record for this book is available from the British Library

Library of Congress Cataloging-in-Publication Data
Names: Anheier, Helmut K., 1954– editor.
Title: The future of the liberal order: the key questions/edited by
Helmut K. Anheier.
Description: 1 Edition. | New York, NY: Routledge, 2022. |
Includes bibliographical references and index.
Identifiers: LCCN 2021054652 | ISBN 9780367772321 (hardback) |
ISBN 9780367772307 (paperback)
Subjects: LCSH: Social sciences–Forecasting. | Liberalism–Forecasting. |
Twenty-first century–Forecasts.
Classification: LCC H61.4 .F87 2022 | DDC 320.51–dc23/eng/20220207
LC record available at https://lccn.loc.gov/2021054652

ISBN: 978-0-367-77232-1 (hbk)
ISBN: 978-0-367-77230-7 (pbk)

Typeset in Bembo
by Deanta Global Publishing Services, Chennai, India

CONTENTS

FIGURES

TABLES

CONTRIBUTORS

Lisa Anderson is Shotwell Professor of International Relations Emerita at the Columbia University School of International and Public Affairs, New York, USA. She served as president of the American University in Cairo from 2011 to 2016 and has published widely on Middle East studies and public policy.

Helmut K. Anheier is Professor of Sociology and past president of the Hertie School, Berlin, Germany, Adjunct Professor of Social Welfare at the University of California, Los Angeles (UCLA), USA, and Editor-in-chief of *Global Perspectives*.

Roland Bernecker is Visiting Professor, Chair of Cultural Management at Brandenburg University of Technology, Germany. Previously, he was secretary-general of the German Commission for UNESCO (2004–19). His research interests include the history and future of liberalism, cultural leadership, global governance, and narrative theory.

Beverly Crawford Ames is Professor Emerita of Political Science at the University of California, Berkeley, USA, and former director of UC Berkeley's Center for German and European Studies. She has published widely on international and comparative political economy, the causes of cultural conflict, and the politics of migration and refugee protection.

Howard Davies is Professor in the School of International Affairs at Sciences Po, Paris, France, where he teaches masters courses on financial regulation and central banking. He is also Chair of the NatWest Group and Inigo Insurance.

Nabil Fahmy is Founding Dean of the School of Global Affairs and Public Policy at the American University in Cairo, Egypt, expert on public policy issues in Africa and the Arab World, and a career diplomat.

Alexandru Filip is Postdoctoral Fellow at the University of Mainz, Germany. He obtained his PhD at the University of Bremen, Germany, in 2017, and was previously Research Associate at Jacobs University Bremen, Germany, and Postdoctoral Fellow for the Dahrendorf Forum at the Hertie School, Berlin, Germany.

Ronald Grätz is Secretary-General of ifa (Institut für Auslandsbeziehungen) in Germany. Before taking up his current position, he was director of the Goethe-Institut in Portugal, having held various positions previously at Goethe-Instituts in Munich, Cairo, Göttingen, Barcelona, and Moscow.

Mark Juergensmeyer is Professor of Religious Studies and William F. Podlich Distinguished Fellow at Claremont McKenna College, California, USA, and Distinguished Professor Emeritus of Sociology and Global Studies at the University of California, Santa Barbara, USA.

Inge Kaul is Senior Fellow at the Hertie School, Berlin, Germany, and Non-resident Fellow at the Center for Global Development, Washington, DC, USA, and served previously as Director of the Human Development Report Office and the Office of Development Studies at the United Nations Development Programme (UNDP).

Kishore Mahbubani is Distinguished Fellow at the Asian Research Institute, National University of Singapore (NUS), former Singapore diplomat, founding Dean of the Lee Kuan Yew School of Public Policy, NUS, and author of eight books including *Has the West Lost It?* (2018) and *Has China Won?* (2020).

Wolfgang Seibel is Professor of Politics and Public Administration at the University of Konstanz, Germany, and Adjunct Professor of Public Administration at the Hertie School, Germany. His latest book is *Collapsing Structures and Public Mismanagement* (2021).

Rudolf Stichweh is Professor of Sociology at the Forum Internationale Wissenschaft and the Bonn Center for Dependency and Slavery Studies at the University of Bonn, Germany. His latest book is *Democratic and Authoritarian Political Systems in 21st Century World Society* (2021).

Linda Yueh is Fellow in Economics at St. Edmund Hall, University of Oxford, UK, Adjunct Professor of Economics at London Business School, UK, and Visiting Professor at LSE IDEAS, UK. She is the author of *The Great Economists: How Their Ideas Can Help Us Today* (2018).

Jan Zielonka is Professor of Politics and International Relations at the University of Venice, Italy, and the University of Oxford, UK. His last book *Counter-revolution.*

Liberal Europe in Retreat (2018) was awarded the 2019 UACES prize for the best book on Europe.

Michael Zürn is Director of the research unit Global Governance at WZB Berlin Social Science Center, Germany, and Professor of International Relations at Freie Universität Berlin, Germany. Since 2019, he has been spokesperson of the Cluster of Excellence "Contestations of the Liberal Script" (SCRIPTS).

PREFACE AND DEDICATION

What are the great questions of our time as they relate to the future of the liberal order? This is the question we posed to a diverse group of social scientists, inviting reflections based on their intellectual interests, curiosity, and expertise. In 1963 Ralf Dahrendorf ([1963] 1969, 51) famously wrote, "As the court-jesters of modern society, all intellectuals have the duty to doubt everything that is obvious, to make relative all authority, to ask all those questions that no one else dares to ask." Nearly 60 years later, we wonder what the questions are today, and what possible answers might be.

The contributions in this volume are in the spirit of this probing, questioning essence of intellectual life that Dahrendorf demanded so passionately. As part of the Dahrendorf Forum (www.dahrendorf-forum.eu), a collaborative project of the Hertie School and LSE IDEAS of the London School of Economics and Political Science from 2010 to 2020, we wanted to honor the legacy of Dahrendorf and invited contributors to address uncomfortable, nagging questions. We therefore left the format of the various contributions open. Some contributions are commentaries in essay form, others are more conventional research articles, and others yet are somewhere in between. They were first published in 2020–2021 in a special collection in *Global Perspectives* (https://online.ucpress .edu/gp/collection/228/Special-Collection-The-Great-Questions-of-Our -Time) and subsequently revised for this volume.

On Ralf Dahrendorf and his legacy

Dahrendorf (1929–2009) rose to academic fame in postwar Germany as a leading social scientist with a wide range of interests in sociology and political thought. As a professor at the University of Konstanz, he entered politics in the late 1960s, first as a liberal member of the Landtag of Baden-Württemberg in 1968 and then as a member of the German Bundestag in 1969. In 1970 he became a commissioner in the European Commission. From 1974 to 1984 he served as director of the LSE, and from 1987 to 1997 he was warden of St. Antony's College at the University of Oxford. He was appointed a member of Britain's House of Lords in 1993. During the last years of his life, he was also a senior member of the Social Science Center Berlin. (On Dahrendorf's life, see his autobiography (2003) and the biography by Maifort (2017).)

Liberalism and the liberal order were at the core of Dahrendorf's intellectual and political concerns. Today, Dahrendorf's vision of a democratic, liberal order remains as relevant as it was during the Cold War period and in the immediate aftermath of the collapse of communism. Pandemics, climate change, growing inequality, the rise of populist movements, and autocratic temptations as well as other recent developments have profound and far-reaching implications, affecting economies, entire societies, and their political culture.

Central to Dahrendorf's intellectual approach was the insight that liberal market societies are prone to tensions and conflicts of many kinds, and yet, at the same time, they are also in a better position to handle them. Unlike statist and autocratic forms of governance, liberal societies prevent conflicts from being bottled up. Instead, social and economic tensions become creative elements that allow societies to move forward. Smart forms of governance turn potential conflicts into opportunities and actual conflicts into solutions. If this is to happen peacefully, societies need some form of conflict management, an agreement among stakeholders that legitimate and viable solutions can be found.

What is the source of conflict in modern societies? For Dahrendorf, it is more than the obvious fact that individuals have different interests and expectations. Rather, it is the outgrowth of unavoidable tensions that modern societies have to negotiate and balance between the competing values of justice, liberty, and economic well-being, and between economic efficiency, identity, and security. How can societies become just, open, and prosperous? How can they aim for efficient economies where people have a sense of community and enjoy internal as well as external security?

Managing such tensions at the national level is hard enough under the best circumstances. It becomes even more challenging in a European Union of diverse member states, or in a United States that is divided along ethnic and socioeconomic lines. If we add to this the complex layers of subregional and international governance, the United Nations, and transnational regimes, it becomes clear that such tensions exist at multiple levels. Identifying latent and manifest tensions at these different levels, their conflict potential, and the options that present themselves for managing and resolving conflicts—that is the essence of Dahrendorf's thinking about the future of the liberal order.

Reflecting on the 1990s globalization spurt, Dahrendorf (1995) argued that growing and globalizing economies would create "perverse choices" for liberal democracies, which became known as the Dahrendorf Quandary: over time, staying economically competitive required either adopting measures detrimental to the cohesion of civil society or restricting civil liberties and political partici- pation. Later, Rodrik (2011) formulated a version of the Quandary in the form of a Trilemma, which rests on the incompatibility of democracy, national sover- eignty, and global economic integration: any two can be combined, but never all three simultaneously and in full. Is this indeed the case?

Dahrendorf feared a vicious cycle: economic globalization, increasingly decoupled from national processes, undermines the nation-state, hence national sovereignty, and, in turn, threatens democracy through loss of legitimacy and the rise of populist opposition groups. While neomercantilist economic policies may strengthen the nation-state, even democracy, they may also ultimately lessen economic growth and competitiveness. By contrast, while open economies may benefit some parts of the population, usually those with higher socioeconomic status, they may at the same time undercut the prosperity of others, even entire regions, weakening social cohesion and commitment to liberal democracy, even though the gross domestic product increases.

Some 25 years ago, Dahrendorf anticipated grave dangers in these tensions and saw the shadow of growing authoritarian temptations arising in increasingly divided societies. Dahrendorf's (1995, 4) great question was and remains in the early twenty-first century, how could countries manage "to square the circle between growth, social cohesion and political freedom"?

References

Dahrendorf, Ralf. (1963) 1969. "Der Intellektuelle Und Die Gesellschaft." In Philip Rieff (ed.). *On Intellectuals*. Garden City: Doubleday. (reprint; originally published 20 March, 1963 in *Die Zeit*).

Dahrendorf, Ralf. 1995. "Economic Opportunity, Civil Society and Political Liberty." UNRISD Discussion Paper 58. Geneva: United Nations Research Institute for Social Development.

Dahrendorf, Ralf. 2003. *Über Grenzen. Lebenserinnerungen*. Munich: C.H. Beck.

Maifort, Franziska. 2017. *Ralf Dahrendorf. Eine Biographie*. Munich: C.H. Beck.

Rodrik, Dani. 2011. *The Globalization Paradox: Why Global Markets, States, and Democracy Can't Coexist*. New York: W. W. Norton & Company.

ACKNOWLEDGMENTS

This volume is the result of countless exchanges and debates with many scholars and policy experts that took part in the Dahrendorf Forum, a ten-year-long joint initiative by the Hertie School in Berlin and the London School of Economics and Political Science (LSE). Funded by Stiftung Mercator, the purpose of the Forum was to honor and advance the intellectual legacy of Ralf Dahrendorf, a British-German sociologist, politician, and public intellectual. Initially a British-German collaboration, the Dahrendorf Forum soon grew into a broader European and ultimately global project, drawing together a wide network from many different countries.

I would like to thank the co-directors of the Forum on the LSE side: Iain Begg, Kevin Featherstone, Robert Falkner, and Arne Westad, next to Mick Cox of LSE IDEAS, Mary Kaldor, and the previous LSE directors and presidents Anthony Giddens, Howard Davies, Craig Calhoun, Julia Black as well as the present director Dame Nemat Shafik. Among Hertie School faculty, special thanks go to Mark Hallerberg, Andrea Römmele, Wolfgang Ischinger, and the late Henrik Enderlein; to Gesa-Stefanie von Stillfried for managing the Dahrendorf Forum and for helping create the idea and the concept of this book; to Edward Knudsen, Charlotte Koyro, and Christoph Abels for research assistance; and to Anna Soczek for administrative support.

The present volume also owes its origins and evolution to a class I taught to undergraduates at UCLA's Luskin School of Public Affairs entitled "Foundations and Debates in Public Thought." This course is an exploration of major debates in public affairs that involve concepts and issues such as power and legitimacy, conflicts and justice, inclusion and exclusion, and questions about the role of the state, governance, the relationship between politics and policy, market systems and the modern corporation, civil society, and citizenship. In this respect, I would like to thank Dean Garry Segura for suggesting that I teach that course,

Jocelyn Guihama and Justin De Toro for their support in offering it, and especially the UCLA students for their challenging questions and many contributions along with four fabulous teaching assistants Jasmine Hennessy, Jason Plumer, Nataly Rios, and Kristen Brock-Petroshius.

With the exception of the introductory and the concluding chapters of this volume, the various chapter first appeared in a special collection of *Global Perspectives* (https://online.ucpress.edu/gp/collection/228/Special-Collection -The-Great-Questions-of-Our-Time). They were revised and updated for this book by the authors. In this respect, I would like to express my appreciation to David Famiano and Liba Hladik of the University of California Press.

Many thanks are due to my longtime collaborator and friend Regina A. List, who carefully edited all chapters with her impeccable skills as a researcher, writer, and editor, and saw the entire project to its conclusion.

Finally, I am grateful to the team at Routledge, in particular Terry Clague and Alexandra de Brauw.

1

THE FUTURE OF THE LIBERAL ORDER AND THE GREAT QUESTIONS OF OUR TIME

Helmut K. Anheier

Fraying trust in institutions, democratic backsliding, increasing inequality with persistent patterns of social exclusion, self-serving elites in the face of lower social mobility, political polarization, and rising authoritarian tendencies—all challenge the liberal democratic order. Already present before the COVID-19 pandemic, these trends seem to have gained added momentum. Many fear that current developments could permanently endanger democratic norms, tear the social fabric of societies apart, and threaten the liberal order at home as well as internationally.

This volume is about the future of the liberal order and some of the key questions provoked by the troubled state of the Western world. There are many critical issues, factors, and developments shaping the future of the liberal order that so many see in jeopardy. To find out which ones stand out, we posed the question to a diverse group of social scientists, inviting reflections based on their intellectual interests, curiosity, and expertise. In 1963 Ralf Dahrendorf ([1963] 1969, 51) famously wrote, "As the court-jesters of modern society, all intellectuals have the duty to doubt everything that is obvious, to make relative all authority, to ask all those questions that no one else dares to ask." Nearly 60 years later, we wonder what the questions are today and what possible answers might be.

The contributions in this volume are in the spirit of this probing, questioning essence of intellectual life that Dahrendorf demanded so passionately. As a concluding project of the Dahrendorf Forum (2010–20), a collaborative between the Hertie School and LSE IDEAS of the London School of Economics and Political Science, we invited contributors to address uncomfortable, nagging questions. We therefore left the format of the various contributions open. Some contributions are commentaries in essay form, others are more conventional research articles, and others yet are somewhere in between. Given this diversity, it is important to have a common understanding of what the liberal order means, what its origins and principles are, and what the nature of the current challenges that face Western countries is.

The liberal order

The liberal order, or as it is often referred to the international liberal order, is the long-term normative political, economic, and social product of two order-building developments. First, there is the modern inter-state order, based on the notion of sovereignty, reaching back to the Treaty of Westphalia in 1648, and today understood as an open and rules-based system enshrined in institutions such as the United Nations (UN) and the norms of multilateralism (Ikenberry 2011a, 56). Second, there is the domestic liberal order within national boundaries, spearheaded by the US and its European allies, that has meant open markets, democratic institutions, and the rule of law (Ikenberry 2011b, 6).

Historically both developments have been closely intertwined, but rarely in clear and linear ways. The combination of the domestic and the international order found its clearest expression in the policy blueprint of the Atlantic Charter (1941), signed by American President Franklin D. Roosevelt and British Prime Minister Winston Churchill in 1941. The Charter is widely regarded as the founding document of the international liberal order that emerged after World War II. It provided a legitimating platform for the UN, Marshall Plan, General Agreement on Tariffs and Trade (GATT), North Atlantic Treaty Organization (NATO), and the like as well as many international treaties and declarations that became part of what we know as the multilateral system today (Borgwardt 2005).

The Atlantic Charter drew on the four freedoms—freedom of speech, freedom of worship, freedom from want, and freedom from fear—President Franklin D. Roosevelt highlighted in his 1941 State of the Union Address to the combined session of the US Congress. The Charter was not a formal treaty but a statement of principles outlining the political and moral foundations for a more just, peaceful, and prosperous world to emerge after World War II. It laid out eight principles that are worth restating (in abbreviated form below) even today as they served as the major building blocks of the liberal order that emerged in the 1950s. That order came to include a growing number of countries over time, and even achieved hegemonic status after the Cold War:

- First, countries seek no aggrandizement, territorial or other;
- Second, there are no territorial changes that do not accord with the freely expressed wishes of the peoples concerned;
- Third, all peoples have the right to choose the form of government under which they will live;
- Fourth, there is equal access of all countries to trade and to the raw materials of the world which are needed for economic prosperity;

- Fifth, all nations collaborate in the economic field with the object of securing for all improved labor standards, economic advancement and social security;
- Sixth, peace will afford to all nations the means of dwelling in safety within their own boundaries and afford assurance that all people in all the lands may live out their lives in freedom from fear and want;
- Seventh, such a peace should enable all people to traverse the high seas and oceans without hindrance;
- Eighth, for realistic as well as spiritual reasons, countries must come to abandon the use of force and disarm.

Born in a time of war and a reaction to all forms of totalitarianism, the Atlantic Charter envisioned a world where the comity of nations would be based on a set of commonly agreed principles: prominent among them the preservation of the territorial status quo, the right to self-defense, the right to self-governance, the rule of law, open societies, economic development and social welfare, free trade, and the preservation of the global commons. These principles, which first emerged sometimes centuries ago and developed over time, have served as the building blocks of the Western liberal order for more than three-quarters of a century.

Of course, since the end of World War II, there has been no shortage of instances when these principles were compromised and violated, even by those countries who propagated them the most. The colonial wars of the 1950s and 1960s and the South-East Asian wars are cases in point of many. In the post-Cold War era, prominent cases are NATO's military intervention in Serbia in 1999, conducted without a UN Security Council mandate, and the 2003 US-led Iraq invasion. As Kundnani (2017, 4) and others have argued, "Western powers were prepared to break the rules when they believed there was a compelling reason."

Yet, on the whole, the liberal order proved not only resilient, but it also expanded its reach and dominance over the decades. It spread, first, through economic and trade liberalization beginning in the 1950s with the establishment of GATT and culminating in the creation of the World Trade Organization in 1994. Second, it reached well beyond the US and UK with the expansion in the number of democratic countries over time, during the 1980s and especially after the fall of the Berlin Wall and then the Soviet Union. Third, in terms of international security, the number of NATO member states rose from 12 in 1949 to 30 by 2020. Fourth and finally, at the domestic level, the liberal order extended its reach generally, but most prominently through the expansion and deepening of the European Union in the 2000s.

However, by emphasizing and propagating the principles of the liberal order, on the one hand, and ignoring them when opportune, even for seemingly good or justifiable reasons, on the other, the West brought itself repeatedly into contradictory positions. These invited other powers like Russia (annexation of the Crimea in 2014, invasion of Eastern Ukraine) and China (increasing its stronghold control of Hong Kong) to violate the international rules as well or to interpret them as they see fit. Likewise, human rights violations in Western countries (e.g., police brutality in the US) has made it easier for autocrats to suppress internal opposition and more difficult for the West to maintain the moral high ground in the face of authoritarianism.

What is more, a problem of over-extension emerged in the field of human rights and genocide prevention, creating serious international tensions. For example, by pushing the policy of Responsibility to Protect and thereby reserving the right to intervene abroad (United Nations 2005), the Western powers seemingly enabled others like Russia to justify their own interventions (Ignatieff 2014). As Kundnani puts it, "by trying to make the liberal international order more 'liberal,'" the West ended up undermining both domestic and international orders. For Kundnani, "there can be a tension between 'liberalism' and 'order'" (2017, 6).

That the liberal order accumulated contradictions over time was not limited to international relations. The open and rules-based economic order became synonymous with neoliberalism. The liberal economic order became the de facto global order when financial and other market regulations eased, ushering in a brief era of hyper-globalization (Rodrik 2011; 2018) that has little regard for social and economic equity. That era came to an end with the global financial crisis of 2008–9, having pushed millions into precarious employment situations and cutting off life chances. Swapping the private debt of economic elite and banks for public debt at the expense of ordinary taxpayers invited distrust and ushered in a lingering legitimacy crisis.

Indeed, sociologists like Dahrendorf (1995) and international relations specialists like John Ikenberry (2018) argue that tensions and contradictions—and the various conflicts they generate—are part of the continuing evolution of the West, and the current challenges of the post-Cold War period are no different. Dahrendorf (1994) referred to the importance of ligatures—flexible cultural bonds between people based on shared identities and interests that find expression in a complex web of group affiliation—as essential in how modern societies manage conflicts and achieve stability amidst change. While these ligatures are the malleable social glue that holds societies together, they are nonetheless fragile and in danger of breaking up. As we will see in the next section, these tensions and contradictions have been key factors in both the emergence and the continued development of the liberal order in the first place. To follow up on this thought, it is useful to review, however briefly, the rise of the liberal order.

Historical accounts

Of course, the Atlantic Charter, the postwar multilateralism, the immense economic expansion, and the spread of democracy since the 1950s did not happen outside a longer-term historical context. They are as much part of the development of capitalism as they are intrinsically grounded in culture and value systems as well as power constellations that evolved over time. There is certainly no shortage of analyses and attempts to explain the rise of the West and with it the liberal order. Indeed, some of the "Great Books" of the social sciences deal with this question.

How can one not start with Karl Marx and his masterful analytic framework and political ideology? History is a history of class conflict, in which structure (systems of property rights) determines superstructure (systems of ideologies, religion, values). England—its economy and society—was the first to pass the threshold from feudalism to capitalism. It was the mirror for other countries in the West, and capitalism its trademark, ready to be exported. The Western order so seen was not at all about matters "liberal"; it was about property rights, profits, and conflict as the powerful bourgeoisie replaced the feudal order. A new class liberated from feudal chains is what made the West, and its rise was driven by conflicts over economic surplus.

That capitalism developed in the West both to a quantitative extent and in type, forms, and directions which have never existed before was the starting point of Max Weber's (2002) analysis of how value changes (from Catholicism to Protestantism) affect social and economic behavior, which in turn lead to the emergence of new institutions, in this case the capitalist economic system. Why did this development occur only in the West, and not in China, India, Persia, or other parts of the world? His general argument was that the rise of Protestantism, particularly in its Calvinist variety, was an important factor contributing to the rise of capitalism. The Western order was not about how liberal values mattered; it was how religion and economy matched, ushering in a period of world mastery through the rationalization of life conduct.

For Norbert Elias, writing a generation after Max Weber, and two genera-tions after Karl Marx, the central question was how Western civilization and its cultural system happened in the first place? In his seminal study, *The Civilizing Process* (1969), he linked modern notions of "civilized behavior" or being a "cul-tured person" to behavioral modifications in the sixteenth and seventeenth cen-turies, when standards regarding violence, sexual behavior, bodily functions, table manners and forms of speech were gradually transformed by increasing thresholds of shame and repugnance. This process developed from a nucleus in court etiquette outward, spreading locally, regionally, and internationally. It was, similar to Max Weber's argument, a dual process: competition among political and economic elites led to increased interdependence and more complex forms of organization and governance as commerce, trade networks, and diplomatic relations expanded. This required more standard-setting and greater predict-ability of human behavior, as increasingly frequent and complex interactions also heightened the potential for miscommunication and misunderstanding, hence conflict. The rise of the West is related to a successful system of devolved social self-organization for avoiding and managing conflicts.

We could easily add more about the longstanding emphasis in the social sci-ences on what accounted for the rise of the West and how the West differs from other civilizations, especially in relation to Islamic civilization and China as both were more advanced prior to the rise of the Occident. Apart from narrower Marxist interpretations, most accounts agree that there was nothing inevitable about that process, and that tensions and conflicts play an important role, be they class conflicts, religious debates, or competition among political elites.

One could also review accounts of the equally longstanding scholarly tradition announcing the demise of the West—from Oswald Spengler's *The Decline of the West* (1926) in the 1920s and Friedrich Hayek's *The Road to Serfdom* (1944) to Samuel Huntington's *The Clash of Civilizations* (1996). Among the more recent is Pankaj Mishra's (2017) *Age of Anger*, in which he argues that we are experiencing nothing less than the latest consequences of the long-term failure of the Enlightenment and of the modernization process that it unleashed on the world. While these accounts, and we could add others, may make some valid points, they are empirically flawed as they cannot explain hundreds of years of growth, resilience, and indeed dominance of the liberal order—despite many and often tragic setbacks.

So, like Karl Marx, Max Weber, and Norbert Elias before, the historian Niall Ferguson (2012) and, as we will see, political economists like Douglass North revisit a key question. Ferguson asks, what "allowed a minority ... originating on the western edge of Eurasia to dominate the world for the better part of 500 years?" (2012, 12). In posing the question, Ferguson reminds us that relative to China and India, the West was a backward region for centuries prior to the 1600s. For him, the answer is found in the significant competitive advantage the West developed and that allowed it to expand and dominate any other civilization.

Niall Ferguson, in deference to today's parlance, refers to the factors behind the West's comparative advantages as the "Six Killer Apps":

1. Competition—a decentralization of both political and economic life, which became a launchpad for nation-states and capitalism;
2. Science—a way of studying, understanding, and ultimately changing the natural world, which yielded military advantages too;
3. Property rights—the rule of law as a means of protecting private owners and peacefully resolving conflicts, which formed the basis for stable forms of representative government;
4. Medicine—a branch of science that brought major improvements in health and life expectancy;
5. Consumer society—a mode of material living in which general production and individual consumption play a central economic role in sustaining capitalism;
6. The work ethic—a value system or moral framework derived from, among other sources, Protestantism, which provides the glue for the dynamic and potentially unstable societies created by apps 1–5.

While the "six apps" amount to a considerable competitive advantage, they are also behind the volatile, uneven, and contradictory developments that are so characteristic of the liberal order as it emerged and endured over the centuries. Among this mix of contradictions are: domestic unity and disunity, peace and war among Western powers; colonialism and suppression of other societies and entire civilizations; development aid and humanitarian assistance and utter neglect and ignorance; calls for universal values such as human rights that are de facto violated by the actual behavior of Western societies; and so on.

The combination of these apps and their inherent contradictions creates fertile ground for both a loss of legitimacy as a global hegemonic civilization and a loss of collective self-confidence, both of which seem to be the situation today, according to Ferguson. Yet what are the processes that led to the killer apps, and how are conflicts and tensions negotiated and settled, and such that social, economic, and moral progress follows?

Put differently: how did Western societies manage to advance despite the many contradictions, conflicts, and setbacks and to reach as well as maintain what North et al. (2009) refer to as open access orders that, compared to limited access orders, are characterized by

- Higher political and economic development;
- Economies that experience much less negative economic growth and volatility;
- Richer and more vibrant civil societies with lots of organizations;
- Bigger, more decentralized governments and administrative systems;
- More widespread impersonal social relationships, including rule of law, secure property rights, a sense of citizenship, fairness, and equality—all aspects of treating everyone the same.

Such open access orders are based on a state holding the monopoly on the use of force, freedom of association, freedom to create organizations, competitive economic and political markets, and mobility. Yet open orders, like the liberal order, continue to run into difficulties and contradictions, and sustaining them means ongoing contestations in search of compromises and conflict settlements, especially during critical transition phases when economic inequalities rise and social mobility declines.

The role of elites in managing conflict and transitions is crucial throughout: why should elites transform the unique and personal privileges which they currently enjoy into impersonal rights shared more equally? Why should they share their largesse when they could even claim more? Or, less abstractly, in today's world: why should the economic elite, in this case the shareholders and CEOs of Amazon, Apple, Google or Facebook agree to a more equitable international taxation system and have them pay a fairer share? The answer lies in the creation of a credible protection of the rights elites hold, while extending rights to others under the promise of expanding economic benefits for all. That way, the promise of a continued and systematic rent creation can induce elites to share economic, social and political rights, thus making greater mobility possible and yielding a positive-sum outcome for elite and non–elite alike.

Of course, the approach taken by institutional economists like North et al. (2009) and Acemoglu and Robinson (2012) is abstract, yet can be illustrated by a brief look at the US following the reconstruction period of the 1870s. It was a period, not unlike today, with significant social and economic inequalities and limited state capacity to react. After the Civil War, unified national markets unleashed rapid economic development, leading to highly unequal access orders, soon dominated by few corporations which often abused their economic and political power ("robber barons"). The government at that time did not possess the institutions to control these "trusts," and an extractive, self-serving elite was on the verge of emerging. However, three activist presidents (Theodor Roosevelt, Republican; William H. Taft, Republican; and Woodrow Wilson, Democrat) working with Congress managed to forge and lead elite coalitions willing to effect change for a greater open access order while producing positive-sum outcomes acceptable to elites as well as non–elites. In other words, they saved the US from falling into the regressive trap.

This included first and foremost a series of major regulations: the Interstate Commerce Act of 1887, which introduced industrial standards; the Sherman Antitrust Act of 1890, which outlawed monopolistic business practices; the Hepburn Act of 1906, which created a regulatory agency to monitor market behavior; and the Clayton Antitrust Act of 1914, which defined unethical business practices, such as price-fixing, and upheld various rights of labor. The activist presidents also expanded centralized state capacity through the 16th Amendment and the creation of a federal income tax in 1913, and corrected democratic deficiencies in the Senate through the 17th Amendment, which ended the hold of local economic interests on state legislatures by disallowing the election of senators by state legislatures.

As a result of these corrective actions, the US managed the transition phase to an industrial market economy without regressing to a limited access order. However, while the outcome was ultimately a success, there was nothing inevitable about it. There is no automatic progression, and societies can, and do, regress. The liberal order is dynamic and subject to continuous as well as unexpected changes. It is intrinsically unstable, which is both a curse and a blessing.

For Daron Acemoglu and James A. Robinson (2019) the role of the state is critical, as the US example illustrates, or more precisely, it is the relationship between the state and society. Going back to the Hobbesian answer that a strong state or despot is needed to prevent unending conflict, they argue that such a state stifles society; by contrast, an absent state may mean liberty and bring comfort for some but dominance and misery for many. They suggest instead that both state and society must be strong and their relations carefully calibrated. The state (i.e., the elites that run it) must agree to its limits in terms of power and rent extraction, and society (i.e., the economic and social elites) must accept the limits of private privilege and the need for public goods production. Society "shackles" the Leviathan, and the Leviathan imposes norms on society.

As their book's title, *The Narrow Corridor*, suggests, Acemoglu and Robinson (2019) argue that achieving and maintaining a state–society balance is hard and requires the very compromises that North et al. (2009) speak of. It is in many cases easier to fall back to despotism (as Russia did under Putin) where the state becomes stronger and society weaker and inert. But nothing is certain, as Acemoglu and Robinson (2019) remind us: Poland and Hungary, which had been well under way to forging a society with a shackled Leviathan, are now drifting in the opposite direction towards despotism. In the long run, however, societies with shackled Leviathans have proven more successful economically and socially, and hence been able to benefit from the competitive advantages of Ferguson's "killer apps" toward greater progress.

In other words, the liberal order has been strong because both the state and society were. Yet, as mentioned, such success has been neither self-evident nor linear. And it is heavily contested. Depending on one's normative position, it is possible to write a history of the Western liberal order as positive as does Victor Hanson (2001), who proposes that the West's global dominance has been a force for good intimately linked to its faith in democracy and personal liberty, under-written by its military strength, or as negative as does Pnakaj Mishra (2017), who emphasizes a centuries-old history of ignorance, terror, and brutality meted out by Western elites. What then are the prospects of the liberal order?

The current challenges

Since the end of the Cold War, when for a very brief period, a sense of stability and superiority set in, as exemplified in the title of Francis Fukuyama's *The End of History* (1992), the liberal order has confronted many internal and external challenges, be it the rise of populism, mass migration, Islamic fundamentalism, a belligerent Russia, or the ascendance of China. In his 2018 essay, "The end of the liberal international order," Ikenberry identified two related challenges. The first is the crisis of governance and authority, and the second, the crisis of social purpose. Both are the result of a "slow-motion reaction to a deep transformation in the postwar liberal international project" (Ikenberry 2018, 18).

The crisis of governance and authority has its origin in the end of the Cold War, which loosened the ties between the Western countries, given that the immediate threat of Soviet domination was over. At the same time, the trilateral coalition—the US, Europe, and Japan—that had constituted the core of the international liberal order faced a very different world order, with new emerging powers pursuing new and divergent agendas and with complex global challenges such as growing economic and monetary interdependence, climate change, and terrorism. Ikenberry sees resolving the unsettled questions "who pays, who adjusts, who leads" (2018, 19) as the core challenge that remains unsettled.

Given the rise of China, the Western liberal order, especially the US, faces a dilemma between two traps: first the Thucydides's Trap, named after the Greek philosopher who studied the changing relationship between Athens and Sparta as Graham Allison (2017) does that between the US and China. It describes a situation in which a great power's position as hegemon is threatened by an emerging power and posits that there is a significant likelihood of war between the two powers, or at least a period of tensions and conflicts.

By contrast, the Kindleberger Trap (Nye 2017) refers to the proposition that the disasters that occurred during the 1930s were the result, at least in part, of the US's failure to take up the UK's role in providing global public goods once it had replaced the UK as the largest global power. With no one ensuring the provision of public goods, the international system collapsed into depression, genocide, and war. We should recall that domestically, governments produce public goods such as policing or clean drinking water, from which all citizens can benefit, and none are excluded. At the global level, public goods—such as financial stability, trade regimes, and security—are provided by coalitions led by hegemonic powers. Typically, small countries have little incentive to pay for such global public goods because their small contributions make little difference to whether they benefit or not. For them, it is rational to ride along for free. But the largest powers can see the effect and feel the benefit of their contributions. So, it is rational for the largest countries to lead. When they do not, global public goods are underproduced. When Britain became too weak to play that role after World War I, an isolationist US continued to be a free rider, with disastrous results. Relative to the US, Japan and Europe, how will China or other emerging powers like Brazil or India behave?

The second crisis, that of social purpose, is more domestic in its implications, but its forces are largely international in origin. It is the result of economic changes caused by globalization and digitalization plus a neglect of appropriate social policies to cushion the impact of these transformations on vulnerable population groups. Like the first, it is to some extent a crisis born out of success after the end of the Cold War. Beginning in the 1970s, successive policies reduced barriers to international trade and capital flows and ushered in an era of economic liberalism. It was a successful ideology for some but created serious problems for others.

A typical problem scenario that emerged from neoliberalism and was reinforced by the global financial crisis of 2008–9 are growing numbers of people with low-paying or precarious jobs and little hope of getting ahead; a growing share of people are stuck in a kind of limbo, earning too little to make ends meet, but too much to qualify for government support. Over time, they have become economically, socially, and culturally more isolated, strangers in their land as the title of Arlie Hochschild's (2018) book about the people living in southern Louisiana suggests. They have grown increasingly resentful of the prosperous economic and political elites in big cities and national capitals, and become vulnerable to appeals by neonationalist populists and aspiring authoritarians. This dynamic is most pronounced in the US, where it contributed to the election of Donald Trump as president, and in the UK, where it fueled support for Brexit, and has become a major political force in France and Italy. But, with much of the Western world having followed neoliberal policies, it is now afflicting all developed economies, dividing societies and stunting their development, as Ambar Narayan et al. (2018) argue.

The notion of a dual crisis challenging the liberal order provides the organizing principle for this volume. Implicit in both crises is the complexity of many of the issues involved, be it democracy, polarization, finance, or civil society. What is domestic and what is international or global interact in various and convoluted ways. This volume's separation between the domestic and the international liberal order is therefore meant rather loosely, and the various chapters typically connect the two.

The domestic liberal order

In our chapter, Alexandru Filip and I ask how the circle can be squared between economic globalization, social cohesion, and liberal democracy and provide an empirical test of two theorems of increasing relevance in the current international political economy. Dani Rodrik's (2011) impossibility theorem posits that democracy, national sovereignty, and global economic integration are mutually incompatible. In short, he argued that it is possible to combine any two of the three, but never have all three simultaneously and in full. A similar impossibility theorem was formulated by Dahrendorf (1995) who argued that a growing and globalizing world economy would create "perverse choices" for liberal democracies: over time, staying competitive required either adopting measures detrimental to the cohesion of civil society or restricting civil liberties and political participation. This chapter examines Rodrik's Trilemma across a sample of mainly developed market economies from 1991 to 2014, showing that it can be overcome in rare cases only, and that the tensions assumed by Dahrendorf's Quandary hypothesis build up to a considerable extent. The findings nevertheless provide considerable nuance, since individual country performance varies too significantly to support the broad assertions Rodrik and Dahrendorf make. While tensions inherent in the Quandary seem to be present in almost all countries, their acuteness or severity varies. In other words, countries can address the challenges of globalizing economies through appropriate policies.

Looking at the US primarily in her chapter, Beverly Crawford Ames takes a sociological and social-psychological approach to explore the reasons why the liberal order is in danger and what might be done to safeguard it. She argues that the decline of the liberal order can partly be attributed to the inherent limitations of liberalism itself, exacerbated in recent decades by neoliberal economic forces and digital technology. The liberal values of equality, tolerance, the rule of law, and rational debate chafe against the entrenchment of the neoliberal free market and its laissez-faire ideology, as well as the neglect of the human need for status, community, heroes, and the impulse to unleash passionate grievances. This chafing continues to open lesions in liberal institutions, exacerbated by disinformation and inequality.

Jan Zielonka explores the future of politics in his chapter, focusing on what effect the COVID-19 pandemic has had on the political "body" and how it might emerge from the crisis stronger rather than weaker. In response to the COVID-19 pandemic, governments around the world introduced measures that shattered our private lives, brought economic life to a virtual standstill, and threw into question the value of international organizations. Zielonka's chapter first shows how the political interventions undertaken throughout 2020–1 have crushed long-standing equilibria on such fundamental issues as the notion of a common good, the limits of individual freedom or the relationship between the state and markets. It then analyzes the battle of power and minds between the main political protagonists, and scrutinizes the policies applied by these actors and their implications for democracy. The final section tries to envisage a democratic politics suitable for the world of viruses, super-bugs, climate change, poverty, and hyper-connectivity.

Linda Yueh is concerned about what economic consensus might emerge now that support for neoliberalism seems to have been shaken. There are times in history when the consensus about our economic system breaks down. It happened after the Long Depression of the nineteenth century, and again in the twentieth century around the Great Depression of 1929–33, as well as after the Great Recession of 2008–9 that followed the global financial crisis. The COVID-19 pandemic, which has carried the risk of a deep downturn, has led governments to take extraordinary measures in all areas of our lives. This has further fueled the need to discuss how to rebuild the consensus about the most appropriate economic system for the twenty-first century as the great question of our time.

And if the economic consensus has been shaken, what about the future of democracy in light of today's polarized societies? This is the question Rudolf Stichweh addresses in his chapter that looks at divisive forces in contemporary societies and links them to the unfulfilled hopes of the revolutions at the beginning of modernity: the hopes for equality, freedom, and solidarity. Stichweh's chapter highlights, first, persistent inequalities that emerge in all the function systems of society and become divisive as soon as there arises a discontinuous split in the distribution of rewards, a split that makes it improbable that someone might switch from one to the other side of a distribution. There are, second, strong, asymmetrical dependencies that are connected to an escalation of controls by which persons and groups control resources wanted by others and furthermore build up controls regarding the actions, communications, exit options, and ways of perceiving the world available to these others. The more control dimensions are implied in a specific social relation, the stronger and more pervasive asymmetrical dependencies become and then definitely separate those who exercise controls from those who are objects of control. There is, third, the rise of sociocultural polarization that creates a split between significant subcommunities of a society, on the basis of which communities perceive the members of other communities as strangers and as dangers to the values one regards as essential for one's own community. Stichweh finally explains these societal divisions by studying them as forms of inclusion and exclusion. Inequalities come from the inclusion dynamics of social and economic systems: over time asymmetrical dependencies accumulate in institutions and groups that absorb persons that are being excluded from relevant participation. This, in turn, leads to polarizations based on reciprocal and totalizing exclusions by which communities define the members of other communities as radical "others."

The notion of citizenship is central to the liberal order. Lisa Anderson asks what citizenship's future is considering experiences in the Middle East. Globalization has eroded borders virtually everywhere in the world. The waning of the modern state as the world's default political unit has been reflected in the simultaneous expansion of supranational norms of human rights and contraction of legal, enforceable citizenship. The upheavals of the "Arab spring" provided eloquent testimony to both the appeal of rights-based political discourse and the catastrophic consequences of reliance on weakened and ineffectual states to enforce such rights. Governments and peoples across the Middle East and North Africa are abandoning citizenship as a sign of belonging and resorting to alternative and sometimes competing identities, from family and sect to class and social media communities, to secure political support and obtain life's necessities. While these social markers may provide access and even solace, they do not bode well for adherence to universal human rights.

State capacity, i.e., the ability of governments to deliver services and maintain administrative order, is essential for building and maintaining legitimacy that underpins the liberal order. Yet can we rely on public administration in these regards, inquires Wolfgang Seibel. Trust is the basis of delegated power, especially where government is entrusted with the protection of human security. Seibel's chapter addresses the question of how to calibrate theories about reliable, and thus trustworthy, public administration when identifying risk zones of unreliability. The relevance of such theorizing is underlined by buildings and bridges that collapse due to insufficient supervision of engineering by the relevant authorities or improper planning and risk assessment in the preparation of mass events such as soccer games or street parades. The basic argument is that conceptualizing differentiated causal mechanisms of organizational failure in public administration is useful for developing more fine-grained variants of conventional theories on "normal accidents" or "high reliability organizations." Appropriate theorizing on risk-increasing mechanisms within public administration needs to address standard pathologies of public bureaucracies and the inevitable trade-offs, such as the tensions between responsiveness and responsibility and between goal attainment and system maintenance, connected with their embeddedness in democratic and rule-of-law-based systems. This implies identifying points of intervention at which permissive conditions with the potential to trigger risk-generating human action can be neutralized and raising the threshold that separates risk-generating human action from actual disaster. These are, in turn, a prerequisite of trust-building when it comes to the reliability of public authorities tasked with the protection of human security.

Max Weber and others identified religion as a major element of the rise of the West. Yet what is the state or role of religion in Western societies today? This is the topic of Mark Juergensmeyer's essay. The rise of strident movements of religious nationalism seems to signal a resurgence of religion. But it can also be read as the last gasp of religiosity as it succumbs to the inevitability of secular globalization. Which is correct, has religion revived or is it in its death throes? Part of the issue is statistical: adherence to religion seems to be on the rise in some parts of the world (Islam in Africa, for instance), though on the decline in others (Christianity in Europe and increasingly in the US) and under attack in China. But part of the issue is definitional: what is meant by religious adherence—social identity or metaphysical belief? Scholarly attempts to define religion are various, though an interesting new definition is provided by the late sociologist, Robert Bellah (2011), in describing religion as "alternative reality." With that definition one can posit that religiosity is a fundamental part of the creative imagination, a constituent of culture as certain as art or music. The question then becomes not whether religion will survive, but in what way it will survive. The popular religious choice of Millennials, "none," may be consistent with the multicultural religiosity of the old Protestant liberals. Liberal Protestants have not disappeared but transformed into the bearers of a global morality and spiritual sensibility. Hence, as Juergensmeyer suggests, we may be witnessing the emergence of new forms of spirituality and ethical community that resonate with the alternative reality of traditional religious experience, but which has no name and no organization. It may become the global religion of the future.

Culture, as Norbert Elias and others remind us, is another core aspect of the liberal order. Yet how do culture and the liberal order relate? Roland Bernecker and Ronald Grätz retrace a significant transformation in our perception of liberty and liberalism, based on Isaiah Berlin's distinction between negative and positive liberty, and confirm its profound linkage to parallel conceptual shifts in our understanding of culture. The authors argue that these shifts reveal a particular dynamic in the increasing political colonization of the spaces which, in the cultural evolution of centuries, seemed destined to favor the continuous expansion of freedoms in the *longue durée*. The current emergence of new kinds of pressure such as tensions in global politics, the perceived success of authoritarian concepts of governance, and crises such as climate change and pandemics, risk significantly augmenting our acceptance of a limitation of freedoms. With its clarity and passion, Berlin's (2002) seminal text is an important reference for intellectual and political ambitions that position themselves in the perspective of a culture of liberty.

The international liberal order

"Is effective multilateralism still possible?" asks Inge Kaul. The world today witnesses a rising number of unmet global challenges, ranging from climate change, cyber-insecurity, disease outbreaks such as the COVID-19 pandemic, and excessive international financial instability, to terrorism and war. Why this, and why today? In her chapter, Kaul argues that the main reason is the present lack of a persuasive change vision indicating how states could have both secure policy-making sovereignty and effective multilateralism. Accordingly, she recommends forging consensus on a new operating principle of multilateralism called the "dual-compatibility principle," because it guides states on how to make multilateralism sovereignty-compatible and the exercise of sovereignty multilateralism-compatible. Judging from the numerous high-level policy pronouncements issued in response to recent global crises such as the COVID-19 pandemic and the rise in more violent weather patterns related to global warming, Kaul concludes that effective multilateralism is now more essential than ever before and more doable because the political will to realize mutual compatibility between multilateralism and sovereignty appears to exist.

What about a political vision in a globalized world? Michael Zürn asks whether the liberal order even needs one. Compelling visions of how political institutions can be effective and democratic in handling globalization problems is one of our most important predicaments. Political institutions were always deficient in that they were neither fully effective nor fully democratic. During the prime of liberal democracies, their problem-solving capacity was limited, and the process of making decisions approached democratic ideals at best. Yet the current predicament goes deeper. We lack a compelling vision of ideal political institutions for handling global problems such as climate change. In order to develop this argument, Zürn first develops two criteria for a compelling vision of ideal political institutions. In a second step he argues that neither of the two currently most crucial institutional visions provides convincing accounts for fulfilling these criteria. The chapter concludes by suggesting that the weaknesses of both sides of the debate contribute to polarization, thus making the predicament worse.

What about the future of the global financial system, a central component of the international liberal order as it emerged under neoliberalism and in the aftermath of the global financial crisis? For Howard Davies, the economic recession resulting from the COVID-19 pandemic will leave both governments and many private sector companies with a greatly increased debt burden. That will have severe consequences for the financial system. To work off the debt overhang, interest rates may be held down by central banks for a long period. Inflationary pressures have started off weak, but fiscal dominance may constrain central banks' freedom to raise interest rates if prices do rise strongly. Financial repression will add to the pressures on banks and other financial institutions. Major banks entered the crisis period with high capital ratios, but expected losses on loan portfolios will put some under strain. Less strongly capitalized new entrants may suffer disproportionately. Other likely changes are more rapid growth in digital financial services and a decline in cash usage. Central banks will probably issue their own digital currencies, which will make maintaining negative interest rates more achievable. At the same time the international financial system will be put under strain by global tensions generated by the crisis. In this complex environment it will be crucial for governments, central banks, and the banking system to collaborate closely, and for the European Union to bolster the Eurozone with long-planned but long-delayed reforms, in particular to promote a Capital Markets Union which could relieve pressure on banks' balance sheets.

If liberalism provided a value framework, does it mean anything today? Nabil Fahmy explores the need for a common social compact or conscience, which the global community seems to have lost. Through this realization, it is important to address issues of global, public order in order to learn from past mistakes and herald a new pathway forward for a more collective, more inclusive global community. This can be achieved through regenerating a collective "social conscience," one that has been lost in the middle of discussions of expenditure and wealth concentration in both liberal and illiberal public orders in the global community. Reflecting on the past for a better future allows for a change from "balance of power and authority"-driven systems to ones driven by different systems in an attempt to achieve a "balance of interest." The issues that arise are in handling and dealing with the common good of the general public and in resolving the intellectual question that divides everything between "liberal" or "illiberal," "democratic" or "authoritarian." All systems of public order are being challenged on a multiscalar level—domestically, regionally and globally—because they have not been able to respond to the needs or aspirations of their constituencies. That is why there is a need to find collective interests that do not necessarily need to be equal. This way, the paradigm shift from a "balance of power" to a "balance of interest" will minimize the marginalization that constituencies face on a global level. Ultimately, achieving interaction based on a global, common good will rebalance the individual ambitions that have been spearheading global interactions and collective interests needed for the twenty-first century global order and onwards.

Referring to geopolitical tensions, rivalries, and traps, Kishore Mahbubani uses the tools of Western empirical reasoning to analyze the origins and driving forces of the ongoing geopolitical contest between China and the US. He argues that the origins of the geopolitical contest lie in China's rapid growth from the Deng era, the relative socioeconomic decline of the US, and the failure of the US to work out a rational, comprehensive strategy for managing China's rise. In the fallout of the global COVID-19 pandemic, in which the relations between the two countries have been further strained, Mahbubani's essay suggests that the two countries can manage their geopolitical rivalry if they concentrate instead on five "noncontradictions" that also characterize their relationship: that between the fundamental national interests of both countries; in tackling climate change;

in the ideological sphere; in the American and Chinese civilizations; and in their worldviews.

Conclusion

Fourteen (sets of) authors pose 14 questions addressing economic globalization and global finance, social cohesion and polarization, liberal democracy and authoritarian tendencies, the future of citizenship and religion, state capacity, culture and liberty, the possibility of a new multilateralism, the role of political visions, and geopolitical rivalries. The authors in this volume examine these questions in both their domestic, nation-bound and their international aspects, as well as the connections between them. They approach them from political, economic, sociological, and cultural perspectives. Given the range of topics, the diversity of perspectives, and the intellectual breadth of the following chapters, it is, therefore, not surprising that their assessments and conclusions diverge. But finding differences and commonalities in the way we interpret the current situation and future of the liberal order, debating them, and questioning them again and again is an integral part of the very tradition that many see in jeopardy.

References

Acemoglu, Daron and James A. Robinson. 2012. *Why Nations Fail*. London: Profile Books.

Acemoglu, Daron and James A. Robinson. 2019. *The Narrow Corridor: States, Societies and the Fate of Liberty*. New York: Penguin.

Allison, Graham. 2017. *Destined for War: Can America and China Escape Thucydides's Trap?* New York: Houghton Mifflin Harcourt.

Bellah, Robert. 2011. *Religion in Human Evolution: From the Paleolithic to the Axial Age*. Cambridge, MA: Belknap Press, of Harvard University Press.

Berlin, Isaiah. 2002. "Two Concepts of Liberty." In Henry Hardy (ed.). *Liberty*, 166–217. Oxford: Oxford University Press.

Borgwardt, Elizabeth. 2005. *A New Deal for the World: America's Vision for Human Rights*. Cambridge, MA: Harvard University Press.

Dahrendorf, Ralf. 1963. "Der Intellektuelle und die Gesellschaft." *Die Zeit*, 20 March. Reprinted as "The Intellectual and Society," in Philip Rieff (ed.). 1969. *On Intellectuals*. Garden City: Doubleday.

Dahrendorf, Ralf. 1994. "Das Zerbrechen der Ligaturen und die Utopie der Weltbürgergesellschaft." In Ulrich Beck and Elisabeth Beck-Gernheim (eds.). *Riskante Freiheiten: Individualisierung in modernen Gesellschaften*, 421–436. Frankfurt am Main: Suhrkamp.

Dahrendorf, Ralf. 1995. *Economic Opportunity, Civil Society and Political Liberty*, UNRISD Discussion Paper 58, Geneva: United Nations Research Institute for Social Development.

Elias, Norbert. 1969. *The Civilizing Process, Vol.I. The History of Manners*. Oxford: Blackwell.

Ferguson, Niall. 2012. *Civilization: The West and the Rest*. New York: Penguin.

Fukuyama, Francis. 1992. *The End of History and the Last Man*. New York: Free Press.

Hanson, Victor Davis. 2001. *Why the West Has Won*. Allen Unwin

Hochschild, Arlie. 2018. *Strangers in Their Own Land: Anger and Mourning on the American Right*. New York: The New Press.

Hayek, Friedrich. 1944. *The Road to Serfdom*. Chicago: University of Chicago Press.

Huntington, Samuel P. 1996. *The Clash of Civilizations and the Remaking of World Order*. New York: Simon and Schuster.

Ikenberry, G. John. 2011a. "The Future of the Liberal Order." *Foreign Affairs*. May-June, 56–68.

Ikenberry, G. John. 2011b. *Liberal Leviathan: The Origins, Crisis, and Transformation of the American World Order*. Princeton: Princeton University Press.

Ikenberry, G. John. 2018. "The End of the Liberal International Order?" *International Affairs*, 94(1): 7–23. https://doi.org/10.1093/ia/iix241.

Ignatieff, Michael. 2014. "The End of Intervention?" presentation at Chatham House, London, March 19. https://www.files.ethz.ch/isn/178208/20140319AgeofIntervention.pdf

Kundnani, Hans. 2017. "What Is the Liberal International Order?" Liberal International Order Project. Policy Essay 17 (April). Washington, DC: The German Marshall Fund of the United States.

Mishra, Pankaj. 2017. *Age of Anger: A History of the Present*. New York: Penguin.

Narayan, Ambar, Roy Van der Weide, Alexandru Cojocaru, Christoph Lakner, Silvia Redaelli, Daniel Gerszon Mahler, Rakesh Gupta N. Ramasubbaiah, and Stefan Thewissen. 2018. *Fair Progress? Economic Mobility Across Generations Around the World*. Washington DC: World Bank.

North, Douglass, John Wallis, and Barry Weingast. 2009.*Violence and Social Orders: A Conceptual Framework for Interpreting Recorded Human History*. Cambridge: Cambridge University Press.

Nye, Joseph S. 2017, January 9. "The Kindleberger Trap." *Project Syndicate*. https://www.project-syndicate.org/commentary/trump-china-kindleberger-trap-by-joseph-s--nye-2017-01?barrier=accesspaylog. Accessed September 22, 2021.

Rodrik, Dani. 2011. *The Globalization Paradox: Why Global Markets, States, and Democracy Can't Coexist*. New York: W. W. Norton & Company.

Rodrik, Dani. 2018. "Populism and the Economics of Globalization." *Journal of International Business Policy*, 1: 12–33.

Roosevelt, Franklin D. 1941. Annual Message to Congress on the State of the Union. Washington, DC: The White House. https://avalon.law.yale.edu/wwii/atcmess.asp

Spengler, Oswald. 1926. *The Decline of the West*. New York: Knopf.

The Atlantic Charter. 1941. The Atlantic Conference: Joint Statement by President Roosevelt and Prime Minister Churchill, August 14, 1941. https://avalon.law.yale.edu/wwii/at10.asp

United Nations. 2005. *World Summit Outcome Document*. New York: United Nations. https://www.un.org/en/genocideprevention/about-responsibility-to-protect.shtml

Weber, Max, Peter R. Baehr, and Gordon C. Wells. 2002. *The Protestant Ethic and the "Spirit" of Capitalism and Other Writings*. New York: Penguin.

PART I

The domestic liberal order and fundamental issues

2

HOW TO SQUARE THE CIRCLE BETWEEN ECONOMIC GLOBALIZATION, SOCIAL COHESION, AND LIBERAL DEMOCRACY?

Alexandru Filip and Helmut K. Anheier

Introduction

At the beginning of the new millennium, an individual may have been forgiven for predicting an ever more globalizing, free, prosperous, and democratic world going forward in the coming decades. The financial crisis and global recession had not yet hit, the larger part of the European continent had adopted a common currency while the European Union (EU) witnessed its largest expansion to date, the fall of the Berlin Wall was not a distant and fading memory yet, and the present geopolitical chilling of the West vis-à-vis countries such as China and Russia would not have lent itself to easy credulity. It would likewise have been hard to predict the populist onslaught that eventually engulfed large tracts of the developed world with Brexit, the election of Donald Trump in the US, the electoral victory of Eurosceptic parties in founding members of the EU, or the surge of a radical right party in Germany.

Yet even in such a "honeymoon" phase of globalization, certain authors were able to see beyond the immediate horizon of socio-economic and political bliss and—unlike many of their peers, not disregarding the costs associated with economic globalization and economic growth brought about by an intertwined world economy—ask whether and to what degree it will remain possible for the countries of the world to remain (socially, politically, economically) on the tracks of the time. Such was the case with Lord Ralf Dahrendorf and Dani Rodrik, whose works envisioned or predicted less fortunate choices that countries around the world might find themselves having to make, and postulating ahead of their time an end to the wave of increasing globalization that seemed to be taken for granted.

During the height of the 1990s' globalization spurt, Dahrendorf (1995) argued that a growing and globalizing world economy would create "perverse choices" for liberal democracies: over time, staying competitive required either adopting measures detrimental to the cohesion of civil society or restricting civil liberties and political participation. For OECD countries, the task ahead for the early twenty-first century, he wrote, was "to square the circle between growth, social cohesion and political freedom" (Dahrendorf 1995, 4). This challenge became known as the Dahrendorf Quandary (Figure 2.1).

Writing at the time of the global financial crisis that began in late 2007, which proved to be the greatest stress test for the global economy since World War II and continues to strain the social fabric and political systems of many developed market countries, Rodrik (2011) suggested a version of the Quandary, the Rodrik Trilemma (Figure 2.2). Phrased as an impossibility theorem, it posits that "we cannot have hyperglobalization, democracy, and national self-determination all at once. We can have at most two out of three" (Rodrik 2011, 200).

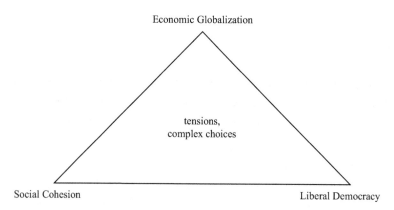

FIGURE 2.1   Dahrendorf's Quandary.

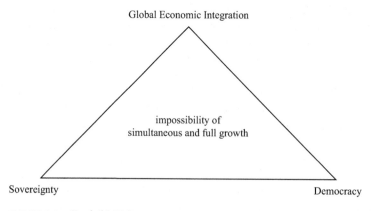

FIGURE 2.2   Rodrik's Trilemma.

It seems that Dahrendorf and Rodrik have pointed to a fundamental challenge of liberal market economies: the incompatibility of the underlying "drivers" involved, the asynchrony of the ensuing processes, and their impacts on different population groups in terms of economic inequalities and opportunities for social advancement. The economic drivers of globalization, increasingly decoupled from national processes and operating in transnational space, undermine the nation state, hence national sovereignty, and in turn, democracy through loss of legitimacy and the rise of disloyal and semi-loyal political opposition groups. Nativist economic strategies may strengthen the nation state, even democracy, but could ultimately lessen economic growth and weaken the economy. Open economic borders may benefit some parts of the population but undercut the prosperity of entire communities and regions and weaken social cohesion and commitment to liberal democracy, even as the gross domestic product increases. Inherent in these tensions are grave dangers, be they left or right populism mixed with identity politics, as Rodrik suggests, or, as Dahrendorf put it, the growing authoritarian temptations of divided societies.[1]

Both authors foresee a world in which states are faced with a choice of what to renounce: the global element, the liberal democratic one, or the national/local social one. And what each author expected as possible paths for the states can be seen as reflections of the contexts in which they were writing.

Rodrik wrote more from the twenty-first century perspective in which the global financial crisis had brought significant damage to public trust in economic globalization and the unfettered international flow of capital as well as the ability of sovereign governments to enact policy aimed at social and economic well-being (the sovereign debt crisis prompting even wealthy countries to enact austerity policies). He also had the hindsight of having witnessed the growth of populist anti-system political actors around the globe, who promoted economic nationalism and protectionism. It should thus come as little surprise that Rodrik assumes it more likely that countries will choose to maintain national sovereignty and liberal democracy over globalization, which he expects is braced for a rollback.

By contrast, when Dahrendorf formulated the Quandary, it was unclear whether the populist advocates of economic protectionism would manage to again make inroads into politics. If anything, the opposite was the case. The eastern socialist bloc had just collapsed, Francis Fukuyama's (1992) "End of History" thesis enjoyed a certain popularity, liberal free trade prevailed. It was hard to assume or expect a reversal of the trend that eliminated ever more barriers to free trade and the growing interconnectedness of the world. In the EU, the era of the Maastricht Treaty had just begun—promising ever more pooled sovereignty and more "community action." This was the era prior to the global financial crisis. "Hard but hardly relevant" is how Deschouwer and Van Assche (2008) described Eurosceptic parties prior to the financial crisis, and it was still debated whether Van der Eijk and Franklin's (2004) fears about the "Sleeping Giant of Euroscepticism" would ever awaken (De Vries 2007).

It thus seems plausible that Dahrendorf deemed scenarios in which states maintain economic globalization but renounce liberal democracy or social cohesion more likely because he saw globalization as more inevitable than Rodrik does. In essence, one could argue that Rodrik foresaw a world in which economic globalization is rolled back, while Dahrendorf's expectation was that more and more countries would opt for the path with either less democracy or cohesion.

Not surprisingly, the Quandary and the Trilemma have received considerable academic and policy attention that can be grouped into three main categories: the conceptual overlap between the two and between them and similar formulations by other scholars; the manifestations they can take in different contexts; and the policy approaches countries have taken, either explicitly or implicitly. Surprisingly, however, despite the attention both received, there has been no systematic empirical assessment of the validity of either the Quandary or the Trilemma over time and cross-nationally. Neither have the important extension of Rodrik's sentence, i.e., "simultaneously and in full," and Dahrendorf's puzzlement over "how to square the circle" been addressed empirically.

Dahrendorf and Rodrik proposed their analysis of the trajectory of liberal market economies independently of each other. Both the Quandary and the Trilemma are statements about sovereign nation states that are to varying degrees integrated in the global economy and have some kind of liberal democracy in place. They address a very similar *problèmatique*. Specific to the Quandary is an emphasis on social cohesion and civil society in the context of economic globalization and liberal democracy. Specific to the Trilemma is an emphasis on sovereignty and self-determination in the context of economic globalization and democracy.

Their different emphases notwithstanding, there is much overlap between the Quandary and the Trilemma, as Buti (2017) and Buti and Pichelmann (2017) have pointed out.[2] We agree with this assessment and for purposes of operationalization, we will merge both into one with three main conceptual components: economic globalization, the nation state as a liberal democracy, and social cohesion and civil society.

The capacity of the state to enact sovereign economic (fiscal, monetary) policy is strongly tied to social policy as well. The development of modern nation state institutions has gone hand in hand with the development of national welfare states and the raising of borders that can exclude non-nationals and their access to welfare entitlements. In addition, increasing feelings of "togetherness" as a community of shared fate directs the state to policies that protect members of particular domestic groups. In other words, social cohesion and protection are tied to a national sovereignty that allows governments to deliver, which, in turn, becomes a source of their legitimacy.

Without the underlying belief in the nation as a shared community of fate, as a social contract that binds individuals mostly unknown to each other, national institutions would be impossible to establish and maintain. Put differently, in the absence of national social cohesion and the presence of transnational cohesion, there is no reason to prefer national institutions like redistributive schemes, pension systems, or health insurance, over transnational ones.

Based on this reasoning, the two approaches can be considered equivalent, and past work has attested to this view. Indeed, Buti (2019) showed how the two theorems mirror each other, with two of the Trilemma/Quandary's corners being self-evidently equivalent (economic globalization and liberal democracy). The third vertex is tied—in an underlying way—by the links between social cohesion and the social contract within the national community of fate on one hand, and the ability of the state to enact policies that protect the vulnerable elements of the national community on the other.

Others have argued against the use of a "trilemma" in this case at all. The argument is that globalization, which entails economic integration, inherently implies a diminishment of national sovereignty, and that as such, Rodrik's theorem actually describes a dilemma, not a trilemma. This is in a way similar to accounts according to which the impossible trinity of macroeconomics (fixed exchange rates, free capital flow, independent monetary policy) is actually a dilemma in which two of the corners can be merged into one. However, Rodrik takes care to describe how the vertex combining globalization and state sovereignty would look (at the expense of liberal democracy): "Another option is to maintain the nation state, but to make it responsive only to the needs of the international economy. This would be a state that would pursue global economic integration at the expense of other domestic objectives" (Rodrik 2007).

Nonetheless, the two schemes differ in one important aspect. The Quandary implies a process whereby globalizing, open economies encounter growing domestic difficulties over time that demand corrective action governments would increasingly find difficult to deliver. The ultimate outcome is a situation where policy-makers have to "square the circle." The Trilemma, however, points to the impossibility of achieving some hypothetical optimum whereby all three "drivers," i.e., democracy, national sovereignty and global economic integration, advance simultaneously and in full. In other words, while the Quandary and the Trilemma suggest a common operationalization, their analysis and interpretations differ somewhat.

Of course, Dahrendorf and Rodrik are not alone in addressing the social and political implications of economic globalization. Prominent in the European context is the distinction between negative and positive integration of national economies and polities, as proposed by Scharpf (1999). For the EU, he warns of the dangers of negative integration, whereby economic globalization and economic liberalization are facilitated not though the policies of democratically legitimated institutions but through administrative-judicial measures, for example, by the European Court of Justice or the European Commission (see also Grimm 2017). By contrast, positive integration would involve democratically legitimated transfers of sovereignty to a supranational body to compensate for the national state's lost capacity to enact policy. Positive integration is a version of dual sovereignty.

Streeck (2018), too, is aware of the imbalances introduced by further European economic integration. Addressing the problems caused by the increasing liberalization of the international trade system and a globalizing economy, he posits more socioeconomic tensions and ever less social cohesion. He anticipates stronger centrifugal forces within countries similar to the regional tensions between Spain and Catalonia, Wallonia and Flanders, or Scotland and England. Weakened social cohesion and regional tensions facilitate and intensify identity politics and populist tendencies (see Crawford Ames, Chapter 3 in this volume).

Like Streeck, O'Rourke (2014) sees the Trilemma inherently at work in the tensions created by the European Monetary Union. *The Economist* (2018) sees trilemma conditions manifesting themselves in how different EU member states and leaders struggle to find solutions acceptable to their electorate, the interests of national and international business, and the need for further integration. Similarly, Merler (2018) concludes that European integration has failed to solve the Quandary as member states became increasingly unable to shield their citizens from the social and economic harms caused by economic globalization. Featherstone (2017) discusses the relationship Norway and Switzerland have with the EU, as well as the Brexit negotiations, and points out the tensions and difficulties in designing institutions that satisfy the diverging concerns inherent in the Trilemma.

Beyond the European context, Aram (1997) concluded already in the mid-1990s that current policy frameworks seem unable to resolve the challenges posed by economic globalization, especially its impact on social cohesion. By contrast, Drache (1999) and Hirst and Thompson (2002) suggest that economic globalization would at some stage approach its limits due to national reactions and come to a halt. Held (1997) proposes cosmopolitan democracy as the way to address the Quandary, as globalization in its various forms reduces the autonomous governance capacity of nation states.

Stein (2016) at first questions some of the underlying assumptions of the Trilemma and explores what each of the three combinations entails. Eventually, he arrives at the same conclusion as Rodrik: the three components become incompatible at some point. One "corner" always remains likely to fall victim to the other two, and possible reconciliations of the three for overcoming the trilemma would only come about in conditions that seem either implausible or impractical.

Throughout, however, authors seem to take the Quandary and the Trilemma as well as the conditions leading to them more or less at face value and focus on some part or another, without examining a systematic evidence base to test the extent to which the relationships posited do in fact exist and lead to incompatibility and perverse choices. As a result, we have incomplete evidence, partial analysis at best, and a patchwork of policy proposals. Given these shortfalls, the purpose of this chapter is to examine the empirical foundations of Dahrendorf's and Rodrik's propositions. Is it indeed the case that countries face the Quandary equally and are trapped in the Trilemma? Or do we find distinct patterns such that some countries are more exposed and in different ways?

Having entered the third decade of the 21st century, an interesting state of affairs is to be found. Across the globe, populist politicians have made significant gains against the backdrop of or in conjunction with the global recession and economic crisis. Harshening economic conditions not only increased economic inequality across various national contexts, leading to higher degrees of social exclusion and deprivation, they offered ample political ammunition to populist political actors maneuvering for economic nationalism and protectionism. Faced with increasing hurdles, globalization has, after a long growth spurt, begun to decelerate and stall. Political polarization, inequality, and other such factors also went hand in hand with a seeming decline in social cohesion. Arguably, the past two decades provide what might be an interesting test bed for both Rodrik's and Dahrendorf's visions. In the remainder of this chapter, we explore the Trilemma and Quandary more minutely by inspecting how individual countries have fared against the backdrop of conditions postulated by the two theses.

Approach

With the country as the unit of analysis, we first look at measures for the three common components or drivers: the degree of economic globalization, the extent to which the nation state is a liberal democracy, and the extent of social cohesion and civil society development. As shown in Figure 2.3, we use one key indicator for each driver. Economic globalization is measured using the KOF Globalization Index (Gygli et al. 2019); democracy and the nation state, i.e., the "health" of democracy at the national level, is based on the Varieties of Democracy (Coppedge et al. 2019) or V-Dem Liberal Democracy Index; and social cohesion and civil society reflects a population's answers to a question of the type "Do you believe that most people can be trusted?" collected in the Quality of Government dataset (Teorell 2019).

We then examine measures of "stressors," i.e., the tensions associated with or accompanying changes in each of the three drivers. As shown in Figure 2.4, each

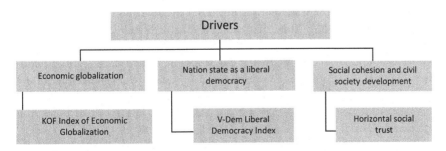

FIGURE 2.3 The drivers.

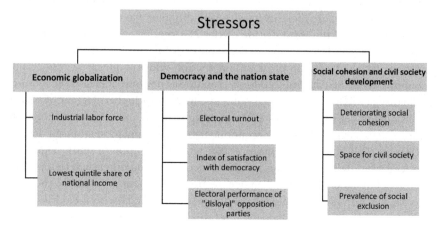

FIGURE 2.4 The stressors.

stressor reflects a combination of two to three indicators. Pressures related to economic globalization, for example, include the extent of industrial deskilling of the national labor force, reflecting a possible trend towards lower-paying and more precarious service employment (Teorell 2019), and the share of national income of the population in the lowest quintile, reflecting income inequality. The democracy stressor aggregates measures of legislative electoral turnout (Coppedge et al. 2019), the electoral performance of anti-system or disloyal opposition parties from the far right and far left (Armingeon et al. 2019), and dissatisfaction with democracy in order to capture politicians' and the electorate's commitment to liberal democracy (Teorell 2019). Finally, pressures relating to social cohesion and civil society are reflected by measures detecting deterioration of social trust (Teorell 2019), space for civil society action (Coppedge et al. 2019), and social exclusion (Smith et al. 2019; European Values Study 2015, 2019; NORC General Social Survey for the US). All indicators are normalized and projected on a scale ranging from 0 to 100.[3]

With these different measures and approaches we can account for the differences in Rodrik's Trilemma and Dahrendorf's Quandary. In the case of Rodrik, we ask whether all three drivers (economic globalization, liberal democracy, social cohesion/sovereign state or institutions) can reach and maintain high levels over longer periods of time. If a country starts off with one of the drivers at a lower level which then climbs higher, how do the other two drivers behave? Rodrik's prediction would be that if the economic driver reaches a high level, then any one of the other two must stay relatively stable or even decline. In the case of Dahrendorf, we put the analytical focus on the stressors that can manifest themselves for liberal democracy and social cohesion as a result of increasing economic globalization.

For the Trilemma and the analysis of the drivers, the data assembled for the various indicators cover 34 countries over a period stretching from 1991 to 2014. Given the focus of the Trilemma, all included countries are members of the OECD and upper-middle to high income market economies. Within that focus, the inclusion of any country is based on data availability across the various data sources and over time. Israel and New Zealand are excluded on that basis, leaving nonetheless considerable geopolitical range: next to the US and Canada, two high-income developed Asian countries (Japan and South Korea), two Latin American countries (Chile and Mexico), and 28 European countries, mostly EU member states with the exception of Iceland, Norway, Switzerland, and Turkey. For the Quandary, as a function of data availability, we have a smaller group of countries. With the exception of the US, the sample consists of 20 European countries, of which 17 are EU member states.

In terms of the time frame, we assume that a longer-term perspective is needed as both the drivers and the tensions involved are not short-term developments; rather, they build up over time, and are at least medium-term phenomena unfolding over several years, and perhaps even longer, and may well show delayed effects over time. Therefore, we examine the data in two ways: for the Trilemma analysis, we look at longer-term changes, and examine the entire period from the early 1990s to 2014; for analyzing the Quandary we examine the period after the global financial crisis from 2009 to 2014 against the background of increases in economic globalization since 1991.

Both Rodrik and Dahrendorf make clear and simple statements about the (co)evolution of certain variables, and the task at hand is to assess to what degree they evolve in the manner predicted or not. We concede that the sample does not allow for extrapolation to non-Western (in the case of the Quandary analysis) or non-OECD countries (for the exploration of the Trilemma). Even so, the sample still has analytical value, since the Quandary and Trilemma, as posited, are intended to apply to advanced market economies.

Exploring the trilemma

Let us take a look first at economic globalization. As shown in Table 2.1, some countries are already fairly globalized by 1991, while other countries begin from a lower level of integration of their national economies. The top five most globalized countries are Luxembourg (85 of 100 points), Belgium (81), Ireland and the Netherlands (both 79), and Denmark (74)—all highly developed yet smaller economies with a limited domestic market. Among the largest economies, the UK (71), Germany (66) and France (66) rank higher than the US (55) and Japan (43). Among the least globalized economies are South Korea (34), Poland (34) and Mexico (37).

By 2014, there is both change and continuity in the country ranking. The top five countries are Ireland (90), Luxembourg, Belgium and the Netherlands (89) and Estonia (86)—again highly developed yet smaller economies. The larger economies of the UK (80), Germany (79) and France (77) continue to have higher scores than the US (67) and Japan (61). Among the least globalized economies are Mexico (60) and Turkey (56).

TABLE 2.1 Economic globalization, democracy and the nation state, and social cohesion and civil society indicators, 1991 and 2014, by country

	Economic globalization		Democracy and the nation state		Social cohesion and civil society	
	1991*	2014	1991	2014	1991**	2014
Average	58	77	75	77	37	49
Australia	52	67	85	84	40	52
Austria	70	83	77	79	32	49
Belgium	81	89	81	82	34	50
Canada	55	70	81	79	53	67
Chile	46	72	75	84	23	49
Czech Republic	58	83	83	78	62	45
Denmark	74	84	88	90	58	68
Estonia	61	86	83	85	22	54
Finland	64	82	83	85	63	62
France	66	77	82	82	23	45
Germany	66	79	86	83	33	51
Greece	46	73	81	75	24	37
Hungary	51	86	72	59	25	42
Iceland	48	70	79	77	44	57
Ireland	79	90	79	79	47	54
Italy	54	68	75	79	35	39
Japan	43	61	76	77	42	39
Latvia	49	81	72	77	25	43
Lithuania	48	75	78	77	22	44
Luxembourg	85	89	77	76	25	50
Mexico	37	60	21	48	33	59
Netherlands	79	89	83	82	53	59
Norway	69	74	87	87	65	62
Poland	34	72	77	80	29	47
Portugal	56	78	80	83	22	44
Slovakia	49	82	57	73	36	39
Slovenia	42	76	73	80	17	42
South Korea	34	67	55	61	34	49
Spain	54	75	78	75	34	46
Sweden	67	84	87	88	66	63
Switzerland	72	86	85	87	37	57
Turkey	45	56	38	42	10	12
UK	71	80	77	83	44	52
USA	55	67	81	87	51	53

Notes:

* For the Czech Republic and Slovakia, the earliest available KOF Globalization data are for 1993, and those values are used here instead of 1991.

** For some countries, the hum_trust variable depicting social cohesion was not available for 1991; in these countries, the earliest available time point is used instead: Australia 1995, Czech Republic 1997, Estonia 1996, Germany 1997, Greece 1999, Latvia 1995, Lithuania 1996, Luxembourg 1999, Slovakia 1998, Switzerland 1996.

But overall, there is a pronounced trend towards more economic globalization indicated by higher scores: all countries show a higher economic globalization score by 2014 than they did some 25 years earlier. The average economic globalization score was 58 in 1991 and increased to 77 by 2014. On average, countries added 19 points, with only six adding fewer than 10 (mostly economies that were already highly globalized in 1991), and 15 countries adding more than 20. Among the latter group are five Central and Eastern European countries (Hungary, Latvia, Poland, Slovakia and Slovenia), as well as Chile, Iceland, Mexico, Portugal, Spain and South Korea—all countries that followed open market policies throughout that period.

How does this pattern of increase compare to democracy and the nation state? As shown in Table 2.1, the highest-ranking countries in 1991 are Denmark (88), Sweden and Norway (both 87), Germany (86), and Australia and Switzerland (both 85). The lowest-ranking countries are Mexico (21), Turkey (38) and South Korea (55). The 34-country average score is 75, and with a standard deviation of 13.9, most countries with fall within the 70s and 80s range. If we remove the three outliers (Mexico, Turkey and South Korea), the standard deviation falls to 6, indicating an overall narrow range.

How does this pattern change by 2014? The average score for democracy and the nation state increases only slightly to 77 and the standard deviation falls to 10.6. Nearly two-thirds (21) of countries in our sample show 2014 scores that are 3 or fewer points higher or lower than they were in 1991. Ten countries made gains greater than 3 points, with Chile, Mexico, Slovakia, and Slovenia standing out. By contrast, two countries showed pronounced declines: Hungary and Greece.

Finally, looking at the social cohesion and civil society driver in Table 2.1, we see a different pattern yet. The average score for the indicator increased from 37 in 1991 to 49 in 2014, with standard deviation dropping from 14.8 to 10.5 during the same period. Around 1991, Sweden, Norway and Finland rank highest with a score of over 60, as does the Czech Republic. By 2014 Denmark joins the other three Scandinavian countries at the top of the ranking, and Canada (67) takes the place of the Czech Republic, whose score drops substantially to 45. Turkey (10) and Slovenia (17) are the only clear outliers in the ranking in 1991, and by 2014 only Turkey (12) remains in that group.

Importantly, no country other than Turkey scores below 35 by 2014, which suggests a general increase in social cohesion and civil society over the 25-year period, with an average increase of 12.3 points per country. Indeed, only one country, the Czech Republic, experienced a major drop of 17 points. What is more, only four other countries, including the three Scandinavian countries at the top of the ranking in 1991, show slightly declining scores of three points or less.

If we summarize the changes of the three drivers over the period in question, we observe a significant increase in economic globalization across all countries; also notable is a general convergence at a relatively high level. For these liberal democracies as nation states, stability is the dominant pattern. In terms of social cohesion and civil society, countries show on average a higher degree of social cohesion and a more vibrant civil society in 2014 than they did in 1991.

What do these results imply for the Trilemma? The aggregate pattern for OECD countries suggests pronounced growth in globalization, moderately more social cohesion, and stability of democracy over a 25-year period. Since only two of the drivers increase and the third does not, this would seem to validate Rodrik's Trilemma. However, recall that the impossibility theorem states the countries cannot sustain growth in all drivers simultaneously and in full over periods of time, in this case the 25 years from 1991 to 2014. We show the changes for each driver in Table 2.2. Of interest are two questions. First, do we, in fact, find that all three drivers grew to at least some extent during that time period? If not, then the Trilemma is confirmed. If we do, then the impossibility theorem can at least be questioned in its generality.

As Table 2.2 reveals, in 32 of the 34 cases, all three drivers failed to increase simultaneously and in full; there the Trilemma does indeed hold. The combination of increases in both economic globalization and social cohesion/ civil societies with a stagnant or decreasing score in liberal democracy as a nation state applies in 21 of the 32 cases. In eight cases, only economic globalization advances while the other two drivers remain stable or decline; in one further case (Norway) all drivers are more or less stable, with no increase worth mentioning.

This leaves Chile and Mexico, the only Latin American members of the OECD, as the two clear cases where over a prolonged period of time all drivers could advance simultaneously and in full, and contrary to what Rodrik's Trilemma would predict. Both countries, however, present unusual cases. Chile emerged from years of dictatorship with an open market policy and a nascent civil society, while Mexico benefited on both the economic and political front. The North American Free Trade Agreement provided an instrument for economic growth while the gradual opening up of the political system invited political engagement. What both countries have in common is that high potential for economic growth opened up and coincided with changes in the political status quo.

The second question we can explore with the data in Table 2.2 is what happens if we loosen the conditions from "simultaneous and in full" to "over a longer period of time and to a measurable, meaningful extent"? As we can see (Table 2.2, column "Trilemma rejected/confirmed only in a broader sense"), several more countries seem to escape the Trilemma. The clearest cases are Slovenia and the UK. In the former, economic globalization expanded 34 points, social cohesion and civil society 25 points, and liberal democracy considerably less but still has a 2014 score 7 points higher than 1991. The UK reveals advances across the board at quite moderate levels. If we loosen up the conditions even more and only require that all three drivers show positive growth rates (however minimal) over time, more countries qualify. Table 2.2 thus shows three outcomes for the Trilemma test: 17 cases for which the Trilemma is confirmed to exist in the narrow sense; 15 cases for which it is confirmed in the broader sense; and, finally, two countries where the Trilemma does not hold.

TABLE 2.2 Changes in driver scores, 1991–2014, by country

Country	Change in economic globalization indicator	Change in liberal democracy as nation state indicator	Change in social cohesion and civil society indicator	Number of drivers with pronounced increase	Number of drivers decreasing or stable	Trilemma confirmed in narrow sense	Trilemma confirmed in broader sense	Trilemma rejected
Australia	14	−1	12	2	1	Y		
Austria	13	2	17	2	1		Y	
Belgium	8	1	16	2	1		Y	
Canada	15	−2	14	2	1	Y		
Chile	26	9	26	3	0			Y
Czech Republic	24	−5	−17	1	2	Y		
Denmark	9	2	10	2	1		Y	
Estonia	25	2	32	2	1		Y	
Finland	18	2	−1	1	2	Y		
France	11	0	22	2	1	Y		
Germany	13	−3	18	2	1	Y		
Greece	27	−6	13	2	1	Y		
Hungary	35	−13	17	2	1	Y		
Iceland	22	−2	13	2	1	Y		
Ireland	11	0	7	2	1	Y		
Italy	14	4	4	1	2		Y	
Japan	18	1	−3	1	2	Y		
Latvia	32	5	18	2	1		Y	
Lithuania	27	−1	22	2	1	Y		

(Continued)

TABLE 2.2 (Continued)

Country	Change in economic globalization indicator	Change in liberal democracy as nation state indicator	Change in social cohesion and civil society indicator	Number of drivers with pronounced increase	Number of drivers decreasing or stable	Trilemma confirmed in narrow sense	Trilemma confirmed in broader sense	Trilemma rejected
Luxembourg	4	−1	25	1	2	Y		
Mexico	23	27	26	3	0			Y
Netherlands	10	−1	6	1	2	Y		
Norway	5	0	−3	0	3	Y		
Poland	38	3	18	2	1		Y	
Portugal	22	3	22	2	1		Y	
Slovakia	33	16	3	2	1		Y	
Slovenia	34	7	25	2	1		Y	
South Korea	33	6	15	2	1		Y	
Spain	21	−3	12	2	1	Y		
Sweden	17	1	−3	1	2	Y		
Switzerland	14	2	20	2	1		Y	
Turkey	11	4	2	1	2		Y	
UK	9	6	8	2	1		Y	
USA	12	6	2	1	2		Y	

In sum, when viewed as the failure of all three drivers to increase simultane-ously and in full, the Trilemma applies to all but two of the countries in our study, which, in turn, means that it is not a universal statement but an empiri-cal generalization that allows for exceptions. In a looser formulation that takes into account lower levels of expansion, the Trilemma still holds for half of the countries we covered, but shows significantly different patterns: in several of these cases, two of the drivers expand significantly while a third, usually liberal democracy as a nation state, advances somewhat but "does not give," as Rodrik suggests. For many of the other half, all three drivers grow slowly or moderately over time, and in a few cases remain constant or even decline. In particular, the finding that drivers can expand at lower to moderate degrees over longer periods of time suggests that the strict Trilemma can be avoided: economic globalization, social cohesion and civil society, and democracy and the nation state can all grow simultaneously - but not in full.

Exploring the Quandary

Dahrendorf's Quandary predicts that countries will be faced with "perverse choices" in the face of the acceleration of economic globalization. Countries would not be able to pursue simultaneously all three goals of economic growth brought by globalization, liberal democracy, and social cohesion, but have to compromise on one to reach the other two. Thus, his stance is very similar to that of Rodrik, postulating an impossibility theorem for the twenty-first century.

Table 2.3 presents changes in the three sets of stressors over the period 2009–14, as well as each country's 1991 economic globalization score and the percent change in that score between 1991 and 2007, just before the global financial crisis began. An analysis then reveals essentially four groups of countries:

- The first group includes Spain, Italy and, marginally, also France where all three stressors increase. The average economic globalization indicator for the group in 1991 is 58, the average rise in globalization by 2007 amounts to 25%, and their combined average stressor scores increased by 23% between 2009 and 2014. These are the quandary conditions Dahrendorf hypoth-esized, in which countries face the difficult choice of "how to square the circle," as he put it;

- There is a second group of countries, where two stressors gain substantially and a third drops or remains stable. This is the case for Slovenia, Slovakia, Hungary, the US, Finland, Norway and the Netherlands. Their average 1991 economic globalization indicator is 60, yet they experienced a higher globalization expansion of 38%, and a lower combined average stressor level increase of 8%. These are countries that generally managed to expand in terms of economic globalization while avoiding some of the tensions implied in the Quandary and thus confirm it in the broader sense;

TABLE 2.3 Percent changes in economic globalization indicator, 1991–2007, and stressors, 2009–2014, by country

Country	Economic globalization indicator 1991	Percent change in globalization indicator (1991–2007)	Percent change in globalization stressor	Percent change in democracy stressor	Percent change in cohesion stressor	Number of stressor increases	Narrow confirmation of Quandary	Broader confirmation of Quandary	Quandary rejected
Poland	34	98%	-1%	-1%	14%	1			Y
Slovenia	42	78%	27%	17%	-18%	2		Y	
Lithuania	48	57%	1%	-13%	-6%	1			Y
Iceland	48	57%	-1%	-9%	-14%	0			Y
Slovakia	49	63%	18%	-16	16%	2		Y	
Hungary	51	67%	29%	12%	-7%	2		Y	
Spain	54	35%	19%	35%	34%	3	Y		
Italy	54	24%	13%	32%	17%	3	Y		
USA	55	23%	0%	36%	13%	2		Y	
Czech Republic	58	36%	0%	20%	-14%	1			Y
Estonia	61	41%	16%	-7%	-25%	1			Y
Finland	64	28%	5%	3%	-9%	2		Y	
France	66	16%	2%	21%	34%	3	Y		
Germany	66	21%	8%	-12%	-37%	1			Y
Sweden	67	26%	7%	-4%	-3%	1			Y
Norway	69	11%	4%	-22%	16%	2		Y	
Austria	70	21%	-6%	5%	-2%	1			Y
UK	71	11%	0%	-7%	-35%	0			Y
Switzerland	72	15%	2%	-8%	-7%	1			Y
Denmark	74	13%	5%	-2%	-13%	1			Y
Netherlands	79	11%	8%	11%	-3%	2		Y	

- Then there is a larger group of countries (Poland, Lithuania, Czech Republic, Estonia, Germany, Sweden, Austria, the UK, Switzerland, and Denmark), where two stressors decline or remain relatively stable, and one stressor increases. For these countries, the 1991 average economic globalization indicator was 61 and its average increase up to 2007 was 36%. The group, however, includes countries with very high rates of increasing globalization such as Poland (98%) and those with substantially lower ones such as Denmark (13%) and the UK (11%). Overall, however, the pattern for this group of countries suggests that a growing globalization of the economy can be accompanied by lower stress levels, and in most cases both for democracy and social cohesion. Thus, we can say that the Quandary does not hold for this group of countries;
- Finally, Iceland is the only country in the sample that shows a decline in all three stressors between 2009 and 2014, while the indicator for economic globalization had increased by 57% in the 16 years prior. In other words, Iceland is a clear case refuting the Quandary.

Based on the results in Table 2.3, we can conclude that for the 2009 to 2014 period, the Quandary seems to apply in three of our 21 cases in a narrow sense and in seven countries in a broader sense. In the remaining 11 countries the Quandary hardly seems to arise, if at all. While tensions inherent in the Quandary seem to be present in all our countries, except Iceland, their extent varies in terms of acuteness or severity.

The Trilemma and the Quandary combined

Examination of the Trilemma and the Quandary resulted in three groups of countries in each case. Knowing that we have a smaller set for the latter, the question still arises of how the country groupings relate. The answer is presented in Table 2.4.

The combination of the "Trilemma overcome" and "Quandary tensions avoided" does not apply to any of the countries included, although, due to data limitations, we do not know how Mexico and Chile would have fared when it comes to the Quandary for the period in question. However, we find that two countries, Spain and France, are strongly exposed to Trilemma and Quandary forces, and six, Poland, Estonia, Austria, the UK, Switzerland, and Denmark, are only moderately exposed to the Trilemma and weakly to the Quandary, with other countries located in between.

The presence of France and Spain in a group in which both Quandary tensions and Trilemma conditions are present coincides with the fiscal and monetary situation of the Eurozone's southern members. Italy's presence in the "strong Quandary tensions" group reinforces that impression: some countries *do* find themselves in a bind between enjoying liberal democratic ideals, social cohesion and a strong degree of state sovereignty, while simultaneously

TABLE 2.4 Trilemma and quandary, by country

Quandary tensions Trilemma conditions	Strong	Moderate	Weak
Strong	France, Spain	Hungary, Finland, Norway, the Netherlands	Lithuania, Czech Republic, Germany, Sweden (Iceland)
Moderate	Italy	Slovenia, Slovakia, USA	Poland, Estonia, Austria, UK, Switzerland, Denmark
Weak		(Mexico, Chile)	

experiencing greater economic globalization. These are countries which have had a difficult time coping with the confines of globalized/Europeanized economic governance.

The conditions of limited policy avenues that Eurozone governments can pursue is often termed the "golden straitjacket of the Eurozone," as it limits the monetary and fiscal toolboxes of elected governments. Italy and France are also countries in which populist anti-system parties have made the most significant inroads in halls of power: in Italy the (northern) League and the Five Star Movement (both Eurosceptic parties) are among the strongest political actors, and in France the National Rally (formerly Front National) led by Marine Le Pen won the most seats in that country's 2019 European Parliament election. Spain, too, is flirting with disloyal opposition, where Euroscepticism, long limited to the left, has been taken up by a right-wing populist party (VOX) as well.

The group of countries in which neither the Trilemma conditions nor the Quandary tensions are decisive consists of two types of countries: some of the Central and East European countries which joined the EU in the 2000s, and several northwest European countries whose economic structures ensured them a degree of insulation from the perils of the tenuous financial circumstances that swept the world in the early twenty-first century. This second group of countries are arguably "not losers of globalization" or at the very least "not there yet." The "losers of globalization" approach to explaining social and political opposition to economic liberalization such as the EU's four fundamental freedoms (unhindered movement of capital, services, goods, and persons across national borders) expresses said opposition in terms of pressure on the least skilled and least educated (and thus least mobile) segments of a workforce. These forces may push the population to vote for parties that are economically and culturally protectionist. Such tension comes in the form of added immigration and competition over low-skilled jobs (which exerts downward pressure on wages and increases the risk of unemployment) as well as the threat of outsourcing or moving production to countries or regions where production and services cost less.

With its variety of socioeconomic contexts, the EU can be seen as a microcosm of the wider global political economy: within the EU there are highly developed (western) countries that attracted high levels of immigration from Central and Eastern EU member states, while production facilities steadily moved east into the new members of the bloc. While the unskilled and socially excluded in Western Europe thus became "losers of globalization/Europeanization," their analogues in the Central and Eastern European member states were relative "winners" (at least compared to their previous position). The latter countries benefitted from new foreign direct investment opportunities and new employers, and with the potential for their less skilled laborers to seek employment in the West, they essentially exported their unemployment and any pressure on local/national welfare states. It is thus to be expected that Central and East European member states are more likely to find themselves near the bottom right corner of Table 2.4.

From another (world systems) theoretical point of view, the countries comprising the second group can be seen as belonging to the so called "Lockean Heartland" (see Van der Pijl 1988), the West European capitalist core whose economic structure (strong export and trade orientation that is not reliant on expansive monetary intervention) makes them more suited to working in an austere environment. It is popular to claim that the austere members of the EU have more competitive industries, which is what shielded them and their socio-economic model since the 1990s (as opposed to the more Keynesian approach in southern Europe).

Perhaps the Trilemma and Quandary are to be read not as axioms but as a sort of cautionary tale: they depict a combination of circumstances in which countries *may* come to find themselves, and the hard choices the countries will face when they do. As of the early 2020s, some countries are more constrained by this set of circumstances (countries closer to the top left corner of Table 2.4), while others are in less danger. This leads to additional questions. First, what policy paths led some countries toward the Quandary/Trilemma and which ones away from it? Second, if countries find themselves subject to the conditions of the Trilemma and/or the Quandary, which combinations of policies and responses have corrective effects, and which interact to amplify inherent tensions? Alternatively, it is also possible that the likelihood that a country will face the Trilemma or Quandary depends not on their governance or policy decisions and paths, but on other combinations of conditions or circumstances that are not under their control. Yet another possible explanation could be a mix of the two: that the ways in which the Trilemma and Quandary manifest themselves is indeed a result of policy decisions, but of those made a longer time ago (not with a view to solving the present situations, but with other objectives in mind), with those decisions manifesting themselves now, with a lag, generating a diverse landscape of conditions in which the Quandary and Trilemma play out. Recent scholarship (Rodrik 2018; Manow 2020; Manow, Palier, and Schwander 2018) has pointed to the different ways in which globalization and the stresses associated with it (including differing scenarios of challenges to national democracy and political health) can present themselves differently as a result of earlier policy.

These are broad and important questions, beyond the scope of the present chapter and merit their own detailed study. Ultimately, adding a layer of analytical operationalization (indicators for comparative policy assessment) on top of the present tabulatory exercise could further restrict the temporal and cross-sectional characteristics of the sample. That is, however, what would be required of any attempt at quantifying the different policy measures of countries in the same way as the drivers and stressors.

Are some countries truly able to avoid the Trilemma and Quandary traps? Is there anything approximating a set of decisions that countries can take to avoid or even reduce the effect of the trilemma(s)? Or is the incidence, and strength, of the Quandary tensions and Trilemma conditions in which countries find themselves a function of other contextual factors such as the development of the international political economy? These are questions with wide-reaching consequences. Finding the right "cocktail" of policy and governance instruments to balance the social, political, and economic tensions that occur with globalization (if at all possible) would be of immense value. In an ideal world of policy analysis, it would even raise the prospect of "fixing" globalization. Still, that would not undermine the validity and initial intuitions of the Trilemma and Quandary, i.e., that the socioeconomic upheavals caused by unfettered globalization are difficult to manage for policy-makers, pushing them towards ever more difficult choices.

Conclusion

The purpose of this chapter has been to examine the empirical foundations of Dahrendorf's and Rodrik's propositions. Dahrendorf's Quandary implies a process whereby globalizing economies with open markets encounter growing domestic tensions over time such that governments have increasing difficulties responding with, and delivering, remedial measures. Rodrik's Trilemma depicts the impossibility of achieving some hypothetical optimum whereby all three "drivers," i.e., global economic integration, democracy, and nation state sovereignty, advance simultaneously and in full.

Assessing developed market economies from 1991 to 2014, evidence suggests that in rare cases, the Trilemma can be overcome and the tensions the Quandary implies can build up to a significant extent. In most cases, however, the performance of the countries examined here is too varied to support the broad claims Rodrick and Dahrendorf put forth in their respective writings. Specifically, next to the small group of three cases where either the Trilemma or the Quandary apply fully (France, Italy, and Spain), there are twice as many countries that generally managed to grow moderately in terms of economic globalization, liberal democracy and social cohesion, while avoiding some of the tensions implied in the Quandary or reaching Trilemma conditions. What is more, for an even larger group of countries the evidence suggests that growing economic globalization can co-exist with lower stress levels and even enhance democracy and social cohesion.

That countries do not fully face up to the Trilemma and the tensions of the Quandary as such does not mean that they are immune to the inherent trade-offs and tensions Rodrik and Dahrendorf described. There are some instances in which globalization increased significantly, others with such increases for the nation state as a liberal democracy, and yet others for social cohesion and civil society. By contrast, economic globalization did not lessen in any of the cases during the time period we studied, but the nation state as a liberal democracy and social cohesion did in many. Countries seem to face challenges to their internal governance, but not always in the same manner.

One interpretation of the finding suggests that countries generally manage to avoid the Quandary, suggesting a pattern of push-and-pull among drivers and stressors. In this interpretation, the drivers of economic globalization find at least some correction in policy action to better deal with stressors. These policy responses address stressors and rein in drivers that seem to transgress and thereby cause governance problems. Could it be that different policy approaches and responses are behind the patterns observed, and in the sense that they prevent a fuller manifestation of the Quandary, perhaps doing so unevenly by privileg-ing one driver or another and hence creating different stressors with varying strengths?

Finally, one may wonder why Dahrendorf's Quandary and Rodrik's Trilemma managed to gain such salience. One reason may well be their crisp, intuitive flavor and their ability to capture the zeitgeist of the era. We are reminded of the historian Huizinga who wrote in his seminal *The Waning of the Middle Ages* (1924/1999) that complex concepts have first to take visual shape to impress peo-ple's mind. What could give a more useful impression than a trilemma?

Yet we should also consider the possibility that a weakening of both liberal democracy and social cohesion may take longer to materialize and were not yet captured here. For example, it could be argued that for much of the 1990s, Central and East European countries were in a profound transition phase that had more to do with changes stemming from some four decades of communism than with globalization and its related stressors. By the late 2010s, the impact of economic globalization would presumably be felt more directly. What is more, for the other countries included, one could suggest that the Quandary's notion of tensions building up during the initial globalization spurt of the 1990s could amplify during the period following the global financial crisis of 2008–9, and only begin to reveal their effects a decade later.

For Dahrendorf, the global financial crisis of 2008–9 and its aftermath proved that many countries failed to find solutions to the Quandary and the vexing ten-sions and choices it entails. As the crisis unfolded, and shortly before his death, he argued in 2009 that the response by most countries (a policy stance he labelled *Pump-Kapitalismus*, i.e., piling up public debt to bail out large business corpora-tions while implementing austerity measures for the population at large) would create many medium- to long-term problems, i.e., reaching into the late 2010s and even the 2020s. In his view, populist and illiberal tendencies were likely to rise, and civil society to be jeopardized, while economic globalization would continue pushing social inequality higher and social mobility lower, ultimately eroding trust in key national institutions (Dahrendorf 2009).

Indeed, had he lived to witness the Brexit referendum and its arduous aftermath, the illiberalism of Victor Orban's Hungary, former US President Donald Trump's repeated challenges to US institutions and political norms, the rise of controlled and well-managed societies like Singapore, the autocratic developments in China, Russia and Turkey, populism in Brazil, Argentina and Italy, uprisings in Chile and Hong Kong, and the growing public indebtedness of many OECD economies, especially the US, Dahrendorf would most likely have uttered despairingly: "Have I not told you so?"

Notes

1 See Dahrendorf's comments on populism: www.eurozine.com/acht-anmerkungen -zum-populismus/.
2 Dahrendorf's Quandary considers social cohesion rather than Rodrik's sovereignty. While social cohesion is not exactly the same as nation state sovereignty, both point to similar issues. Social cohesion depends on some underlying belief in a shared community of fate, and a sovereign nation state can to some extent represent it. Could a nation state and its institutions function without social cohesion? Certainly not as a liberal democratic order, and only as a highly controlled, authoritarian society. Likewise, can social cohesion at the national level retain its fiber if the institutions of the nation state are functionally overtaken by supranational ones? A purpose of democratic politics is to guide and channel decisions over distributive questions. How public resources are used, how markets work and what rules govern and regulate them, and the design and workings of redistributive policy are all phenomena which—ideally—are subject to democratic oversight and decisions at the level corresponding to the operational level of the economy. In a globalized economy with corresponding supranational common rules and forms of redistribution, these would be subject to democratic oversight as well.
3 See Anheier and Filip (2020) for more details on indicators and data sources.

References

Anheier, Helmut K. and Alexandru Filip. 2020. "The Rodrik Trilemma and the Dahrendorf Quandary: An Empirical Assessment." Working Paper. The Dahrendorf Forum. https://www.dahrendorf-forum.eu/publications/the-rodrik-trilemma-and -the-dahrendorf-quandary-an-empirical-assessment/. Accessed 28 June 2021.
Aram, John D. 1997. "Challenges to the Social Foundations of Capitalism in an Age of Global Economics." *Human Relations*, 50: 967–986. https://doi.org/10.1023/A :1016929011357
Armingeon, Klaus, Virginia Wenger, Fiona Wiedemeier, Christian Isler, Laura Knöpfel, David Weisstanner and Sarah Engler. 2019. Comparative Political Data Set 1960- 2017. Bern: Institute of Political Science, University of Bern.
Buti, Marco. 2019. "Renewing the (Damaged) Social Contract." https://ec.europa.eu/ info/sites/info/files/economy-finance/mb-dahrendorf_forum_v3.pdf

Buti, Marco. 2017. "Globalization and Inequality: Implications for European Integration." https://ec.europa.eu/info/sites/info/files/21.06.2017_villa_mondragone_m.buti_.pdf

Buti, Marco and Karl Pichelmann. 2017. *"European Integration and Populism: Addressing Dahrendorf's Quandary."* http://sep.luiss.it/sites/sep.luiss.it/files/Buti_PB_01302017.pdf

Coppedge, Michael, John Gerring, Carl Henrik Knutsen, Staffan I. Lindberg, Jan Teorell, Kyle L. Marquardt, Juraj Medzihorsky, Daniel Pemstein, Josefine Pernes, Johannes von Römer, Natalia Stepanova, Eitan Tzelgov, Yi-ting Wang, and Steven Wilson. 2019. "V-Dem Methodology v9." Varieties of Democracy (V-Dem) Project.

Dahrendorf, Ralf. 1995. *Economic Opportunity, Civil Society and Political Liberty*, UNRISD Discussion Paper 58. Geneva: United Nations Research Institute for Social Development.

Dahrendorf, Ralf. 2009. "Nach der Krise: Zurück zur protestantischen Ethik?" *Merkur*, 63: 373–381.

De Vries, Catherine. 2007. "Sleeping Giant: Fact or Fairytale?: How European Integration Affects National Elections." *European Union Politics*, 8(3): 363–385.

Deschouwer, Kris and Jose Van Assche Martine. 2008. *Opposing Europe. The Comparative Party Politics of Euroscepticism*. ed. / A. Szczerbiak; P. Taggart. Oxford: Oxford University Press, pp. 75–92.

Drache, Daniel. 1999. "Globalization: Is There Anything to Fear?" CSGR Working Paper No. 23/99. http://dx.doi.org/10.2139/ssrn.153089. Warwick: University of Warwick.

European Values Study. 1981-2008. Longitudinal Data File. GESIS Data Archive, Cologne, Germany, ZA4804 Data File Version 3.0.0 (2015-07-30), doi:10.4232/1.12253.

European Values Study. 2019. European Values Study 2017: Integrated Dataset (EVS 2017). GESIS Data Archive, Cologne. ZA7500 Data file Version 2.0.0, doi:10.4232/1.13314

Featherstone, Kevin. 2017. "The EU and its Neighbours Reconciling Market Access, Governance and Democracy." http://www.dahrendorf-forum.eu/publications/the-eu-and-its-neighbours-reconciling-market-access-governance-and-democracy/

Fukuyama, Francis. 1992. *The End of History and the Last Man*. New York: Free Press.

Grimm, Dieter. 2017. *The Constitution of European Democracy*. Oxford: Oxford University Press.

Gygli, Savina, Florian Haelg, Niklas Potrafke, and Jan-Egbert Sturm. 2019. "The KOF Globalisation Index—Revisited." *Review of International Organizations*, 14(3): 543–574. https://doi.org/10.1007/s11558-019-09344-2

Held, David. 1997. "Democracy and Globalization." *Global Governance*, 3(3): 251-267.

Hirst, Paul and Grahame Thompson. 2002. "The Future of Globalization." *Cooperation and Conflict*, 37(3): 247–265.

Huizinga, Johann. 1924/1999. *The Waning of the Middle Ages*. London: Dover.

Manow, Philip. 2020. "Welche Rolle spielen Wohlfahrtsstaatlichkeit und Globalisierung für die Ausprägungen des Populismus?." *Totalitarianism and Democracy* 2020, 17(1): 35–44.

Manow, Philip, Bruno Palier, and Hanna Schwander (ed.). 2018. *Welfare Democracies and Party Politics: Explaining Electoral Dynamics in Times of Changing Welfare Capitalism*. Oxford: Oxford University Press.

Merler, Silvia. 2018. "Europeans and Globalization: Does the EU Square the Circle?" In Diamond, Patrick (eds.). *The Crisis of Globalization: Democracy, Globalization, and Inequality in the Twenty-First Century*, 73–90. London and New York: I.B. Tauris.

O'Rourke, Kevin H. 2014. "A Tale of Two Trilemmas." In Louis Brennan (ed.). *Enacting Globalization*, 287–297. London: Palgrave Macmillan.

Rodrik, Dani. 2007. "The Inescapable Trilemma of the World Economy." http://rodrik .typepad.com/dani_rodriks_weblog/2007/06/the-inescapable.html

Rodrik, Dani. 2011. *The Globalization Paradox: Why Global Markets, States, and Democracy Can't Coexist*. New York: W. W. Norton & Company.

Rodrik, Dani. 2018. "Populism and the Economics of Globalization." *Journal of International Business Policy*, 1: 12–33.

Scharpf, Fritz. 1999. *Governing Europe: Effective and Democratic?* Oxford: Oxford University Press.

Teorell, Jan, Staffan Kumlin, Stefan Dahlberg, Sören Holmberg, Bo Rothstein, Natalia Alvarado Pachon, and Richard Svensson. 2019. "The Quality of Government OECD Dataset, version Jan19." University of Gothenburg: The Quality of Government Institute, http://www.qog.pol.gu.se. https://doi.org/10.18157/qogoecdjan19

The Economist. 2018. "The Tension between Globalization and Democracy," *The Economist*, https://www.economist.com/europe/2018/10/27/the-tension-between -globalisation-and-democracy.

Smith, Tom W., Michael Davern, Jeremy Freese, and Stephen Morgan. 2019. General Social Surveys, 1972–2018 [machine-readable data file] /Principal Investigator, Tom W. Smith; Co-Principal Investigators, Michael Davern, Jeremy Freese, and Stephen Morgan; Sponsored by National Science Foundation. --NORC ed.-- Chicago: NORC.

Stein, Arthur A. 2016. "The Great Trilemma: Are Globalization, Democracy, and Sovereignty Compatible?" *International Theory*, 8(2): 297–340.

Streeck, Wolfgang. 2018. "*Norbert Lechner Lecture on Globalization and the Transformation of the International State System*." Diego Portales University, November 14, 2018. https:// wolfgangstreeck.com/2019/01/21/globalization-and-the-transformation-of-the -international-state-system/

Van der Eijk, Cees and Mark Franklin. 2004. "Potential for Contestation on European Matters at National Elections in Europe." In G. Marks and M.R. Steenbergen (eds.). *European Integration and Political Conflict*, 32–50. Cambridge: Cambridge University Press. https://doi.org/10.1017/CBO9780511492013.004

Van der Pijl, Kees. 1998. *Transnational Classes and International Relations*. London: Routledge.

3

WHY THE FUTURE OF THE LIBERAL ORDER IS IN DANGER AND WHAT WE CAN DO TO SAFEGUARD IT

Beverly Crawford Ames

The question: why?

At the turn of the century, Freedom House reported that liberal democracy was on the march. Revolutionary digital technologies were creating new sources of information, available to all, from newly minted "citizen journalists." Global trade and migration expanded, creating the expectation that globalization would create wealth and opportunities across the globe. But 20 years later, liberal democracy was on the decline (Freedom House 2021), a trade war between the US and China simmered, Brexit became a fact, and reciprocal tariffs threatened an open global economy. Walls to keep out migrants and asylum-seekers multiplied seismically, from 11 countries who built them before the Berlin Wall collapsed to more than 70 countries in 2018. We have watched the decline and destruction of respect for the rule of law and the election of authoritarian rulers around the globe. Aided and abetted by the US Republican Party, Donald Trump, once the "leader of the free world," proved that it was easy to undermine venerable liberal democratic institutions by suppressing voting, spreading disinformation, vilifying the free press, closing borders, turning away asylum-seekers, and sending federal troops to quell peaceful domestic protests. Almost half of the American public supported him in the 2020 election. He may now be gone, but he lit the fuse of a bomb that had long been planted under liberal democratic institutions, waiting for that fuse to be lit. Why that bomb was built and why it exploded now is the subject of this chapter.

Liberal democracy was in decline long before Trump. Why? This chapter provides the answer: liberalism itself is a force that is tearing us apart. To rely on liberal principles as a foundation for social order is to lean on a weak reed. That reed can bend and break in the face of entrenched inequality, skyrocketing poverty, weakened communities, and new technologies that spread disinformation.

These forces have exposed the bending and breaking of principles that are the foundation of liberal democratic institutions. If liberals are not careful, liberalism will dig its own grave after living for a mere three hundred years of human history. Why is the reed of liberalism not as resilient in the twenty-first century as it seemed to be in the past?

Ironically, answers to this question are obscured by liberalism's own moral strength. Liberal values, while a powerful moral force, are weak and sometimes harmful underpinnings of social institutions. Freedom, equality, tolerance, the rule of law, and rational debate leading to the peaceful settlement of disputes are the heart of liberalism. These values, however, chafe against the sacrosanct entrenchment of the "free" market and the liberal neglect of the human need for status, community, and heroes. This chafing has now opened wounds in liberal democratic institutions that have deepened with the rise of neoliberal economics and the digital revolution. As weaknesses are exposed, deep and threatening cracks in the institutions upon which we have depended to ensure freedom, social harmony, rational discourse, social equality, and the protection of "inalienable" rights have become unavoidably visible.

Like a runaway immune system that sickens the body rather than protecting and healing it, liberal principles of free speech, free markets, individualism, and even equal rights protection have run amok, threatening to destroy the liberal democratic body politic. Unrestricted "free" markets have led to unprecedented economic inequality and deep and widespread economic precarity (Azmanova 2020). Precarity destroys freedom of choice in housing, schooling, employment, and healthcare for millions. Precarity, individualism, and laws against discrimination have, each in its own way, undermined community, caused status insecurity, and splintered social reality along economic lines. Unbridled free speech has led to a post-truth information environment that destroys rational discourse and further destroys a shared reality.

Ironically, naive belief in "self-evident" liberal "truths" has blinded much of Western society to forces that have debilitated liberal institutions. Hamstrung by a false certainty that liberal principles provide a strong foundation for liberal democracy, liberals have become complacent, depending on those institutions to uphold their values and translate them into laws, norms, and behaviors that create social trust and progress. But the very values that liberals hold dear leave many deep human needs and desires unfulfilled and cannot support the institutions that they believe in.

For these reasons, liberalism's foundations have always been unstable, and liberal institutions have long been distorted and subverted. But technological, economic, social, and geopolitical forces that reared their heads in the twenty-first century expose the weakness of those institutions, threatening them as they have never been threatened before. In this chapter, I briefly lay out the principles of liberal democracy and of the institutions that constitute the "international liberal order." I then discuss the fragility of those principles and argue that their weakness lies both in their internal contradictions and in their conflict with basic human needs and desires. I discuss how the COVID-19 pandemic revealed these contradictions and conflicts. I then focus on one failure of liberalism and its cause: the twenty-first-century viral spread of disinformation, which strikes at the heart of social trust and rational debate. Although much of the argument applies to liberal democracies in general, my reference point and the focus of most of my examples is the US.

Liberal principles

Despite its historical mutations and ambiguity, "liberalism" is a set of commonly understood principles codified in the impersonal laws and institutions of most democracies and international institutions. These principles include freedom (of discussion, assembly, religion, press, movement, trade, and elections), tolerance of other cultures and religions and of opposing views, reasoned debate, rule of law as the basis of governance, peaceful settlement of disputes and transfer of power, legal protection of fundamental human rights, legal equality, equality of economic opportunity, and limitations on state power.

These principles of what we can call political liberalism accompany but rub against the principles of economic liberalism that underpin the "free" market. Market competition creates winners, losers, economic inequality, and precarity. Liberals have varying degrees of tolerance for the economic inequality that markets inevitably produce. For economic liberals, economic inequality is simply a side effect of functioning free markets that must be tolerated. They believe that market "losers" have only their own inefficiency to blame and that economic equality—and even equity—produces scarcity for all. Neoliberals believe in a self-regulating, impersonal market that requires little or no state intervention protecting those most vulnerable. Ralf Dahrendorf (1968) argued that inequality is not compatible with freedom if it limits individuals' chances to participate in the political community. He and other progressives believed that government should offer the economic support needed to give all citizens the opportunity to participate in liberal democratic society. The debate between neo- (right-wing) liberals and progressive (left-wing) liberals has long raged in the halls of government. The exponential growth of economic inequality now, however, renders this debate moot and both amplifies and is overshadowed by the forces of extreme right-wing illiberalism.

Liberal institutions and the rule of law

Liberal principles provide a blueprint for the social construction of liberal democratic institutions, both domestic and international. These institutions are intended to create shared social norms and a shared social reality that also respects different opinions. For example, it is a widely shared norm that market discrimination between rich and poor, winners and losers, is tolerated as a legitimate impersonal force for the welfare of all, whereas personal and organizational discrimination based on race, gender, sex, or religion is not to be tolerated. It is also a widely shared norm that political conflict should be resolved by established laws rather than by coercion or violence. The basis of shared norms and shared reality is the rule of law, restricting the arbitrary exercise of power by subordinating it to established laws that codify "the will of the people." The rule of law is the foundation of liberal constitutions because it depersonalizes political power. Alexander Hamilton (1787) wrote that the rule of law is necessary

> because the passions of man will not conform to the dictates of reason and justice without restraint [and when] the whole power of government is in the hands of the people, there is less pretense for the use of violent remedies in partial or occasional distempers of the State.

Unable and unwilling to eschew "passions," liberal democracies have institutionalized restraints on antiliberal behavior. One restraint is the separation of powers into legislative, administrative, and judicial branches of government, each of which is designed to limit the power of the other two and represent different points of view. Under systems that enshrine universal (or near universal) suffrage, government representatives of the people assume power through free elections. The judiciary is designed to be independent from the other branches and from the whims and illiberal desires of both citizens and politicians in office. Its role is to interpret the constitution as the ultimate basis of law, ensure that the rule of law prevails in governance, ensure equal justice for all, and protect "inalienable" human rights and the rights of minorities, which could otherwise be weakened or rescinded by the majority. Together these domestic institutions can be said to constitute "the liberal order."

Post–World War II international institutions enshrine many of these principles and provide the basis for what is called "the liberal international order." This "order" was constructed to ensure that the political and economic failures that led to two world wars in the twentieth century would not reoccur. Its creators built institutions of global governance to promote peaceful international cooperation, universal human rights, free markets, and economic development (see Kaul, Chapter 13 in this volume, for more on multilateralism). The liberal international order, as this narrative goes, succeeded in freeing trade, preventing another world war, and spreading prosperity to Western allies.

Many argue that these institutions must have a "leader" to survive. Why? States participating in these organizations must relinquish some of their sovereignty and sacrifice their own self-interest for the common good if the rules demand it. But they look first to their own interests, and only secondarily to the common good. Also, unlike in domestic society, there is no enforcement mechanism for liberal international rules. Therefore, the creation and maintenance of a liberal rule-based global order would not have been possible without the power and willingness of the strongest country to use its great might to create incentives for cooperation and make sacrifices for the common good. That power was the US. It shaped the rules of liberal institutions and agreed to pay the costs of international cooperation by providing "side payments" to those who believed their participation might not serve their interests. For example, through a system of extended deterrence and alliances, the US offered and paid for security to those who cooperated. And by providing a reserve currency and an open economy, the US greased the wheels of a global economic system, even if that meant suffering a trade deficit. As the story goes, the US sacrificed some of its own power for the common good.

Under the aegis of the US, these rule-based institutions and their underlying norms and principles were the dominant form of domestic and international governance in the last half of the twentieth century. Liberal democracy became the most widespread political system in the world. To this day, no new institutions have emerged to challenge those that have long constituted this "liberal international order."

As the twenty-first century opened, however, this vision of the liberal world order showed signs of weakness. For the first time in a century, a set of large, populous, increasingly wealthy, and undemocratic or fragile democratic states with governments hostile to liberalism—China, Russia, Brazil, and India—were becoming "great powers" that refused to accept the principles of a liberal international order. The US had already begun its slow relative economic decline with the growing economic strength of Europe and Japan. Some countries thus began to challenge the Western conception of order based on the primacy of the US and liberal post-World War II rules. Now the liberal hegemon had lost much of its power and willingness to lead. China's growing power and ambition in Asia; cracks in the international consensus on free trade; Russia's snubbing of international law and invasion of Ukraine; the rise of illiberal regimes among the European Union's members; the (re)emergence of authoritarian rulers and their successful efforts to fragment and undermine liberal democratic governance around the globe; the rise of the extreme political right—all these combined to put the postwar liberal order at risk. Four years of an antiliberal US president who scoffed at liberal institutions was simply the latest blow.

There is, however, another way to tell the story: the international liberal order has never been international, liberal, or orderly. During the Cold War, much of the world did not participate in it. The US used coercion to get its way in international organizations. Governments in the Global South, struggling to quickly establish democracies so that they could receive US aid, held perfunctory elections while refusing to establish an independent judiciary, protect human rights, or permit fundamental freedoms. In the "one-party democracies" of Mexico, South Korea, and Taiwan, elections were held and opposition parties appeared on the ballot, but for many decades, rulers manipulated elections to maintain their authoritarian power with the blessing of the US. And while loudly advocating democratization across the globe, the US supported corrupt regimes and instigated coups and assassination plots against democratically elected leaders. Its military unilaterally intervened abroad, breaking the rules of the multilateral security institutions it had created. Based on the lie of the Gulf of Tonkin incident, it escalated its war with Vietnam, which killed thousands of Americans and millions in Southeast Asia. With the Cold War long over, the US launched an unlawful invasion of Iraq—also based on a lie—and engaged in horrific acts of torture. Liberal international institutions were only a thin ideological curtain behind which US power was exercised and legitimized.

No matter which version of the story is emphasized, the question remains: how could these institutions fail so quickly after so many apparent successes in achieving (what some might say is simply the appearance of) relative peace and prosperity, at least for the Western world? In the latter version, the institutions themselves were an illusion and a distraction from the machinations of power politics driving the international system. Nonetheless, they did spread the idea of liberal democracy, and they healed many wounds of World War II. So, what is causing them to fail so spectacularly now, if the foundation of liberalism, as I will show below, was weak from the outset? I turn first to the fatal flaws of three liberal principles—equality, individual freedom, and rational discourse—and then to the current conditions leading to failure.

The weakness of liberalism

Many in liberal democracies admit that there are aspects of their societies that are painfully illiberal. Over time, they believe, reforms have brought the liberal promise closer to reality. Incremental reforms, for example, to realize the principle of equality in education have benefited some immigrants and people of color. Infrastructure reforms have enabled the formerly disabled. Market regulation has reduced environmental disaster. But liberalism itself and the remedies it offers cannot eradicate the disease of illiberalism. Reforms may treat the symptoms, but because they do not target the causes, they can neither kill illiberal pathogens, nor inoculate society against them. Ironically, the successes of reform and widespread belief in liberal democratic principles—particularly the principle of individual freedom—have staved off controversy over liberalism's inherent weaknesses and have blinded us to the real problems caused by its contradictions. I begin with the central problem: the frailty of the principle of equality in liberal democracies.

Inequality, precarity, and the dissolution of shared reality

The American narrative venerates the principle of equality. But its conflict with the principle of freedom—the "free" market—is at the heart of liberalism's weakness. The Declaration of Independence acknowledged human equality to be a self-evident truth, and the notion is a core value of liberal democracy.

In this document, however, the "self-evidence" of equality did not apply to "all men." Thomas Jefferson intended his words "All men are created equal" only to convince the British that American colonists were equal to them and that they must therefore dissolve the hierarchical relationship between Crown and colonies. "Equality" did not apply to slaves, Native Americans, or women. Jefferson rejected the universality of individual equality when, in *Notes on the State of Virginia* (1782, 2017), he declared "that the blacks…are inferior to the whites in the endowments both of body and mind." Black males, he wrote, prefer white women, and orangutans prefer black women. If slave owners were to abolish slavery, former slaves should be deported to Africa, and free blacks should be eliminated from Virginia. As a "founding father" of the US, Jefferson argued that there was no place for free and equal black people in American society. That belief remains alive to this day. The white people who stormed the US Capitol on January 6, 2021, believed that the 2020 election was stolen from them because votes of Black people should not be counted.[1]

Nonetheless, the declaration of universal equality was transformative on many levels. It was enshrined in US law with the widening of the franchise. Politicians of all political stripes declare that, in the name of equal rights, racism, misogyny, and religious discrimination have no place in American society. But in fact, the inequality of rights based on gender and skin color is inherent in the DNA of US institutions. It is embedded in the healthcare, criminal justice, election, and education systems, housing, and the physical infrastructure of the country. These institutions were built for the exclusive benefit of white people. And they harm groups that face discrimination. Equal rights are not a promise: they are the law. And in order to lay low centuries of white (and white male) dominance, women, workers, people of color, the disabled, LGBTQ people, and immigrants have each had to fight long and hard to achieve their "inalienable rights." Those fights are still ongoing.

Precarity affects people of all colors

Equality of rights stops at the economy's edge. There, freedom trumps equality. Liberal society vilifies the idea that people should share income and wealth equitably. "Free market competition" is classical liberalism's motto and political battle cry. While liberal democratic societies tolerate the economic inequality that is inevitable in capitalist economies, they substitute "equality of economic opportunity" as a compromise to express both freedom of choice and equality.

Understanding the ideological basis for this liberal tolerance of economic inequality and inequity helps us to understand why the crisis of economic inequality and precarity persists and why it weakens liberal democracy. Liberalism assumes that obscene economic inequality and precarity result from an inability to compete in the market. By this sleight of hand, these indignities cannot be caused by discrimination.

Economic inequality poisons the entire liberal project, and COVID-19 strengthens the poisonous brew. The wealth of the world's billionaires reached a new record high in the pandemic, and the stock market soared, while millions—primarily low-wage workers—lost their jobs and were unequipped to manage without income. Despite the stimulus packages, the US cut back on revenue redistribution while the Federal Reserve propped up asset values by acting as the buyer of last resort. This dramatically increased the wealth of those who held stocks. The poor and the middle class of all colors risk illness and death because they must go out to work, while the rich retreat to their isolated homes and zoom-equipped computers.

Public acceptance of economic inequality undermines economic opportunity and "freedom of choice." The poor have little freedom to choose where they live; their homes are crowded, often in polluted areas, and far from amenities. Poor people disproportionately die of heatstroke because they work outside and live in neighborhoods surrounded by asphalt. Dependent upon property taxes, public schools in less affluent areas are substandard. As economic inequality grows, precarity grows with it. Access to medical care, for example, is restricted by income. As a result, the US has among the largest income-based health disparities in the world. Precarity kills: the life expectancy of the wealthiest Americans now exceeds that of the poorest by ten to fifteen years.

Economic inequality also diminishes a shared perception of reality in liberal society. The "winners" of market competition and those lucky enough to have inherited wealth experience a daily reality of relative comfort. The "losers" experience varying degrees of economic and social struggle. During the pandemic, a white-collar worker's reality has been shaped by the ability to comfortably zoom from the safety of home, while the blue-collar worker's reality is shaped by working a "frontline" minimum-wage job with exposure to deathly illness. Access to healthcare shapes the experience of pain, illness, and death. While a person of means attends yoga classes for spiritual sustenance, a poorer person pleads with God for economic sustenance. Those with sufficient wealth have a more positive experience of globalization, while those who live on the margin and lose their jobs to overseas workers have a negative experience. Wealth is also a conduit for emotional experience: whether one has it and how much one has shapes divergent hopes and fears, confidence, and emotional security, as well as respect for liberal democratic institutions. While the economic "losers" are driven by fear of what lies ahead for them, the economic "winners" express more confidence in the future and more respect for institutions of liberal democracy.

A puzzle

Oddly, this absence of a shared economic reality is not echoed in public opinion (Pew Research 2019). What is expressed is a fractured and polarized social and cultural reality that correlates with stark differences in economic and racial realities. While all white US voters react to good or bad news about the aggregate economy, there is little evidence that their own financial situation similarly influences their voting behavior. If the aggregate economy is doing well but they are struggling to make ends meet, they believe it is their own fault or the fault of their immediate employer. In numerous surveys, white working-class men express little criticism of the "1 percent" and its growing wealth, even as their own economic situation worsens. But a high percentage of these same men express disdain for political liberalism's emphasis on diversity and equality, and they show contempt for "liberal coastal elites" while they praise wealthy CEOs as "winners."

The above discussion suggests that commitment to economic liberalism and its emphasis on "freedom of choice" is deeply entrenched across classes in American society, but a commitment to political liberalism with its emphasis on freedom and equality is much more tenuous. Why? First, while it is difficult to rage at an impersonal force like the free market, political and social institutions and the people who populate them are easy targets for the expression of hatred, even if the actual cause might be despair over a worsening personal economic situation. Therefore, the fragmentation of a shared social reality is most obvious in the expression of support for or opposition to particular policies protecting equality and the politicians and bureaucrats who write them. A second explanation is expressed in different experiences of injustice and favoritism. Those who struggle to survive in the market report that they experience increasing political discrimination against them due to government efforts to decrease racial, sexual, and gender discrimination. In fact, white men feel equal to other white men, no matter their economic status. It is their feeling of superiority to women and people of color that defines their equality to one another. Their equality to each other depends on their superiority and on inequality of those "below them" in social status.

An influential study by the National Academy of Sciences (NAS) (Mutz 2018) suggests that white working-class males fear that greater social and political equality will result in a loss of their place in a social hierarchy that has historically privileged white Christian men. Though they express little opposition to the fact that their wages have stagnated while the affluent grow richer, they feel that their dominant status (white, male, Christian) is threatened by demographic shifts and policies to ensure equal rights. The fear that a person of color could take their job translates into anger, despondency, and distrust of political institutions that protect equal rights. They vote for those they believe will protect their dominance. Many support right-wing politicians who promise to rein in globalization and to weaken or abolish policies and laws that promote equality. The NAS study shows that in the 2016 presidential election, white working-class men turned to Trump for the reasons noted above. They have voted Republican in every election since the 1968 civil rights law was enacted. White rural voters stayed with Republicans in 2020, despite a large defection, largely of women, to Democratic presidential candidate Joe Biden in the metropolitan suburbs. The January 6, 2021, mobs that stormed the capital were composed mostly of white men, many of them members of white supremacist groups.

Many of those white men who fear the toppling of their social status have formed modern illiberal "tribes"—communities that tout their own superiority and victimhood and feel threatened by demographic shifts and liberal protection of equal rights for all others. These tribes are characterized by exclusive collective identities—nativist, racist, sectarian, supremacist, misogynist, antigovernment, and the like—that prevail over individual and even national identity. They feel superior to other identity groups and communities of women and people of color. Members of these communities may be citizens of a liberal democracy, but their deeper loyalties are to their own ethnic, racial, or sectarian groups. These groups provide a sense of connection, status, and belonging, which they believe is denied to them by liberal principles, institutions, and elites.

Liberal neglect of the need for community

The rise of this so-called "tribalism" reveals a second weakness of liberalism: its role in the weakening of community. A root cause of liberalism's malaise is that its focus on individual freedom and equality neglects the human need for social solidarity. Most people crave an identity larger than themselves, an identity that community provides. Community gives a sense of safety and offers resources that most people cannot obtain on their own. It produces emotional bonds that promise feelings of belonging and security. Those feelings become the source of reciprocity, trust, and solidarity. Liberal principles do not oppose community, and liberal institutions provide ample space and freedom for religious, social, athletic, ethnic, and other identity groups to form. And liberals defend the protection of a "national" community from threatening outsiders. But liberal principles of individual merit, competitiveness, and freedom are often at odds with the norms of community.

In his seminal study, *Bowling Alone*, Robert Putnam (2000) shows that communities have weakened in liberal societies and the need for community has gone unfulfilled. As the community-destroying principles of free market competition and free movement of people spread, neoliberalism ushered in an age of globalization in which the borders of a liberal national community are weakened. In the US, for example, there has long been simmering conflict between those who would seal off the national community to both migrants and trade and those who believe in free mobility. In 2016 Trump translated the fear of "aliens" in the national community into electoral success with his promise to build a wall to keep them out. President Biden is likely to maintain many of Trump's antiliberal restrictions as well as those that Obama put in place. Liberal nationalism has always faced deep internal contradictions between opening borders and protecting the national community.

Liberal principles prevent homogeneous ethnic, religious, and ideological communities from determining who can teach in their public schools, live in their neighborhoods, or provide them with healthcare. The law gives most anyone the freedom to enter a local community. That freedom, however, can tear the boundaries of traditional, ethnic, or religious groups asunder. And it has caused friction, particularly when outsiders have entered lower-middle-class, rural, and poorer white communities. When a homosexual teacher was hired at a school in a small, Christian, white rural community in 2019, residents protested for fear that their community values would weaken. A liberal would argue that those values are discriminatory and that their fear is the price of living in a liberal democracy. But as their boundaries are transgressed, these communities weaken, and their members are driven to extremism in hopes of community protection through exclusion of outsiders.

Community "heroes"

Particularly in a time when liberal laws seem to gnaw away at their communities, many want their political leaders to be "heroes" who promise to ignore or rescind the law in order to protect them. But heroic leaders of liberal democracies are few and far between. Bound to follow the rule of law, their leaders are, at worst, faceless and rational or, at best, mild-mannered and boring administrators of impersonal rules. So, it is no wonder that some of these groups circle the wagons and seek as their political leader a charismatic authoritarian hero who will banish faceless bureaucracies and uphold their communities by undermining liberalism, rather than a leader who is considered "weak" because she upholds the law.

While many of these communities and their "heroes" are peaceful, some have joined extremist tribes of radical right-wing white supremacists and have followed antigovernment activists whose principal hero was Donald Trump. Many have turned to violence. The Proud Boys, QAnon, and Aryan Nations are good examples of extremist communities that have gained national and even international traction. With Trump's blessing, they joined with others to show their deep contempt for liberal institutions by violently storming the US Capitol. Supporters of these and other right-wing extremist hate groups, like Marjorie Taylor Green, are even being elected to US public office. Most Republican representatives openly support QAnon and/or armed extremist right-wing groups in their efforts to silence the free press, undermine liberal democratic politicians, weaken judicial independence, and undermine efforts to dismantle racist institutions and symbols.

The radical left: loose communities, dead heroes

The radical left, also bereft of community and alienated from liberal democracy, has formed its own antiliberal communities. The Communist Party USA, for example, founded in 1919, continues to exist. Other examples include the Socialist Workers Party, the Freedom Socialist Party, and CrimethInc. Unlike right-wing extremist groups, most are loosely organized and antihierarchical and—while many revere revolutionaries long dead—do not venerate their current leaders. Many encourage anonymity. And the most recent groups have emerged in response to the menacing behavior of white supremacist militias. Antifa, which is leaderless, is the oldest and most visible. Black Bloc and Pastel Bloc, also leaderless, often appear at white supremacist rallies to protect antiracist counterprotesters. The NFAC (the Not F**king Around Coalition) is a Black armed group formed to protect peaceful protesters from white militias.

Pandemic weakens community

The COVID-19 pandemic created an environment that has hastened this weakening of community. Lockdowns, masks, social distancing, work disruptions, travel bans, and sudden unemployment easily led to social isolation. These measures hobbled communities already weakened by liberal policies that place individual rights above community cohesion. The virus further unmasked the deficiencies of unregulated globalization. Government restrictions triggered an angry backlash, weaponized by the extreme right wing. Public health restrictions are called a government assault on "liberty." Many angry dissenters joined existing antigovernment hate groups. The virus has triggered open racial discrimination with increasing calls to close borders and exclude Asians from local communities.

The hard truth is this: the task of liberal institutions is to destroy discriminatory boundaries, not to build community. Focused on individual freedom and equality, liberal democratic policymakers ignore the fact that liberal institutions undermine community. Their blindness to both structural inequality and the weakening of community deepens resentment and feeds the popularity of right-wing politicians who insult, vilify, and mock liberalism, unleashing a viral hatred of liberals. By their refusal to nurture community, liberal institutions can exacerbate social conflict.

The impact on social discourse is obvious. Both the absence of a shared social reality and the rise of illiberal "tribes" cultivate misinformation, disinformation, and a vast dissemination of falsehoods. Widespread belief in these falsehoods further fragments an already tattered sense of shared social reality. This phenomenon is the third weakness of liberalism.

Threats to rational discourse

The free exchange of information is the lifeblood of a liberal society. Liberal political discourse distinguishes itself in that it demands logic, reasoned argument, and persuasion in order to shape rational public policy. Its liberal democratic quality hinges on the integrity of public language and its responsible and accountable usage. Liberal principles emphasize the importance of truthful information as the basis for political bargaining, debate, and adherence to the rule of law. In the hope that rationality and evidence can defeat irrational emotion and hardened opinion, liberal democracies have attempted to unite disparate groups through reasoned discourse over competing norms, interests, and interpretations of factual information.

Human emotion cannot and should not be banned from liberal democratic politics but must be restrained. Why? Free speech is a "sacred" liberal principle, and appealing to human emotion is a natural and powerful tool of persuasion. Politicians can inspire potential voters and draw on their feelings of pride and admiration to win them over. But they have also long invoked fear of their opponents—often with lies—to gain support. Lyndon Johnson used images of a nuclear explosion to raise voters' fear of nuclear war if they voted against him in 1964. Both Johnson and George W. Bush perpetrated lies to justify war. Upstart candidates often stir up anger over "Washington insiders" to win votes of those who distrust "the system." Unharnessed emotion is at the root of intolerance, and unchecked emotional appeals increasingly rely on misinformation and lies to sway the opinions of others. It is to these two threats to rational discourse—intolerance and misinformation—that the discussion now turns.

Intolerance

When politicians stoke the fires of fear and hatred, they undermine the liberal norm of tolerance. Political tolerance is the willingness to extend basic rights and civil liberties to persons and groups whose viewpoints, economic status, or ascribed characteristics such as race, religion, sexual orientation, or gender differ from one's own. Intolerance, an unwillingness to extend basic rights to groups that differ from one's own, is a blatant rejection of the liberal norms of freedom and equality for all. Political scientists have shown that intolerance is a key obstacle to the consolidation of liberal democracy in newly democratic states. But only recently have scholars seen it as a threat to the institutions of established democracies. Political psychologists argue that intolerance is a behavioral expression of fear, anger, and hatred. Indeed, Bar-Tal and Teichman (2005) argue that those who express hatred of the other also express a willingness to harm and even annihilate the other.

Liberals are exhorted to extend basic rights and freedoms, even to the intolerant. But liberal practices are seldom possible when confronted with hardened intolerance. Because nonviolent acts of intolerance are rarely penalized, the intolerant believe that their behavior makes them stronger, and they see tolerance as a sign of weakness.

Misinformation and disinformation

The second threat to rational debate is that discourse grounded in unharnessed passion can be distorted by half-truths and lies contrived to win arguments and manipulate emotions. This is not new. In 1828 Andrew Jackson's presidential election campaign planted a false rumor that Jackson's opponent, John Quincy Adams, had procured an American girl to pleasure the tsar of Russia. Mainstream media is also tempted to lie: "yellow" journalists—abandoning their professional responsibility to report only the facts—have long tried to stir up passions to sell their papers. In the nineteenth century, amid tensions with Spain over its colonial oppression of Cuba, William Randolph Hearst and Joseph Pulitzer, in fierce competition for industry dominance, tried to outdo one another with sensational headlines and false claims.

Believing that their communities would be invaded by minorities and immigrants, extreme nationalists in the nineteenth and early twentieth centuries spewed hatred, fear, and lies to keep their communities "racially pure." The environments that nurtured them were marked by the spread of deceptive propaganda from a few central and powerful sources—media moguls like Hearst and Pulitzer, or the regime in power like the Nazis in Germany and fascists in Italy. They spread falsehoods for the purpose of maintaining political and economic domination. As noted above, in the early twentieth century, the *New York Times* and the *Nation* raised the specter of white people losing status, power, and influence to nonwhite or the wrong kind of white people. On Capitol Hill, Republicans and Democrats alike converged on the idea that America was a white man's country. Watching from across the Atlantic, Nazi leaders noticed. They copied restrictive American immigration and Jim Crow race law, with one exception: they believed that the Fourteenth Amendment to the US Constitution, allowing freed slaves to vote, codified an ideal of equality at odds with human experience and with the type of country whites wanted to live in. In the eyes of many Americans today, the Nazis were correct.

In the twenty-first century, the message of intolerance and exclusion and the emotions of fear and hatred driving it echo these historical examples, but the medium and the purveyors are more diverse. Today's environment is marked by two new forces: new digital technologies and social media that can disseminate information from numerous unconnected sources for a multitude of reasons. Lashing out against the gutting of their communities or simply attempting to muddy the political waters, disconnected groups and individuals joined President Trump and bolstered his message of fear and hatred, using these technologies to spread lies and scoff at liberal principles. These forces emerged long before Trump and continue to persist in his absence.

Twenty-first-century technology

With lightning speed, thousands of groups and individuals can cast their votes and share views they agree with around the world via social media. In disseminating information this way, illiberal individuals and groups join journalists, scientists, and political authorities to spread what they know, think, wish, believe, and feel. Truth is often tinged with falsehood and falsehood with truth, making truth and falsehood difficult to distinguish.

As these groups and individuals compete for attention, content and entertainment take precedence over truth. Speed blurs the line between information, misinformation, and disinformation. Exaggeration and the packaging of falsehoods as entertainment have more persuasive power than the dry presentation of facts. Instant "sharing" allows posts and tweets—true, false, distorted, and magnified by retweets and shares—to dominate social media. With digital communication technologies, millions who want their voices heard compete for the attention of those who might hear them. Both "citizen" and professional journalists vie for a scoop and exaggerate their narratives, hoping to attract attention. These practices have spread to mainstream media. As it did in the past, it manipulates readers' emotions with sensational headlines to get more clicks on digital platforms. Mainstream media is increasingly guilty of purveying misinformation, ironically cultivating general distrust of professional information sources. It is difficult to spot the difference between factual and false information in both social and mainstream news and opinion.

In 1858 C. H. Spurgeon (2014) stated, "A lie will go round the world while truth is pulling on its boots." In the twenty-first century, this statement came true. The current digital environment not only ensures the most rapid spread of falsehoods in human history but also facilitates widespread degradation of legitimate information and propagates social distrust in factual knowledge. Those who spread lies are diverse and often unconnected. They include government officials and far-flung members of antiliberal groups, spewing anti-immigrant, antiminority, and misogynist views.

This is a phenomenon now permeating Western liberal democracies. The so-called "immigration crisis" serves to illustrate. Skillfully using social media, the far right seized upon the refugee crisis of 2015 to gain a foothold throughout Europe and the US, describing refugees fleeing for their lives as invaders, jihadists, and human garbage. Their emotion-laden narratives tell of rape, murder, chaos, job snatching, and a takeover of their communities by violent Islam, all intended to strike fear and hatred into the hearts of believers. One German conspiracy theory, "the great replacement," holds that German chancellor Angela Merkel planned to swap out the ethnic German population for foreigners. In 2018 this was one of the most shared conspiracy theories circulating in Germany, and it has spread to the US through social media. These technological innovations go far in explaining the current slide of liberal democracies into a labyrinth of lies.

The global spread of this labyrinth of lies has led to the creation of a powerful alternative reality based on fantasy, opinion, and manufactured falsehoods. Antiliberal "tribes" base their reality on beliefs, not facts. They scorn rational argument and mock those who base their arguments on factual or scientific information and methods. They dismiss evidence-based claims and express opinions that call for no verification. They denigrate liberal norms of tolerance, compromise, and forbearance; they try to lower the social status of those who adhere to those norms. They often act to impose their own exclusive antiliberal identity on the identity of the nation by mocking and attacking liberal institutions. They believe that they are locked in a deadly battle with liberals, and they loathe them as the enemy. Their partisanship becomes stronger as traditional political parties weaken. Populist "heroes" work to weaken them. Their battles are part of a larger war on liberal democracy and open society itself.

Hot cognition and tribal epistemology

This belief in lies is bolstered by the social-psychological forces of "hot cognition" (Redlawsk 2002) and "tribal epistemology" in illiberal communities. There, belief replaces thought and is influenced by emotion over reason. Social psychologists call this "hot cognition." The dominant gut feelings of fear, anger, and hatred of "the other" crowd out factual narratives. Heightened emotions forge hardened opinions. Opinion becomes a sacred value, an affirmation of allegiance to one's community. If the opinion conforms to that of the community, its content, truth, or verifiability does not matter. This is a kind of *tribal epistemology*, in which information is evaluated based not on a widely shared reality or conformity to common standards of evidence, but on whether it supports the community's values and goals and is vouchsafed by its leaders. "Good for our side" and "true" begin to blur into one.[2]

Forged in the furnace of hot cognition, hardened opinion dominates cool, fact-based knowledge and provides fertile ground for the spread of falsehoods. Hot cognition provides the emotional basis for Republican lawmakers' adherence to Trump's "Big Lie" that the 2020 election was stolen from him. But in a more practical sense, it provides an excuse for their campaign of voter suppression.

Confirmation bias, social sharing, and "doubling down"

Falsehoods are packaged in the form of information. All humans share information that confirms their values, beliefs, passions, and opinions. In general, they are biased toward confirmation: they wish to believe only that which confirms what they already believe. They pass on to others stories that conform to the beliefs and values of their communities. Information is shared, not just to inform or even to persuade but as a marker of identity with a particular community. Social media users often declare their affiliations by posting links to information—true, partly true, or false—that reflects their community's taste, beliefs, and grievances and that denigrates, mocks, or scorns those they wish to exclude.

Digital sharing among illiberal and extreme right-wing communities is more pervasive than digital sharing among liberal communities (Benkler et al. 2017). The impulse to share in liberal communities is lower because liberals tap into norms and information already widely known, while illiberal communities offer up a new, more sensational counter-reality not present in mainstream discourse. If that counter-reality taps into their grievances, they are inclined to accept it and reject the mainstream liberal narrative. And if it conforms to the beliefs of their communities and community "heroes" and signals their loyalty, it becomes part of their worldview.

Although political polarization drives most citizens into mutually hostile communities, the difference between social sharing in liberal versus illiberal tribal communities often boils down to the difference between evidence-based claims and simple belief as an impetus for sharing (Chai and Ma 2012). For members of both communities, collective identity and community affinities are important. Liberals are moved by an emotional impulse to share, but they most often cling to the established practice of reasoned debate to hone, strengthen, and sometimes change their positions. They seek out evidence that supports their positions, but they also believe that they come to their positions based on factual evidence.

Members of illiberal tribal communities tend to double down on beliefs that bolster their alternative realities, especially after being presented with contradictory factual evidence, which causes uncomfortable feelings of cognitive dissonance. "Doubling down" helps resolve those feelings by dismissing the evidence or creating "alternative facts." When outsiders claim a piece of information to be false that an illiberal tribal community believes is true, that false belief becomes entrenched in the community as an article of faith. Sharing that belief demonstrates both the believers' loyalty to their community's worldview and disdain for liberal outsiders who wish to undermine that worldview with facts. In this way, the practice of fact-checking that liberals naively use to gain the upper hand in political debate can backfire (Nyhan and Reifler 2010), actually strengthening illiberal tribalism.

For the reasons cited above, liberal and illiberal communities create mutually exclusive "information bubbles." While the liberal bubble is more open to argument, the antiliberal bubble is closed: only opinion that conforms to tribal beliefs, group loyalty, and community identity is permitted to enter. With each community ensconced in its own bubble, there is no chance for opposing communities to talk to each other. In the absence of rational debate, illiberal communities often double down with inflammatory, exaggerated denunciations in order to weaken the liberal "enemy" by strengthening their own tribe with falsehoods that deepen fear, hatred, and mistrust in liberal democracy.

Liberals are slow to learn that they are not engaging in "normal" discourse or debate. They therefore have few means to resist. Isaiah Berlin warned long ago of this enduring strength of "the forces of anti-rational mystical bigotry" (2013). Because illiberal tribes believe they are at war with liberals, their goal is to bully them. They attempt to drown out their voices with swarms of bots and trolls, rumors, half-truths, and speculation on social media to overwhelm honest dialogue and denigrate those who disagree. This intimidates and unnerves liberals who attempt to counter falsehoods with fact.

This kind of bullying is not new; only its methods are. A commitment to rational discourse, negotiation, and compromise has long been exploited as a weakness of liberalism. Toward the end of World War II, Jean-Paul Sartre (1948, 13) wrote in his essay "Anti-Semite and Jew" that anti-Semites "delight in acting in bad faith, since they seek not to persuade by sound argument but to intimidate and disconcert." They "are amusing themselves, for it is their adversary who is obliged to use words responsibly, *since he believes in words*" (emphasis mine). In

1967 Hannah Arendt summed up the goals of powerful politicians who spread inflammatory lies:

> *the result of a consistent and total substitution of lies for factual truth is not that the lies will now be accepted as truth, and the truth be defamed as lies, but that the sense by which we take our bearings in the real world…is being destroyed.*
>
> (quoted in Adler 2019, 290; emphasis mine)

If they become powerful leaders, bullies fragment a shared social reality and attempt to alter the sense by which we all take our bearings.

Adherents are drawn to lying bullies who argue that factual evidence signals liberal weakness. A seminal article published in *Science* (Vosoughi, Roy, and Aral 2018) examines how falsehoods propagated through Twitter reached far more people than truth: "Whereas the truth rarely diffused to more than 1000 people, the top 1% of false-news cascades routinely diffused to between 1000 and 100,000 people." Falsehoods reached more people at every depth of a cascade than the truth, meaning that many more people retweeted falsehoods than they did the truth. Lies did not spread simply through broadcast dynamics but rather through peer-to-peer, i.e. human, sharing. Because illiberal communities are more digitally close-knit than liberal communities, it appears that falsehoods outperform the truth at every turn.

Finally, it is important to note that many liberals, too, have propagated big lies and bullied those who do not believe them. One is the lie about racial and gender equality and meritocracy in America. Laws were created and passed to ensure that all would be treated equally and that all would have "equal opportunity" to succeed. Those who ignored the law went about constructing institutions that propagated norms and behavior that kept women, African Americans, and other people of color down while privileging white American males, often under the fig leaf of the law. But the official lines that "all men are created equal" and "the merit system ensures equal opportunity" in employment and education meant that African Americans should therefore blame themselves and not the liberal system for any inability to achieve equal economic status with white males. The lie persists and helps ensure continuing inequality. Another is the lie about the "free market," discussed above, leading those who fail in the market to blame themselves, believing that they are inefficient losers and that their lack of success is their own fault. Liberals who believe these lies often double down when their beliefs are challenged.

The infodemic: how the assault on truth aided the viral spread of COVID-19

Throughout the history of pandemics, truth has been the first casualty; the coronavirus pandemic is no exception. Before the 1918 flu reached the US, government officials, including President Woodrow Wilson, covered up the extent of the disease, and many were told it was caused by malnutrition among the soldiers. Just as Wilson dismissed the danger of the pandemic in 1918, Trump dismissed the severity of COVID-19 in 2020. What distinguishes the spread of misinformation about COVID-19 today is that it comes from myriad sources, confounded by the rise and strength of illiberal communities and their disrespect for liberal government regulations.

The ubiquity of digital misinformation made the coronavirus pandemic spread more easily and quickly than it might have otherwise. In the early weeks of the outbreak, viral posts called it a hoax. Later, YouTube videos appeared, showing "why" it was caused. Some argued, for example, that Bill Gates had planted chips in human bodies, or that the virus was a biological weapon engineered by the Chinese (or by the US), or caused by 5G technology or myriad other villains.

Quickly traveling from one platform to another, these and other falsehoods about the pandemic appeared on 4chan, Telegram, Gab, Parler, Facebook, Twitter, and others. Torrents of misinformation emerged from Russian and Iranian sources, intended to deepen social and political divisions by stoking fear and weakening the credibility of restrictive measures, thereby hastening the spread of the virus. More false conspiratorial stories went viral (so to speak) than reports that debunked them. Misinformation about the virus primarily reached the ears of illiberal communities, while most liberals focused on health advice from scientific authorities. Cognitive biases clouded the truth by making readers and viewers less discerning, thereby allowing the virus to spread faster. Many, clinging to a liberal belief in "individual liberty," refused to be vaccinated, endangering the larger community.

Three remedies to heal the liberal order

Liberal principles must be drastically reformed to include (1) redefinition of the principle of freedom to include a strong repudiation of hate speech and intolerance, and strict regulation of digital technologies, (2) a reversal of the growth of economic inequality and precarity, and (3) respect for community and a way to incorporate "the other" into communities without threatening their boundaries. Without such reforms, liberal communities will not have the ability to oppose antiliberal forces. Below I briefly elaborate on remedies that can strengthen the liberal order.

Regulating digital technology and social media

I have argued here that facts, upon which a shared social reality/shared discourse is based, have been thrown onto the fires of fear and rage, fueled by twenty-first-century technology. Social media companies long resisted calls for reining in misinformation by claiming steadfast allegiance to the legal fig leaf of "freedom of speech." But in 2021, under pressure from government and the spread of deadly misinformation on the coronavirus, the companies began to rein in content on their platforms. They removed or labeled as false voting misinformation, claims of election rigging, coronavirus hoaxes, and conspiracy theories. They began to educate consumers about how to spot false content. Twitter made it more difficult to retweet false information, and Facebook began to remove some false content and ban their purveyors.

It is easy to thwart these efforts. Those banned from some platforms find others to spread their falsehoods. Users of Facebook can easily change the background color of their false messages to bypass AI fact-checking. There are not enough human fact-checkers to stamp out a post before it goes viral.

Current legislative efforts do nothing to address problems of misinformation and the viral spread of falsehoods. Social media platforms currently block rhetoric that unambiguously threatens violence and the explicit malevolent targeting of particular people and groups. They do not block hate speech that demonizes and threatens people based on their skin color, religion, or sexual orientation, Holocaust deniers, or those who implicitly incite violence. This rhetoric creates an environment that sanctions the use of violence.

In short, social media's efforts to reign in unacceptable speech only shear off the tip of the iceberg of misinformation. Only liberal democratic governance can correct the weaknesses of liberalism that produce the viral spread of misinformation. I have argued here that the sources of these weaknesses are the breakdown of shared reality, the neglect of community, and the shockingly rapid growth of economic and social inequality that give rise to fragmented and divisive realities. It is to these deeper causes that the discussion now turns.

Reducing racial and economic inequality to build and rebuild a shared reality

To bring the realities of diverse groups closer together is a necessary basis for a healthy, well-functioning liberal democracy. Achieving consensus and compromise through rational discourse grounded in factual information can be an important step in bringing realities closer together. But rational discourse is blocked by skyrocketing racial and economic inequality and poverty in which the social realities of millions of people sharply diverge.

The "free market" weakens liberal democracy. Because it is considered an impersonal, self-regulating institution from which we cannot escape, it pursues its destructive path with little complaint or notice. It is a myth that the market is an impersonal force and that it is free. It is a complex human construction, increasingly dominated by monopolies and oligopolies that set prices, manufacture demand, create barriers to entry, and take most of the winnings.

Since the 1980s, tax changes in the US benefiting the wealthy have not improved the lot of working people. While the wealthy pay little or no tax on their surging wealth, they use that wealth to influence politicians to enact policies that favor them. This undermines liberal democracy at the very top.

Taxes should be skewed toward the "ability to pay," and the wealthy have a growing capacity to pay, while the ability of the middle and working classes has diminished. The middle class, which once made up the majority of Americans, is shrinking. Its percentage of national income is falling, while upper-income households are taking the lion's share. The wages of the average American worker once kept pace with the growth of the US economy, but over decades, workers' real wages stagnated, driving many into poverty, while total wealth and the gains that accrue from assets—in addition to income and wages—soared. Wealth inequality in the US, where the top 1% of the population holds more wealth than the bottom 90%, is more glaring than in any other developed country.

What is desperately needed is a new tax on wealth. Wealth is now given special treatment in the US tax system, where the wealthy pay low rates on income derived from their assets. Revenue from a fair income and wealth tax could be redistributed to healthcare, education, infrastructure, renewable energy, and housing. Redistributive policy in Europe provides a model for the US to follow. Typical European benefits include an unemployment allowance, job training, state pensions, one-parent-family payments, illness benefits, disability allowances, rent and mortgage supplements, universal healthcare and education, childcare supplements, and more. Not all social benefits are means-tested, but for those that are, the largest share goes to the bottom 40% of the income distribution, significantly reducing economic inequality.

Reducing the realm where money matters

Tax policies and equitable redistribution can significantly reduce economic inequality and provide a larger realm of shared reality in liberal democratic society, but it does not usher in real equality or strengthen community. Social equality is possible when economic inequality is reduced and neighborhoods become more racially and socially integrated and less isolated from one another. Contact theory (Allport 1954) tells us that interaction between members of different groups can reduce prejudice and improve social relations. The more social exchanges there are, the less people of different groups will fear each other, and the more tolerant people can be toward one another. But there must be space and reasons for social exchange to take place. And because illiberal "tribes" feed off cultural and social grievances rather than economic disparity or their own precarity, they are likely to remain isolated unless they have reason to integrate with other communities.

Thirty years ago, gadfly journalist Mickey Kaus proposed that government and wealthy citizens could enhance community solidarity and social equality by providing resources to create and maintain public spaces and public institutions that reduce the realm where money and wealth matter and where everyone inhabits the space and participates in that space as an equal (Kaus 1995). Public parks, public sports facilities, beaches, city parks and parklets, racially and socially integrated churches, and public libraries may be good examples. Where social and economic inequality do not "count," then social realities can begin to converge, and all can mingle in "public space," rather than fence themselves off from one another.

Two of those spheres exist now and can provide a model for more: the military and public schools. The military—while not a "liberal" institution—exposes its members to a multitude of opinions, experiences, and ethnic, religious, and income groups. That exposure creates shared realities that demand mutual tolerance and help strengthen social cohesion. While racial discrimination is still deeply entrenched, the military is constructed as a social equalizer: the salaries at the top are much closer to those at the bottom than in the civilian world. Senior officers and enlisted personnel live and work together. Their children go to the same schools. Military values instill a sense of community, which, as noted above, creates mutual trust and a shared social reality. A civilian national service can be created along the same lines. Spending time serving one's country in a civilian capacity can both strengthen the national community and create local community for those who participate. A shared commitment to a goal that requires collective effort provides community cohesion for those who participate. Participation can counter the false claim that the only national service necessary is protecting one's country against an armed enemy.

Similarly, adequately funded public schools can act, as Horace Mann said in 1848, as a "great equalizer" (quoted in Growe and Montgomery 2003). The basic but unrealized idea of public education is that if people are admonished to "pull themselves up by their own bootstraps," they first need to have boots. Public school can level the playing field by providing boots filled with equal learning opportunities for all students. An educated population is crucial to the success of liberal democracy. Thomas Jefferson (1820) wrote, "I know no safe depository of the ultimate powers of the society but the people themselves: and if we think them not enlightened enough to exercise their control with a wholesome discretion, the remedy is not to take it from them, but to inform their discretion by education." Horace Mann underlined these words when he said that a good education is the birthright of every American child, rich and poor alike (Growe and Montgomery 2003). Education can help push people out of the poverty trap.

But because they depend on property tax revenue, public schools in affluent areas flourish while schools in poor areas often fail due to inadequate funding. Poorer schools are forced to hire inexperienced and uncertified teachers. They cannot afford enrichment, gifted, remedial, and sports programs. Furthermore, the rich and upper middle class increasingly receive tax breaks to send their children to private and charter schools (funded with public moneys), leaving all public schools to flounder. Underfunded public schools produce students who are inadequately trained for employment and who earn less when they do find a job. Students at poorly funded schools drop out at a higher rate, and their life expectancy is shorter. Students who receive a good education are likely to be more affluent than those who do not, and their divergent earning capability widens the inequality gap even further. Of course, funding alone cannot fully address inequality—good instructors, a rigorous curriculum, and strategies to meet the needs of at-risk students are also necessary. But funding is an important start in providing equity.

Public schools also offer students a sense of community. For some, it is the only community they have. Students from all walks of life can sit together; they take part in the same rituals; they share pride in the same sports team. A sense of school pride is important in building a successful school community; parent participation and pride in their children's school widens social cohesion. Student participation in cleaning up school grounds, in peer tutoring programs, and in student clubs all contribute to student cohesion through working together on common tasks and collective activities.

Conclusion

I am an avowed liberal. I bristle at the fact that the Republican Party in the US has recast the term *liberal* as a pejorative word. I do not want the principles and institutions of liberal democracy to be relegated to the dustbin of history. What I have suggested here is that if liberals do not want this to happen, they can no longer cling to an ideology of economic freedom that tolerates obscene inequality. They must do the work of opening their eyes to the structural racism that benefits white people. They enshrine individualism and ignore the human impulse to form community at their own peril. Liberals can no longer tolerate hate speech and lies in the name of "freedom of speech."

I return to the question that began this chapter. Why are the things that are supposed to bring us together driving us apart? The answer I have presented here is that liberalism, which should bind us together, has fatal weaknesses that divide us into opposing camps, each experiencing separate truths and different realities. Liberals self-righteously blame conservatives, right-wing extremists, white supremacists, and illiberal tribalism for undermining liberal institutions. To be sure, these are powerful antiliberal forces attempting to destroy all that is good about liberal democracy. But the weakness of liberalism has prepared the ground in which these forces have risen to power. Now is the time for liberals to acknowledge their part in weakening liberal democratic society, to recognize human needs and liberal contradictions, and to repair what is broken.

Notes

1 The Trump campaign targeted Detroit, Philadelphia, and Milwaukee, falsely accusing them of voter fraud and corruption. These cities either are majority Black or have large Black populations.
2 David Roberts, "Donald Trump and the Rise of Tribal Epistemology," Vox, May 19, 2017 www.vox.com/policy-and-politics/2017/3/22/14762030/donald-trump-tribal-epistemology.

References

Adler, Emanuel. 2019. *World Ordering: A Social Theory of Cognitive Evolution*. Cambridge: Cambridge University Press.

Allport, Gordon. 1954. *The Nature of Prejudice*. Cambridge, MA: Perseus Books.

Azmanova, Albena. 2020. *Capitalism on Edge: How Fighting Precarity Can Achieve Radical Change Without Crisis or Utopia*. New York: Columbia University Press.

Bar-Tal, Daniel and Yona Teichman. 2005. *Stereotypes and Prejudice in Conflict: Representations of Arabs in Israeli Jewish Society*. Cambridge: Cambridge University Press.

Benkler, Yochi, Robert Faris, Hal Roberts, and Ethan Zuckerman. 2017. "Study: Breitbart-led Right-wing Media Ecosystem Altered Broader Media Agenda." *Columbia Journalism Review*. https://www.cjr.org/analysis/breitbart-media-trump-harvard-study.php.

Berlin, Isiah. 2013. *The Crooked Timber of Humanity: Chapters in the History of Ideas*. Princeton, NJ: Princeton University Press.

Dahrendorf, Ralf. 1968. "On the Origin of Inequality among Men." In Ralf Dahrendorf, Essays in the Theory of Society, 151–78. Stanford, CA: Stanford University Press.

Freedom House. 2021. *Freedom in the World 2021*. Washington, DC: Freedom House.

Growe, Rosilyn and Paula Montgomery. 2003. "Educational Equity in America: Is Education the Great Equalizer?" *The Professional Educator*, 25(2): 23.

Hamilton, Alexander. 1787. "The Insufficiency of the Present Confederation to Preserve the Union." Federalist No. 15. *The Independent Journal*. https://guides.loc.gov/federalist-papers/text-11-20#s-lg-box-wrapper-25493286.

Jefferson, Thomas. 1820. "Letter to William Charles Jarvis." National Archives. https://founders.archives.gov/documents/Jefferson/98-01-02-1540

Jefferson, Thomas. 2017. *Notes on the State of Virginia*. London: Forgotten Books.

Kaus, Mickey. 1995. *The End of Inequality*. New York: Basic Books.

Chai, Lee and Long Ma. 2012. News Sharing in Social Media: The Effect of Gratifications and Prior Experience. *Computers in Human Behavior*, 28(2): 331–339.

Mutz, Dianna C. 2018. "Status Threat not Economic Hardship Explains 2016 Presidential Vote." *Proceedings of the National Academy of Sciences*, 115(19, Spring): 4330–4339. https://doi.org/10.1073/pnas.1718155115.

Nyhan, Brendan and Jason Reifler. 2010. "When Corrections Fail: The Persistence of Political Misperceptions." *Political Behavior*, 32(2): 303–330.

Pew Research. 2019. *In a Politically Polarized Era, Sharp Divides in Both Partisan Coalitions*. December 17. https://www.pewresearch.org/politics/2019/12/17/in-a-politically-polarized-era-sharp-divides-in-both-partisan-coalitions/.

Putnam, Robert D. 2000. *Bowling Alone: The Collapse and Revival of American Community*. New York: Simon and Schuster.

Redlawsk, David P. 2002. "Hot Cognition or Cool Consideration? Testing the Effects of Motivated Reasoning on Political Decision Making." *Journal of Politics*, 64(4): 1021–1044.

Sartre, Jean Paul. 1948. *Anti-Semite and Jew*. New York: Schocken Books.

Spurgeon, Charles. 2014. *Spurgeon's Gems*. Apollo Pennsylvania: Ichthus Publications.

Vosoughi, Soroush, Deb Roy, and Sinan Aral. 2018. The spread of true and false news online. *Science*, 359(6380): 1146–1151. https://doi.org/10.1126/science.aap9559

4

WHAT FUTURE FOR POLITICS?

Jan Zielonka

The outbreak of COVID-19 prompted the greatest political intrusion in our lifetime. Governments around the world introduced measures that shattered our private lives, brought economic life to a virtual standstill, and threw into question the value of international organizations. These stringent measures were adopted in a war-like fashion in order to combat an invisible enemy which has infected millions of people globally. Only some interventions have been long-lasting, and efforts are since being made to soften the impact of restrictions. Governments have spent plenty of money to protect businesses, for instance. We can argue about the wisdom of individual measures, but we cannot negate their magnitude. Our basic rights to privacy, to work, to move, and to associate freely have been brushed aside by states aspiring to a quasi-absolute power. No wonder the Russian conservative intellectual, Alexander Dugin, announced with a visible satisfaction "the total collapse of open society" (Dugin 2020). We may find his declaration premature and biased, but we cannot deny that the unprecedented interventions undertaken by states have left a durable impact on our polities and on citizens.

This chapter addresses the far-reaching political implications of the pandemic: what effect the pandemic has on our political "body" rather than our physical bodies and how it can emerge from this crisis stronger rather than weaker. The shock may leave us shattered and divided, but it may also mobilize us to rebuild and enlarge the public sphere, to offer citizens meaningful forms of participation in public affairs, to bring markets under democratic scrutiny, and perhaps to even create a kinder market society able to respect labor (including migrant labor), the environment, and citizens' health.

Revolution by default

The scale and form of governmental actions during the pandemic amount almost to a revolution, but this revolution was not plotted by angry citizens inspired by a radical ideology. It is a revolution by default, resulting from policies aimed at combatting a deadly virus rather than overthrowing leaders and regimes. Yet the measures introduced in 2020–2021 have shifted the key boundaries of the political, and the world will never be the same.

Political systems reflect a certain equilibrium. Their complex balance of competing values, rights, and prerogatives is the product of hard and long bargaining and in some cases even war, either civil or international. The equilibrium—or compromise if you prefer—governs procedures for adopting laws, the powers of state institutions, and catalogues of citizens' rights. The latter limit state intervention in our family life, economic activity, and leisure. Most of these rights are protected in our constitutions. This equilibrium also concerns issues which are difficult to legislate, but which form the basis of an unwritten "social contract" between the state and its people. They define the notion of the common good, demarcate the public sphere from the private one, and shape the relationship between the state and markets. If this fundamental equilibrium is overturned, then we may witness a revolution. This chapter will argue that the political interventions undertaken to fight COVID-19 have destroyed most of the existing equilibria beyond repair. This is why the impact of these intrusions is not just massive in scale, but also bound to be long-lasting.

The scale of governmental interventions is most vividly manifested by the politics of time and space. Time and space are, as Charles S. Maier put it, "two of the scarcest social resources" that politicians must handle with great care (Maier 1987, 16). Both have been subject to brutal intervention during the pandemic. Lockdowns have not only confined us to narrow spaces defined by the authorities; they have also turned upside-down our future planning and changed the implications of past decisions regarding our work and family life. The process of easing the lockdowns has often been arbitrary, and it is not yet complete. We do not yet know when, if ever, we will be moving across space in the ways we did before the pandemic, but we suspect that our pre-COVID thinking about the past and the future cannot be restored.

Political interventions have also effectively curbed our political freedom. During lockdowns it is hard to exercise the right to assembly or peaceful demonstration. Lockdowns also curb our access to information and our freedom of speech. In China whistleblowers have been brutally silenced, and in Russia some of them have "accidentally" fallen from high windows. Even in established democracies, scientific reports have been censored by governments, and journalists have publicly been reprimanded by officials for being "too negative" and "unpatriotic." Former United States President Donald Trump's press conferences during the pandemic will be watched by students of journalism for many years. In the United Kingdom scientists condemned "Stalinist" attempts to censor COVID-19 advice.

Political interventions in private business have been unprecedented. Many factories were ordered to shut down. The movement of goods, services, and labor was stopped by the closure of borders and flight cancellations. Millions were asked to work online, while millions of others found themselves without a job. Governments have tried to soften the economic impact of the decreed lockdowns by spending huge sums to support affected entrepreneurs and workers. This support in itself represents an enormous political intervention with uneven and controversial distributive results. In Poland the government was denounced for favoring local political cronies, while the Dutch government was accused of wasting money on indebted euro members. Some have criticized the governmental help for distorting the markets, while others condemned it for failing to help the unemployed or migrant laborers.

The burden of these political interventions has been shouldered not just by individuals, but also by their families. In fact, governments openly declared private homes to be the frontline in the war against the pandemic. Yet lockdowns have physically divided many families, and those squeezed in small flats have struggled to cohabit peacefully. Some governments went as far as to define who belongs in a family or not. In France the "lovers amendment" was voted down in parliament to prevent separated couples from reuniting for the lockdown unless they are officially married.

The relationship between the private and public spheres has thus been shifted considerably by these political intrusions. Public authorities assumed more powers, and these were not always exercised in rational, effective, and fair ways. The relationship between the individual and the market has also changed through political intervention. Initially, policies were guided by ethical considerations rather than by concerns about profit. The aim was to save lives regardless of the economic implications. With time, however, this relationship has been reversed. Workers have been asked to return to their workplaces to restart the economy, whilst the risk of further waves of the pandemic loomed large. The relationship between local, national, and universal identities has also been changed through these interventions. As states began to rally people under national flags, new enemies were created, and some of us discovered ourselves to be on the wrong side of the newly erected borders, physical or virtual.

The case for hope amid despair

Social media is full of conspiracy theories suggesting that these unprecedented intrusions have been orchestrated by a small group of people with power and money, that Danton or Saint-Just would call the aristocracy of the twenty-first century. Bill Gates and George Soros are the favorite targets of conspiracy theorists. Some "experts" have even questioned the dangers related to COVID-19. I find these speculations groundless, and in some cases malign. There is ample evidence suggesting that many governments across the world acted in good faith; they all tried hard to save lives in their own imperfect way. Draconian laws were usually drafted by doctors rather than politicians; the information to guide decisions was patchy; and each measure hurriedly adopted was bound to have unintended side effects. Those in charge have often been partisan, and some of them have misused the emergency powers they were granted. At the end of the day, however, this is not the most important factor behind the revolutionary change. The boundaries of the political would have shifted even if someone else was occupying the White House, 10 Downing Street, or the Élysée Palace. COVID-19 has prompted a politics of fear, with all its destabilizing implications. This virus could not be treated in a benign manner; it required an extraordinary, rapid, and largely improvised response.

However, even the noblest of intentions can generate poor, if not malicious, results. All political interventions create winners and losers. Revolutions can be a force for good, but they can also be a force of evil, generating violence and injustice. Democracy and capitalism have been temporarily suspended, and various partisan actors will try to redefine the rules of the game in the coming years. We have already observed a clash of power and ideas between scientists, industrialists, and politicians. National politicians have come into conflict with local and regional leaders, and also with each other. We have seen the World Health Organization (WHO) and the United Nations (UN) struggling with their national paymasters. The European Central Bank in Frankfurt clashed with the German Constitutional Court in Karlsruhe. The European Union also came under fire for either doing too little, or too much, depending on who was doing the criticizing. Most citizens were either confused or scared, which opened the door for speculators and demagogues.

The result of this systemic breakdown is not necessarily bad news, as citizens can find ways of turning this crisis into an opportunity rather than a tragedy. Inequality has reached unprecedented levels in recent years, and those who find themselves at the bottom of our societies may welcome a shock to the existing equilibrium. But if they find themselves without a job and with no state able to support them, they may well look for support beyond the state: in Calabria and Campania we have already observed citizens turning to the mafia. International organizations have done little to arrest climate change or the spread of viral diseases. No wonder some citizens rejoice in their demise. But are we sure that closing pompous buildings in Geneva or Brussels will help rather than hinder our efforts to avert another pandemic or environmental disaster? We need to comprehend the nature of the ongoing changes and steer political interventions in a direction reflecting the interests and aspirations of the majority of citizens.

Shifting political priorities

We often hear that politics and economics will be different after this pandemic, but we do not know how different exactly. In the field of politics at least three major changes can be expected. First, we can imagine that issues of time and space will become more contentious than the traditional political and economic concerns. Second, since the public sector is regaining its importance, we can expect competition for power and resources between different levels of public governance. Third, the pandemic has revealed that we were preparing for the wrong war, and we can presume that there will be increased pressure to see health and the environment as the key security issues demanding relevant institutional and financial resources.

History is full of battles for political or economic power. The former is chiefly about the control of state institutions, and the latter is about making and distributing profits. I suspect that in the future key battles are likely to be about time and space. Over years, citizens have learned how to stand up for their political and economic rights. However, during the pandemic they realized that an unprecedented intrusion in their time and space could be introduced overnight by a hastily drafted law. At stake was not just the freedom of assembly or uneven economic burdens, but something much more personal. We suddenly realized how precious time and space is for us. Initially, most citizens accepted the imposed restrictions on medical grounds, but they gradually realized that many policies were imposed or lifted randomly with no clear logic or scientific evidence underpinning these decisions. As a consequence, we entered a new era of political contestation centering chiefly around issues of time and space impinging directly on individual and collective rights. Some of this contestation aimed at preventing a power grab by politicians misusing emergency measures. Yet a large part of this contestation was about the uneven implications of the adopted policies for different groups of citizens. Only some groups could continue working remotely from home. Quarantine affected people in large cities differently than those in the countryside. Older people were more vulnerable to the virus than younger ones, although the latter were usually more affected by the economic implications of the adopted policies. Gender, race, and wealth were also differentiating factors, with black and ethnic minority groups disproportionately affected in many countries.

COVID-19 is likely to stay with us for some time, and then another virus (or bacteria) will arrive, prompting more contentious political interventions affecting citizens' time and space. Citizens may respond in either chaotic or organized ways to these interventions. There is a danger that social distancing rules will generate self-centered citizens unable to form what sociologists refer to as social and political capital. As Rafael Behr put it in *The Guardian*: "Each handshake or shared bag of chips is a little social contract—a declaration of affinity. And without physical proximity we have to work harder to negotiate those alliances" (Behr 2020). Citizens' quests for collective rights emerge from such social bonds based on trust and affinity. An atomized society is easy prey for autocratic politics and economic exploitation. We have seen this repeatedly during the pandemic.

The battle against COVID-19 has placed public institutions on the front line, but it is debatable which level of public governance has performed better in this battle. Initially the nation-states tried to take things into their own hands by issuing decrees binding local governments and ignoring or even attacking transnational institutions such as the WHO or EU. With time, however, it has become clear that many nation-states are not effectively using the powers they claimed. The virus has spread unevenly across individual countries and one-size-fits-all policies applied by national governments were clearly at odds with the realities on the ground. No wonder that conflicts between national, regional, and municipal authorities have multiplied. Although most states sealed their respective national borders, medical arguments argued for sealing the borders around the epicenters of infections. These national rather than regional shutdowns also defied logic: why should people living in a heavily infected Lombardy be banned from travel to the United Kingdom or France but not to Sardinia or Basilicata where there were hardly any infections? The real battle against COVID-19 has seldom been fought in state capitals, but rather in different cities, sometimes quite small and remote from national ministries. Local communities quickly realized that their municipal or regional authorities are more skillful in pandemic politics than their national governments. In France, public trust in mayors jumped to 70%, while the central government only enjoyed 30% of the public's trust. The governor of the state of New York, Andrew Cuomo, and the mayor of Moscow, Sergei Sobyanin, fared much better through the crisis than the respective presidents at the time, Trump and Vladimir Putin.

With the passage of time, it has also become clear that most national states will not be able to shoulder the economic burdens of the pandemic on their own. Europe is a very good example here, where states most affected by the virus have proved dependent on the arrangements negotiated within the eurozone. Although these national leaders have prided themselves on being the most skillful in combatting the virus, it became plainly obvious that medics learn from the experiences in other countries, and they are dependent on international suppliers of even basic medical items. Even then, President Trump had to acknowledge that it is hard to invent and produce effective vaccines without international collaboration. Claims that nation-states have effectively reclaimed sovereignty and glory during the pandemics have proved premature. In the future, the public sphere is likely to be stronger vis-à-vis the private sphere than was the case in the past decades. However, it is not yet clear which level of public governance is likely to prevail. As always, the outcome will be decided through a long-lasting political battle for access to decision-making and resources. This battle among different levels of public governance is likely to dominate politics in the coming years.

The politics of pandemics has largely been driven by fear. In this sense, it could be conceived as a kind of security policy albeit of a different type than traditional military security. "We are at war!" declared France's President Macron in March 2020, and the emergency measures adopted in most countries were very much war-like and involved the armed forces in various capacities. In fact, deaths from COVID-19 have exceeded the number of deaths resulting from most of the post-1945 wars. Economic devastation caused by the pandemic has also been described in war-like terms. Clearly, this was a very lethal "war," for which states and their armed forces were poorly prepared. In the past decades, most efforts and money were invested in combatting traditional military threats, even though infectious diseases were time and again identified as real, if not imminent, threats. Even the most basic defensive equipment against the virus was lacking in wealthy countries, let alone in the poorer ones. International security alliances such as the North Atlantic Treaty Organization have proved irrelevant in the "war" against the pandemic. Expensive military aircrafts or battle ships proved useless in combatting the virus. In fact, the very symbol of the French defense system, the aircraft carrier Charles de Gaulle, has been "defeated" by the virus; a thousand sailors were infected on this "armed to the teeth" ship.

The traumatic experience of the pandemic is likely to revolutionize security calculations and policies. Of course, nuclear or terrorist threats will not disappear, but citizens will demand that states address health security in its various forms and shapes. Security institutions and their budgets will have to be rethought and adjusted to these new threat perceptions. This process of adjustment will challenge not only vested interests within the military, but also within the industrial military complex that is dependent on the maintenance of the traditional security structures and related profits. We can therefore expect hard political bargaining over the new meaning of security and the related policies. Pressure to address these new security threats will come not only from medical concerns, but also from environmental worries, each of them demanding new policies and budgets.

Legitimizing the new policies

The pandemic has raised new apprehensions and called for new policies to address them. However, major changes are always contentious, and novel policies do not always meet expectations. The pandemic has struck various groups of citizens unevenly, and policies to cope with the effects of the pandemic will have uneven impacts on the population. Unless those in charge of public institutions are able to secure the legitimacy of the measures undertaken, we can expect civic conflicts or perhaps even in some cases, civil wars.

Legitimacy is a precious political good, but there is no hard science that tells us how to acquire legitimacy, especially in periods of major change. Two types of legitimacy are popular in the literature: input and output legitimacy (Easton 1965; Scharpf 1999). The latter depends on the quality of government services and the former on the quality of democratic governance (Rothstein 2009). The majority of citizens support certain policies either because they had an opportunity to shape them through democratic devices or because they believe that these policies generate the desired results and impacts, regardless of the democratic input. The pandemic has showed that governments, even in Western Europe and the US, are neither particularly effective nor democratic. Why is this so?

Democracy is under fire for numerous reasons, but the crisis of parliamentary representation is certainly one of them. We elect politicians once every four or five years to represent us in running the state, but our vote usually does not result in the envisaged policy changes. As a result, we have a vote but not voice; we can change the government, but this change of government fails to reduce inequalities, curb racism, or protect the natural environment. Therefore, we must try to build democracy on pillars other than representation alone: deliberation, contestation, transparency, and most crucially, participation. As one of our most respected political scientists, Giovanni Sartori, put it: "Real democracy can only be, and must be, participatory democracy" (Sartori 1989, 39).

Participation is chiefly about localism: the larger the unit the more difficult it is to offer citizens valuable forms of participation. This means that we should shift more decisions to the urban and regional level and embrace genuine grassroots initiatives such as the Barcelona-style *municipalismo*. Local governments found themselves on the front line of the fight against the pandemic, but their records of performance were uneven. This is because most of the recent reforms aimed at devolution and decentralization were organized by top party echelons, and they empowered local elites rather than local citizens. This must be reversed. We also should utilize the various grassroots and voluntary initiatives which spontaneously emerged during the pandemic to help those most vulnerable. The vast strata of local activists engaged in helping thousands across local communities represents a solid foundation of the envisaged participatory democracy. Digital technology can also be utilized to enhance citizens' participation, especially at the national and European level. The internet can narrow the space between governments and the people; it can enhance transparency and offer novel ways of deliberation and decision-making. Of course, the internet can also be a means of manipulation, but there are ways to avert this.

Without boosting democracy, it would be hard to see post-pandemic policies enjoying widespread legitimacy. However, the system needs not only to be democratic; it must also be effective. We used to identify effectiveness with the private sector, while the public sector was often seen as unresponsive, slow, and incompetent. As a result, policies of privatization and deregulation have been in vogue since the 1980s. We have been trying to privatize virtually everything including schools, hospitals, and even prisons. The public sector has increasingly been understaffed, underpaid, and poorly trained. However, the pandemic has demonstrated that without public health services and state support for the economy, it was impossible to combat COVID-19 effectively. Thus, post-pandemic reconstruction can hardly rely on the private sector alone. However, the question is how to make the public sector more professional and less bureaucratic. How can we create a public sector that is not only big, but also wise, cost-effective, and responsive to citizens?

My answer is: start to rebuild a competent public administration (see Seibel, Chapter 8, for more on reliance on public administration). Without a skilled public administration, the state is brainless and toothless. Neoliberals treated the public service as redundant, and they cut its size, tasks, and autonomy. Then populists came to power, here and there, and started to staff state institutions with their political cronies who were loyal but lacked competence. Today most countries lack a bureaucracy that is able to effectively plan and implement policies. This will obviously hamper all post-pandemic efforts. Public admin-istrations ought to be trained practically from scratch, made independent from political games, and democratized. The latter can be achieved through enhanced transparency, clearer lines of responsibility, and stronger societal ties helped by non-discriminatory recruitment processes. Our administrators should be neither policy-motivated "zealots" nor policy indifferent "slackers," to use Gailmard and Patty's expression (2007, 874). They should be helped to rediscover the meaning of the noble term "civil servants" at various levels of government. Teachers in public schools, nurses in public hospitals, and the police officers on our streets are also public servants. They should be properly trained, rewarded, and appreciated by all of us, and especially by those at the top of the decision-making process.

Different levels of government are in a better or worse position to acquire either input or output legitimacy. Citizens' participation is easier to secure at the local rather than European level, for instance. Yet local governments usually lack the means to cope effectively with transnational actors such as pharmaceutical multinational firms or with transnational issues such as climate change. Large units such as the EU are in a better position to handle climate change or firms such as Microsoft, but they are further away from citizens than small units such as cities or regions. Nation-states are somewhere in the middle of this equa-tion, although some states are very small, some are dysfunctional, and some are autocratic. As Robert A. Dahl has pointed out, the arguments over the optimal democratic and efficient unit go around in circles, as with a set of Chinese boxes:

> Any unit you choose smaller than the globe itself can be shown to be smaller than the boundaries of an urgent problem. Yet the larger the unit the greater the cost of uniform rules, the larger the minorities who cannot prevail, and the more watered-down control of the individual citizen.
>
> *(Dahl 1970, 372–3)*

This means that the post-pandemic policies cannot be confined to one level of government only. Policies will enjoy broader public support if the local, national, and transnational governments act in concert, "trading off" their different types of legitimacy. The pandemic showed that harmony between different levels of governance is not easy to secure, and yet it is important to keep in mind that without such harmony policies will ultimately lack legitimacy. The units able to offer input legitimacy are usually unable to offer output legitimacy, and vice versa. This finding should primarily reach national leaders trying to monopolize decision-making at the expense of both local and transnational government.

Conclusions: defending open society

Alexander Dugin was right: the politics of pandemics represent a mortal chal-lenge to open society. However, he was wrong to announce the total collapse of open society. Open society can be saved, and the way to do this was shown by a group of intellectuals born a century ago in my native part of Europe: Hannah Arendt, Isaiah Berlin, and Karl Popper. They knew what society they were striving for, but they refrained from advocating any revolutionary utopia. For them the process of arriving at the destination was as important as the final product. They urged us to move forward towards a better future through reasoning, deliberation, and bargaining. Key values advocated by them, such as individual liberty and equality, tolerance and anti-racism, the rule of law and accountable power, fair trade and diplomatic multilateralism, have not lost their relevance during the pandemic. These values ought to be defended in the post-pandemic context. This is not an endorsement of the status quo, because the pandemic urged us to alter the way we relate to each other, distribute goods, and organize government. This is a call for change guided by liberal values and not by shallow oratory promising glorious prospects through the application of a few simple soundbites. For Karl Popper society is open when it "sets the critical powers of man," and he contrasted it with the "closed" or "tribal" society with its "submission to magical forces" (Popper 1991). Most people would like to see their countries doing "great," but this can hardly be achieved through individual greed, national jingoism, and political gambling. COVID-19 has exposed human weakness, but we can certainly bounce back if we act wisely and stick together.

References

Behr, Rafael. 2020, April 28. "The Lockdown in Our Minds Will Be the Last Restriction to be Lifted," *The Guardian*, https://www.theguardian.com/commentisfree/2020/apr/28/lockdown-restrictions-solidarity-coronavirus-social-distancing. Accessed July 16, 2021.

Dahl, Robert A. 1970. "Democracy and the Chinese Boxes." In Henry S. Kariel (ed.). *Frontiers of Democratic Theory*. New York: Random House.

Dugin, Alexander. 2020. "This Coronavirus Epidemic Represents the End of Globalization," MEMRI. Russia/Special Dispatch No. 8710. https://www.memri.org/reports/anti-liberal-russian-philosopher-dugin-new-multi-polar-world-order-upon-us-where-russia. Accessed July 16, 2021.

Easton, David. 1965. *A Systems Framework for Political Analysis*. Englewood Cliffs, NJ: Prentice Hall.

Gailmard, Sean and John W. Patty. 2007. "Slackers and Zealots: Civil Service, Policy Discretion, and Bureaucratic Expertise." *American Journal of Political Science*, 51(4): 873–889.

Maier, Charles S. (ed.). 1987. *Changing Boundaries of the Political. Essays on the Evolving Balance Between the State and Society, Public and Private in Europe*. Cambridge & New York: Cambridge University Press.

Popper, Karl. 1991. *The Open Society and Its Enemies*. London: Times Books.

Rothstein, Bo. 2009. "Creating Political Legitimacy: Electoral Democracy Versus Quality of Government." *American Behavioral Scientist*, 53(3): 311–330.

Sartori, Giovanni. 1989. "Video-Power." *Government and Opposition*, 24(1): 39–53.

Scharpf, Fritz W. 1999. *Governing in Europe: Effective and Democratic*. Oxford: Oxford University Press.

5

WHAT FUTURE FOR THE ECONOMIC CONSENSUS?

Linda Yueh

Introduction

There are times in history when the consensus about our economic system breaks down. It happened after the Long Depression, also known as the Great Depression of the nineteenth century, and again in the twentieth century around the Great Depression of 1929–1933, as well as after the Great Recession of 2008–2009 that followed the global financial crisis. The COVID-19 great crash, which carries the risk of a deep downturn, has led governments to take extraordinary measures in all areas of our lives (IMF 2021). This has further fueled the need to discuss how to rebuild the consensus about the most appropriate economic system for the twenty-first century as the great question of our time.

The dissatisfaction over the past decade and for many years before then stems from a number of factors which are difficult to generalize about. But they seem to share in common an anti-establishment sentiment, that is, that the current economic system does not work well enough for the middle class, wage growth or the environment. This sentiment has manifested as a backlash against globalization, dissatisfaction about a system with high levels of inequality and a desire to reform or even to reject the current capitalist system.

After all, globalization does lead to "losers" even if the economy as a whole gains (Ricardo 1817). This has led to discontent in advanced economies (see e.g., Stiglitz 2017). Also, developing countries have not benefited as much as developed ones, which resulted in the protests of the late 1990s against the World Trade Organization (WTO) (Stiglitz 2002). The launch of the WTO's Doha Round in 2001 was an attempt to liberalize global markets in a more inclusive fashion. That Round has stalled after 14 years of discussions (Pakpahan 2012; Donnan 2015).

Furthermore, inequality is a huge concern, particularly with the top 1% getting ever richer while the middle class see their incomes stagnate across major economies (Piketty 2013). According to some measures, the US is as or in some respects more unequal than during the Gilded Age of the late nineteenth century, which coincides with a previous period of a breakdown in consensus (Yueh 2018).

Unsurprisingly, these and other factors, including not doing enough to address the climate crisis, have contributed to discontent with the current economic system. This leads to the great question of our time, which is how to reform the economic system to make it more inclusive and equitable and to protect the environment. Or the current system risks being discarded in favor of an alternative. The resurgence in interest in socialism is one example (see e.g., Chatiner 2020).

Just as the factors contributing to the breakdown in consensus are complicated, even a definition of the current economic system is complex, much less reforming the entire way the economy works. Yet, for society to come together again, it is imperative that we address this question of how the economic consensus can be rebuilt. One step to help rebuild that consensus is to look to lessons from history and learn from previous periods when the economic consensus broke down and was rebuilt.

The creation of welfare state capitalism

The nineteenth-century breakdown in consensus about the appropriate economic system led eventually to a significant reform of the capitalist economy through the creation of the welfare state. But it took decades.

The breakdown had happened a few decades after a new economic consensus around free trade had seemingly been reached. The repeal in 1846 of the protectionist Corn Laws, which levied high tariffs on imports of grain that protected English landowners, seemed to mark a new era for globalization (Irwin and Chepeliev 2020). The previous consensus that countries should aim for trade surpluses, known as mercantilism, was rejected in favor of openness. It took decades to achieve the new consensus that nations would follow the theory of comparative advantage whereby countries specialized and exchanged rather than protected their borders. This was the economic idea of the great economist, David Ricardo (Ricardo 1817).

An increase in tariffs on imported wheat in 1815 under the Corn Laws prompted Ricardo's "Essay on the Influence of a Low Price of Corn on the Profits of Stock." The argument against the protectionist Corn Laws then formed the foundation for his seminal work that set out the basis for trade models in 1817. In *On the Principles of Political Economy and Taxation*, he set out his theory of comparative advantage that countries should specialize and trade. Ricardo's arguments eventually led to the repeal of the Corn Laws after his death. He was not the first to make this case against these protectionist tariffs, but he formalized the model of comparative advantage that captured the benefits of international trade over protectionism which helped to change the mind of the British Prime Minister Sir Robert Peel. Peel broke with his own party to repeal the Corn Laws, which had great support among landowners, and seemingly heralded a new period of support for globalization and openness.

That consensus did not last. Fewer than three decades later, the global economy was shaken by the panic of 1873 (Barreyre 2011). A railroad speculative bubble burst, and the financial crisis spread from the US to Europe and affected the global economy. It led to the Long Depression, also called the Great Depression of the nineteenth century. That was the first time that the word "unemployment" appeared in the dictionary (Yueh 2018).

This downside of global links and globalization added to the backlash. The misery of unemployment and poverty were in stark contrast to the excesses of the Gilded Age. That period of the late nineteenth century was indeed a time of high levels of income and wealth inequality. The capitalist system seemed to work for the very rich but provided no safety net for the rest.

The late nineteenth century also marked the late Victorian period. There was a social focus on helping the "deserving poor." There was growth in charitable organizations funded by private benefactors, such as the UK's first female peer, Baroness Angela Burdett-Coutts, who was recognized for her philanthropy and had worked with Charles Dickens at that time (Healey 2004).

But welfare supported by the state was initially resisted, particularly by economists. Neo-classical economists such as Alfred Marshall at Cambridge University were initially skeptical about creating a welfare state (Yueh 2018). Their concern was over the disincentivizing effects on work of giving people benefits. Instead, Marshall believed in a prescribed set of roles for the government to improve welfare for the society where these measures can provide opportunities to advance in a capitalist economy. For instance, he supported state provision of universal education so that even the poorest children could gain skills and compete for jobs. When it came to improving social conditions, Marshall believed in the market forces of supply and demand to raise wages for the poor rather than welfare.

Therefore, Alfred Marshall initially did not support fiscal redistribution through taxes. He viewed income taxes as inefficient because of their disincentivizing effects on work. But, with the introduction of a graduated death tax (higher rates on larger estates) in 1894, the forerunner to an inheritance tax, there was no disincentivizing effect on the willingness to work. That helped change Marshall's mind, since more needed to be done to reduce poverty and inequality. So, during and after the First World War, Marshall came to believe in the benefits of progressive tax rates. He gradually accepted fiscal redistribution. This change in mindset among the neo-classical economists helped pave the way for the introduction of the welfare programs that characterize advanced economies today, e.g., Social Security in the US, the National Health Service (NHS) in the UK, among others.

They did so under great pressure from others such as Karl Marx who preferred an entirely different economic system altogether (Yueh 2018). Marx had experienced the same Industrial Revolution as the neo-classical economists, albeit somewhat later in his native Germany. But he came to a different conclusion.

During the late nineteenth and early twentieth centuries, his theories were influential. Marxism transformed the economies of some of the largest countries in the world. From Russia to China, communism took hold in some form as these nations sought an alternative to the US-led capitalist model. The notions of economic equality and communal effort were among the reasons Russia turned to Marx. Their communist revolution in 1917 led to the establishment of the Soviet Union, which vied with capitalist US as the economic model *du jour* during the Cold War which lasted from the end of the Second World War until the fall of the Berlin Wall in the late 1980s.

The end of the nineteenth century was when Marx's communist theories gained traction. The last quarter of the 1800s saw frequent economic downturns, including the Long Depression or the Great Depression of the nineteenth century. In the 1870s, economic crises plagued Europe and North America. Stock market crashes led to deep recessions, which generated high unemployment, labor unrest and strikes. During the Long Depression, nineteen socialist and labor parties were founded in Europe as were trade federations. So, the downsides of industrialization paved the way for the workers' movement.

The rise of Marxism in the twentieth century led other economists to argue for a reformed capitalist system or risk losing the battle of ideas (Yueh 2018). The Austrian economist Joseph Schumpeter was one of them. His *Capitalism, Socialism, and Democracy* (1942) began as a series of essays, which reflected a time of turmoil that encompassed the Great Depression of the 1930s, the rise of Marxism that challenged capitalism and the Second World War. It was published in 1942, but due to the Second World War it was not until the second edition in 1947 and the third edition in 1950 that *Capitalism, Socialism, and Democracy* became prominent. The book became popular because it captured the great debate of the time. During the early twentieth century, around 40% of the global population was living under communism and another quarter or so in at least partly socialized economies.

Schumpeter was not alone. As the Second World War started to wind down, another Austrian economist Friedrich Hayek published *The Road to Serfdom* in 1944. It would make him one of the world's best-known thinkers (Yueh 2018). The Great Depression before the war had shaken belief in the capitalist system and people had even become used to centrally planned wartime economies. Hayek warned about the dangers resulting from government control of economic decision-making, whether communist or fascist. He argued that the abandonment of individualism led not only to a loss of freedom and the creation of an oppressive society, but inevitably also to totalitarianism and effectively the serfdom of the individual. In his view, government-imposed centralized planning was undemocratic because the will of a few was imposed on the people and the rule of law and individual freedoms were sacrificed.

The 1944 volume was to make Hayek famous, and not just in economic or academic circles. Hayek's influence was notable behind the "Iron Curtain" and contributed to the shift in opinion against the communist regimes that eventually ended with the collapse of the Soviet Union in the late 1980s and early 1990s. The former Soviet states reintegrated with the global economy, and many joined or sought to join the European Union (EU), for instance, Poland, Hungary, Romania and Bulgaria. These nations embraced marketization and openness to international trade. Even those economies which did not abandon communism, such as China and Vietnam, still introduced market-oriented reforms during the 1980s and 1990s.

By that point, the capitalist system of the twentieth century was not the same as that of the nineteenth century during the Long Depression. For instance, the US economy had been transformed through the New Deal in the 1930s that followed Keynesianism and introduced a role for government intervention. This followed from the change in mindset of the neo-classical economists who accepted the need to have a redistributive system to provide a social safety net. In the postwar period, some form of welfare state was found across advanced economies and changed the economic system into one characterized by welfare state capitalism.

With the Soviet Union disintegrating and communist China adopting market-oriented reforms, that seemingly brought about a new consensus by the late 1980s. This new consensus was not without exception. But most major economies were characterized by welfare state capitalism. The role of the market, with a social safety net, was deemed to be a better system than the previous system and the alternative communist and socialist approaches.

With the former Soviet Union states adopting democracy along with marketization that completely transformed their previous communist and planned economies, this period of the 1990s onwards seemed to be characterized by liberal democracies which embraced free trade and a welfare state. This new consensus was captured by Francis Fukuyama's 1992 book, *The End of History and the Last Man*, which saw the ascendancy of liberal democracy and the reformed capitalist economy over the alternatives.

But this new consensus did not last. Fractures were evident during the late 1990s' protests against globalization at the WTO meeting in Seattle. Even before then, the excess of the capitalist system was captured by movies like *Wall Street* and captured by the dotcom bubble which burst in the early 2000s. Throughout this period, inequality continued getting worse in the US and elsewhere (Piketty 2013).

Then, the 2008 global financial crisis struck. A bubble in the US housing market generated shockwaves across the global economy, linked closely to the American financial system (Tooze 2018). The slow recovery from the Great Recession that followed highlighted the many ways in which the economic system did not seem to work. It revealed the inadequacy of the social safety net in many economies when unemployment skyrocketed. The 2010s were also characterized by movements such as Extinction Rebellion and activists like Greta Thunberg who grew impatient with the inability of the current system to address the climate crisis.

Just as the recovery appeared to be taking hold and the end of austere economic policies were in sight, the COVID-19 pandemic struck in late 2019 and early 2020. This crisis was not only a demand shock but also a supply shock, which further revealed the global linkages that meant that health and economic disruptions in one country can quickly affect others. This crisis has again highlighted the inadequacy of the social safety net to cope with a pandemic, which meant that governments quickly devised and put in place new benefit and loan programs to help people and businesses (IMF 2021). Seeing what can be done has reignited the debate over whether governments should do more for the welfare system in normal times (*The Economist* 2021).

We are again at a point in history where the economic consensus has broken down. There is a backlash against the current economic system, which does not adequately address environmental concerns and permits too much inequality. There is also a backlash against globalization and an interest in alternative systems, such as socialist policies proposed by the economist Thomas Piketty in *Capital and Ideology* (Piketty 2019).

Lessons from history

What happened in the late nineteenth century has resonance for this century, i.e., a US financial crisis led to a global crisis which contributed to the brewing discontent with the economic system. Some of the lessons that might be drawn are below.

First, there is an urgent need to explore reforms to the current economic system, e.g., is there a twenty-first century equivalent to when the capitalist system was transformed into welfare state capitalism? Are there alternative economic systems which can address the myriad of concerns over inequality, the environment, or globalization, to name a few, which have been expressed in different ways over the past few decades?

Another lesson is that it took a long time to form a new consensus. Whether the historical breakdown in consensus is dated from the late nineteenth century or the early twentieth century, it took the better part of a century for the battle of ideas between a reformed capitalist system and a communist or socialist one to be temporarily won by a changed market-based economy.

Finally, the road was not straightforward in getting to a new consensus. There was a time during the Cold War during the postwar period when it was a battle for hearts and minds. The growth of communist and socialist regimes only gradually gave away to welfare state capitalism throughout the early twentieth century until the 1980s.

Therefore, a great challenge for our time is to rebuild the economic consensus. The final lesson is that to agree on this consensus will require a robust debate that involves all in society. It cannot be done by economists or specialists alone. Though they play an important part in proposing economic reforms, the concerns around the environment, inequality and globalization need to be addressed by a wide range of stakeholders and those from a wide range of fields.

Conclusion

The future of the economic consensus is at stake. Rebuilding it will take time. But history teaches us that it can be done and that there are lessons that we can learn from those who have done it before us.

Perhaps Mark Twain was right when he reportedly said: "History doesn't repeat itself, but it often rhymes."

References

Barreyre, Nicolas. 2011. "The Politics of Economic Crises: The Panic of 1873, the End of Reconstruction, and the Realignment of American Politics." *The Journal of the Gilded Age and Progressive Era*, 10(4): 403–423. JSTOR. www.jstor.org/stable/23045120.

Chatiner, Isaac. 2020, March 2. "How Socialist Is Bernie Sanders?" *New Yorker*. https://www.newyorker.com/news/q-and-a/how-socialist-is-bernie-sanders

Donnan, Shawn. 2015, December 20. "Trade Talks Lead to 'Death of Doha and Birth of New WTO,'" *Financial Times*, https://www.ft.com/content/97e8525e-a740-11e5-9700-2b669a5aeb83

The Economist. 2021, March 6. "Covid-19 Has Transformed the Welfare State. Which Changes Will Endure?" *The Economist*, https://www.economist.com/briefing/2021/03/06/covid-19-has-transformed-the-welfare-state-which-changes-will-endure.

Fukuyama, Francis. 1992. *The End of History and the Last Man*. New York: Free Press.

Hayek, Frederick. 1944. *The Road to Serfdom*. London: Routledge.

Healey, Edna. 2004. *Coutts, Angela Georgina Burdett-, suo jure Baroness Burdett-Coutts (1814–1906)*. Oxford Dictionary of National Biography. https://doi.org/10.1093/ref:odnb/32175

International Monetary Fund (IMF). 2021. "Policy Tracker." https://www.imf.org/en/Topics/imf-and-covid19/Policy-Responses-to-COVID-19 (This policy tracker summarizes the key economic responses governments are taking to limit the human and economic impact of the COVID-19 pandemic. The tracker includes 197 economies. Last updated on July 2, 2021. Accessed July 26, 2021.)

Irwin, Douglas and Maksym Chepeliev. 2020, December 9. "The Economic Consequences of Sir Robert Peel: A Quantitative Assessment of the Repeal of the Corn Laws." VoxEU.org, https://voxeu.org/article/quantitative-assessment-repeal-corn-laws

Pakpahan, Beginda. 2012. "Deadlock in the WTO: What Is Next?" World Trade Organization Research and Analysis, https://www.wto.org/english/forums_e/public_forum12_e/art_pf12_e/art19.htm

Piketty, Thomas. 2013. *Capital in the Twenty-First Century*. Cambridge, MA: Harvard University Press.

Piketty, Thomas. 2019. *Capital and Ideology*. Cambridge, MA: Harvard University Press.

Ricardo, David. 1817. *On the Principles of Political Economy and Taxation*. London: John Murray.

Schumpeter, Joseph. 1942. *Capitalism, Socialism and Democracy*. London and New York: Routledge.

Stiglitz, Joseph. 2002. *Globalization and Its Discontents*. New York: W.W. Norton & Company.

Stiglitz, Joseph. 2017. *Globalization and Its Discontents Revisited*. New York: W.W. Norton & Company.

Tooze, Adam. 2018. *Crashed: How a Decade of Financial Crises Changed the World*. London: Penguin Random House.

Yueh, Linda. 2018. *The Great Economists: How Their Ideas Can Help Us Today*. London: Viking.

6

HOW DO DIVIDED SOCIETIES COME ABOUT?

Rudolf Stichweh

The rise of global modernity

When Émile Durkheim (1893) published *De la division du travail social* in 1893, the "division" he analyzed was the "division of labor," and the division of labor or "organic solidarity"—the major term for it in his book—is not at all "divisive" but is the most important cooperative force in modern society. The transformations of modern society turned organic solidarity into the contemporary structures of "functional differentiation" (Stichweh 2013); once more functional differentiation is not at all divisive but establishes relations of complementarity and rich textures of interaction among the function systems. Probably the most important among these integrative structures is the separation of individuals and their life trajectories from function systems. Individuals do not live in or do not belong to function systems. In principle, all individuals are included in all the function systems of society. Patterns of participation vary from individual to individual, and it is this diversity of patterns of participation that probably generates the strong integrative force of societal differentiation. There are many other aspects. One of them is the representation of other function systems (representation by cognitions and specialized structures) that arises in every function system: the policies regulating other function systems, the differentiation of markets dealing with the specificities of other function systems, the cognitive perspectives science invents to understand the idiosyncrasies of other function systems and to transform this understanding in disciplines internal to science, the specialized corpora of law. The diversity of individual inclusions and the multiplicity of functionally specific reconstructive perspectives (on other function systems) are both good candidates for understanding the integration of society.

There are strong divisive forces in modern society, nonetheless. It is the goal of this chapter to give a systematic overview of these forces of division in an interpretation focused on early twenty-first century world society. But I will locate these divisions in circumstances that arose in the genesis of modern society, late in the eighteenth century, and in the unfulfilled promises and unrealized values that may be seen as constitutive for the self-understanding of modern society. There are three of these promises and values, and these three are semantically closely tied to the self-description of the French Revolution.

The three promises we identify with the French Revolution are equality, liberty and fraternity/solidarity, although the semantic consolidation of this tripartite formula probably occurred later than the 1790s, around and after 1848 (Ozouf 1997). The three terms in this formula are values or promises or preferences. They obviously do not describe realities, but as values they are indicators of a significant semantic transformation that is characteristic of modernity in a general sense and is not limited to France.

In modern society observers are no longer able and willing to admire inequality and to venerate persons with high social status. Instead they prefer equality. Furthermore, since the eighteenth century there are no longer semantic resources available that allow for articulation of a preference for dependency over freedom or liberty. The education of young people is no longer perceived as a training for submission, and political education is not oriented toward obedience—and similar theses can be formulated for all the function systems of world society. There may exist authoritarian aspects in the training of the student physician (Merton et al. 1957) or the future research scientist and other professionals. But these partial authoritarian patterns are perceived as preparation for a future in which the person trained clearly will have become a colleague in a situation characterized by symmetry. Even the military does not instill obedience as an invariable habit of a person but only as military role behavior one should be able to change if one becomes a commander. The case for fraternity/solidarity is slightly more difficult. But it can clearly be said that a core value of modern society is not to look any longer to most other people as enemies and dangerous competitors, opting instead for ever widening circles of solidarity (Banfield 1958; Nelson 1969) that may include the whole of humanity at some point.

The three core values mentioned here and the desirable type of society (Kluckhohn 1951) they project is a society that is based on extremely complicated patterns of functional differentiation and other forms of structure formation that emerge together with the global social system (global networks, world organizations, epistemic communities as forms of structure formation complementary to functional differentiation; see Stichweh 2007). But it is a non-divided society as long as it is based on universal equality, on personal freedom instead of dependencies and on basic solidarities including all other humans. This, obviously, is not the society we live in. The basic value preferences and promises of modernity remain unrealized. We will look at some major reasons and social forms in the following.

Persistent inequalities

Premodern societies are in many respects based on ascriptive inequalities. Inequalities are ascribed via membership in estates, castes and strata into which one is born. In one's life-course one lives these inequalities, one has to practice a lifestyle that demonstrates every day where a person finds its place in the inequalities society consists of. Persons are explicitly taught inequality; they are incessantly reminded of their station in life.[1]

These ascriptive inequalities mostly disappear with the rise of modern society. This disappearance is the major legitimation for the claim of modernity to bring about a society of equals. The real shift is, however, a shift from ascriptive, monodimensional and stable inequality (singular) to dynamic inequalities (plural inequalities). Inequalities reproduce the primary differentiation of modern society, functional differentiation. Even if, in function systems, there are institutional arrangements that try to guarantee an equality of starting conditions for all participants (a homogenization of the start (Luhmann 1990)), there soon arise small differences, and these small differences often trigger bigger differences that may grow continuously. There is the idea of the "Matthew effect" or the theory of cumulative advantages that has been proposed by Robert K. Merton (1988; see also DiPrete and Eirich 2006). This theory seems to be the best explanation for the dynamics and expansion of inequalities to be observed in all the function systems of world society. The basic mechanism proposed by this theory postulates that persons who achieve early successes in a functional context will get bigger rewards for later successes than other persons who did not produce these early results. Therefore, differences expand and may become ever bigger.

This theory is a very good approach for explaining inequalities in function systems. But it is not the only one, and it is not in itself a sufficient one. Another complementary approach will not look at the escalation of performances and rewards. Instead it will only study the (preordained) social distribution of rewards, prizes and prestige or elite positions in a given social system. If there is such an institutionalized distribution it will clearly limit or expand the effects that can be produced by cumulative advantages. If there is only a very small number of prizes and positions, there will probably arise enormous disparities among participants, and these disparities cannot be explained by cumulative advantage as they are somehow instantaneous and arise in the moment the prizes/positions are attributed (Nobel prizes that discriminate among scientists of equal standing are probably a good example). An opposite case are the professions that are institutionalized by creating a considerable number of professional roles that realize a professional monopoly in a certain field of professional activity (often dominating a function system) (Stichweh 2008). These professional roles are often described by a fundamental equality among professional role bearers (an equality of doctors, professors, lawyers, etc.), and these institutionalized equalities in many cases neutralize cumulative advantages that had already been there. This equalizing effect of professional roles has in a number of social systems the effect of stabilizing an asymmetrical relation of professional performance roles and all others who are as clients the public of professional roles. But these relations are asymmetries and not inequalities.

Besides Matthew effects (= cumulative advantages) and positional effects there exists a third type of inequalities in function systems. These are network effects. In networks one does not collect rewards or prizes/positions. Instead one acquires ties. And there is "preferential attachment" as a mechanism of the growth of personal networks that operates very similar to "cumulative advantage." If some participants already have a significant number of "ties," it becomes ever more probable that the next actor entering the network will, in establishing ties, look for those actors who already have many ties. Network ties and the social structures and inequalities coming with them (especially "structural holes" (Burt 1992)) are not the core rewards of the function systems. But they obviously channel access to core rewards. From "preferential attachment" may arise "cumulative advantages" in terms of the core resources/rewards defining a system.

The inequalities in function systems discussed here that are the dominant inequalities in present-day world society do not in themselves bring about a divided society. As long as inequalities produce continuous gradations one may have the idea and the hope that individuals could in principle manage a stepwise ascent in a relevant dimension of inequality and that it might be exactly this possibility and hope of a gradual ascent that somehow prevents discontinuities that place individuals on two sides of a discontinuous distribution with no chances to switch from the one to the other side of such a distribution. As soon as such discontinuities arise and are perceived as such, we probably have to do with a divided society. A good example for such a discontinuity is the 1%-phenomenon in economic systems. If one studies the present-day global income distribution one realizes that from 1988 to 2008 the top 1% of the global income distribution achieved a cumulative global real income gain of 65% in these 20 years. This 1% group consists of 70 million people, half of which live in the United States, most of the others in Europe, Canada and a few Asian countries (Milanovic 2016, Ch. 1; Autor 2014). The lower middle classes of the European and North American countries and Japan cluster around the 80th percentile of the global income distribution—that is they might even be called "rich" in global, comparative perspective. But their cumulative real income gain in the same 20 years was near to 0% and is the lowest among all income groups of the world in these 20 years. This difference between a 65% and a 0% real income gain seems to be a plausible example of a discontinuity or gap arising in a number of countries that produces a divided society. The consequences of these developments are easily perceived in terms of conflict levels, political polarization, the rise of populism and the support for former US President Donald Trump and Brexit.

Besides discontinuities arising in specific function systems there is one other possibility: discontinuities arising in a specific function system that become causally relevant for inequalities in one or several other function systems in society. The most important case in our days is education, especially higher education. For hundreds of years participants in higher education were a small elite segment of populations that in those countries that established higher educational institutions between 1200 and 1945 only included 1–5% of the male population and minimal numbers of females, if any at all. This has changed dramatically in the twentieth century, especially after 1945. If one compares the years 1980 and 2010 the OECD average and the G20 average of the share of the young population who gets a higher education degree grew from around 20% to nearly 40% (now true for males and females) (OECD 2011).

From the point of view of functional differentiation, this primarily means that the knowledge one acquires in higher education is no longer one relevant form or source of knowledge among others. It becomes universal knowledge that is relevant in all function systems of society and more or less becomes a precondition for elite positions in all the function systems of society. This makes visible that higher education may become a source of societal inequality that transcends the boundaries of function systems, and it implies the possibility of a division of society that separates all those with higher education from all others who have no higher education. There are some strong economic indicators that point in this direction. The OECD average of earnings of persons with higher education compared to persons with the highest secondary school degree shows in 2011 a 55% advantage for persons with higher education. In this respect there is a range from 15% to 160%, and the countries with the lowest higher education income advantage are (besides New Zealand) the three Scandinavian countries Sweden, Denmark and Norway that in other respects, too, are probably the most equal countries in the world.

It seems to be the case in contemporary systems of stratification that if there is a dividing line that separates the higher from the lower strata it is mostly connected to education. This is a very dynamic development with rapidly increasing differences. If one only looks at the US this country surely is one of the most unequal countries in the world (if one measures inequality by the higher education wage premium) (Autor 2014): the earnings advantage for people with a college degree increased from 1979 to 2012 (in constant dollars) from US$13,000 to $23,000 for females and from US$17,000 to $35,000 for males. In a slightly longer period (1964 to 2012) the higher education wage premium (again in comparison to people with a high school degree) rose from 45% to 95%. This is astonishing as in the same 48 years the share of college graduates in the total number of hours worked in the US economy rose from 18% to 52%. This can be seen as a strong indicator of a split in the US economy and society. Half of the workload in the US is done by college graduates, and for these hours they are paid more than 100% (the 95% noted above refers only to all high school graduates; for all other educational levels the college wage premium is higher than 100%) more per hour than all the other contributors to the American economy.

Pervasive asymmetrical dependencies

The second promise of modernity was freedom as being based on the disappearance of asymmetrical dependencies. In one famous formula it was called "enlightenment" as the "exit of man from his self-inflicted immaturity" (Kant 1783). Of course, postulates such as "freedom" and "enlightenment" can never mean that there are no dependencies. Social life consists of dependencies, and a complex, differentiated society is a system that multiplies and diversifies dependencies. Especially in terms of knowledge there are ever more knowledge systems that nearly everyone living in society does not understand well and that establish universal dependencies on experts and professionals. But the experts and professionals are as dependent as everybody else. The range of their expertise is strongly limited, and their need for other experts and professionals is as strong as everyone's.

What is really problematic are pervasive asymmetrical dependencies that impact on the entire range of life practices of a person. I propose a hierarchy of five conditions that sequentially define what pervasive asymmetrical dependencies are about. There is as a first condition the control a person has over resources another person wants to own or to use. This situation is near to market exchange, and as long as there are effective markets no significant dependencies will probably arise on this basis. The second condition postulates the existence of rights of control (sometimes only the facticity of control) that someone exercises over the actions of another person (Coleman 1990). This second condition implies the possibility of pervasive rights of control over nearly all the actions of another person that would establish a very strong asymmetrical dependency between two persons. In some societies the relations between parents and young children/ teens come near to such a pervasive control over potentially all actions of a person. Slavery is obviously another case of complete action control. The control of actions in many cases includes the control of resources a person owns as the use of resources consists in actions that may be controlled by somebody else even if this controlling person is not the owner of the resources.

Even if the resources I want and my actions are controlled by somebody else, there is the possibility of arguing about and protesting against control. I still can initiate conflicts about control. This points to a third condition for asymmetrical dependencies. This condition arises when the possibility of conflictual communication (Luhmann 1984, Ch. 9) or the possibility of "voice" (Hirschman 1970) is cut off. As long as one can protest openly, there is the hope to change asymmetrical dependencies by consistent argument and to do it over time. If there is no possibility of "voice" a fourth condition has to be taken into account. This is the possibility of "exit" (Hirschman 1970). For pervasive and stable asymmetrical dependencies this possibility is the *ultima ratio* if one wants to escape these dependencies. One simply has to leave the system—and the effect of this exit option can be as pervasive as asymmetrical dependencies can be. But if there are strategies that effectively block exit, this establishes the most complete dependency one can think of. Even in this condition of nearly complete dependency there is one last option and one last freedom coming from this option, and this is the fifth and last condition to be mentioned here. This is the possibility of retreat into a private way of experiencing the world (Luhmann 1978). It is difficult to control the way somebody else experiences the world, and this is the reason why this can be seen as the last domain of freedom. It is probably characteristic of totalitarian societies that they try to invade even this domain. Reeducation camps are one of the social institutions by which they try to establish this improbable type of control.

This hierarchy of five conditions that determine how pervasive asymmetrical dependencies are is here formulated in a general understanding for nearly all types of social systems. But what about modern society? Into many of its structures and values are built strong biases against asymmetrical dependencies. Looking first at socialization and education: both are understood as training for autonomy and independence and not at all as a training for submission. Society is based on the autonomous individuals produced by education, and the political system of society is understood as a self-organized democracy that includes everyone on one's own and not in a relational perspective that embeds the possibilities of participation in social relations and social dependencies (Ahlers et al. 2020, Ch. 1). It is remarkable how much late nineteenth-century political systems begin to protect the act of political voting against the influence potentials of the persons nearest to everyone. Over time "voting" is redefined as a completely individual act. No pressures and influences are wanted or allowed (Mares 2015). Finally, one has to look to culture. Transcending the contexts just mentioned there seem to be no dependency values in modern society and instead very strong preferences for freedom and equality.

But there are significant asymmetrical dependencies nonetheless, and it is important to look at the circumstances under which they arise. In some way they seem always to be related to "exclusions." To be strongly dependent on individual others or several others or on institutions of dependency seems to be related to forms of social exclusion. We will distinguish two major forms of institutionalized asymmetrical dependency in contemporary society.

The first of these forms is what has been called "including exclusion" by several authors (Bohn 2006; Stichweh 1997; Stichweh 2016). The starting point of "including exclusion" is the diagnosis or attribution of disabilities, deficiencies and deviances to persons, a diagnosis that is characteristically made by one of the many experts of modern society. If the deficiency is significant, exclusions may result from it: one finds no job, is seriously ill or disabled or has committed a crime. For modernity it is characteristic that these exclusions take the form of an inclusion: one becomes a client of public labor administration, a patient in a hospital or in a care home, a disabled person in a special school or a criminal in prison. These organizations are rather restrictive contexts that create strong asymmetries and dependencies. They can often be described as "total institutions" in Goffman's understanding (Goffman 1961). The strong, pervasive asymmetries that arise this way claim to be self-limiting. The declared intention of most of these institutions is to lead the persons they include back into mainstream society. But if they fail in realizing their institutional intentions—and they often fail—they may contribute to the rise of an "outer class" (Ifill 1993) that is one of the indicators of a divided society.

The second form of social exclusion that is of enormous local and global relevance should be called "excluding inclusion" (Stichweh 2009). The persons, groups and populations involved are partially the same that are the objects of including exclusion. In this second form of social exclusion processes do not start with a negative event (loss of work, major illness or disability) or a negative sanction (penal judgment). Instead there is a seemingly positive sanction that offers to persons in marginal situations a membership in a total way of life. This can be membership in a gang, an all-inclusive religious sect, a terrorist group, a world-defining radical party, an unsuspected occupational offer in a far-distant country, a place for years on a ship. But in all these cases the new context of membership may prove to be a total and totalizing context and a context that blocks off all other and all future memberships and options in society. There often is no way out. The organization never wants and never allows the person to leave again. There is already a significant descriptive literature (and social activism) on "modern slavery" (O'Connell Davidson 2015; Roberts 2015). But on a conceptual level, we are still at the beginning. Our hypothesis is that most cases of "modern slavery" have to do with the structures of excluding inclusion. At the start there is often an offer of inclusion and a hope and a promise to be able to leave marginality. But this deceptive offer results in permanent exclusion, with small chances of return to societal "normality."

Sociocultural polarization

For the greatest part of human history most societies were hunter-gatherer societies. These are small social systems—mostly including a few hundred members—in which everybody knew everybody else, and social control and obligatory solidarity had their basis in a "presence society" that consisted of interactions among members (Schlögl 2014). For these small social systems all other humans living on earth were "strangers," and societal members had good reasons to consider strangers as enemies (Stichweh 2010; Stichweh 2017). Strangers who met accidentally knew nearly nothing about one another. This is nearly the purest case of "double contingency" (Luhmann 1984, Ch. 3).[2] It seems reasonably risk averse to attribute the most hostile intentions possible to these unknown strangers and therefore to look at them as enemies.

Sociocultural evolution and the rise of large territorial systems and finally of global society widens the circle of those about whom one knows enough not to consider them as enemies. It is the third promise and hope of global modernity to anticipate fraternity and solidarity with all other humans living on earth. This idea is present in the Enlightenment and the French Revolution and many later social and intellectual movements.

This third hope becomes the third disappointment of modern society. "Tribal brotherhood" does not become "universal brotherhood." Benjamin Nelson (1969) proposes instead "universal otherhood" as the adequate description of modern society. This is a good proposal as it takes into account the institutionalization of individuality as a core invention of modern society. "Otherhood" is more compatible with diversity and differentiation as signatures of world society. The great disappointment, however, is that "the other as enemy" comes back in the form of sociocultural polarization. There are many forms and variants.

There is first the fear and the practice of violence (Elias 1976), the fear of criminality (Merry 1981) and the fear of terrorism. All three are themata that produce and symbolize divisions of society, a split of society into those who are thought to endanger social order and to fight against it and those who claim to sustain it. Uncontrolled physical violence can be seen as the early modern form. It is practiced by those who are violent and by the defenders of order who punish the violators in extremely violent forms.

Criminality is the modern equivalent of premodern violence. Criminal behavior is often goal-oriented and rational and may insofar be seen as a part of the society of social disciplining (Oestreich 1980). But it negates constitutive norms and values, and the criminal is for many the representative figure of the other as enemy. It is no surprise that those who perceive migrants and refugees as dangerous others often spend a lot of energy on trying to prove that most criminals come from these groups of migrants and refugees. There is an obvious contradiction in modern attitudes toward criminals: on the one hand there is the tradition from Beccaria and other authors of the European Enlightenment that sees punishment as a way of reforming criminals. On the other hand, the fear of criminals and the negative stereotypes describing them are very strong. It is characteristic that the first wholly negative and intentionally destructive presidential campaign in modern American history, the fight of George Bush against Michael Dukakis in 1988 that Bush clearly won (with 40 states) after first having trailed Dukakis by 17 points, had as its most prominent campaign subject the story of an Afro-American criminal on weekend furlough who had committed a rape and an assault. The fact that the criminal on furlough who committed the criminal acts was black was not explicitly mentioned by the Bush campaign. But it was a potent implicit message that combined the sociocultural otherhood of black people with the radical deviance of criminal acts ascribed to them. This strict coupling of different in themselves non-coupled identities that is strengthened by implicit communication is often the material from which sociocultural polarizations are built (Mendelberg 2001).

The other core issue is "negativity." One does not argue for the life forms or policies one favors. Instead one paints a complex picture of the other as radically different and therefore as enemy. In looking at American politics Ezra Klein speaks of "negative partisanship": "partisan behavior driven not by positive feelings toward the party you support but negative feelings toward the party you oppose" (Klein 2020, 9–10)—and he explains a higher consistency in voting over time by the prevalence of negative feelings: "we became more consistent in the party we vote not because we came to like our party more … but because we came to dislike the opposing party more" (Klein 2020, 10). This is connected to a switch from issues to identities. Klein makes the interesting point that there is a "diversity divergence" in American politics. The increasing demographic diversity of the American society finds its place nearly only in the Democratic Party, and that means that the difference between the two parties becomes ever bigger. In 1952 among self-identified Democrats there were 6% nonwhites, for Republicans the percentage was 2%. In 2012 the difference was 43% to 9% (Klein 2020, 36–42). As migrants live primarily in cities the "diversity divergence" additionally produces a "density divergence." You can predict the political orientation of a locality on the basis of its population density. And, finally, there arises this link to identities. Voters who have a weak political engagement look at political issues and policies in terms of their material interests. The stronger the political engagement of voters becomes the more they look at issues in terms of identities: "What does a specific policy decision say about me?" (Klein 2020, 63).

A last core dimension of sociocultural polarization is education. The college/non-college divide that is central to inequality is strongly linked to sociocultural polarization, too. As we already pointed out, in the US this educational split nearly divides the US into two equal halves. Hillary Clinton who won and lost the 2016 election made the point in favor of the urban educated elites in somehow extreme form in 2018: "I won the places that represent two-thirds of America's gross domestic product. So I won the places that are optimistic, diverse, dynamic, moving forward" (Klein 2020, 41). What becomes visible here is how the sides in a situation of sociocultural polarization exclude one another reciprocally. And they do this as they fear the exclusion from the other side, as they reciprocally fear becoming "strangers in their own land" (Hochschild 2016).

Inclusion and exclusion

Looking back to the three dimensions of societal division examined in this chapter the question arises whether there is a form of societal differentiation that allows us to understand the rise and the interconnectedness of these divisions. My proposal is to look at the two primary aspects of the differentiation of society that define global modernity. These are functional differentiation and inclusion/exclusion.

The function systems of modern world society are more or less based on universal inclusion (of individuals). One could postulate that they start with the premise (and promise) of equality of inclusion of everyone. The inequality we observe is not a contradiction but is the result of the extremely dynamic processes that arise in all the function systems on the basis of millions and finally billions of individual inclusion addresses. Inequality is not traditional inequality. It comes from the inclusion revolutions of modernity.

It is different with the genesis of strong and pervasive asymmetrical dependencies. They are not connected to the inclusion side of the distinction inclusion/exclusion. Instead they are related to exclusions. This is true in different ways for both of the major types of exclusion: on the one hand the exclusions that emerge from deficiencies and deviances and that are administered by inclusive organizations that build strong dependencies; on the other hand the seductive inclusions of deviant organizations, which one may never be able to leave again.

The third divisive force is sociocultural polarization. It is again related to exclusion but in a wholly different way. Sociocultural polarization introduces a division in a population, a division that is based on a fear that one will be excluded in society by the preponderance of the opposite group. This fear of exclusion is shared on the other side of the polar distribution. This reciprocal fear of exclusion or reciprocal fear of being made a stranger creates a kind of negative double contingency in which the buildup of trust does not come about and instead mistrust is intensifying on both sides of the polarized distribution.

Notes

1 A good example is Mr. Dombey in Charles Dickens' *Dombey and Son* (Oxford University Press, 2008, 65): "I am far from being friendly to what is called by persons of levelling sentiments, general education. But it is necessary that the inferior classes should continue to be taught to know their position, and to conduct them properly. So far I approve of schools."

2 Only civilizations meeting in space know still less about one another. Cixin Liu, author of *The Three-Body-Problem, Vols. 1–3 (Head of Zeus, 2015–2017)* has constructed an extraordinarily inventive "cosmic sociology" on the basis of this idea of cosmic double contingency.

References

Ahlers, Anna L., Damien Krichewsky, Evelyn Moser, and Rudolf Stichweh. 2020. *Democratic and Authoritarian Political Systems in 21st Century World Society. Vol. 1 - Differentiation, Inclusion, Responsiveness.* Bielefeld: Transcript.

Autor, David H. 2014. "Skills, Education, and the Rise of Earnings Inequality among the 'Other 99 Percent'." *Science*, 344: 843–851.

Banfield, Edward C. 1958. *The Moral Basis of a Backward Society.* New York: Free Press.

Bohn, Cornelia. 2006. *Inklusion, Exklusion und die Person.* Konstanz: UVK.

Burt, Ronald S. 1992. *Structural Holes. The Social Structure of Competition.* Cambridge, MA: Harvard University Press.

Coleman, James S. 1990. *Foundations of Social Theory.* Cambridge, MA.: Harvard University Press.

DiPrete, Thomas A. and Gregory M. Eirich. 2006. "Cumulative Advantage as a Mechanism for Inequality." *Annual Review of Sociology*, 32: 271–297.

Durkheim, Émile. 1893. *De la division du travail social.* Paris: P.U.F. [1973.]

Elias, Norbert. 1976. *Über den Prozeß der Zivilisation. Soziogenetische und psychogenetische Untersuchungen.* Frankfurt a.M.: Suhrkamp.

Goffman, Erving. 1961. *Asyle. Über die soziale Situation psychiatrischer Patienten und anderer Insassen*. Frankfurt a.M.: Suhrkamp.

Hirschman, Albert O. 1970. *Exit, Voice and Loyalty. Responses to Decline in Firms, Organizations, and States*. Cambridge, MA: Harvard University Press.

Hochschild, Arlie Russell. 2016. *Strangers in Their Own Land. Anger and Mourning on the American Right*. New York: The New Press.

Ifill, Gwen. 1993, November 15. "Clinton's Tightrope; Presidency Takes on Shifting Politics Of U.S. Role in Curbing Violent Crime," *The New York Times*, Section B: 8.

Kant, Immanuel. 1783. "Beantwortung der Frage: Was ist Aufklärung?" In Wilhelm Weischedel (ed.). *Werke Bd. 9*, 51–61. Darmstadt: Wissenschaftliche Buchgesellschaft. [1975.]

Klein, Ezra. 2020. *Why We're Polarized*. New York: Avid Reader Press.

Kluckhohn, Clyde. 1951. "Values and Value Orientations in the Theory of Action: An Exploration in Definition and Classification." In Talcott Parsons and Edward A. Shils (eds.). *Toward a General Theory of Action*, 388–433. New York: Harper & Row.

Luhmann, Niklas. 1978. "Erleben und Handeln." In Niklas Luhmann (eds.). *Soziologische Aufklärung 3*, 67–80. Opladen: Westdeutscher Verlag.

Luhmann, Niklas. 1984. *Soziale Systeme: Grundriß einer allgemeinen Theorie*. Frankfurt a.M.: Suhrkamp.

Luhmann, Niklas. 1990. "Die Homogenisierung des Anfangs: Zur Ausdifferenzierung der Schulerziehung." In Niklas Luhmann and Karl Eberhard Schorr (eds.). *Zwischen Anfang und Ende: Fragen an die Pädagogik*, 73–111. Frankfurt a.M.: Suhrkamp.

Mares, Isabela. 2015. *From Open Secrets to Secret Voting. Democratic Electoral Reforms and Voter Autonomy*. Cambridge: Cambridge University Press.

Mendelberg, Tali. 2001. *The Race Card. Campaign Strategy, Implicit Messages, and the Norm of Equality*. Princeton: Princeton University Press.

Merry, Sally Engle. 1981. *Urban Danger. Life in a Neighborhood of Strangers*. Philadelphia: Temple University Press.

Merton, Robert King. 1988. "The Matthew Effect in Science, II. Cumulative Advantage and the Symbolism of Intellectual Property." *ISIS*, 79: 606–623.

Merton, Robert King, George G. Reader, and Patricia L. Kendall. 1957. *The Student Physician: Introductory Studies in the Sociology of Medical Education*. Cambridge, MA: Harvard University Press.

Milanovic, Branko. 2016. *Global Inequality. A New Approach for the Age of Globalization*. Cambridge, MA: The Belknap Press of Harvard University Press.

Nelson, Benjamin. 1969. *The Idea of Usury. From Tribal Brotherhood to Universal Otherhood*. Chicago: University of Chicago Press.

O'Connell Davidson, Julia. 2015. *Modern Slavery: The Margins of Freedom*. London: Palgrave Macmillan.

OECD. 2011. *Education at a Glance. OECD Indicators*. Paris: OECD Publishing.

Oestreich, Gerhard. 1980. *Strukturprobleme der frühen Neuzeit*. Berlin: Duncker & Humblot.

Ozouf, Mona. 1997. "Liberté, égalité, fraternité." In Pierre Nora (ed.). *Les Lieux de mémoire*, 4353–4388. Paris: Gallimard.

Roberts, John. 2015. *Freedom as Marronage*. Chicago: University of Chicago Press.

Schlögl, Rudolf. 2014. *Anwesende und Abwesende. Grundriss für eine Gesellschaftsgeschichte der frühen Neuzeit*. Konstanz: Konstanz University Press.

Stichweh, Rudolf. 1997. "Inklusion/Exklusion, funktionale Differenzierung und die Theorie der Weltgesellschaft." *Soziale Systeme*, 3: 123–136.

Stichweh, Rudolf. 2007. "The Eigenstructures of World Society and the Regional Cultures of the World." In Ino Rossi (ed.). *Frontiers of Globalization Research: Theoretical and Methodological Approaches*, 133–49. New York: Springer.

Stichweh, Rudolf. 2008. "Professionen in einer funktional differenzierten Gesellschaft." In Irmhild Saake and Werner Vogd (eds.). *Moderne Mythen der Medizin. Studien zur organisierten Krankenbehandlung*, 329–344. Wiesbaden: VS Verlag.

Stichweh, Rudolf. 2009. "Leitgesichtspunkte einer Soziologie der Inklusion und Exklusion." In Rudolf Stichweh and Paul Windolf (eds.). *Inklusion und Exklusion. Analysen zur Sozialstruktur und sozialen Ungleichheit*, 29–42. Wiesbaden: VS Verlag für Sozialwissenschaften.

Stichweh, Rudolf. 2010. *Der Fremde. Studien zu Soziologie und Sozialgeschichte*. Berlin: Suhrkamp.

Stichweh, Rudolf. 2013. "The History and Systematics of Functional Differentiation in Sociology." In Mathias Albert, Barry Buzan, and Michael Zürn (eds.). *Bringing Sociology to International Relations. World Politics as Differentiation Theory*, 50–70. Cambridge: Cambridge University Press.

Stichweh, Rudolf. 2016. *Inklusion und Exklusion. Studien zur Gesellschaftstheorie*. Bielefeld: Transcript.

Stichweh, Rudolf. 2017. "Gibt es Fremde der Weltgesellschaft? Der Fremde und die soziokulturelle Evolution des Gesellschaftssystems." In Ilse Fischer and Johannes Hahn (eds.). *Europa Neu Denken, Bd. 4*, 245–253. Salzburg: Anton Pustet.

7

DILEMMAS OF CITIZENSHIP IN THE TWENTY-FIRST CENTURY

Does the Middle East show us the future?

Lisa Anderson

Seventy years ago, Hannah Arendt warned us that "[t]he danger is that a global, universally interrelated civilization may produce barbarians from its own midst by forcing millions of people into conditions which, despite all appearances, are the conditions of savages" ([1951]1968, 302). Globalization has eroded borders, fostered mobility, and deepened inequality virtually everywhere. The waning of the modern state as the world's default political unit has had myriad consequences; among the most challenging may be the simultaneous expansion of supranational norms of human rights and contraction of legal, enforceable citizenship. The upheavals of the "Arab spring" provided eloquent testimony to both the appeal of rights-based political discourse, as protesters across the region called for "bread, freedom and social justice," and the catastrophic consequences of reliance on weakened and ineffectual states to enforce such rights. The baleful landscape of the Middle East a decade later suggests a warning for the rest of the world: enfeebled states may herald the demise of universal human rights.

The Middle East as the future

Between 2010 and 2019, most of the countries of the Middle East and North Africa witnessed major popular revolts. The earlier American invasion of Iraq in 2003 precipitated repeated insurrections against its United States-backed central government throughout this period, but the most dramatic upheavals, in 2010–2011, led to spasms of instability the region had not seen since the turmoil that attended independence in the 1950s. By 2020 several countries—Algeria, Bahrain, Egypt, Sudan, Tunisia—teetered between brutal authoritarian restorations and fragile political compromises, while others—including Iraq, Libya, Syria, and Yemen—had dissolved into bitter and apparently intractable internecine war.

The prospects for Palestinian statehood seemed more remote than ever while, according to the United Nations High Commissioner for Refugees (UNHCR), one in every six people in Lebanon was a refugee—the highest proportion in the world (Jordan was second and Turkey third).[1]

As the end of the decade approached, Syria had seen more than half its population displaced, and a quarter had fled the country. In Libya, more than a million people were in need of humanitarian assistance—almost 20% of the population, including both internally displaced Libyans and refugees and asylum-seekers from other countries (UN High Commissioner for Refugees 2019a). In Yemen, more than 22 million people—over three-quarters of the population—needed humanitarian aid. Astonishingly, Yemen also hosted hundreds of thousands of refugees from other countries, including Somalia, Eritrea and Syria (UN High Commissioner for Refugees 2019b). By 2016, given the rapid rise in the number of people looking for security and livelihoods, the Middle East had the fastest growing international migrant and displaced population in the world (Connor 2016).

The spectacular implosion that led to the scattering of humanitarian crises across the region was not entirely homemade; as Sharro (2019, 39) observed, "the precarious moment in the Middle East and North Africa is, simultaneously, the product of political failures within the region and of a global retreat of political models that could guide the process of transition to an alternative." The ambiguities of citizenship in the Middle East, where even functioning regimes routinely failed to provide their nationals with basic government services and where both legal and illegal commerce in people across borders was widespread, provides a sobering lens through which to consider the conceptual and empirical puzzles of citizenship in the twenty-first century.

Citizenship's link to the state

Citizenship has two fundamental dimensions, linked to the two faces of the modern state, or what Elizabeth Picard (2012, 259) has succinctly described as sovereignty "based on Westphalian criteria (the world was organized into independent and equal state units) and Weberian criteria (the state was meant to be the only legitimate holder of physical force)."[2] The Westphalian state system, born in Europe in the seventeenth century and exported globally in European imperialism, reached its apogee after World War II, when the then-new United Nations (UN) codified the worldwide reach of the mutually exclusive and exhaustive system of formally sovereign independent countries. In theory, and to a large degree in practice, the people of the world were assigned to states defined by territorial boundaries and those states were given free rein in pursuing their domestic arrangements; the UN charter prohibited interference in the internal affairs of states.[3]

The people for whom these states are responsible were termed "nationals" or "citizens." Because each of these terms has secondary connotations—nationality is associated with membership in a community or culture; citizenship is associated with legal rights—this terminology has been a source of confusion in both the scholarly and policy literatures. Nonetheless, as Piattoeva (2016, 2) put it,

> citizenship and nationality are commonly treated as synonyms, or at least, as two sides of the same political coin. The bundling of the terms is essentially a product of the modern territorial nation-state and the ideology of nationalism that asserts congruity between the state and the nation.[4]

The Weberian face of the modern state looks to its domestic role and its responsibilities to the people assigned to it. Citizenship in this context reflects various theories of membership and types of regime.[5] Here too the terminology is confusing. As Naujoks (2020, 2) points out, there are numerous "conceptions of citizenship. In particular, they may focus on citizenship as a legal status; a system of rights; a form of political activity; any form of political identity and solidarity." Moreover, some commentators use "citizen" for all members of all states, as if by courtesy, while others distinguish "citizens" from "subjects," for example, on the basis of the extent of their civil and political rights or the ability to secure and sustain government accountability (Mamdani 1996).

The confusion attending citizenship is not simply terminological, however. Two features of the UN era contributed to complicating the relations between states and citizens. The first was the Universal Declaration of Human Rights, which recognized "all members of the human family" as having rights typically associated with citizenship. As the UN itself puts it:

> The Universal Declaration promises to all the economic, social, political, cultural and civic rights that underpin a life free from want and fear. They are not a reward for good behaviour. They are not country-specific, or particular to a certain era or social group. They are the inalienable entitlements of all people, at all times, and in all places.[6]

There was no provision for the enforcement of these inalienable and universal rights, however; that responsibility was left to individual states. The provision for mutual noninterference was to mean that, in practice, the realization of these rights was uneven at best. But the language of rights associated with modern citizenship was universalized, and the global human rights movement was born.

The second confounding feature of the structure of the post-World War II international system was expressed in the debates about statelessness. Technically, statelessness is defined as "the condition of having no legal or effective citizenship" (Weissbrodt and Collins 2008, 246). We will return to the profound ambiguities entailed in the notion of "effective" citizenship, but even "legal" citizenship is vexed. The extension and stabilization of the international state system represented by the UN was expected to extinguish the status of statelessness except in very unusual individual circumstances. The end of the Cold

War saw renewed attention to the problem of people without a claim on any state, however, as the successor states of, for example, the Soviet Union and Yugoslavia debated the citizenship status of residents of their territories while refugee populations, from Palestinians to Rohingya, found themselves apparently permanently unrecognized by both their erstwhile home and present-day host countries.

Statelessness deprives individuals of rights associated with the international obligations of a state, such as a passport, but more importantly, membership in a state confers a domestic status as well, as Arendt ([1951] 1968, 177) famously put it, "the right to have rights." While the Universal Declaration asserts that all people are endowed with inalienable rights by virtue of their being human, Arendt's formulation suggested that, even if that is true, these rights cannot be realized in the absence of a state that is responsible for and capable of enforcing them: as Weissbrodt and Collins (2008, 249) pointedly put it, "as a practical matter…international protection is still a problem" (see also Donnelly 2003).

Moreover, even if all people were nationals of one state or another, they would not necessarily be "citizens." Sometimes this is formally acknowledged: numerous countries distinguish "nationals" from "citizens"—residents of American Samoa, for example, are American nationals but not American citizens, meaning that they may obtain a US passport but may not vote in US elections. Although the term "subject" has fallen out of favor, thanks to its association with imperial dominion—at the end of World War II, His Britannic Majesty ruled over "British subjects" throughout the Commonwealth but by the turn of the century, the independent countries of the Commonwealth had designated their people "citizens"—it is often an accurate description of the actual relationship of people with their governments.

Indeed, as we shall see, many putative citizens have no effective recourse in asserting these rights. For example, as Naujoks (2020) observed, where "citizen" applies only to those who have full political rights,

> [i]t is important to bear in mind that non-democratic states do not provide such powers to their citizens while the formal concept of citizenship as state membership remains unchallenged…Classifying state members without political rights as subjects and only those with political powers as citizens may be a relevant terminological differentiation for political philosophy, but it seems less important from the perspective of legal state membership.
>
> *(9)*

In fact, the distinction is important from the perspective of the substantive rights and responsibilities of the state and their "members"—the exercise of "effective citizenship." Labelling subjects "citizens" does not make them so. Effective citizenship constitutes "a package of liberal rights (e.g. freedom of association, freedom of speech and conscience and the general freedom to lead meaningful lives) and responsibilities (e.g. to exercise autonomous and critical reasoning in elections and surveillance of political leaders)." Although "it is by virtue of belonging to the national community that individuals are granted the privileges of citizenship" (Piattoeva 2016, 1), those privileges are quite robust and adhere to all members of the community equally. As Mamdani (1996, 18) showed in his aptly named book, *Citizen and Subject*, the legacy of European imperialism in Africa was a bifurcated system of rights and obligations, framed in the competing languages of "civil society and civil rights" and "community and culture."

These ambiguities of both language and structure were artifacts of a legal and political process that had begun after World War I, when the ill-fated League of Nations tried unsuccessfully to reconcile the formal, egalitarian aims of an international state system with the informal hierarchical imperatives of imperialism. As its successor, the UN system served to globalize these conceptual tensions without resolving them—and, indeed, added a further complication in the assignment of rights not simply to communities (the "self-determination" of the League) but to individuals. Yet this modern rights-bearing individual is itself a reflection of the state; as Mitchell (1991, 93) has argued, the modern state is distinctive as an apparatus standing apart from the rest of the social world, formal, abstract and predicated on the production of the modern individual, "an isolated, disciplined, receptive, and industrious political subject."

Citizenship reflects a formal, abstract, legal relationship between the individual and the state, outlining the mutual rights and responsibilities of these modern individuals and the public authorities. In theory, and by the late twentieth century to a great extent in European and North American practice, citizenship was to supersede other sources of political identity and authority. As the inhabitants of a state were integrated into the public sphere, traditional identities and primordial authority structures were to be dispatched to the realm of private relations; public obligations were to be expressed in legally codified universalist rights and obligations.

In fact, while some countries define citizenship as conferred by where the individual was born (*jus soli*), acknowledging the territorial basis of the modern state, many others look to the individual's parentage (*jus sanguinis*), linking notions of formal citizenship to ethnic or ancestral nationality. Parolin's (2009, 128) dissection of the history of definitions of citizenship in the Middle East and North Africa highlights the distinction between nationality, via descent, and citizenship "as a vehicle for the principles of equality and territoriality." Even as a vehicle for principles, the notion is complex: *jinsiyya*, the right of abode, is not the same as *muwatana*, the right of equal access to the civil, political, social and economic resources of the state (Davis 2000, 53). And empirically, of course, as Turner (2000, 30) reminds us, "citizenship is the exception, not the rule; it is politically fragile and socially precarious, and it is not historically cumulative."

The erosion of the state and the weakening of citizenship

The accelerated and uneven erosion of state autonomy through the movements of goods, people and ideas fostered by globalization after the end of the Cold War reshaped the international authority of the world's states and magnified the precariousness of citizenship. Intensified trade and global finance created vast international supply chains; cosmopolitan networks of business and labor spanned the globe, reaching from the conference rooms of Davos to the worker's camps of Dubai; international human rights norms contested the imperatives of a "global war on terror;" states struggled to respond to a global pandemic, seeming to pit national interests, economic incentives and international welfare against each other. Moreover, as Piattoeva (2016) pointed out, "new forms of citizenship, such as European, global, cosmopolitan, environmental and others, are simultaneously on the agenda [and] the processes of international migration that diversify national societies and increase the number of people who hold identities distinct from...national identity" (3).

As the autonomy and capacity of the states of the Middle East shrank under the pressures of globalization, regimes deliberately fostered alternative identities, as ways to distinguish among claimants in the face of increasingly scarce benefits, growing demands by clients and cronies, and mounting pressure from foreign investors and donors. By the turn of the century, the erosion of the state began to reveal the outlines of alternative political communities in the region, many of them reflections of the longstanding reliance of state authorities on informal, personal loyalties.

Historically, both imperial and nationalist governments had paid lip service to universalist mandates, from liberalism to socialism, but from the outset of European influence both supporters and foes of the governments in the Middle East were encouraged, often by deliberate policy, to organize around familial, patronage and sectarian identities. European efforts to carve out states for religious communities in Lebanon and Palestine, to rule a Shi'i population through a Sunni monarchy in Iraq, to recruit Alawis in the military in Syria, or to provide economic privileges to Berbers in North Africa, all established patterns that outlasted European rule, even if they were sometimes obscured by facades of commitment to Weberian-style bureaucratic order (Robson 2017, 3).[7] Mamdani's (1996) observations about Africa obtained in the Middle East as well:

> The form of rule shaped the form of revolt against it. Indirect rule at once reinforced ethnically bound institutions of control and led to their explosion from within. Ethnicity (tribalism) thus came to be simultaneously the form of colonial control over natives and the form of revolt against it. It defined the parameters of both the Native Authority in charge of the local state apparatus and of resistance to it.
>
> (24)

In fact, from independence to the late twentieth century, state elites in the Middle East often found themselves better served by nonstate ideologies: Iraqi, Libyan and Iranian patriotism paled in comparison to the pan-Arab nationalism of the ruling Ba'th in Iraq, the internationalist vocation of the Libyan revolution and the Islamic republic in Iran, all of which constituted efforts to inspire loyalty on bases—ethnicity, ideology, religion—that denied the primacy of the state as an object of fidelity. What Davis (2000, 57) called, "other kinds of belonging or membership: kinship (common ancestor), tribal homeland (common motherland), confession (common religious tradition)" were very durable.

This ambivalence was codified in various ways. Syrian laws on naturalization discriminated in favor of Arabs; as Parolin (2009) tells us: "for Syrian legislation, the world is divided into three categories: Syrian nationals, Arabs, and foreigners" (88). For all other Arab countries except Algeria and Lebanon, candidates for naturalization must exhibit a knowledge of Arabic, while being Muslim is an explicit requirement under Kuwaiti and Yemeni law and an element of "good character" in many other countries (Parolin 2009, 102–103).

In a number of Middle Eastern countries, there was virtually no pretense to universalist ambitions. Shallow as the veneer of state-based political identities may have been in post-independence republican regimes, it was entirely absent in the monarchies of the Middle East. As the very name of Saudi Arabia, called after its ruling family, suggested, these domains embodied and celebrated political affiliation and authority based on family, tribe, and sect (Longva 2000, 194). As Parolin (2009) attests, this was not universally appreciated: "Arab intellectuals and activists who are engaged in the struggle for equality and full citizenship condemn the current system and call for the eradication of all forms of discrimination between citizens based on any voluntary or involuntary membership" (115). By the turn of the century, however, the hope of a Middle Eastern version of European nation-building—that the transformation of "peasants into Frenchmen" (Weber 1976) would have its analogue in the making of "tribes into Bahrainis" or "sects into Syrians"—was proving illusory.

In fact, effective citizenship was eroding within the states of the region. As Weissbrodt and Collins (2008) explained,

> de facto statelessness can occur when governments withhold the usual benefits of citizenship, such as protection, and assistance...[P]ersons who are de facto stateless might have legal claim to the benefits of nationality but they are not, for a variety of reasons, able to enjoy these benefits.
>
> *(253)*

What makes for "effective statelessness"? Sometimes it is simple bureaucratic ineptitude, as when births and deaths go unrecorded in rural areas, but Weissbrodt and Collins argue that it "typically results from state discrimination...One mechanism of de facto statelessness is slavery and human trafficking" when trafficked or enslaved people are deprived of travel documents; another is when "governments commit what is known as administrative ethnic cleansing or erasure," by removing people, such as the Roma in Slovenia, from administrative files. As they point out, "Being without identity documents...makes it difficult to obtain basic social services, [including] acquiring jobs, receiving medical care, marrying and starting a family, enjoying legal protection, travelling owning property, gaining an education, or registering the birth of their children" (Weissbrodt and Collins 2008, 264–265).

Although the security apparatus of many of the states of the Middle East appears to be robust and intrusive, the administration of the rights of citizenship is arbitrary and capricious. As Butenschon (2000) observed,

> The power of citizenship is probably best known to those who are denied it: the right to carry a passport and be protected by a state; the right to abode; the right to membership in a political community with access to decision-making institutions and public welfare. Citizenship is a scarce public good that is distributed by the state, a source of collective identity and an instrument of political control.
>
> *(5)*

By the opening of the twenty-first century, thanks to rapid population growth, inattentive and often erratic public administration and even deliberate policy (including the neoliberal structural adjustment programs of the International Monetary Fund), many governments in the Middle East were unable to provide the services they had once guaranteed. The gaps were filled by private sources: family networks and charitable associations. As urban slums proliferated, charitable associations assumed welfare responsibilities and corruption ate away at the public bureaucracy (Bayat 2010; Nucho 2016; Singerman and Amar 2006; Cammett and McLean 2014; Cammett 2014; Ruiz de Elvira et al. 2019; Hibou 2017), regimes saw their control—even their knowledge—of their citizenry slip away (Anderson 2018, 320–321). As Ismail (2006, 165) reported, in the slums of Cairo the residents claim that "'here there is no state; here people live in a state other than the state.'" Most of the activity of the informal economy, in Egypt and elsewhere, depended upon personal networks of family, friends and associates and seemed to provide the economic foundation for alternative loyalties, identities and communities. Salame (1994) put it this way:

> Gangs, nepotistic privatizations, trafficking in influence, tolerance of drugs, militia corruption, the so-called black or informal economy, and para-statist rackets have all been obstacles to democratization. But...these gangs are also the instruments of survival of groups marginalized by the state as well as forces maintaining those states.
>
> *(15)*

At the same time, growing numbers of unemployed university graduates, increasingly aware of the global standards of universal rights, also grew disenchanted with the apparently empty promises of citizenship (see Bishara 2018).

Alternatives to citizenship

In the absence of reliable access to rights-based government services, people in the Middle East turned to alternative identities and communities. As Alsayyad and Roy (2006) put it,

> If modern citizenship was constituted through a set of abstract individual rights embedded in the concept of the nation-state, then now there is the emergence of forms of citizenship that are…linked either to patronage or to associational membership and in both cases is fundamentally about protection…Some such forms of citizenship substitute for or are even hostile to the state. From the private homeowner's associations to the neighborhood-level Islamic republics being declared by religious fundamentalist groups, these are private systems of governance that operate as medieval fiefdoms, imposing truths and norms that are often contrary to national law.
>
> *(3)*

Some of the bases for nonstate "citizenship" in the Middle East are well-known; as we have seen, the region's sectarian and ethnic identities are notoriously politicized. Other kinds of identities—Alsayyad and Roy's "private homeowner's associations" among them—are also being constructed and deployed to overcome the deficiencies in state-sponsored citizenship. In all cases, they are discriminatory, precisely what the UN insisted rights were not to be: "particular to a certain social group" or a "reward for good behaviour." As Jamal (2015) describes the United Arab Emirates (UAE), for example, a complex system of rights and privileges distinguishes and sustains "the numerical minority status of its local population, an ambiguous 'tiered system' of economic, political and social rights among permanent residents (including a reversal of rights for some), and a fluctuating, informal hierarchization of migrant communities" (602).

Family as the "foundation of society"

For political arrangements that contravened formal rights-based state–citizen relations, there was no better place to start than with the monarchies. As Longva (2000) described Kuwait, for some, the state was "the political embodiment of a specific 'imagined community,' located on a specific territory and with a specific common history; for others, the important aspect of the state is its leadership, in this case the Al Sabah ruling family" (180). In fact the accent on family was important and deliberate in all of the monarchies: the Qatari Constitution stipulated that "the family shall be the foundation of the society" (Kassem and Al-Muftah 2016, 214), explicitly rejecting the individuality of the citizen as the building block of the polity. In this, male heads of households were privileged; in the monarchies, citizenship, like political authority, was gender-specific (Al-Malki 2016, 248; see also Charrad 2001; Joseph 2018). In fact, across the region, debates about the legal rights of women were usually less about women as such than about the competing claims of citizenship and family as the basis of social and political life. But rulers embraced paternalism: Sheikh Zayed of the UAE was styled the "father of the nation," a title a number of other Middle Eastern rulers, including King Hussein of Jordan, Mohammed V of Morocco, and President Habib Bourguiba of Tunisia, also adopted (De Bel-Air et al. 2018).

The rulers not only accentuated family and tribal affiliations at home, they extended them in regional networks. Soon after Saudi troops helped put down popular protests in Bahrain in 2011, a son of the Bahraini king was engaged to marry a daughter of the Saudi king. Another of his sons had already married a daughter of the ruler of Dubai, who had himself married a sister of the king of Jordan (al-Qassemi 2019; Al-Khaladi 2019). Just as migrant laborers spun self-protective networks of money transfers across the region (El Qorchi et al. 2003), so too rulers made alliances across national boundaries, supplementing and sometimes supplanting allegiance to their states with loyalty to transnational dynasties or, at least, the idea of transnational dynasties. As Al-Qassemi (2019) put it:

> In the continuous absence of credible federal institutions, this inter-marriage network has…no doubt contributed to the survival of the UAE as a federation over the past four decades…Tribal loyalty continues to be employed even within state borders as a tool of managing populations when the criteria for citizenship in a modern state should be measured in different metrics altogether.

The apparent erosion of esteem for authority based in distinctive Weberian-style bureaucratic state office in favor of more "traditional" sources, including family, was hardly limited to monarchies, however, as the growing visibility of the sons of rulers, even in ostensible republics suggested. Indeed, precisely this observation landed Egyptian sociologist Saad Eddin Ibrahim in jail in Egypt in 2000 after he published an article on political succession, "al-Jumlikiyya (the republico-monarchy): the Arab Contribution to Politics in the 21st Century," in which he suggested that after a decade or so in power, rulers in the Arab world seemed to view their countries as their personal domain (El-Ghobashy 2002). This increasing resort to "sanguine relations in the design of rule" (Sadiki 2014, 14) may have reflected the growing economic clout of the region's monarchies, which of course made no pretense otherwise.

Beyond putative kin relations, monarchs also grant privileges to their retainers. The King of Bahrain, for instance, has the power to grant and revoke citizenship, and he often deploys that power to reward loyalty and reshape the sectarian balance of the country, which is how thousands of foreign Sunnis who served in the security forces were accorded citizenship (Jones 2002, 742).

Ethnicity and sect

As the Bahraini king's preference for Sunni loyalists suggests, it was not only the apparently growing emphasis on kinship that consistently and deliberately weakened citizenship. Indeed, from the very early days of the modern states of the Middle East, there were numerous examples of efforts, government and non-governmental alike, to manage domestic populations, not as citizens of a state, but as members of an ethnic or sectarian community. Lebanon's entire political system formally codified such discrimination, a pattern adopted explicitly in Iraq after the American invasion in 2003 (see Haddad 2019; Hashemi and Postel 2017). In Syria, it was less formal: while the majority of the Syrian population was Sunni, former president Hafez al-Assad built a political system in which minority Alawis controlled the country—both through recruitment into positions of authority and by re-drawing the ethnic map, bringing Alawis from the mountains and installing them in the suburbs of surrounding Damascus, from where they were drafted into the security services. His son Bashar relied on this Alawi support during the Syrian civil war (Khatib and Sinjab 2018).

The experience of Palestinians is a much examined case of the ambiguity of "citizenship without a state," as their status—whether second-class citizens, residents with travel documents or stateless asylum-seekers—varied across time and space in Israel, the West Bank and Gaza, Jordan, under the jurisdiction of the United Nations Relief and Works Agency for Palestine Refugees in the Near East (UNRWA), as refugees in Lebanon, Libya, Kuwait, Egypt and elsewhere over more than half a century. In Israel, where many of the rights of formal citizenship were extended to non-Jewish residents in the 1960s, as Rebecca Kook (2000) put it, "the tension between the universalist and particularist elements of the Israeli state render[ed] the distribution of rights unequal and biased in favor of the Jewish citizens of the state and [did not] afford the Palestinian inclusion within Israeli society" (267; see also Kassim 2000; Molavi 2013).

Yet it was not only the Palestinians whose status was ambiguous and precarious. Across the region, the experience of what Lori (2019, 30–31) calls, "the structured uncertainty of inhabiting a limbo status and being unable to secure permanent access to citizenship rights," was common. From the half-million residents of the Western Sahara, which had been on the UN list of Non-Self-Governing Territories since 1963, to the Bidun, the more than 106,000 stateless persons who claimed Kuwaiti nationality but remained without legal status since the country's independence, people across the region were left to fend for themselves (see Fernández-Molina and Porges 2019; Human Rights Watch 2011). And this does not include the millions of migrant workers, formally citizens of their sending countries, who lived and worked in the region, often without access to legal protection in either their host states or home countries (Vora 2013). The ability of the notorious Islamic State to recruit adherents reflected the powerful draw of sectarian identity, particularly among young people whose formal allegiance to their own state was largely unrequited. As Gerges (2016) put it, "ISIS is tied to the raging sectarian fires in Iraq and Syria and the clash of identities that is ravaging Arab countries…a manifestation of the breakdown of state institutions" (22).

The "shareholder," the bourgeois, and the commodity

The reliance on family, ethnic group, and sect as an alternative to citizenship drew on longstanding, albeit ostensibly "private" identities and networks, but a novel form of "private" identity was also being politicized in the first decades of the twenty-first century: for a number of the governments of the Middle East and North Africa, the neoliberal foundations of globalization presented a new opportunity to reframe state–society relations. If family may have seemed old-fashioned, and ethnicity and sect sometimes constraining, the burgeoning interest in business and the private sector seemed to hold out new opportunities to avoid the responsibilities states have to citizens.

For the small population, oil-producing countries of the region, the world of international trade and investment was already familiar. The Kuwait Investment Authority, the oldest sovereign wealth fund in the world, was founded in 1953; by the 1990s, when its returns surpassed oil revenues, many countries in the region adopted the model, often deploying more "experimental and high-risk strategies" (Young 2019). In Saudi Arabia, the Vision 2030 diversification plan assigned its Public Investment Fund responsibility not only for generating domestic growth and employment opportunities—not typically sources of high returns—but also for partnering with international private funds, which typically made investments in higher risk ventures such as technology firms, entertainment companies and real estate projects, as befit with private investment funds responsible not to citizens, but to shareholders.

In fact, the adoption of the role of "shareholder" created claims on governments based less on citizenship and more on "the idea of getting a fair return on one's share" (Beaugrand 2019, 59). How such "shares" were determined and how "fair" returns should be calculated were increasingly complicating and even supplanting rights-based claims on governments. Particularly in the Gulf, regimes characterized themselves less as stewards of states than management committees of family-owned businesses. Indeed, Muhammad Bin Rashid Al Maktoum called himself the "CEO of Dubai" (Kanna 2011, 139). As Abulkhaleq Abdulla wrote, "There is no difference in the age of globalization between the commodity, the state, merchandising, the city, cultures, and services. All are equivalent… for the surface, in this day and age, is as important as content itself" (quoted in Kanna 2011, 137).

In many ways, the ruling families of the Gulf were among the most eager proponents of the retreat of the state as they adopted the watchwords of the global private sector, positioning their countries as "flexible, adaptive, entrepreneurial, and innovative" in meeting the changing demands of the global environment. Calvert Jones (2017) put it this way: theirs was a "vision of a citizen as a loyal, entrepreneurial bourgeois" (2). Of course, a different legal regime governed the proletariat; as Babar (2020) observed, "labor rights have been cast in a nonessential basket and divorced from citizenship...labor rights are presented in Gulf states as a replacement for citizens' rights" (768–769).

This citizen-as-economic actor idea may have been born in the Gulf, but it was transregional; wherever there was foreign investment, there were local partners, agents and representatives looking for shares. And to service them— that is, to attract private investment and global talent—there were various kinds of exceptional jurisdictions and privatized enclaves that operated under special legal regimes, profiting and protecting their investors. From special economic zones, self-contained "techno-cities" and science parks, gated residential communities and offshore cruise ships to labor compounds and private islands, such enclaves provided a regional and even global class of wealthy entrepreneurs with bespoke legal regimes, including not only tax exemptions but dispute arbitration rather than the jurisdiction of national courts, and private security in lieu of the local police (Murray 2017). Dubai Media City, for example, which was the headquarters for major global news outlets in the UAE, allowed freedom of speech not technically permitted elsewhere in Dubai. Qatar Education City in Doha and Saudi Arabia's King Abdallah University of Science and Technology—the latter the country's only co-education establishment—were designed to foster research in an atmosphere of academic and social freedom unavailable elsewhere in their countries (Murray 2017, 272).[8] As Alsayyad and Roy (2006, 2) put it, "in urban enclaves, citizenship is linked to patronage or associational membership and in both cases fundamentally about protection" substituting "private systems of governance" that are often inconsistent with, even contrary to, national law.

In a related development, what Somers (2008, 2) called "the contractualization of citizenship" was fast moving from metaphor to reality. Between 2008 and 2010, the UAE paid the government of the Comoros Islands to issue passports to between 80,000 and 120,000 Bidun—stateless residents. Abrahamian (2018b) estimated that the purchase of 40,000 Comoran passports for UAE residents cost the UAE government more than $200 million, or about a third of the Comoros annual GDP.[9] The holders of passports of a place they had never seen and to which they had no other connection, these newly minted "Comorans" were now able to travel out of the UAE but had few other rights, in either the Comoros Islands—it was not clear that they could take up residence there if they wanted—or the UAE itself, where they were now classified as foreign nationals (Abrahamian 2018b; see also Beaugrand 2015). In 2019, the Saudi government announced the launch of a new "golden visa" program that targeted wealthy foreigners. At the same time they extended citizenship to 50,000 refugees and provided identification papers to another 800,000. As Bsheer (2020) pointed out, however, "the millions of workers and decades-long residents of Saudi Arabia—sometimes second and third generation—were not privy to Saudi nationality" (753).

But the appeal of arbitrary and capricious, or merely commercial, deployment of citizenship was rapidly becoming apparent across the region. To relatively poor countries it was obvious: by 2020, the Egyptian government was considering a proposal to grant Egyptian citizenship to foreigners who will pay for it ("deposit a non-refundable USD 250k into a local bank account that goes directly to the government") or invest in local projects or property.[10] As Deckard and Heslin (2016) summed it up, economic viability trumps moral equality.

Facebook "friends," "data subjects," jokes

Finally, new information and communications technologies were creating new identities and new opportunities to expand, and perhaps distort, definitions of citizenship. Perhaps the most famous and, at least for a time, consequential, online community in the Middle East was Facebook. Building social identities and group cohesion is a purpose that Facebook itself embraces, providing a "one-stop resource center for building a thriving community,"[11] and the political potential of such communities was amply demonstrated in the Arab uprisings of 2011 (Ghonim 2012; see also Vargas 2012; Alaimo 2015; Hammami 2016).

This early example of cross-border inspiration and solidarity proved somewhat ephemeral, as regimes also went online to battle local and regional opponents in what appeared to be escalating surveillance and censorship in the name of cybersecurity. Human Rights Watch (2005) had observed a two-pronged approach to the new technologies already well before the uprisings: "faced with this new technology, many regional governments have pursued contradictory policies. With varying degrees of enthusiasm, they have sought to facilitate the spread of information and communications technologies with economic benefits in mind. At the same time, they have sought to maintain their old monopolies over the flow of information." By 2018, facilitating the spread of information had given way, and it was reported that "large-scale sales of sophisticated surveillance technology to Arab states, including the UAE, [illustrated] the growing trend of state repression and control of the internet through surveillance. Authorities say surveillance is necessary to keep citizens safe" (Miller 2018). As Jones (2002) put it, "with all this talk of digital technology transcending boundaries and de-spatializing geographically rooted politics, states still matter" (744).

If states were struggling to retain, if not strengthen, their stability and authority, the denizens of the states were confronting challenges to the strength and control of their very identities. As Abrahamian (2018a) argued, the increased harvesting of online data about individuals and their activities meant that "we are not only clients of a company, residents of a state or citizens of a country but data subjects of the world. Data is currency; creating and holding it is power." The political implications of this development were unclear; Abrahamian (2018a) suggested that "algorithmic citizenship" can "produce combinations of affiliations to different states" and, like their counterparts earlier in the century, governments seem to have been taking divergent, if not contradictory, positions:

> The increasing adoption of biometric technology by governments, aid organizations, and other stakeholders in the Middle East has critical implications for regional developments in business, governance, and society. And while some observers and stakeholders have noted the potential for such tools to streamline security infrastructure and provide opportunities for sectors as diverse as mobile payment and financial security, a growing chorus of voices has raised concern about the potential of biometric data to similarly streamline violations of human rights, particularly those of the region's most vulnerable populations.
>
> *(Johnson and Campbell 2020)*

As Petrozziello (2019) put it, biometric technologies seemed to herald a "shift toward citizenship as identity management" (143).

But perhaps the most dramatic indication of the kind of citizenship envisioned by the regimes of the region was in the October 2017 announcement that the Saudi Arabian regime had granted citizenship to Sophia, a humanoid robot developed in Hong Kong. As Bsheer (2020) put it, "Sophia became the world's first robot citizen...The spectacle delineated the boundaries of a reconceptualized national identity...[T]he conferral on Sophia reified the archetype of the good citizen: obedient, politically passive, and economically productive" (748–749).

Rights as privileges: the death of citizenship?

It is worth repeating what the UN says about human rights:

> The Universal Declaration promises to all the economic, social, political, cultural and civic rights that underpin a life free from want and fear. They are not a reward for good behaviour. They are not country-specific, or particular to a certain era or social group. They are the inalienable entitlements of all people, at all times, and in all places.[12]

Virtually no one in the Middle East and North Africa can rely on that "promise to all." Instead, the rights we cavalierly call "universal" are privileges accorded to certain social groups and rewards for good behavior. The "bread, freedom and social justice" for which protestors called during the Arab uprisings are still distant aspirations; the "conditions of acute legal, physical and psychological insecurity" (UNHCR 1997) in which stateless people find themselves are the norm. It is hardly surprising that people have turned for recognition and protection to "new forms of belonging and attachment [that] sometimes substitute for, or are even hostile, to comprehensive citizenship rights associated with the sovereign nation-state" (Murray 2017, 223).

Naujoks (2020) has argued, in fact, that "from a cynical perspective, the label-dimension of citizenship appears to be nothing but a psychological trick to manipulate citizens' sense of belonging…and ease the exercise of power" (16). This would hardly seem worth preserving although he suggests that the label may also serve as "the seed for future expansions" of claims to belonging and to rights.

The ambiguity of the term—its use as a "label" with little agreed upon substance—makes it liable to manipulation by both states and aspiring right-bearers. If a useful life for the notion is to be recuperated, it will require reviving—or perhaps establishing—a common understanding of the content of citizenship for the twenty-first century, and this will require disaggregating at least three elements of the term.

In the first instance, the UN campaign to "end statelessness," slated to conclude in 2024, highlights the importance of nationality, of belonging. Indeed, in the absence of a prohibition on depriving individuals of their legal citizenship, the need for such a campaign will never actually end. Between 2010 and 2020, Saudi Arabia stripped a number of erstwhile Saudi nationals of their citizenship. As Bsheer (2020) reports,

> With a stroke of a pen, they lost access to financial, educational, medical, bureaucratic, institutional, and other state services. At the same time, they could neither work nor leave the country. They exist in a liminal space, somewhere between life and death. This severe sanction—more common in some other Gulf states—wholly unmade their social world.
>
> *(751)*

Not coincidentally, because this deprivation bans the victims from traveling, it also prevents them from claiming asylum in a place where they might advocate on their own behalf or criticize the regime (Jones 2002, 742).

Citizenship entails not merely technical recognition, however, but belonging to a community with which the individual has an "effective connection" (Vlieks et al. 2017). The sale of "citizens" to countries to which they have no link, such as the Comoros Islands, should be prohibited. Knowing, as we do, that some states sometimes produce statelessness to design the citizenry they want, such ploys should elicit more than a legalistic or formulaic response. That said, since in the contemporary world life chances are often shaped by citizenship at birth, "forum-shopping" for rights by acquiring multiple citizenships or hoping to guarantee rights through "birth tourism" would also seem to violate the requirement of an effective or genuine connection (Aneesh and Wolover 2017).

Finally, citizenship entails not only recognition as a human belonging—in other words, as more than a savage or an "abstraction…displaced from political community" (Gessen 2018)—in a community to which the person has a genuine connection but also as having effective use of the associated rights. In many parts of the world, and certainly much of the Middle East, the economically disempowered are "the neoliberal citizenship regime's newly stateless" (Deckard and Heslin 2016, 301). Rendering squatter settlements, refugee camps or migrant transit sites "illegal" has much of the same consequence as formally depriving their residents of citizenship, pushing them outside the state's purview and relieving the state of any obligations to those now deemed "beyond the law." Citizenship entails recognition of the right to exercise a host of rights and fulfill a variety of duties—and, moreover, equal access to such rights and duties. As we have seen, "stratification of rights and entitlements for those considered more or less desirable" (Bsheer 2020, 751) is usually by state design, but it is antithetical to the notion of effective citizenship which is, as Patrick Heller (2012) put it, "the actual capacity of citizens to make use of formal and civic political rights" (643).

Citizenship entails three levels of rights: (1) to belong to a community—what we would call nationality—with which one (2) has a "genuine connection" and in which one (3) can effectively exercise civil rights. It is difficult to imagine that today's states will serve to guarantee realization of those rights. The UN itself (UNHCR 1997) has argued that

> Statelessness is first and foremost a problem for states to resolve…Given the frequency with which governments have denaturalized and expelled their citizens, coupled with the protracted nature of so many citizenship disputes, an appeal to the notion of state responsibility might seem somewhat naive.

And yet there is no other mechanism designed to establish a formal community and to enforce compliance with its abstract, legal provisions for "the inalienable entitlements of all people, at all times, and in all places." If we value those entitlements, we need to acknowledge the role of the state in creating and realizing them. Perhaps we can take heart in Yadav's (2020) observation about Yemen that citizenship is "less a set of de jure rights that originate with the state and more a set of practical capacities for action that are built through, around, and sometimes against state institutions" (754).

Notes

1 These figures relate only to the refugee population under UNHCR's mandate, and Lebanon and Jordan respectively hosted an additional half a million and 2.2 million Palestine refugees under the UNRWA's mandate (United Nations High Commissioner for Refugees 2018).
2 This distinction might also be termed external and internal or positive and negative sovereignty. See Tetreault (2000, 71).
3 "UN Charter" *United Nations* (1945), Article 2, paragraph 7.
4 See also the succinct and useful, if dated, discussion in Koessler (1946). As he points out, "national" had "two accepted denotations: 1. The status of belonging to a state; 2. The quality of membership in an ethnological group" (61). These two meanings were to vex discussions of the "nation-state" not least because, following Max Weber,

most scholarly definitions of the modern "state" emphasize its territorial rather than ethnic underpinnings, while in international law, "nationality" designates the status of a person's belonging to a state, whether or not it is ethnically coherent or consistent with that person's ethnic identity.

5 Weber (1947) emphasized the state's compulsory and coercive character; he did not develop criteria for membership, defining the state as "a compulsory political association with continuous organization whose administrative staff successfully upholds a claim to the monopoly of the legitimate use of force in enforcement of its order in a given territorial unit" (154).

6 "Introduction, The Universal Declaration of Human Rights," *United Nations* (2015, v). www.un.org/en/udhrbook/pdf/udhr_booklet_en_web.pdf.

7 See Parolin (2009, 27), who tells us that "Upon attainment of independence, tribal courts, confessional judges and state tribunals operated simultaneously almost everywhere in the Arab world." See also Anderson (2018).

8 See Education City homepage: www.qf.org.qa/education/education-city; KAUST homepage: www.kaust.edu.sa/en

9 The numbers vary, as Lori's (2002) wonderful essay explains.

10 "Gov't mulls granting citizenship in exchange for increasing working capital," *Enterprise*, August 2020 https://enterprise.press/stories/2020/08/12/govt-mulls-granting-citizenship-in-exchange-for-increasing-working-capital-20241/. The value of people as tradeable goods extended beyond citizenship as such: even people were useful for rent-seeking regimes. As Arar (2017) pointed out, Jordan's recognition as "a world leader in refugee hosting" positioned it to access substantial international aid, while Yaghi (2019) reported that Tunisian workers working abroad to send home remittances were said to feel like "a commodity that can be bought and sold" (128).

11 www.facebook.com/community/.

12 "Introduction," The Universal Declaration of Human Rights," www.un.org/en/udhrbook/pdf/udhr_booklet_en_web.pdf, p. v.

References

Abrahamian, Atossa Araxia. 2018a, May 28. "Data Subjects of the World, Unite!" *New York Times*, https://www.nytimes.com/2018/05/28/opinion/gdpr-eu-digital-privacy-law-data-subject-europe.html

Abrahamian, Atossa Araxia. 2018b, January 5. "Who Loses When a Country Puts Citizenship Up for Sale?" *New York Times*, https://www.nytimes.com/2018/01/05/opinion/sunday/united-arab-emirates-comorans-citizenship.html

Alaimo, Kara. 2015. "How the Facebook Arabic Page 'We Are All Khaled Said' Helped Promote the Egyptian Revolution." *Social Media + Society*, 1(2): 1–10.

Al-Khalidi, Suleiman. 2019, July 31. "Jordan Keeps Silent in Case Pitting Princess Against Sheikh," *Reuters*, https://www.reuters.com/article/us-britain-dubai-court-jordan/jordan-keeps-silent-in-case-pitting-princess-against-sheikh-idUSKCN1UQ2AX

Al-Malki, Amal Mohammed. 2016. "Public Policy and Identity." In M. Evren Tok et al. (eds.). *Policy-Making in a Transformative State: The Case of Qatar*, 241–270. Palgrave Macmillan.

Al-Qassemi, Sultan. 2019. "Tribalism in the Arabian Peninsula: It Is a Family Affair," *Jadaliyya*. https://www.jadaliyya.com/Print/25199

Alsayyad, Nezar and Ananya Roy. 2006. "Medieval Modernity: On Citizenship and Urbanism in a Global Era." *Space and Polity*, 10(1): 1–20. doi:10.1080/13562570600796747.

Anderson, Lisa. 2018. "The State and Its Competitors." *International Journal of Middle Eastern Studies*, 50(2): 317–322.

Aneesh, Aneesh and D.J. Wolover. 2017. "Citizenship and Inequality in a Global Age." *Sociology Compass*, 11(5): 1–9.

Arar, Rawan. 2017. "Leveraging Sovereignty: The Case of Jordan and the International Refugee Regime." POMEPS. https://pomeps.org/leveraging-sovereignty-the-case -of-jordan-and-the-international-refugee-regime. Accessed August 2, 2021.

Arendt, Hannah. 1951/1968. *The Origins of Totalitarianism*. Harcourt, Brace & World.

Babar, Zahra R. 2020. "The Vagaries of the In-Between: Labor Citizenship in the Persian Gulf." *International Journal of Middle East Studies*, 52: 765–770.

Bayat, Asef. 2010. *Life as Politics: How Ordinary People Change the Middle East*. Stanford: Stanford University Press.

Beaugrand, Claire. 2015. "Torn Citizenship in Kuwait: Commodification versus Rights-Based Approaches." In *Challenges to Citizenship in the Middle East and North Africa Region*, LSE Middle East Centre Collected Papers, Volume 2. http://eprints.lse.ac .uk/61773/1/Challenges%20to%20citizenship%20in%20the%20Middle%20East %20and%20North%20Africa%20region.pdf

Beaugrand, Claire. 2019. "Oil Metonym, Citizens' Entitlement, and Rent Maximizing: Reflections on the Specificity of Kuwait." POMEPS Studies 33.

Bishara, Dina. 2018. "Why Unemployed Graduates' Associations Formed in Morocco and Tunisia but not Egypt." POMEPS Studies 31.

Bsheer, Rosie. 2020. "The Limits of Belonging in Saudi Arabia." *International Journal of Middle East Studies*, 52(4): 748–753.

Butenschon, Nils A. 2000. "State, Power and Citizenship in the Middle East." In Nils A. Butenschon, Uri Davis, and Manuel Hassassian (eds.). *Citizenship and the State in the Middle East*, 3–27. Syracuse: Syracuse University Press.

Cammett, Melani. 2014. *Compassionate Communalism: Welfare and Sectarianism in Lebanon*. Ithaca: Cornell University Press.

Cammett, Melani and Lauren M. McLean. 2014. *The Politics of Non-state Social Welfare*. Ithaca: Cornell University Press.

Charrad, Mounira. 2001. *States and Women's Rights: The Making of Postcolonial Tunisia, Algeria, and Morocco*. Berkeley: University of California Press.

Connor, Phillip. 2016. "Middle East's Migrant Population More Than Doubles Since 2005." Pew Research Center. https://www.pewresearch.org/global/2016/10/18/ middle-easts-migrant-population-more-than-doubles-since-2005/

Davis, Uri. 2000. "Conceptions of Citizenship in the Middle East." In Nils A. Butenschon, Uri Davis, and Manuel Hassassian (eds.). *Citizenship and the State in the Middle East*, 49–69. Syracuse: Syracuse University Press.

De Bel-Air, Françoise, Jihan Safar, and Blandine Destremau. 2018. "Marriage and Family in the Gulf Today: Storms over a Patriarchal Institution?" *Arabian Humanities*, 43. https://journals.openedition.org/cy/4399

Deckard, Natalie Delia and Alison Heslin, 2016. "After Postnational Citizenship: Constructing the Boundaries of Inclusion in Neoliberal Contexts." *Sociology Compass*, 10(4): 294–305.

Donnelly, Jack. 2003. *Universal Human Rights in Theory and Practice*. Ithaca: Cornell University Press.

El-Ghobashy, Mona. 2002. "Antinomies of the Saad Eddin Ibrahim Case." MERIP. https://merip.org/2002/08/antinomies-of-the-saad-eddin-ibrahim-case/

El Qorchi, Mohammed, Samuel Munzele Maimbo, and John F. Wilson. 2003. *Informal Funds Transfer Systems: An Analysis of the Informal Hawala System*. The International Monetary Fund and The World Bank.

Fernández-Molina, Irene and Matthew Porges. 2019. Western Sahara. In Gëzim Visoka, John Doyle, and Edward Newman (eds.). *Routledge Handbook of State Recognition*, 376–390. London: Routledge.

Gerges, Fawaz. 2016. *A History of ISIS*. Princeton: Princeton University Press.

Gessen, Masha. 2018, May. "'The Right to Have Rights' and the Plight of the Stateless," *The New Yorker*, https://www.newyorker.com/news/our-columnists/the-right-to-have-rights-and-the-plight-of-the-stateless

Ghonim, Wael. 2012. *REVOLUTION 2.0 The Power of the People Is Greater Than the People in Power: A Memoir*. Boston & New York: Houghton Mifflin Harcourt.

Haddad, Fanar. 2019. *Understanding "Sectarianism": Sunni-Shi'a Relations in the Modern Arab World*. London: C. Hurst & Co Publishers Ltd.

Hammami, Sadok. 2016. "The Three Phases of Facebook: Social Networks and the Public Sphere in the Arab World—the Case of the Tunisian Revolution." In L. Jayyusi and A.S. Roald (eds.). *Media and Political Contestation in the Contemporary Arab World. The Palgrave Macmillan Series in International Political Communication*, 35–61. Basingstoke & New York: Palgrave Macmillan.

Hashemi, Nader and Danny Postel, eds. 2017. *Sectarianization: Mapping the New Politics of the Middle East*. Oxford: Oxford University Press.

Heller, Patrick. 2012. "Democracy, Participatory Politics, and Development: Some Comparative Lessons from Brazil, India and South Africa." *Polity*, 44(4): 643–665.

Hibou, Beatrice. 2017. *The Force of Obedience: The Political Economy of Repression in Tunisia*. Cambridge, UK and Malden, MA (USA): Polity Press.

Human Rights Watch. 2005, November 14. False Freedom: Online Censorship in the Middle East and North Africa. https://www.hrw.org/report/2005/11/14/false-freedom/online-censorship-middle-east-and-north-africa#. Accessed October 17, 2021.

Human Rights Watch. 2011, June 13. Prisoners of the Past: Kuwaiti Bidun and the Burden of Statelessness. https://www.hrw.org/report/2011/06/13/prisoners-past/kuwaiti-bidun-and-burden-statelessness. Accessed October 17, 2021.

Ismail, Salwa. 2006. *Political Life in Cairo's New Quarters: Encountering the Everyday State*. Minneapolis, MN (USA): University of Minnesota Press.

Jamal, Manal. 2015. "The 'Tiering' of Citizenship and Residency and the "Hierarchization" of Migrant Communities: The United Arab Emirates in Historical Context." *The International Migration Review*, 49(3): 601–632.

Johnson, Madelyn and Eliza Campbell. 2020. "Biometrics, Refugees, and the Middle East: Better Data Collection for a More Just Future." Middle East Institute. https://www.mei.edu/publications/biometrics-refugees-and-middle-east-better-data-collection-more-just-future. Accessed October 17, 2021.

Jones, Calvert. 2017, *Bedouins into Bourgeois: Remaking Citizens for Globalization*. Cambridge: Cambridge University Press.

Jones, Marc Owen. 2002. "Digital De-Citizenship: The Rise of the Digital Denizen in Bahrain." *International Journal of Middle East Studies*, 52: 742–747.

Joseph, Suad. 2018. *Arab Family Studies: Critical Reviews*. Syracuse: Syracuse University Press.

Kanna, Ahmed. 2011. *Dubai: The City as Corporation*. Minneapolis: University of Minnesota Press.

Kassem, Lina M. and Esraa Al-Muftah. 2016. "The Qatari Family at the Intersection of Politics." In M. Evren Tok et al. (eds.), *Policy-Making in a Transformative State: The Case of Qatar*, 213–240. Basingstoke & New York: Palgrave Macmillan.

Kassim, Anis F. 2000. "The Palestinians: From Hyphenated to Integrated Citizenship." In Nils A. Butenschon, Uri Davis and Manuel Hassassian (eds.). *Citizenship and the State in the Middle East*, 201–244. Syracuse: Syracuse University Press.

Khatib, Lina and Lina Sinjab. 2018. *Syria's Transactional State: How the Conflict Changed the Syrian State's Exercise of Power.* London: Chatham House.

Koessler, Maximilian. 1946. "Subject," "Citizen," "National," and "Permanent Allegiance." *Yale Law Journal*, 56: 58–76.

Kook, Rebecca. 2000. "Citizenship and its Discontents: Palestinians in Israel." In Nils A. Butenschon, Uri Davis, and Manuel Hassassian (eds.). *Citizenship and the State in the Middle East*, 263–287. Syracuse: Syracuse University Press.

Longva, Anh Nga. 2000. "Citizenship in the Gulf States." In Nils A. Butenschon, Uri Davis and Manuel Hassassian (eds.). *Citizenship and the State in the Middle East*, 179–197. Syracuse: Syracuse University Press.

Lori, Noora. 2002. "Time and its Miscounting: Methodological Challenges in the Study of Citizenship Boundaries." *International Journal of Middle East Studies*, 52: 721–725.

Lori, Noora. 2019. *Offshore Citizens: Permanent Temporary Status in the Gulf.* Cambridge: Cambridge University Press.

Mamdani, Mahmood. 1996. *Citizen and Subject: Contemporary Africa and the Legacy of Late Colonialism.* Princeton: Princeton University Press.

Miller, Elissa. 2018, August 28. "Egypt Leads the Pack in Internet Censorship Across the Middle East." MENASource. https://www.atlanticcouncil.org/blogs/menasource/egypt-leads-the-pack-in-internet-censorship-across-the-middle-east/. Accessed October 17, 2021.

Mitchell, Timothy. 1991. "The Limits of the State: Beyond Statist Approaches and Their Critics." *American Political Science Review*, 85(1): 77–96.

Molavi, Shourideh C. 2013. *Stateless Citizenship: The Palestinian-Arab Citizens of Israel.* Leiden & Boston: Brill Academic Publishers.

Murray, Martin J. 2017. *The Urbanism of Exception: The Dynamics of Global City Building in the Twenty-First Century.* Cambridge: Cambridge University Press.

Naujoks, Daniel. 2020. "Atypical Citizenship Regimes: Comparing Legal and Political Conceptualizations." *Comparative Migration Studies*, 8(1): 2–20.

Nucho, Joanne Randa. 2016. *Everyday Sectarianism in Urban Lebanon.* Princeton: Princeton University Press.

Parolin, Gianluca P. 2009. *Citizenship in the Arab World: Kin, Religion and Nation-State.* Amsterdam: Amsterdam University Press.

Petrozziello, Allison. 2019. "Statelessness as a Product of Slippery Statecraft." *The Statelessness and Citizenship Review*, 1(1): 136–155.

Piattoeva, Nelli. 2016. "Citizenship and Nationality." In John Stone, Rutledge M. Dennis, Polly S. Rizova, Anthony D. Smith, and Xiaoshuo Hou (eds.). *The Wiley Blackwell Encyclopedia of Race, Ethnicity, and Nationalism*, 2–5. Hoboken: Wiley Blackwell.

Picard, Elizabeth. 2012. "The Virtual Sovereignty of the Lebanese State: From Deviant Case to Ideal-Type." In Laura Guazzone and Daniela Pioppi (eds.). *The Arab State and Neo-Liberal Globalization*, 247–274. Reading: Ithaca Press.

Robson, Laura. 2017. *States of Separation: Transfer, Partition and the Making of the Modern Middle East.* Oakland, CA (USA): University of California Press.

Ruiz de Elvira, Laura, Christoph Schwarz and Irene Weipert-Fenner (eds.). 2019. *Clientelism and Patronage in the Middle East and North Africa.* London & New York: Routledge.

Sadiki, Larbi. 2014. "In-Formalized Polity and the Politics of Dynasty in Egypt and Libya." In Luca Anceschi, Gennaro Gervasio, and Andrea Teti (eds.). *Informal Power in the Greater Middle East: Hidden Geographies*, 11–23. London & New York: Routledge.

Salame, Ghassan (ed.). 1994. *Democracy without Democrats? The Renewal of Politics in the Muslim World*. London: I.B. Tauris Publishers.

Sharro, Karl. 2019. "The Retreat from Universalism in the Middle East and the World." In Thanassis Cambanis and Michael Wahid Hanna (eds.). *Citizenship and Its Discontents: The Struggle for Rights, Pluralism and Inclusion in the Middle East*, 38–64. New York: The Century Foundation Press.

Singerman, Diane and Paul Amar (eds.). 2006. *Cairo Cosmopolitan*. Cairo: American University in Cairo Press.

Somers, Margaret. 2008. *Genealogies of Citizenship: Markets, Statelessness, and the Right to Have Rights*. Cambridge: Cambridge University Press.

Tetreault, Mary Ann. 2000. "Gender, Citizenship and State in the Middle East." In Nils A. Butenschon, Uri Davis and Manuel Hassassian (eds.). *Citizenship and the State in the Middle East*, 70–87. Syracuse: Syracuse University Press.

Turner, Bryan. 2000. "Islam, Civil Society and Citizenship." In Nils A. Butenschon, Uri Davis and Manuel Hassassian (eds.). *Citizenship and the State in the Middle East*, 28–48. Syracuse: Syracuse University Press.

United Nations High Commissioner for Refugees (UNHCR). 1997. *The State of The World's Refugees 1997: A Humanitarian Agenda*. Geneva: UNHCR.

United Nations High Commissioner for Refugees. 2018. *Global Trends: Forced Displacement in 2018*. Geneva: UNHCR.

United Nations High Commissioner for Refugees. 2019a. *2018 Year-End Report. Operation: Libya*. Geneva: UNHCR. https://reporting.unhcr.org/sites/default/files/pdfsummaries/GR2018-Libya-eng.pdf. Accessed October 17, 2021.

United Nations High Commissioner for Refugees. 2019b. *2018 Year-End Report. Operation: Yemen*. Geneva: UNHCR. https://reporting.unhcr.org/sites/default/files/pdfsummaries/GR2018-Yemen-eng.pdf. Accessed October 17, 2021.

Vargas, Jose Antonio. 2012, February 17. "Spring Awakening," *The New York Times*, https://www.nytimes.com/2012/02/19/books/review/how-an-egyptian-revolution-began-on-facebook.html

Vlieks, Caia, et al. 2017. "Solving Statelessness: Interpreting the Right to Nationality." *Netherlands Quarterly of Human Rights*, 35(3): 158–175.

Vora, Neha. 2013. *Impossible Citizens: Dubai's Indian Diaspora*. Durham, NC: Duke University Press.

Weber, Eugen. 1976. *Peasants into Frenchmen: The Modernization of Rural France, 1870–1914*. Palo Alto: Stanford University Press.

Weber, Max. 1947. *The Theory of Social and Economic Organization*. New York: The Free Press.

Weissbrodt, David and Clay Collins. 2008. "The Human Rights of Stateless Persons." *Human Rights Quarterly*, 28: 245–276.

Yadav, Stacey Philbrick. 2020. "Effective Citizenship, Civil Action, and Prospects for Post-Conflict Justice in Yemen." *International Journal of Middle East Studies*, 52(4): 754–758.

Yaghi, Mohammad. 2019. "Neoliberal Reforms, Protests, and Enforced Patron-client Relations in Tunisia and Egypt." In Laura Ruiz Elvira, Christoph Schwarz and Irene Wepert-Fenner (eds.). *Clientelism and Patronage in the Middle East and North Africa*, 118–142. London & New York: Routledge.

8

CAN WE TRUST PUBLIC ADMINISTRATION?

Wolfgang Seibel

Introduction: public administration and human security

The relevance of properly working public administration for the overall well-being of states and people became suddenly apparent in the COVID-19 pandemic that started to spread in 2020. Whether or not governmental agencies were working efficiently and effectively turned out to be a crucial factor in more or less successful crisis management and, consequently, infection rates and death tolls. What was thus revealed is that the realm of critical infrastructure is much larger than is usually assumed. It entails not only electricity grids, telecommunication, water supply and the entire public health system but also the wide array of public administration in general—its resources, professional capacity and resilience.

Yet it is indicative that it took a crisis to make visible the fact that large parts of public administration are of crucial importance for human security. Whether or not a bridge or a building is sound and safe depends on construction oversight by incorruptible authorities. Whether particularly vulnerable people—for example, elderly people in retirement homes or children living under precarious social conditions—are being protected against carelessness, neglect, and physical violence depends on properly working local administration equipped with sufficient professional staff. Whether or not large crowd events such as soccer games or street parades remain peaceful and enjoyable events or turn into deadly traps when panic breaks out and people are trampled to death depends on proper planning and licensing by the local civil administration.

Although the bulk of public administration outside critical infrastructure is usually not defined as a high reliability organization (HRO) zone, public authorities usually act as de facto HROs as soon as they are concerned, one way or another, with the protection of health and physical integrity. Conscious carelessness, neglect, sloppiness or substandard professional performance are rare, unlikely, and, accordingly, unexpected phenomena. Yet these phenomena do occur even under the unlikely conditions of rule-of-law-based public administration in rich democracies with sound accountability structures (see a selection of examples in Table 8.1). Bridges and buildings collapse, claiming the lives of many people and leaving many more injured even when public licensing and oversight authorities are in place and sufficiently equipped with professional staff. Vulnerable groups are exposed to structural and personal violence despite the supervision of related facilities and critical conditions in families. Mass events get out of control despite licensed crowd management plans and sufficient security staff on the ground.

So it would be a reasonable normative statement to declare public authorities HROs as soon as their action or inaction impacts human security. In what follows, I will argue that while this normative impulse is entirely justified, it misses the point as far as the nature of public administration itself is concerned. Outside the immediate realm of critical infrastructure, democratic rule-of-law-based government with its deeply echeloned administrative substructure has to do justice to a variety of partly convergent and overlapping and partly divergent and rival requirements. As Boin and Schulman (2008) pointed out, it is the very multiplicity of purposes and both functional and political necessities that may relativize the imperative of human security. Elected and appointed officials may find themselves exposed to counterincentives that make them neglect "safety first" principles even when those principles are laid down in legal prescriptions and clear-cut stipulation.

More specifically, the argument is that an ontologically more realistic concept of public administration entities as HROs has to be more nuanced and differentiated on the epistemological end as well. For that purpose, conventional high reliability theory is undoubtedly helpful but only to a limited degree. Standard HRO theory strongly emphasizes the necessity of general awareness and mindfulness (Hopkins 2007; Weick and Sutcliffe 2007) in acknowledgment of the actual relativity of safety as an organizational goal and the resulting necessity to renegotiate related standards and practices (Schulman 1993; Roe and Schulman 2008). Yet that strand of literature remains focused on two main areas and challenges: on the one hand, critical infrastructure, and on the other hand, crises, emergencies, and high-risk technologies. Accordingly, the fact and the systemic nature of risks to human security emerging out of regular public bureaucracy under regular circumstances remain unaddressed.

A similar though complementary weakness characterizes the main "contender" of HRO theory, which is normal accident theory (NAT) (Perrow 1984; 1986, 146–154). Much of what goes wrong in public administration at the expense of safety and human security has its root indeed in normal structural risk zones of the bureaucratic organization such as lack of flexibility due to hierarchized governance and horizontally fragmented division of labor, the proverbial red tape and rigid standard operating procedures. By the same token, however, those risk zones cannot be eliminated the way Perrow recommended

TABLE 8.1 Public administration and human security: sensitive fields and exemplary cases

Field of regulation and implementation	Human security issue	Administrative failure, examples
Construction Supervision and Licensing	Collapsing buildings and bridges	Collapse of the Canterbury TV Building, Christchurch, New Zealand, 2011 Canterbury Earthquakes Royal Commission, Volume 6: Canterbury Television Building (CTV) http://canterbury.royalcommission.govt.nz/Final -Report-Volume-Six-Contents
Child Protection	Child abuse	North Wales Child Abuse Scandal Department of Health: Lost in Care. Report of the Tribunal of Inquiry into the Abuse of Children in Care in the Former County Council Areas of Gwynedd and Clwyd since 1974. Prepared by The Stationery Office. February 2000 ("Waterhouse Report"). webarchive.nationalarchives.gov.uk
Fire Protection	Fire and wildfire	Fire at the Detention Centre Schiphol-Oost, 2005 Report of the Dutch Safety Board https://www.onderzoeksraad.nl/en/page/392/ brand-cellencomplex-schiphol-oost-nacht-van -26-op-27-oktober
Licensing and Managing Mass Events	Panic	The Hillsborough Disaster, 1989 The Report of the Hillsborough Independent Panel. Ordered by the House of Commons to be printed on September 12, 2012. HC 581 London: The Stationery Office. www.gov.uk/government/publications/ hillsborough-the-report-of-the-hillsborough -independent-panel
Law Enforcement, Domestic Intelligence	Improper criminal investigation	Serial Killings of Immigrants, Germany, 2000–2007 Bericht des NSU-Untersuchungsausschusses Deutscher Bundestag, 17. Wahlperiode, Beschlussempfehlung und Bericht des 2. Untersuchungsausschusses nach Artikel 44 des Grundgesetzes, Drucksache 17/14600, August 22, 2013.
Disaster Preparedness and Relief	Insufficient preparedness and response	Hurricane Katrina, 2005 A Failure of Initiative. Final Report of the Select Bipartisan Committee to Investigate the Preparation for and Response to Hurricane Katrina, 109th US Congress, Report 109-377 www.gpo.gov/fdsys/pkg/CRPT-109hrpt377/pdf/ CRPT-109hrpt377.pdf

Source: Author's compilation.

in his classic *Normal Accidents* (1984), namely through the elimination of an entire organizational field. After all, public administration epitomizes division of labor-based professionalism and incorruptible rule of law standards just in accordance with Max Weber's classic characterization (cf. Kettl 2006; Olsen 2008).

Rather, control and containment of risks to life and limb under the condition of properly working public administration is about the conscious control of standard organizational pathologies that themselves are inevitable and irremovable but, for this very reason, require focused attention very much in the vein of HRO theory and the quest for mindfulness. That mindfulness, however, needs to take into account the nature of public administration and its political embeddedness in a democratic polity in an attempt to define as accurately as possible the very points of intervention at which human action can neutralize risks and avert their disastrous consequences.

Hence the structure of this chapter. In the next section, I briefly summarize what HRO theory and NAT do and do not explain when it comes to standard risk zones of public authorities with potential consequences for human security. That entails a brief discussion of strengths and weaknesses of those theories and how the weaknesses could be overcome while the elements of strengths could be combined to the benefit of the analysis of public authorities as potential HROs. From that, I derive my own argument that the risk zones of public administration as the locus of failure with severe consequences for human security appear in two distinct shapes: avoidable standard pathologies and inevitable trade-offs. Both are illustrated through a case of organizational and managerial failure in a German municipal agency that claimed human lives and left hundreds of people injured.

The main theoretical statement of this chapter is that HRO theory and NAT can be fruitfully combined in process-tracing analyses of disasters based on the diagnosis of general causal mechanisms and their configuration. It is through a differentiated mechanism-based perspective that general points of intervention may be identified at which, to the benefit of human security, bureaucratic standard pathologies and inherent trade-offs can be neutralized as risk generators.

Standard theories for standard risks: approaches to high reliability organizations and normal accidents

The very notion of high reliability organizations (HROs) gained prominence in the early 1990s in the wake of major disasters affecting critical infrastructure, primarily major blackouts such as the one in New York City in July 1977 or in San Joaquin County, California, in 1982 and, above all, the Three Mile Island nuclear power plant disaster of 1979. These incidents made the actual reliability of power plants and grids and the consequences of their malfunction an issue of both public policy and scholarly literature (cf. the seminal article by LaPorte and Consolini 1991).

Pretty soon, that literature discovered and discussed a fundamental dilemma of risk management and, consequently, the management of organizations dealing with high-risk technology. On the one hand, improving performance for the sake of security requires learning and, accordingly, an intra-organizational culture of admitting, acknowledging, and thus, within a certain margin or bandwidth, tolerating errors for the sake of learning and piecemeal improvement of performance. On the other hand, accepting errors for the sake of learning implies trial-and-error tactics that are just too costly and ethically unacceptable when "error" translates into immediate threats to human life and limb. Accordingly, similar to what in urban policing is known as "broken window" theory, even minor errors have to be avoided from the very outset in accordance with zero-tolerance principles.

From this explicit or implicit definition, two lines of thought emerged. One was HRO theory proper; the other was normal accident theory (NAT), based on Perrow's trailblazing analysis of the Three Mile Island nuclear plant disaster (Perrow 1984; cf. also Shrivastava, Sonpar and Pazzaglia 2009). Perrow's analysis was radical by virtue of both its exclusive focus on organizational structure and its normative conclusions. According to Perrow, organizational fields with particularly risk-generating structural properties should be defined as a kind of no-go area beyond acceptable structural choices. Not surprisingly, nuclear power plants served as a plausible example. However, what made Perrow's argument compelling was its theoretical justification. It was based on the distinction between two basic dimensions of structural properties: degrees of coupling of organizational subunits and the mode of interaction between them. Loosely coupled organizational systems allow for complex interaction since errors in one subunit do not instantly impact other subunits. Tightly coupled organizational systems, by contrast, are both indispensable and manageable when it comes to linear interaction without particular necessities of time-consuming mutual adjustment. But the combination of tight coupling and complex interaction, Perrow argued, represents an unsolvable dilemma: tight coupling requires centralized governance for the sake of effective coordination. Complex interaction, however, requires decentralization for the sake of cooperative governance and mutual adjustment. Since centralization and decentralization are mutually exclusive, organizations combining tight coupling and complex interaction are, according to Perrow, high-risk organizations from the very outset (Perrow 1986, 146–154). To tolerate them anyway creates a permissive environment for what he termed "normal accidents"—accidents that are just as normal as the structural risk zones they emerge from.

HRO theory, by contrast, directly addresses the dilemma of simultaneous indispensability and unaffordability of trial-and-error learning techniques for the improvement of organizational performance in a high-risk environment. There are two variants of this rather optimistic school of thought when it comes to organizational risk management. One is the modified error-tolerance school, the other the mindfulness school.

Roe and Schulman (2008) reject what they call the "misguided … hard-and-fast distinction between error-tolerant and error-intolerant organizations" and suggest instead adopting some elements of what in a different strand of literature had been termed the "error-tolerant organization under failure-tolerant leadership" (Roe and Schulman 2008, 109, with reference to Farson and Keyes 2002). A core element, here, is to admit one's own mistakes rather than covering up or shifting the blame, fostered and facilitated by a culture of leadership that "routinely reinforce(s) the company's mistake-tolerant atmosphere by freely admitting their [the management's] own goofs." And they add: "The same can be said, almost word by word, for HROs" (Roe and Schulman 2008, 109). Nonetheless, these authors state that, rather than treating error tolerance as an end in itself, it must be tied to the ultimate and indispensable goal of avoiding error altogether: "Error tolerance must be vital to eventual error intolerance, that is, 'learning to avoid failure'" (Roe and Schulman 2008, 110). By the same token, according to these authors, organizational reliability is not as nonnegotiable as it may appear from the perspective of conventional wisdom. The constant balancing of tolerance and intolerance when it comes to errors implies constant mutual adjustment of rigidity and partial pragmatism on a learning-by-doing and case-by-case basis. Again, the point here is that strict inflexibility and rigidity even for the sake of human security may be ultimately as detrimental as sloppiness and neglect in real organizational life. In their 2016 book, Roe and Schulman stress the importance of multiple reliability standards and the indispensable role of accomplished leaders with expertise and an incorruptible professional ethos when it comes to walking the tightrope between error tolerance and error intolerance.

It is here where writings of the pioneers in the field overlap with a second wave of HRO literature that can be denoted as the "mindfulness" school. Unlike classic HRO literature that necessarily focuses on a particular organizational field and, in a normative vein, on the establishment of learning patterns devoted to reliability, the "mindfulness" school focuses on high-risk environments (cf. Hopkins 2007, 2009) and/or crisis and emergency situations (Weick and Sutcliffe 2007). While Hopkins (2007, 103–125) emphasizes the necessity to standardize risk assessment through what he terms the TARP philosophy (Triggers and Corresponding Action Response Plans), Weick and Sutcliffe (2007, 139) suggest a particular technique of coping with the dilemma; as they put it, "you can't just shut your organization down while you figure out ways to make it more reliable and resilient." To that extent, their approach resembles Roe and Schulman's emphasis on learning and productive balancing of error tolerance and error intolerance. Weick's and Sutcliffe's key notion is "small wins strategy," a plea for small and even "opportunistic" (Weick and Sutcliffe 2007, 139) steps in the "right direction" to less risk-prone organizational structures and managerial attitudes. It is also reminiscent of the "muddling through" philosophy developed in political science in the late 1950s, but, unlike Lindblom (1959), Weick and Sutcliffe maintain that the "small wins" have to have a distinct and nonnegotiable objective, which is reliability for the sake of security. They end up with recommendations for mindful managerial attitudes that center around the preoccupation with failure rather than positive (and positivist) portrayals of high reliability principles and practices. It is, according to Weick and Sutcliffe, about "mistakes that must not occur," "creating awareness for vulnerability," "creating an error-friendly learning culture," and explicitly addressing the question of whether something that *almost* went wrong (a "near miss") "is a sign that your system's safeguards are working or as a sign that the system is vulnerable" (Weick and Sutcliffe, 2007, 151–152).

When it comes to a comparative evaluation of the strengths and weaknesses of the NAT and the HRO theory, it is complementarity rather than rivalry or mutual exclusion that prevails. The strength of NAT is its focus on structural risk zones, emphasizing that particular organizational fields entail particular risks of failure and even disaster. After all, some organizational structures are more permissive than others when it comes to lack of coordination, information asymmetry, organized irresponsibility, and the like. Even though Perrow's original diagnosis of particular types of structural complexity might be criticized as not being nuanced and differentiated enough, the perspective on organizational structure as a risk factor in its own right remains analytically productive. NAT's weak flank is obvious too, though (viz. the neglect of human agency and coping capacity). Just as Scott Sagan pointed out in his account of *The Limits of Safety* (1993), human agency is a critical and indispensable factor in keeping even extreme risks to human safety under control, an argument specifically directed against Perrow's somber portrayal of human inability to handle the risks of nuclear energy in both the civil and the military context. This includes, however, the near miss or close call phenomenon— the absence of disasters that *almost* happened. Undetected near misses may create the illusion of safety in virtually vulnerable systems (cf. Sagan 1993, 250–279).

Conversely, emphasis on human agency in the form of learning and mindfulness is what characterizes the strength of HRO theory. Both the traditional school of thought connected to the work of LaPorte (1996), Roe and Schulman (2008), and others and the "mindfulness" school represented by Hopkins or Weick and Sutcliffe emphasize the indispensability of awareness, anticipation and preparedness and thus critical cognitive and actor-related factors of human efforts to enhance organizational reliability and to reduce structural risk zones as potential threats to human security. By the same token, however, a characteristic weakness of the HRO literature is the emphasis on reason and pedagogy and a neglect of organizational structures, their wider institutional embeddedness and related incentive structures. After all, mindfulness might not be enough. It might not even be helpful as an actual strategy when it comes to risks that are inherently structural and counterincentives that prevent real-world actors from learning and drawing consequences from the proverbial "lessons learned" (cf. March and Olsen 1975 and Argyris 1999 for skeptical assessments of organizational learning capacities).

Moreover, neither NAT nor HRO theory contributes very much to the understanding of public bureaucracies as risk generators in their own right when it comes to threats to life and limb. The next section gives an outline of peculiar risk-generating components of public administration and of both the deficiencies and the potential of NAT and HRO theory when it comes to related analyses.

Public authorities as risk generators: avoidable standard pathologies and inevitable trade-offs

Public authorities are formal organizations, just like private businesses (cf. Puranam 2018) from which they differ substantially, however, in terms of resource mobilization, production and output (cf. Kettl 2006, Olsen 2008). The resources come from individual and corporate taxpayers, and the "production" of public goods and services is regulated by legislation and protocol while the output has to be indiscriminate and evenly accessible for everybody according to standardized eligibility criteria. So on the one hand, public authorities are exposed to standard pathologies of any formal organization such as principal–agent problems (bottleneck issues at the top of hierarchies), departmentalization and, consequently, selective perception, and negative coordination, groupthink phenomena, learning constraints, and similar challenges.

On the other hand, however, there are trade-offs peculiar to public admin-istration embedded in a democratic polity. One is connected to the necessity of maintaining overall legitimacy and comes to bear as a tension between respon-siveness and responsibility (Peters 2014): public agencies need to respond to what citizens would like them to do, especially when, at the local level, the action or inaction of authorities impacts directly on the conditions of everyday life. Hence the notion of the "listening bureaucrat" (Stivers 1994) or "street level bureau-cracy" (Lipsky 1980): public agencies need to be responsive. By the same token, however, public agencies and their representatives cannot be held accountable by individuals or social groups in their immediate societal or political environment alone. They are bound by legislation and to be held accountable in accordance with legal and professional standards. Just as the rigidity of rule-boundedness and protocol entails the risk of inadequate reaction to individual and local require-ments, unrestrained responsiveness entails the risk of arbitrariness, clientelism and corruption. Hence there is a trade-off between responsiveness and respon-sibility, which is inevitable and irremovable since it is part and parcel of pub-lic administration and a democratic political order. It is only in authoritarian regimes or outright dictatorships that bureaucrats can afford to ignore the legiti-mate demands of citizens and legal and professional standards at the same time.

Yet another inevitable trade-off is the one between goal attainment and sys-tem maintenance (cf. Seibel 2019, with reference to Deutsch 1963, 182–199, and Talcott Parsons's [1951] distinction between adaptation, goal attainment, inte-gration and latency/pattern maintenance). It is not necessarily limited to public bureaucracies and a democratic polity, but, again, the peculiarities of the politi-cal system impact decisively on the way the trade-off can possibly be handled by appointed and elected public officials.

Goal attainment is an easy-to-understand category since it is directly connected with the effectiveness of public administration. Whether or not and to what degree public policy is being implemented through its administrative substructure is necessarily an important issue of both political reality and scholarly analysis. As a matter of fact, policy effectiveness is the underlying normative yardstick of the entire subdiscipline of policy analysis. System maintenance refers to the complex machinery of governmental apparatuses at all levels. It is about internal coordination, day-to-day cooperation, adjustment of internal protocol, recruitment and education of staff, interface management and "bureaucratic politics" in an attempt to mobilize resources and to defend or enhance one's bureau's standing and influence. Public authorities are, to a large extent, occupied just with themselves, but this ostensibly unproductive activity is an indispensable prerequisite for maintaining the internal cohesion and stability of the administrative system as a whole.

System maintenance activity may collide with goal attainment efforts. Goal attainment may necessitate coordination, and coordination is a resource-absorbing and time-consuming process. Accelerating coordination processes for the sake of goal attainment may put a strain on interpersonal and interorganizational relations whose stability has to be kept intact for the sake of system effectiveness in general. As far as ultimate effectiveness is concerned, overemphasizing goal attainment may be just as detrimental as overemphasizing system maintenance.

Both standard pathologies and principal trade-offs are risk factors of organizational failure in general and failure at the expense of human security in particular. A decisive difference between standard pathologies of formal organizations and the specific trade-offs of public authorities in a democratic polity is, however, that the former can be influenced, thus mitigated, by organizational design while the latter is an integral and necessary component of the democratic polity and its complex bureaucratic substructure, which has consequences for the analytical relevance of the HRO and normal accident theories. Both HRO theory and NAT are helpful for an appropriate understanding of organizational standard pathologies, but they cannot contribute very much to the understanding of the responsiveness versus responsibility or the goal attainment versus system maintenance trade-offs.

The emphasis on structural fault lines that characterizes NAT is helpful for identifying principal-agent problems connected with organizational hierarchy, notorious coordination problems as a result of fragmented division of labor, the risk of diluted responsibilities in collaborative governance structures, and the like. Conversely, building awareness of such structural fault lines and the pitfalls attached to them is what HRO literature would suggest. Certainly, NAT entails more limitations as far as viable coping strategies concerning standard organizational pathologies are concerned. After all, the radical plea for the removal of inadequately risk-prone organizational structures is not applicable to the necessarily bureaucratic substructure of government itself. Still, in support of a structure-conscious strategy of risk assessment, NAT may be instrumental in identifying risk-generating institutional arrangements of all types, which is compatible with what HRO theory suggests in terms of controlled error-friendliness for the sake of learning and systematic "mindfulness" as far as step-by-step risk reduction is concerned.

What neither NAT nor HRO theory has systematically addressed, though, is the peculiarities of both the standard pathologies and the inevitable trade-offs that characterize public administration. Neither of these influential theories was specifically designed for public sector organizations. Accordingly, both strands of literature treat organizations as changeable and their weaknesses and fault lines as restrictable. Public authorities, however, are changeable only to a limited degree within the limits of the constitutional and otherwise legal order, while the very core of their bureaucratic structure is, by definition, not restrictable or changeable at all. Hierarchy as well as departmentalization, protocol as well as red-tape procedures, interagency cooperation as well as rivalry and competition for funds and competences remain part and parcel of public administration and, in that sense, standard pathologies that elected and appointed officials have to cope with rather than overcome, let alone eliminate. Even less eliminable are the trade-offs between responsiveness and responsibility and between goal attainment and system maintenance although they too may qualify as risk factors in their own right when it comes to human security.

So the argument here is that, precisely because of the robustness of standard pathologies and potentially detrimental trade-offs between performance standards of public administration, mindful coping in the sense of HRO theory matters. In its mainstream version, however, HRO theory remains unnecessarily vague as far as the peculiarities of public administration are concerned. Once standard pathologies and the characteristic trade-offs of performance requirements of public sector institutions have been identified, the complementary strengths of HRO theory and NAT can be brought to bear in the form of more fine-grained analyses and for the sake of targeted interventions that may eliminate security risks altogether. Prior to the development of the theoretical argument itself, an empirical case is presented in an attempt to illustrate the ontological relevance.

An illustrative case: standard pathologies and mismanaged trade-offs

On July 24, 2010, a techno-music street parade known as "Loveparade" in the German city of Duisburg ended in a crowd panic that claimed the lives of 21 people and left 652 injured (for a full account, see Seibel and Wenzel 2017). The responsible organizer was an event management firm, Lopavent GmbH (Gesellschaft mit beschränkter Haftung, the equivalent of a limited liability company in Britain or the United States). The event had several predecessors, most in Berlin and two in the cities of Dortmund and Essen. As a street parade, it required the permission of public authorities, in this case the municipal administration of the city of Duisburg. Under the aegis of the head of the Division of Security and Law (Dezernat für Sicherheit und Recht, or Dezernat II), the municipal administration convened a task force in charge of planning and preparing the Loveparade in September 2009. It initially consisted of representatives of the Duisburg city administration, Lopavent GmbH, the owner of the compound envisaged for the concluding segment of the Loveparade, and a public marketing firm, Wirtschaftsförderung metropoleruhr GmbH (cf. Document no. 2; see list of cited documents).

It soon became apparent that the envisaged compound was the critical factor as far as the security of the one million or more estimated visitors was concerned. Moreover, not only the compound itself but also the routes of access and evacuation turned out to be especially problematic since they led through a tunnel 24 meters wide with a single ramp branching off to the compound itself. That 18-meter-wide ramp had to serve as way in and way out, creating the obvious risk of congestion given the expected size of the crowd that would have to use it. The related security risks were clearly articulated by the task force. According to the records (cf. Document no. 4), this happened as early as October 2009.

It was also clear from the very outset, however, that the event enjoyed strong political support since it was an integral part of a publicity and marketing campaign not only for the city of Duisburg but for the entire Ruhr area. The Ruhrgebiet, the heartland of what used to be Germany's coal mining and iron ore industry, is a disadvantaged region that nonetheless had been designated as a "European Capital of Culture," a prestigious initiative of the European Union. The very Wirtschaftsförderung metropoleruhr GmbH was in charge of an entire program under the headline "Ruhr. 2010 Kulturhauptstadt Europas" (Ruhr. 2010 European Cultural Capital), of which the Loveparade was an integral part.

Political pressure to put on the Duisburg Loveparade 2010 under any circumstances increased when the city of Bochum, also located in the Ruhr area and thus participating in the very same program, canceled its own Loveparade scheduled for the summer of 2009. What was at stake in the perception of regional politicians was the prestige of the Ruhr area altogether as far as the capability of planning and organizing a spectacular event with a particular appeal to young people was concerned. When concerns about security issues connected to the Loveparade were voiced by the head of the Duisburg police department months before the task force even met, public criticism was so harsh that the resignation of the police chief was requested (Document no. 1). When the task force met on October 2, 2009, the head of division of Dezernat II, who chaired the meeting, explicitly reminded the participants that after the cancellation of the Loveparade in Bochum on short notice, the Duisburg Loveparade was definitely "politically desired" (cf. Document no. 3).

However, it was only in early March 2010, more than four months into the planning process, that the municipal administration of Duisburg realized that the design of the Loveparade (i.e., closed compound with limited access and evacuation routes) implied a transfer of jurisdiction for risk assessment and public permission to the Office of Regulation and Supervision of Construction (Bauordnungsamt). The Bauordnungsamt (or Amt 62, according to the organizational chart of the Duisburg city administration) clearly stated that permission could not be given for the envisaged event site; its officials also made it clear that violation of the relevant legal provision (the Sonderbauverordnung Nordrhein-Westfalen, or decree for special construction of the state of North Rhine-Westphalia) would make any official involved liable under criminal law (Document no. 5).

From this point on, four and a half months before the event in question, both the substantial security risks and the incompatibility of the conditions at the event site and the related legal stipulations were known to the officials in charge and documented. In the files of the Duisburg city administration, it was also clearly stated that an indispensable prerequisite for any permission was a formal application to be submitted by Lopavent GmbH with substantiated documentation of the relevant security measures (Document no. 5).

What followed was a protracted planning and preparation process in which part of the Duisburg city administration sided with the event management firm in a blunt attempt to manipulate the facts and figures and to obstruct the clear and binding stipulation of the relevant security regulation, while the responsible Amt 62 remained determined to enforce the law.

Ironically, the leading figure among those determined to ignore the law and to issue permission to organize the Loveparade under any circumstances was the head of the city's Division of Security and Law (Dezernat II). This man was a close associate of the mayor, who had expressed unmistakably his will to have the Loveparade take place in his city. His opposite number was the head of the Division of Urban Development (Dezernat für Stadtentwicklung, or Dezernat V), to which the Amt 62 belonged. He, however, kept a low profile and did nothing to buttress the position and action strategy of the administration belonging to his own jurisdiction. Hence, as depicted in Figure 8.1, a power asymmetry emerged in favor of those determined to push through permission for the event

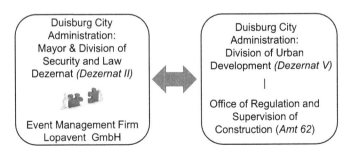

FIGURE 8.1   Public-private coalition building and interagency rivalry within the Duisburg Municipality in the run-up to the Loveparade Event of July 24, 2010.

under any circumstances and to the disadvantage of those compliant with the existing safety regulation.

Under these conditions, Lopavent GmbH managed to outmaneuver the Bauordnungsamt. The head of Dezernat II, in transgression of his own competent jurisdiction, commissioned several separate expert reports that focused on crowd management issues. This was clearly intended to circumvent the unmistakable security stipulations of the law whose enforcement was, in turn, the task of Amt 62. None of these expert reports submitted just a couple of weeks or even days (June and July 2010) before the Loveparade itself referred to the relevant legal provisions (cf. Documents no. 9, 10, 11). Moreover, they were vague and peppered with severability clauses. Nonetheless, they served as justification to grant permission for the Loveparade, which was ultimately pushed through by the head of Dezernat II. Instead of backing the responsible unit of his own administration vis-à-vis an applicant (Lopavent GmbH), he even formed an alliance with that very private firm against the relevant security regulation and the administrative unit tasked with enforcing it.

Not only was the borderline between the rule of law and a compliant public administration and private interests blurred, but the role and competence of public and private actors were virtually inverted. In a meeting on June 18, 2010, the representatives of Lopavent GmbH admitted one more time that they were not able to guarantee more than one-third of the overall width of evacuation routes on the event site of what the legal security provisions required (cf. Document no. 7). While this was astonishing and yet another unmistakable warning that authorization of the Loveparade was just not possible, the head of Dezernat II instructed, again in transgression of his own competent jurisdiction, the Office of Regulation and Supervision of Construction (Bauordnungsamt) to "cooperate" with Lopavent GmbH and to support the latter in the development of a security concept for the Loveparade scheduled to be held within just over a month. This meant not only to provoke a conflict of interest—after all, the Bauordnungsamt as a public authority was tasked with drafting a security concept that it subsequently would have to evaluate and to certify—but also to task Amt 62 with a job it was not competent to do; namely, the development of an accurate evacuation plan on the basis of crowd management data and simulation models it could not possibly have at its disposal.

The representatives of Amt 62 participating in the meeting of June 18, 2010, articulated precisely this, but to no avail. Their superior, the head of the Division of Urban Development (Dezernat V), supported this stance through a handwritten remark on the margin of the report written by the head of Amt 62 stating that the envisaged procedure did not conform to proper administrative practice and that Dezernat II—instead of his own division—would have to make all the relevant decisions.[1] This statement was right and wrong at the same time. While it was entirely correct that the envisaged procedure violated basic principles of proper administrative practice, the head of Dezernat V was wrong in assuming that it was at his personal discretion to concede the jurisdiction for the relevant decision to Dezernat II. On the contrary, it was his obligation to make sure that the Bauordnungsamt evaluated Lopavent's security concept in accordance with the legal requirements and, if necessary, to deny authorization of the Loveparade as long as the requirements were not met. Instead, the head of Dezernat V bluntly refused to be involved in the relevant decisionmaking—a classic case of blame-shifting that was itself improper and an act of irresponsibility.

It was, ironically, the private event management firm Lopavent instead of the public authority actually in charge that filled the vacuum created by the failure of the head of Dezernat V to insist on a proper evaluation and certification of the security concept. Representatives of Lopavent GmbH participated in yet another meeting, held on June 25, 2010, devoted to the unresolved security issues. The primary purpose of this meeting was not the development of a security concept itself but an agreement on how to evaluate such a concept. That agreement entailed the intent to commission yet another expert report on the evacuation plan to be developed, according to the previous instructions, by the head of the Division of Security and Law (Dezernat II) in cooperation with Lopavent GmbH and the very Bauordnungsamt that ultimately would have to certify it. This agreement was, according to the minutes of the meeting of June 25, 2010, "approved" by the participating representatives of Lopavent GmbH (cf. Document no. 8). Thus, the private firm that, according to the legal provisions, was obliged to submit a security and evacuation plan and to have it evaluated and certified by the relevant public agency participated in deliberations whose subject was the very procedure of evaluation and certification whose result directly affected the private firm applying for permission.

Another telling detail of the replacement of what should have been an independent and unfettered examination by an irregular procedure was that the group of consulting engineers authorized to evaluate the security concept was, according to information provided on their website, a spin-off of the chair of the very professor of physics at the University of Duisburg who himself was authorized to evaluate and to certify the report of the engineers who were his former students and PhD candidates. Not only was this series of conflicts of interest not corrected or terminated; they were, instead, literally designed and organized by the Duisburg city administration with the obvious intent to suspend the regular procedure of an independent assessment of the security and evacuation concept for an event involving approximately one million visitors.

Exhausted by what may be called a war of attrition against an alliance of high-ranking public officials and the private event management firm, the Bauordnungsamt, Amt 62, finally gave in and issued permission to hold the Loveparade as planned. That happened on July 23, 2010—24 hours before the event. In revealing clarity, the wording of the authorizing permission made apparent that the security requirements of the relevant legal provision, the Sonderbauverordnung, were not met by the security concept submitted by Lopavent GmbH (Document no. 12). In issuing the permission anyway, the Bauordnungsamt, under the relentless pressure of the head of Dezernat II, invoked the right of administrative discretion whose existence it had explicitly denied up to that point (cf. Document no. 6, p. 5).

On the afternoon of July 24, 2010, panic broke out in the totally overcrowded tunnel leading to the event site and on the ramp that branched off to the actual compound where the final segment of the Loveparade was taking place. Most of the 21 casualties were caused by thorax contusion. The ramp, serving as access and exit at the same time, turned out to be a fatal trap without escape routes—a fact that was known to the private organizer and the relevant authorities from the very outset but that had not prevented the relevant authority from issuing a permission that should never have been given.

Case analysis: neither normal accident nor insufficient reliability management

The Loveparade catastrophe was a man-made disaster in the classic sense. It did not happen by accident. Nor did it happen because of carelessness or lack of skill of those involved in planning and preparation. Neither was it the consequence of structural complexity of governance, bureaucratic inflexibility, "wicked problems," or unsolvable managerial issues. It happened because key actors within the relevant municipality purposefully undermined and successfully circumvented the relevant security regulation. That they did with great skill and, yes, mindfulness and explicit agility in a quasi-entrepreneurial style. What the prehistory of the disaster reveals is in fact the mutual reinforcement of inevitable trade-offs among legitimate performance parameters, on the one hand, and standard pathologies of any bureaucratic organization, on the other hand. What were the actual conditions of this vicious circle, why was it not neutralized by the officials in charge, and what are relevant implications for NAT and HRO theory?

The standard pathologies and, thus, "normal" risk structure in the Perrow sense were connected to the duality of intra-administrative departmentalization, on the one hand, and the hybrid arrangement of municipal authorities and a private event management firm—a classic public-private partnership (PPP)—on the other hand. Frictions and eventually open conflict broke out between the office (Amt 62) directly in charge of licensing the Loveparade event according to the relevant security regulation and a division (Dezernat II) of the Duisburg city administration at the interface between the intra-administrative security screening, the political leadership of the municipality and the private event management firm. None of this was unusual or unmanageable. It was just a matter of priorities. And the priority should have been crystal clear: safety first. According to the relevant safety regulation, this would have implied denying permission to hold the Loveparade event right away.

So the obvious question is why high-ranking municipal decisionmakers did not do what they were undoubtedly supposed to do. One simple answer is that they did not realize that, under the given circumstances, they had to act as representatives of a high reliability organization. Not only was it entirely obvious and evident that at a mass event of the anticipated scale on a compound of limited size and with narrow access and exit routes, the protection of physical integrity was of prime importance from the very outset, it was also beyond reasonable doubt that the event could not be organized in accordance with the unmistakable legal safety regulation.

Under these circumstances, the standard argument of mainstream HRO theory according to which the officials in charge should have been more "mindful" would be misleading and therefore useless. After all, there *were* rank-and-file officials within the Duisburg municipal administration who, as civil servants obedient to the law, were entirely "mindful" and determined to insist on compliance with the legal safety stipulations and to deny permission for the Loveparade event. The problem was that their superiors were not willing to listen to them. Instead, these higher-ranking officials mobilized all the political and organizational resources available in the attempt to obstruct the regular vetting and verification procedures for the planned mass event. It is not that they were not smart enough to understand what was at stake. Rather, they were acting under the influence of strong counterincentives that prevented them from doing what they, in all likelihood, would have usually done, which is just to enforce the law and to follow bureaucratic protocol.

One could argue, in accordance with Perrow's normal accident theory, that one of those counterincentives was already the hybrid arrangement in the form of a PPP tasked with the planning of the event. After all, this partnership meant sharing not just tasks and jobs but also jurisdiction and responsibilities and, accordingly, it implied particular requirements of coordination and reintegration. Undeniably, PPPs generate particular coordination problems due to fragmented jurisdiction, diluted responsibilities and opportunity structures for blame avoidance (Hood 2011). However, during the run-up to the Duisburg Loveparade, those coordination and reintegration problems were neither new nor particularly complex. Accordingly, they could have been easily solved, especially since the decisive ingredient of unmanageable complexity, in the Perrow sense, was missing—namely, tight coupling. Decisionmaking stretched over a long period of time and was subject to lengthy deliberation. The decision to ignore and thus violate unambiguous security regulation in order to pave the way for the Loveparade event under any circumstances was made in full consciousness. What could be easily anticipated, though, was that denying permission to perform the Loveparade would trigger massive negative reactions from the overall public. This must have been a much stronger impulse shaping the motivation of the higher-ranking public officials than the objections of their own subordinates and the "bureaucratic" logic of the legal restrictions that made permitting the Loveparade virtually impossible.

Quite ironically, the relevant key actors were "mindful" in their own way. Certainly, these municipal officials mismanaged the structural fault lines of a fragmented intra-administrative jurisdiction and an indispensable cooperation with a private firm, but that was due to their mishandling of the trade-off between responsiveness and responsibility, on the one hand, and goal attainment and system maintenance, on the other hand. The higher-ranking officials were determined to respond to the expectations of political stakeholders to make the high-profile Loveparade event possible, literally against all odds. They were determined to demonstrate their ability to overcome "bureaucratic" obstacles even if those obstacles consisted of legal constraints designed to guarantee human security. In other words, in all their mindfulness, they lost their sense of responsibility. And, consequently, they made goal attainment the absolute priority at the expense of system maintenance since system maintenance would have implied protecting the integrity of the "bureaucratic" vetting and licensing process. Instead of fending off the political pressure to dilute the licensing criteria, the pressure was amplified and focused at the same time, targeting the licensing office (Amt 62) as the weakest link in the chain of hierarchy. Moreover, a quasi-entrepreneurial style of goal-oriented decisionmaking was much easier to sell on the political market than sober-minded bureaucratic decisionmaking according to some legal prescriptions.

The question of why public officials set wrong priorities when balancing the trade-off between responsiveness and responsibility and/or between goal attainment and system maintenance is beyond the grasp of NAT and conventional HRO theory. Normal accident theory is good at identifying risk-generating organizational structures as permissive conditions of public mismanagement, but it does not address the ability of human actors to realize precisely this and to develop successful coping strategies for the sake of risk reduction. By contrast, the ability to be mindful and to learn is precisely what HRO theory emphasizes. However, HRO theory cannot explain why even mindfulness may be based on priorities that ultimately undermine rather than strengthen organizational reliability.

Yet combining the relative strengths of both theories is helpful for a better understanding of organizational failure with severe consequences and, therefore, generalization for the sake of prevention. While NAT is helpful in identifying risk-prone structures, HRO theory is helpful in identifying both counterstrategies and counterincentives to develop mindsets designed to neutralize risks. What the present chapter suggests is that combining these complementary strengths requires a particular analytical perspective that focuses on actual causal processes rather than on structural variables or abstract normative statements. It is only through a process-analytical perspective that both the permissive conditions and their actual impact on risk-generating human action and the relevant points of intervention or critical junctures can be identified. In what follows, a related explanatory model and its application to the Duisburg Loveparade disaster will be described.

An alternative perspective: causal mechanisms and points of intervention

In their respective conventional versions, NAT and HRO theory focus on either structural properties (NAT) or behavioral attitudes (HRO theory) as risk factors and frames of reference for risk reduction. The common blind spots of these theories are (1) the actual risk- and failure-generating "machinery" of organizations and (2) the points of intervention at which human actors can actually stop that machinery from generating undesirable results, especially when it comes to risks to human security. The analytical challenge, then, is to identify predictable elements of risk-generating organizational machineries—in other words, causal mechanisms—and, likewise, typical points of intervention. One way to address that challenge is to systematize the linkages between permissive conditions, related risk-increasing patterns of human action and the actual materialization of risks in the form of disastrous outcomes. These linkages or joints mark the points of intervention at which disastrous causal processes can, in principle, be neutralized.

A model that responds to these analytical requirements is Hedström and Swedberg's (1998) and Hedström and Ylikoski's (2010) distinction of layered causal mechanisms in combination with Mario Bunge's (1997, 2004) characterization of mechanisms as being systemic in nature. Hedström and Ylikoski (2010) distinguish three types of mechanisms, as depicted in Figure 8.2.

This analytical scheme is derived from what in the jargon of social science methodology (methodological individualism, in particular) is known as Coleman's bathtub (or Coleman's boat): the quest for disaggregated causal analytic steps in an attempt to identify at the micro level of individual human agency the origins of causal effects at the aggregate (or macro) level (Coleman 1990, 10). What Hedström, Swedberg, and Ylikoski add to Coleman's original "bathtub" is, first, the language of "mechanisms" previously introduced by Jon Elster (1989) and, second, an explicit account of the disaggregation and reaggregation of causality. Hence they identify three types of mechanisms: action formation mechanisms as core mechanisms shaping individual human agency embedded in,

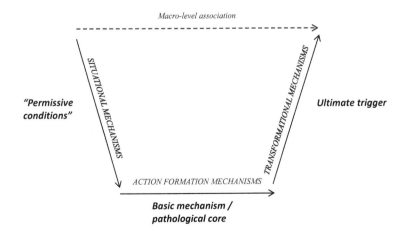

FIGURE 8.2 Typology of causal mechanisms, adapted from Hedström and Ylikoski (2010, 59), with author's addenda.

and shaped by, situational mechanisms and ultimately turned into an aggregated result through transformational mechanisms.

Moreover, Bunge's (1997, 2004) particular contribution to the conceptualization of causal mechanisms is the reference to the system specificity[2] of mechanisms in the first place. We do not expect biochemical mechanisms to occur in a social system, nor do we expect social mechanisms to occur in a mechanical system. The ontology of systems of any sort implies specific mechanisms that, under particular circumstances, may turn out to be causal mechanisms for various outcomes. Formal organizations, by their very ontological nature, entail hierarchy, and hierarchy implies principal-agent problems (Akerlof 1970; Grossmann and Hart 1983). Moreover, organizations operate on the basis of division of labor, which implies requirements of coordination and related risk zones of coordination deficiencies (Thompson 1967). Decisionmaking in organizations, as long as not strictly rule bound, usually takes place in groups, which implies the risk of groupthink in the sense of deviant opinions being restrained or suspended by social pressure or implicit hierarchy (Janis 1972).

What Bunge also emphasized—unlike mainstream literature on causal process tracing and causal mechanisms (cf. Beach and Pedersen 2019; Bennett and Checkel 2015)—is that mechanisms in social systems are not visible, so that they can only be conjectured. It is only on the basis of appropriate theorizing that we are able to identify mechanisms in social systems regardless of whether the analysis is descriptive or causal analytic in nature. Principal-agent problems cannot be observed, deficiencies of coordination or the logic of bargaining processes are not visible either, and neither is groupthink or a prisoner's dilemma. On the basis of an appropriate diagnosis of the actual ontology, however, visibility is reached through conjecturing. Disputes may remain, such as the debate on whether "authority" actually exists or can be redefined as a quasi-contractual relation (cf. Alchian and Demsetz 1972 for the latter position and Arrow 1974 for the former), but this is, after all, what theoretical reasoning is about.

What makes, again, the analytical differentiation of situational, action formation, and transformational mechanisms in the Hedström, Swedberg, and Ylikoski sense particularly helpful for understanding the failure of risk assessment and risk control is the exposure of points of intervention and their implicit ambivalence. Situational mechanisms that either represent or aggravate standard pathologies of organizations may be tolerated as long as they are neutralized at the level of the action formation mechanisms. Similarly, risk-increasing action formation mechanisms may be tolerated as long as they are neutralized at the threshold separating them from "transformational" mechanisms.

Accordingly, there are two "natural" points of intervention, one at the interface between situational mechanisms and action formation mechanisms and one at the threshold between action formation mechanisms and the actual occurrence of the outcome. Situational mechanisms, due to necessary division of labor or to collaborative governance, may split up jurisdiction and dilute responsibility, but these potentially harmful forces can be checked by existing protocol or mindful leaders, or both. And even if that is not the case and risk-increasing behavior does take place, fateful consequences can be averted when no transformational mechanisms are available or mobilized. This is actually the logic of the "near miss" phenomenon, characterized by risk-increasing mechanisms whose impact is finally neutralized, even if sometimes at the very last moment (cf. Hayes 2009, 124–125).

Hence we find a productive complementarity of the NAT and HRO theories: it might be precisely "mindfulness" in the Hopkins (2007) and Weick and Sutcliffe (2007) sense through which harmful effects at the interface between situational mechanisms and action formation mechanisms and at the threshold between action formation mechanisms and transformational mechanisms are neutralized; at the same time the situational mechanisms themselves might represent exactly the type of structural fault lines whose inevitability is emphasized in Perrow's classic version of NAT. In the real world of an ongoing process of decisionmaking, actors may or may not realize that the point of intervention exists, but even when they do realize its existence, it remains uncertain if and how they make use of related cognitions and recognitions. This ambivalence is exactly what skeptical theories of organizational learning have underlined (Argyris 1999; Argyris and Schön 1978; Janis 1972; March and Olsen 1975).

A case reanalyzed

Those who flocked to the event site of the so-called Loveparade in the city of Duisburg on July 24, 2010, had every reason to trust that the public authorities in charge were in full control of all necessary safety measures. After all, the event as such was not unusual and there was no reason to doubt the professionalism of the Duisburg municipal administration. While it is highly unlikely that anybody among those hundreds of thousands of visitors of the event had any idea about the fragmented responsibilities and internal rivalry within the city administration, whatever skepticism arose would have been overcome by a natural trust in the ability of seasoned and experienced bureaucrats to deal with related challenges. Certainly, it would have been beyond anybody's imagination that key actors within the Duisburg city administration not only did not mitigate frictions and tensions in a division of labor-based process of planning and organization but, rather, aggravated their undesirable consequences—which is, however, what happened. A differentiated analysis of the relevant causal mechanisms reveals how that kind of disastrous behavioral pattern emerged.

Applied to the run-up to the Duisburg Loveparade disaster and depicted in Figure 8.3, the differentiation of three different types of causal mechanisms combined with the productive complementarity of the NAT and the HRO theories reveals not only distinct categories of mechanisms but also the very points of intervention at which the path to disaster could have been interrupted. Which is, in turn, what did not happen. There were clearly permissive conditions and terms of organizational structure and, particularly, a political climate that paved

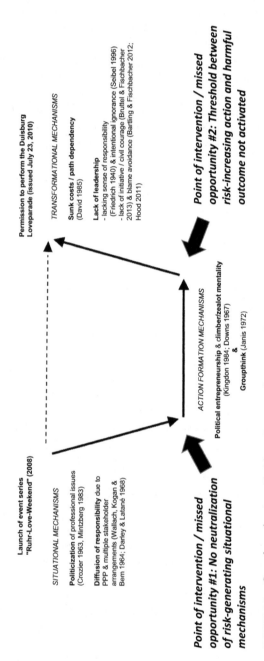

FIGURE 8.3 Causal mechanisms Duisburg Loveparade: points of intervention/missed opportunities.

the way to negligence of security issues and the final issuance of permission that, according to the law and the expertise of the relevant officials in charge, should never have been given. What theory-based conjecturing discovers is what Crozier (1963) has described as the use of remaining zones of uncertainty in bureaucracy for the mobilization of power (cf. also Mintzberg 1983), thus politicization, and what is known in behavioral psychology and economics as the negative impact of a multitude of actors on the readiness to assume responsibility (Darley and Latané 1968; Wallach, Kogan, and Bem 1963) and the temptation for blame-shifting (Bartling and Fischbacher 2012; Hood 2011). The politicization impacted on the process of administrative licensing while the diffusion of responsibility resulted from the PPP between the Duisburg municipality and the private event manage-ment firm. Both factors were interacting: without the politicization of what was basically a banal process of administrative verification and approval, the event management firm would have been just one applicant among many others asking for some sort of authorization or permission. In that case, no implicit coalition would have emerged between a private business and one part of the city admin-istration against a different part of the same administration. In reality, however, this was precisely what happened. What should have been clear and distinct pat-terns of division of labor and related responsibilities were blurred and diluted at the expense of the actual integrity of the city administration as the guardian of the public interest in human security. So politicization and diffusion of responsi-bility turned out to be the very situational mechanisms that shaped the patterns of action at the actual decisionmaking level.

What happened at the level of decisionmaking was that two opposing camps within the Duisburg city administration were competing for influence, a fight in the course of which the micropolitical entrepreneurship of a division chief who was not even jurisdictionally competent pressed relentlessly to permit the Loveparade to go forward under any circumstances. What one recognizes as action formation mechanisms is what Downs (1967, 109–110) has denoted as zealot-style attitude, Finer (1941) as over-feasance, or Kingdon (1984) as policy entrepreneurship. In addition, signs of groupthink (Janis 1972) were unmistak-able. It was the personal zeal of the head of Division II, the mayor's right-hand man, that shaped the climate of internal meetings in which the jurisdictionally competent officials soon found themselves on the defensive. In the final stage of what may be called a war of attrition, nobody dared to raise objections anymore against a clearly illegal strategy to make possible a public event whose security status was more than dubious. The combination of zeal and groupthink made the reversal of an ultimately disastrous process of decisionmaking increasingly unlikely.

And yet, even at that stage, the process itself was still not unstoppable. It could have been halted by the immediate superior of the officials in the licensing authority (Amt 62), the head of Division V. This, however, would have required overcoming strong path dependencies (David 1985) through determined lead-ership in defense of institutional integrity (Selznick 1957, 118–133) as well as a clear and incorruptible sense of responsibility (Friedrich 1940). The fact that this did not happen turned out to be the condition sufficient for a permission that cleared the way to disaster. The actual transformational mechanisms through which the relevant series of decisions passed the proverbial point of no return were path dependency and blunt lack of leadership. A decision to stop the run-up to a popular mass event at the eleventh hour would have implied having wasted a considerable amount of investment of both financial and political capital. All the political, organizational and monetary efforts to make the Loveparade possible would have been in vain. Anticipating precisely this, it would have taken not just sober judgment but, above all, a tremendous amount of courage and resolve to cancel the event (Bruttel and Fischbacher 2013; 't Hart and Tummers 2019, esp. 50–51). The official in charge, the head of Division V, had none of these personality traits.

The definition of different types of causal mechanisms as depicted in Figure 8.3 also makes discernible the relevant points of intervention and the consequences of nonintervention. The opportunity to neutralize the harmful effect of the situational mechanisms was not just missed. Rather, the harm's impact was reinforced through purposeful action. Still, the resulting action formation mechanisms did not make a disastrous outcome inevitable. It took a second missed opportunity at the threshold between risk-taking behavioral attitudes and actual decisions to activate the transformational mechanisms triggering the actual occurrence of the disaster.

Not only can we discern the points of intervention, we also know the individual actors who missed the opportunity to make use of them. This knowledge, in turn, not only implies pinpointing personal responsibility but also building assumptions about motivational forces. It would be overly simplistic to classify the apparent neglect as recklessness and blundering. It was not just personal failure that made high-ranking and accomplished public officials purposefully violate unambiguous security regulations. Those officials had to respond to divergent requirements of justification and legitimacy shaped by the trade-offs between responsiveness and responsibility and between goal attainment and system maintenance. Within that framework of legitimization, the immediately responsible officials made entirely plausible choices. They prioritized responsiveness over responsibility and goal attainment over system maintenance. The head of Division II of the Duisburg city administration, when pressing for issuing permission for the event under any circumstances, responded to the political expectations of the general public. The head of Division V, in denial of his own skepticism, ultimately did the same thing. We do not know anything about their cognitive dissonances or if they felt any. If so, they could have mitigated them by referring to the necessity to do justice to what was politically requested and to avoid what would have frustrated hundreds of thousands of people—namely, canceling the popular mass event altogether. Assuming responsibility for actual law enforcement and protecting the institutional integrity of the licensing office in charge would have been costly in terms of reputation and personal standing.

Normative quests to mindfully resist those incentives are entirely appropriate, but a more promising approach is to make their occurrence less likely.

Conclusion

High reliability in pursuing stated purposes is the basis of trust when it comes to power and resources delegated to public administration in general. This is particularly salient where and when public authorities are tasked with the protection of human security. While the applicability of the high reliability concept to public sector organizations has been generally challenged by some authors (cf. especially Boin and Schulman 2008), this chapter maintains that public authorities should and can be treated as high reliability organizations under conditions in which risks to life and limb are involved. It comes with the very nature of public administration that their operations are standardized and regulated, which implies a limited range of both standard procedures and standard pathologies and, consequently, typical patterns of risk-generating mechanisms. Conceptualizing and differentiating those mechanisms is useful for developing a more fine-grained variant of both normal accident theory (NAT) and high reliability organization (HRO) theory, taking into account the very standard pathologies of public administration and inevitable trade-offs connected to their political embeddedness in democratic and rule-of-law-based systems. This, the chapter argues, makes it possible to identify distinct points of intervention at which permissive conditions with the potential to trigger risk-generating human action can be neutralized, while the threshold that separates risk-generating human action from actual disaster can be raised to a level that makes disastrous outcomes impossible or, at least, less probable.

It is quite in the vein of natural accident theory (NAT) that permissive conditions in the form of situational mechanisms and standard pathologies of a given organizational arrangement can be diagnosed as risk zones connected to particular institutional structures and their societal and political environments. Such diagnoses require a distinct ontological definition of the organizational system at hand and, hence, the basic mechanisms that "make the system work" (Bunge 2004) and, by the same token, may also indicate standard pathologies and trade-offs. In the present chapter, this is illustrated for public authorities whose ontological nature is characterized not only by hierarchy, division of labor, legal prescriptions, and related standard operating procedures but also, for the sake of effectiveness and legitimacy, by trade-offs between responsiveness and responsibility and between goal attainment and system maintenance, in particular institutional integrity.

In the reality of public administration, those trade-offs have to be balanced by human decisionmakers in an attempt to neutralize the undesirable effects of standard pathologies. As standard pathologies and typical trade-offs, they are, in principle, predictable as risk-generating factors. It is here where the emphasis on "mindfulness" as stressed in the HRO literature is helpful and analytically relevant. While, in real organizational life, that mindfulness cannot be taken for granted, accomplished officials in public administration can be assumed to be mindful enough when it comes to the recognition and acknowledgment of bureaucratic standard pathologies such as insufficient vertical communication, selective perceptions and negative coordination, bureaucratic politics, red tape, narrow-mindedness, defensive routines, and the like. They are probably also mindful enough to develop coping strategies designed to mitigate or even to avoid the undesirable effects of those pathologies. The same is true for the basic trade-offs between responsiveness and responsibility, on the one hand, and goal attainment and system maintenance, on the other hand. Mindfulness is what, in a nutshell, characterizes the average "responsible administrator" (cf. Cooper 2012).

Yet mindfulness as such is an insufficient normative requirement as long as the operational leeway remains unspecified where the "mind" can actually come to bear in shaping decisionmaking at the operational level of public authorities in an attempt to neutralize standard pathologies and to balance inherent trade-offs. The argument of the present chapter is that a mechanism-based perspective on organizational standard pathologies and systemic trade-offs makes a valuable contribution to the required specification. The differentiation between situational action formation and transformational mechanisms according to Hedström and Swedberg (1998) and Hedström and Ylikoski (2010) allows for the identification of critical points of intervention at which, according to NAT, structural and situational risk zones can be recognized, and, according to HRO theory, mindful actors should be able to neutralize their undesirable effects (see Figure 8.4).

The joint between situational and action formation mechanisms can be characterized as the permissive conditions / actual agency interface. It is here where a first point of intervention is located since mindful individual or collective actors should be able to make sure that the negative effects of situational mechanisms

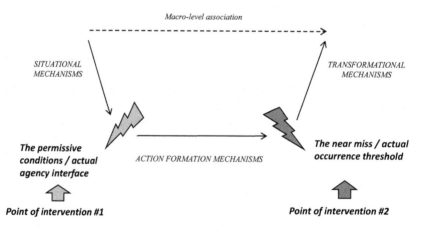

FIGURE 8.4 Causal mechanisms and points of intervention.

or permissive conditions do not materialize. The second—and decisive—point of intervention is located at the joint between action formation mechanisms and transformational mechanisms. That joint can therefore be characterized as the near miss / actual occurrence threshold. Risk-generating action formation mechanisms may be kept under control by key decisionmakers that combine mindfulness with determination and resolve.

One relevant empirical question emerging from the suggested combination of NAT and HRO theories in a mechanism-based perspective is why and under what circumstances the relevant points of intervention remain unrecognized and/or unused. The contention of the present chapter is that identifying structural risk zones of public administration and normative appeals insisting on mindfulness remain insufficient as long as predictable counterincentives to recognize risk zones and to take measures to contain their harmful effects are not systematically addressed. Furthermore, predictions about structural risk zones and applied mindfulness require an analysis of how basic trade-offs of democracy impact on discretionary decisionmaking in public administration.

The run-up to the Duisburg Loveparade disaster is indicative also in this particular respect. Massive political pressure on the licensing authority in charge of vetting and verifying planning and preparation ultimately caused professional and institutional integrity to collapse. That pressure did not originate at random; rather, it was the consequence of choices of upper-rank public officials who had to balance conflicting priorities of democratic decisionmaking. They had to be responsive in terms of goal attainment and responsible in terms of system maintenance at the same time. Canceling a mass event with an anticipated one million visitors, while doing justice to both legal requirements and the professional responsibility for safeguarding human security, would have violated the legitimate expectations of the public at large and thus the requirements of responsiveness. Issuing permission for the event, while doing justice to effective goal attainment in terms of public management and agility, inevitably resulted in violating the professional and institutional integrity of the decisionmaking process itself.

This chapter is intended to demonstrate, first, the necessity to specify general conditions under which structural risk zones of public authorities as high reliability organizations can possibly be recognized and kept under mindful control and, second, the possibility to identify points of intervention at which existing risks can be neutralized. Whether or not actors in public administration make use of those points of intervention is not only a matter of knowledge and mindfulness but also, if not decisively so, a matter of personal resolve and public support. While resolve is, in turn, a matter of personality, and personality is ultimately a matter of recruitment and training, support is a matter of public values. Insisting on personal responsibility for the sake of maintaining professional and institutional integrity is, from that normative perspective, a crucial ingredient of making public authorities high reliability organizations in the real world of a democratic polity.

Acknowledgment

The present chapter is a slightly revised reprint of my article "Are Public Bureaucracies Supposed to Be High Reliability Organizations?," *Global Perspectives* (2020) 1 (1):17643. It is based on the research project "Black Swans in Public Administration: Rare Organizational Failure with Severe Consequences" (https://issuu.com/euresearcher/docs/black_swans_in_public_administration_eur20_h_res), funded by the German Research Foundation (DFG) in the framework of the DFG Reinhart Koselleck program. I would like to express my gratitude to the Utrecht University School of Governance (USBO) for its hospitality during an extended stay as a guest scholar when the present work was in the making. I am also indebted to Stavros Zouridis and the Oderzoeksraad voor Veiligheid (Dutch Safety Board) for the opportunity to discuss the analytical concept of this chapter at the occasion of a talk given in The Hague in January 2020. Finally, I am indebted to Annette Flowe and Paulina Ulbrich for technical assistance in completing the manuscript.

Notes

1 The German original (Document no. 7) reads: "Ich lehne aufgrund dieser Problemstellung eine Zuständigkeit und Verantwortung von [Amt] 62 ab. Dieses entspricht in keinerlei Hinsicht einem ordentlichen Verwaltungshandeln und einer sachgerechten Projektsteuerung. Die Entscheidung in allen Belangen obliegt [Dezernat] II." (Author's translation: Due to the nature of the problem, I reject jurisdiction and responsibility of [Amt] 62. It is in no way in accordance with proper administrative procedure and an appropriate control of the project. In every respect, the decision lies with [Division] II.)

2 Author's wording. Despite the parallel, both in language and in substance, Bunge himself makes no reference to the microeconomic concept of *asset specificity* developed by Oliver E. Williamson (1985)—that is, that the productivity of assets (e.g., skills, investments) is not universal but context dependent.

References

Akerlof, George A. 1970. "The Market for 'Lemons': Quality Uncertainty and the Market Mechanism." *Quarterly Journal of Economics*, 84: 488–500.

Alchian, Armen A. and Harold Demsetz. 1972. "Production, Information Costs, and Economic Organization." *The American Economic Review*, 62: 777–795.

Argyris, Chris. 1999. *On Organizational Learning*. 2nd ed. Oxford: Wiley-Blackwell.

Argyris, Chris and Donald A. Schön. 1978. *Organizational Learning: A Theory of Action Perspective*. Reading, MA: Addison-Wesley.

Arrow, Kenneth J. 1974. *The Limits of Organization*. New York: Norton & Company.

Bartling, Björn and Urs Fischbacher. 2012. "Shifting the Blame: On Delegation and Responsibility." *The Review of Economic Studies*, 79: 67–87.

Beach, Derek and Rasmus Brun Pederson. 2019. *Process-Tracing Methods: Foundations and Guidelines*. 2nd ed. Ann Arbor: University of Michigan Press.

Bennett, Andrew and Jeffrey T. Checkel. 2015. "Process Tracing: From Philosophical Roots to Best Practices." In Andrew Bennett and Jeffrey T. Checkel (eds.). *Process*

Tracing. From Metaphor to Analytic Tool, 3–38. Cambridge: Cambridge University Press.

Boin, Arjen and Paul Schulman. 2008. "Assessing NASA's Safety Culture: The Limits and Possibilities of High-Reliability Theory." *Public Administration Review*, 68: 1050–1062.

Bruttel, Lisa and Urs Fischbacher. 2013. "Taking the Initiative: What Characterizes Leaders?" *European Economic Review*, 64: 147–168.

Bunge, Mario. 1997. "Mechanism and Explanation." *Philosophy of the Social Sciences*, 27: 410–465.

Bunge, Mario. 2004. "How Does It Work? The Search for Explanatory Mechanisms." *Philosophy of the Social Sciences*, 34: 182–210.

Coleman, James S. 1990. *Foundations of Social Theory*. Cambridge, MA: Harvard University Press.

Cooper, Terry L. 2012. *The Responsible Administrator: An Approach to Ethics for the Administrative Role*. 5th ed. San Francisco: Jossey-Bass.

Crozier, Michel. 1963. *Le phénomène buraucratique. Essai sur les tendances bureaucratiques des systems d'organisation modernes et sur leurs relations en France avec le système social et culturel*. Paris: Éditions du Seuil.

Darley, John and Bibb Latané. 1968. "Bystander Intervention in Emergencies: Diffusion of Responsibility." *Journal of Personality and Social Psychology*, 8: 377–383.

David, Paul A. 1985. "Clio and the Economics of QWERTY." *American Economic Review*, 75: 332–337.

Deutsch, Karl W. 1963. *The Nerves of Government: Models of Political Communication and Control*. New York: The Free Press.

Downs, Anthony. 1967. *Inside Bureaucracy*. Boston: Little, Brown and Company.

Elster, Jon. 1989. *Nuts and Bolts for the Social Sciences*. Cambridge: Cambridge University Press.

Farson, Richard and Ralph Keyes. 2002. "The Failure-Tolerant Leader." *Harvard Business Review*, 80: 64–71.

Finer, Herman. 1941. "Administrative Responsibility in Democratic Government." *Public Administration Review*, 1: 335–350.

Friedrich, Carl J. 1940. "Public Policy and the Nature of Administrative Responsibility." In Carl J. Friedrich, and Edward S. Mason (Eds.). *Public Policy. A Yearbook of the Graduate School of Public Administration*, 3–24. Cambridge, MA: Harvard University Press.

Grossman, Sanford J. and Oliver D. Hart. 1983. "An Analysis of the Principal-Agent Problem." *Econometrica*, 51: 7–45.

Hayes, Jan. 2009. "Incident Reporting: A Nuclear Industry Case Study." In Andrew Hopkins (ed.). *Learning from High Reliability Organisations*, 117–134. Canberra: CCH Australia.

Hedström, Peter and Richard Swedberg. 1998. "Social Mechanisms: An Introductory Essay." In Peter Hedström and Richard Swedberg (eds.). *Social Mechanisms. An Analytical Approach to Social Theory*, 1–31. Cambridge UK: Cambridge Univ. Press.

Hedström, Peter and Petri Ylikoski. 2010. "Causal Mechanisms in the Social Sciences." *Annual Review of Sociology*, 36: 49–67.

Hood, Christopher. 2011. *The Blame Game. Spin Bureaucracy and Self-preservation in Government*. Princeton, NJ: Princeton University Press.

Hopkins, Andrew. 2007. *Lessons from Gretley. Mindful Leadership and the Law*. Canberra: CCH Australia.

Hopkins, Andrew (ed.). 2009. *Learning from High Reliability Organisations*. Canberra: CCH Australia.

't Hart, Paul and Lars Tummers. 2019. *Understanding Public Leadership.* 2nd ed., London: Red Globe Press.

Janis, Irving L. 1972. *Victims of Groupthink: A Psychological Study of Foreign-Policy Decisions and Fiascoes.* Boston: Houghton Mifflin Company.

Kettl, Donald F. 2006. "Public Bureaucracies." In R.A.W. Rhodes, Sarah A. Binder, Bert A. Rockman (eds.). *The Oxford Handbook of Political Institutions,* 366–384. Oxford, UK: Oxford University Press.

Kingdon, John W. 1984. *Agendas, Alternatives, and Public Policies.* Boston: Little, Brown & Co.

LaPorte, Todd R. and Paula M. Consolini. 1991. "Working in Practice but not in Theory: Theoretical Challenges of 'High-Reliability Organizations'." *Journal of Public Administration Research and Theory,* 1: 19–48.

LaPorte, Todd R. 1996. "High Reliability Organizations: Unlikely, Demanding and at Risk." *Journal of Contingencies and Crisis Management,* 4: 60–71.

Lindblom, Charles E. 1959. "The Science of 'Muddling Through'." *Public Administration Review,* 19: 79–88.

Lipsky, Michael. 1980. *Street-level Bureaucracy: Dilemmas of the Individual in Public Services.* New York, NY: Russell Sage Foundation.

March, James G. and Johan P. Olsen. 1975. "The Uncertainty of the Past: Organizational Learning under Ambiguity." *European Journal of Political Research,* 3: 147–171.

Mintzberg, Henry. 1983. *Power in and Around Organizations.* Englewood Cliffs, NJ: Prentice-Hall.

Olsen, Johan P. 2008. "The Ups and Downs of Bureaucratic Organization." *Annual Review of Political Science,* 11: 13–37.

Parsons, Talcott. 1951. *The Social System.* New York: The Free Press.

Perrow, Charles. 1984. *Normal Accidents: Living with High-Risk Technologies.* New York: Basic Books.

Perrow, Charles. 1986. *Complex Organizations: A Critical Essay.* 3rd ed., New York, NY: McGraw-Hill.

Peters, B. Guy. 2014. "Accountability in Public Administration." In Mark Bovens, Robert E. Goodin and Thomas Schillemanns (eds.). *The Oxford Handbook of Accountability,* 211–225. Oxford: Oxford University Press.

Puranam, Phanish. 2018. *The Microstructure of Organizations.* Oxford: Oxford University Press.

Roe, Emery and Paul R. Schulman. 2008. *High Reliability Management: Operating on the Edge.* Stanford, CA: Stanford Business Books.

Roe, Emery and Paul R. Schulman. 2016. *Reliability and Risk: The Challenge of Managing Interconnected Infrastructures.* Stanford: Stanford University Press.

Sagan, Scott D. 1993. *The Limits of Safety: Organizations, Accidents, and Nuclear Weapons.* Princeton, NJ: Princeton University Press.

Schulman, Paul R. 1993. "The Negotiated Order of Organizational Reliability." *Administration & Society,* 25: 353–372.

Seibel, Wolfgang. 2019. "Professional Integrity and Leadership in Public Administration." In Tobias Bach and Kai Wegrich (eds.). *The Blind Spots of Public Bureaucracy and the Politics of Non-Coordination, Executive Politics and Governance,* 71–86. Basingstoke: Palgrave Macmillan.

Seibel, Wolfgang and Timo Wenzel. 2017. "Die Loveparade-Katastrophe vom 24. Juli 2010." In Wolfgang Seibel, Kevin Klaman, Hannah Treis (with Timo Wenzel), *Verwaltungsdesaster. Von der Loveparade bis zu den NSU-Ermittlungen,* 23–112. Frankfurt/New York: Campus.

Selznick, Philip. 1957. *Leadership in Administration. A Sociological Interpretation*. New York, Evanston and London: Harper & Row.

Shrivastava, Samir, Karan Sonpar, and Federica Pazzaglia. 2009. "Normal Accident Theory versus High Reliability Theory: A Resolution and Call for an Open Systems View of Accidents." *Human Relations*, 62: 1357–1390.

Stivers, Camilla. 1994. "The Listening Bureaucrat: Responsiveness in Public Administration." *Public Administration Review*, 54: 364–369.

Thompson, James D. 1967. *Organizations in Action. Social Science Bases of Administrative Theory*. New York: McGraw-Hill.

Wallach, Michael A., Nathan Kogan, and Daryl J. Bem. 1963. "Diffusion of Responsibility and Level of Risk Taking in Groups." *Journal of Abnormal and Social Psychology*, 68: 263–274.

Weick, Karl E. and Kathleen M. Sutcliffe. 2007. *Managing the Unexpected: Resilient Performance in and Age of Uncertainty*. 2nd ed. San Francisco, CA: Jossey-Bass.

Williamson, Oliver E. 1985. *The Economic Institutions of Capitalism*. New York: Free Press.

Cited documents

[1] Letter Thomas Mahlberg MdB, February 9, 2009, *Brief an den Innenminister Dr. Ingo Wolf von Thomas Mahlberg MdB, Internet:* www.cduduisburg.de/index.jsp?index =presseandmid=20andcontent=jaandid=147, [downloaded: March 11, 2015].

[2] Minutes, meeting of September 25, 2010, *Niederschrift über ein Gespräch zum Thema Loveparade 2010 in Duisburg*, Internet: http://file.wikileaks.org/file/loveparade2010/ loveparade-2010-anlage-03-protokoll-25-09-09.pdf, [last access: June 27, 2020].

[3] Minutes, meeting of October 2, 2009, *Ergebnisniederschrift zur Besprechung Loveparade 2010,* Internet: http://file.wikileaks.org/file/loveparade2010/loveparade-2010 -anlage-04-protokoll-02-10-09.pdf [last access: June 27, 2020].

[4] Presentation Lopavent, October 29, 2009, *Loveparade 2010 in Duisburg— Präsentation Lopavent, Internet:* https://www.duisburg.de/ratsinformationssystem/bi/getfile.php?id =1458557andtype=do [downloaded: March 11, 2015].

[5] Minutes, meeting of March 2, 2010, *Niederschrift über ein verwaltungsinternes Gespräch*, Internet: http://file.wikileaks.org/file/loveparade2010/loveparade-2010-anlage-20 -protokoll-02-03-10.pdf [last access: June 27, 2020].

[6] Letter Bauordnungsamt, City of Duisburg, to Lopavent, June 14, 2010, *Eingangsbestätigung— Nachforderung fehlender Unterlagen von der Unteren Baubehörde*, Internet: http://file.wikileaks.org/file/loveparade2010/loveparade-2010-anlage-24 -nachforderung-fehlende-unterlagen-14-06-10.pdf [last access: June 27, 2020].

[7] Minutes, meeting of June 18, 2010, *Protokoll eines Gesprächs bei Lopavent*, Internet: http://file.wikileaks.org/file/loveparade2010/loveparade-2010-anlage-25 -aktenvermerk-und-ablehnung-dressler-18-06-10.pdf, [last access: June 27, 2020].

[8] Note for the files, meeting of June 25, 2010, *Aktenvermerk über ein Gespräch bei Lopavent des Bauamtes*, Internet: http://file.wikileaks.org/file/loveparade2010/loveparade -2010-anlage-26-aktenvermerk-abnahme-sv-25-06-10.pdf [last access: June 27, 2020].

[9] Note for the files, July 12, 2010, Aktenvermerk, *Bewertung des Zu- und Abwegekonzepts durch Prof. Schreckenberg*, Internet: https://www.duisburg.de/ratsinformationssystem/ bi/getfile.php?id=1458579andtype=doXIV [last access: June 27, 2020].

[10] Expert report, July 13, 2010, *Entfluchtungsanalyse zur Loveparade 2010 der Firma TraffGo HT GmbH*, Internet: https://www.duisburg.de/ratsinformationssystem/bi/getfile.php?id=1458601andtype=do [last access: June 27, 2020].

[11] Expert report, July 16, 2010, *Stellungnahme zur Entfluchtungsanalyse durch Prof. Schreckenberg*, Internet: https://www.duisburg.de/ratsinformationssystem/bi/getfile.php?id=1458602andty pe=do [last access: June 27, 2020].

[12] Permission, dated July 21, 2010, issued July 23, 2010, *Loveparade 2010 Anlage 34 Genehmigung der Bauaufsicht mit Abweichungsgenehmigungen*, Internet: https://file.wikileaks.org/file/loveparade2010/loveparade-2010-anlage-34-genehmigung-bauaufsicht-21-07-10.pdf [last access: August 27, 2015].

9

IS RELIGION DEAD?

Mark Juergensmeyer

Despite the dark predictions of religion's future by such scholars as Karl Marx, Sigmund Freud, and Friedrich Nietzsche, religion at the beginning of the twenty-first century seems strangely alive. I say "strangely" since the forms of religiosity that come to public notice are indeed strange. The right-wing Christian militia in the US and the terrorism of the Islamic State are only two examples of the extreme forms of religious nationalism and violent sects that have vaulted into public attention.

There is more to religion's revival than that, of course. In areas of Latin America where evangelical Protestantism is flourishing and in the vast swaths of Africa where Islam is on the rise, the devout are neither weird nor vicious, and their religion seems to be an amicable part of their personal and social lives.

Elsewhere, especially in the urban centers of Europe, Asia, and the Americas, religion is clearly on the decline. The once proud cathedrals of spirituality with their marvelous stained glass windows and ornate stone filigree are increasingly monuments to a religious past, relics of another age. What few faithful still attend can be seen as emitting the last gasps of religiosity before the phenomenon succumbs to the inevitability of secular globalization.

Which is it, has religion revived or is it in its death throes?

Dead or alive?

One way of answering the question of whether religion is reviving or dying is to look at the statistics. The statistical picture, however, is not consistent. Adherence to religion seems to be on the rise in some parts of the world (Islam in Africa, for instance), though on the decline in others (Christianity in Europe and increasingly in the US) and under attack in China.

Of the 7.3 billion people in the world the largest percentage, roughly 33%, are Christian. From 2010 to 2015 that percentage stayed the same even though the numbers of Christians rose slightly, especially in Africa and South America, while they declined elsewhere; on balance they kept pace with the general rise of the population worldwide.

The number of Muslims is exploding. Islam is currently the second largest religion in the world, with some 24% of the world's population. That percentage has continued to rise as the absolute number of Muslims expands both through large families (Muslims have the highest birth rate of any religious group in the world) and through conversion, especially in sub-Saharan Africa. Pew research reports indicate that by 2035 the number of children born to Muslims will outpace those born to Christians, and Islam is by far the fastest growing religious community in the world (Pew Research Center 2017).

Though in general Christianity continues to have the same 33% of the population it has had for some years, that percentage is not distributed equally. It has risen in Africa and South America. But Europe is one area of the world where Christianity is in decline. From 2010 to 2015, the number of Christians in Europe dropped by 5.6 million people (Hackett and McClendon 2017). One reason is that the number of deaths of older Christians outpaced the births of Christian parents; another reason is due to the changing demographics in Europe with the rise of new immigrant groups, especially from Muslim countries.

In the US, the erosion of Christian affiliation continues at what the Pew Research Center describes as "a rapid pace" (Pew Research Center 2019). According to the Pew study, in 2019 only 65% of Americans described themselves as Christian, down 12 percentage points in scarcely ten years. Part of this decline is due to the negative birthrate of American Christians compared to their death rates; part is due to the rise of new immigrants with non-Christian faiths; and part is because of the abandonment of any religious affiliation by the rising number of young people who declare their religious faith as "none."

Though European and American Christianity is declining in numbers, it is not doing so evenly across all the Christian denominational affiliations. Internally within Europe and the US, there are dramatic shifts. At one time the mainstream Protestant denominations (such as Methodist, Baptist, Lutheran, Episcopalian, Presbyterian, Congregational, and the like) rivaled the Roman Catholic church in numbers, especially in the US. But from 1972 to 2017, the number of mainstream Protestants in the US dropped precipitously from 28% to almost 10% (Stetzer 2017). The average age of the surviving mainstream Protestant members is 52, indicating that the denominations are quite literally dying out. The decline of mainstream Protestants has been in part due to the strength of Evangelical Protestantism, earlier reported as 26% of the population, but that number has also dropped significantly, especially in the second decade of the twenty-first century (Pew Research Center 2015; Blake 2021).

The decline of a liberal Protestant

What happened to the mainstream liberal Protestants? In the discipline of anthropology, scholars sometimes focus on one example of a general trend and use the life story of that case study to illumine larger aspects of social change. In this spirit, I have searched for a good example of the decline of liberal Protestantism in the global era and sought one person whose story might shed light on the larger transformation of the faith. After some effort, I have finally found a perfect case: me.

So bear with me for a moment while I tell you my story. I am doing so not to impress you with my own religiosity. Quite the opposite, since it is a story of the fall from religion, at least a certain kind of religion. And from my observation of fellow former liberal mainstream Protestants, I think my own pattern is not uncommon.

I am a child of the "silent generation," growing up as a mainstream Methodist in the Eisenhower years. In the small farming community of southern Illinois (US) where I was raised, everyone went to church on Sunday morning, it seemed. My family was very pious and fiercely loyal to our congregation, where the message was a mix of mild social concerns and inspirational homilies. I was equally active in the Boy Scouts and the Methodist Youth Fellowship, and they seemed to me to be quite similar. Both urged us youths to do good and help others.

I served as a boy preacher when I was in high school, pastoring two small rural congregations. When I went to the University of Illinois I majored in philosophy, thinking it a good preparation for seminary. To the dismay of the local Methodist clergy in central Illinois, the seminary I chose was Union Theological Seminary in New York City, touted as the most liberal of liberal theological institutions, and the academic home of America's best known theologian of the era, the staunch progressive Reinhold Niebuhr.

It was in fact Niebuhr with whom I wanted to study. In college increasingly my attention had turned to the aspects of religion that were related to ethics, especially social and political ethics. Niebuhr was the leading figure in this field. Featured on the cover of *Time* magazine as the "prophet to politicians," he was known to have had a major influence on the thinking of President Franklin Delano Roosevelt's New Deal administration.

Niebuhr was a theologian, but as he himself described it, a religious thinker "with one hand on the Bible and the other on the *New York Times*." Taking theologian Karl Barth's insistence on the original sinfulness of all humanity, Niebuhr tried to explain how social ethics was possible given the inherent greediness of humans, an exploitative attitude especially evident when they joined in collectivities such as business corporations. In Niebuhr's view corporations were definitely not "persons, my friend," as Mitt Romney once said, since they lacked the capacity for *agape,* sacrificial love. They were incapable of forgiveness or mercy or even fundamental justice, since they were extensions of people's acquisitive nature.

He suggested that two things could provide "countervailing power" over the dominance of corporations. One was government regulations—which gave philosophical legitimacy to the expanded role of government during FDR's administration. The other was the countervailing power of collective action—among workers this meant the legitimation of labor unions, which during Niebuhr's day were becoming a major force in American economic and political life. Niebuhr also suggested as early as 1932 that collective protest could be an effective means of bringing racial justice in the US (Niebuhr 1932). It was this reading of Niebuhr that made a striking impact on another young seminarian, Martin Luther King, Jr., who wrote about Niebuhr and corresponded with him.

Niebuhr was a lifelong socialist. He once supported communism as many left-wing thinkers in the US did, but like them he became disillusioned with Stalin and became fiercely anticommunist, at least regarding the Soviet variation of the ideology. He remained supportive of socialist causes, however, and helped to found the Liberal Party in New York as the progressive alternative to mainstream Democrats.

I studied with Niebuhr all three years that I was at Union Seminary and wrote two long papers for him. One was on the way automation was changing the nature of work, creating even greater alienation than before. The other paper was on "Sin in the Civil Rights Movement," based on my own observation of being involved in movements for racial justice at the time, and seeing how some leaders could use the platforms for personal power and petty infighting. Niebuhr liked both papers, and I still prize his comments, "you have surveyed the whole field," and "perceptive analysis." My autographed copy of his magnum opus, *The Nature and Destiny of Man* (Niebuhr 1939), where he scrawled, "with great respects," is among my cherished possessions.

With Niebuhr's blessing I became deeply involved in the civil rights struggle of the day, working for the Mississippi Freedom Democratic Party in 1964 and helping to organize a Seminarians Movement for Civil Rights. I also helped to produce a radio program on social ethics for WOR radio station in New York City exploring a range of contemporary issues. Increasingly we progressive Christians were becoming concerned about the expanding war in Vietnam.

The summer after I graduated from seminary I became ordained in the United Methodist Church, an event that thrilled my mother, though it was unclear what that would mean for my future. At the time my main concern was on how to avoid being drafted into the Vietnam War. I took the opportunity of accepting a two-year study and service project abroad, sponsored by the Presbyterian Church, as a way of applying my newly minted ministerial deferment.

I had never been outside the US at that point in my life, and when the program suggested that there was a slot available in India, teaching political ethics at Punjab University, it seemed an interesting opportunity. Because India and Pakistan were at war at the time, and the place to which I was assigned, the Punjab, was at the heart of the fighting, I delayed my arrival in India for three months. Initially I was based in Hong Kong, teaching English, but I took the opportunity of going to nearby Vietnam to see firsthand what the war was about. In Saigon I produced a series of radio programs for my old New York City station, WOR, on the Buddhist and student rejection of both sides in the war and their own movements for peace.

When I finally arrived in India it was a revelation to be immersed in another culture, one so different in some ways and yet so humanly similar in others. I loved the vibrant religiosity of Hindu temples, Sikh gurdwaras and Muslim mosques. My Midwestern American morality and spirituality seemed to adapt easily to these new milieu. I also found a form of progressive Hinduism with which I could identify. I joined a Gandhian ashram in the state of Bihar and became involved in famine relief. It was a form of social service for me, but also a direct education on the social ethics of Gandhi and his understanding of Hinduism.

After India I still needed to find a way to keep from being drafted into the military, so I sought a new student deferral as a graduate student in political science. I chose Berkeley as a place where I could study political ethics, religion, and South Asia studies in the same place, and from which I could launch my academic career. It was also attractive because it was, well... Berkeley. And this was in the mid-1960s, shortly after the "summer of love."

It was also a center of political activism, and for a time my studies took second place to helping to organize protests against the Vietnam War. I continued to have connections with progressive activists in the campus ministry programs and at the adjacent Graduate Theological Union. But church attendance increasingly fell by the wayside. I married a fellow graduate student, one whose family was Chinese Buddhist, though she had little interest in religion of any kind. So for years church was not a factor in my life.

I cannot say that I ever turned away from church religion. It just did not seem very important to me. And besides, the kind of moral urgency and resolute spirituality of my progressive Protestant past could be expressed in a myriad forms of social activism and cultural appreciation. I had not changed; but increasingly the organization of religion seemed unimportant. Later in life I have started attending church again, perhaps out of nostalgia, perhaps out of appreciation for the insights that it provided me when I was young. But I can understand why many of my peers have fallen away from the church and not looked back.

Recently I returned to Union Seminary for the fiftieth reunion of my old class. I was a bit shocked at how old everyone else had become (though I noticed some looking strangely at me as well). But I was also surprised at how few of my fellow classmates had maintained connections with organized religion. Only a handful had become clergy, and many of them had left after a while to take up positions in social work or as organizers with service organizations. Like me, none appeared to be hostile to the church. It was just not a necessary part of our lives.

We were also somewhat uncomfortable to be called "Christians." We certainly were, in that we came from a Christian background, studied theology, and for a time were closely involved with the liturgical roles of ministry. But we bristled with a term that has been largely coopted by Evangelical Protestants. These strident right-wing Christian enthusiasts with their demands that one be "born again" and "saved" did not represent the sort of socially concerned religion of our pasts. We were not that kind of Christian.

Religion as alternative reality

The reluctance of my generation of progressive Protestants to be called "Christians" brings up a more basic issue—what the words associated with religion signify. Our hesitation in being labeled Christian, and perhaps also the disinterest that many of us have had in the organized church, was in part to make clear that we were not Christian in the same way that the Evangelicals were Christian. Our religion was something different.

Not all religion is the same. In the multicultural era of globalization, religion has often been used as a badge of identity politics. It is used by extremist Muslims to demarcate what they regard as the true definition of the faith, and with it a clear distinction between those who are legitimately Muslim and those who are not. It creates a religious in-group. Exactly the same phenomenon is at work among right-wing Evangelical Christians who want to assert the social and political primacy for their kind of people—an identity that is partly defined by race and ethnicity and partly by religious affiliation.

We old progressive Protestants, however, do not want to build walls; we want to tear them down. We feel quite comfortable in the multicultural societies of the globalized world. We see in the better features of other faiths—Islam, Judaism, Hinduism, Buddhism, and Sikhism, among others—a resonance with our own religiosity. It is easy for us to embrace the idea of the commonality of all people in a global civil society. This means that we are uncomfortable with being labelled with one religious identity, especially one that has been coopted by a xenophobic right-wing segment of society.

Are we still religious? That depends on what you mean.

Scholarly attempts to define religion are various, though an interesting new definition is provided by the late sociologist, Robert Bellah, in his magnum opus, *Religion in Human Evolution* (Bellah 2011). It is a huge book, as impressive in its scope as it is rich in detail and insight. In it he takes the long view, beginning 13.8 billion years ago with the Big Bang and the creation of stars and planets, including our own, and then the emergence of living cells in the primal ooze and the beginning of animate life forms. He ends the book at the Axial Age, the rise of new modes of conceptual activity in the sixth century BCE, a period when intellectualism was sprouting around the world, from Greek thought to philosophical developments at the end of India's Vedic period.

It is in this grand historical narrative that he addresses the idea of what religion is, and relates it to the development of living species, an idea that I explore in a recent book (Juergensmeyer 2020). Early life forms, Bellah suggests, are focused on material things, survival and procreation. But later in the evolutionary process more evolved life forms have the leisure of spare time. Freed from the necessities of existence they can do whatever they want. And what they often do is unstructured and arbitrarily structured activity, doing things for no apparent purpose. They are like school children finally released from their boring classrooms for a few precious moments for recess. What they do during recess time is to run around and have fun and explore the world. It is something that we call "play."

Following the lead of the Dutch historian, Johan Huizinga, Bellah affirms that play is the beginning of all forms of culture, including religion (Huizinga 1944). It is the ability for humans to be creative, to roam and discover. Initially it is primarily an activity. This is true of religion as well. The early forms of religiosity—such as the rituals described in Leviticus and the rites detailed in the Vedas of ancient India—are focused on activity, on what priests do to interact with God or the gods. It is only later, in the Axial Age of the sixth century BCE that religion becomes more introspective and cerebral, and this is when we can describe religion as a product not just of creative activity but of creative thought: the religious imagination.

Though it is currently popular in the scholarly community to question whether religion is a thing, something that has agency on its own, Bellah demurs somewhat. In his understanding religion is something, or rather some perception. It is an imagined world of being, "a general order of existence," as the anthropologist Clifford Geertz (1966) describes it. Bellah goes further in labelling it "religious reality," one of various multiple realities that "calls the world of daily life into question" (Bellah 2011, 5). Here Bellah is relying on a whole school of sociology associated with the Austrian philosopher, Alfred Schütz, regarding the notion that reality is socially constructed (Schütz 1967), and before him the American philosopher, William James, who thought about cultural forms as constructions of the social imagination (James 1902). According to this point of view, made popular by the book, *The Social Construction of Reality* by Peter Berger and Thomas Luckmann (1966), what we perceive as everyday reality is a social construction of what things are and what they mean. A wooden table, to most humans, is a place to put books and plates of food, but to a termite it is an edible feast. It all depends on your point of view. What Bellah adds to this conversation—aided by the thinking of the pioneering French sociologist, Émile Durkheim—is the insistence that religious perceptions are one of these constructions of reality (Durkheim 1912). The table might be, for instance, an altar in a religious reality. These religious realities are among the various multiple realities that most people navigate among every day. These multiple realities are often overlapping views, and sometimes contesting ones, but they can present levels of meaning and reality that are quite different from one another even though they relate to the same thing, just as we and termites see tables differently though the table remains the same.

Thinking about this—thinking about religion as alternative reality—provides a way of accepting religiosity as a part of human creativity that may come in myriad forms and adopt many names. With that definition one can posit that religiosity is a fundamental part of the creative imagination, a constituent of culture as certain as art or music. The question then becomes not whether religion will survive, but in what way will it survive?

The religion of the "nones"

This question brings us back to the dilemma that we old liberal Protestants have when confronted with a request to describe our religion. We hesitate being called Christian, in the way that Evangelical Protestants have possessed that term. But we are certainly not atheists, or even agnostics. We are like the "nones."

Though a couple generations older, we are similar to the young Millennials of today who register their religious preference as "none." They do not regard themselves as atheists or agnostics, but they do not see any need for religious organizations or affiliations. They describe themselves as "spiritual, not religious."

In the Pew Research Center's 2019 survey that indicated that affiliation to Christianity in the US had dropped 12 percentage points to 65% of the population over the previous ten years, it indicated that the percentage of those describing their religion as "none" or "nothing in particular" rose from 12% to 16%. The numbers are even more dramatic when one factors in age. Among the Millennials born between 1981 and 1996, only 49% regard themselves as Christian, 9% adherents of other faiths, and 40% unaffiliated, and so so-called "nones" (Pew Research Center 2019). Among those in this generation, the "nones" are America's largest single religious category—more than Catholics, Mainstream Protestants, Evangelical Protestants or Jews. And their numbers are growing, not just in the US but in Europe and elsewhere in the world.

In this regard we may be witnessing the emergence of a new form of global spirituality and moral community that resonates with the alternative reality of traditional religious experience, but which has no name and no organization. This no-name religion is increasingly, however, a major form of religiosity, especially in multicultural societies.

In a five-year Luce Foundation-supported project on the role of religion in global civil society that I directed, one of our tasks was to look at where religion was going, how it was becoming transformed in global society. We saw both tendencies that I have described in this chapter. On the one hand adherents of religion have become more defensive and stridently protective about their identities. On the other hand there are the multiculturally religious, including old liberal Protestants like myself and the young new "nones" who affirm spirituality but do not give it a name or suggest that it needs a formal organization.

It is this latter form of spirituality that intrigued us. Would it be possible if two new developments on the planet, global civil society and global religion, could be linked? The latter could be the cultural expression of the former.

To probe this idea we turned again to Robert Bellah, who had been a colleague of mine in the religious studies program at Berkeley years earlier and was intrigued by our project. Bellah had just finished *Religion in Human Evolution* and was thinking about how religion had continued to change since the period at the end of that book, the Axial Age in sixth century BCE. In particular, Bellah was interested in the way that religion has become linked with individualism in the years since the European Enlightenment. But he was also interested in how religion might be transformed in the global age, in the context of a global community.

We invited Bellah to Santa Barbara to discuss the possibilities of a global civil religion. Typical of Bellah, he had prepared a paper that laid out his ideas. Though never published, I have summarized much of the paper in a chapter of my co-authored book that reports on the Luce project, *God in the Tumult of the Global Square* (Juergensmeyer, Griego, and Soboslai, 2015). The full paper is online in our project's digital archive (Bellah 2012). What we wanted to know was whether the idea of "civil religion" that Bellah advanced in a widely-discussed essay in 1967 could characterize not only national civil societies but also global civil society (Bellah 1967).

To respond to this, Bellah first explained how global civil society was possible. In Bellah's paper he traced the development of the idea of civil society from its inception in eighteenth-century Europe, when it was a part of the complex of ideas related to Enlightenment thinkers such as Jean-Jacques Rousseau and John Locke. "Civil society" in the Enlightenment context described what Bellah calls "the public sphere, a realm of thought, argument, and association independent of the state, but leading to the formation of what came to be called public opinion."

It is this notion of citizenship that is explored more recently by Jürgen Habermas in *The Structural Transformation of the Public Sphere* (Habermas 1989). The concepts of freedom of speech and freedom of religious expression are essential to the sense of citizenship in the public sphere, and they were enshrined in all of the leading Enlightenment documents, including those of the American Declaration of Independence and its Constitution. The idea of universal human rights also became a part of the shared values of the civil society of the public sphere.

The Enlightenment thinkers had particular national communities in mind when they discussed this notion of civil society, but it can be more generally applied. Civil society is not necessarily the province only of national societies. Increasingly in recent years the notion of civil society has gone global, and the phrase, *global civil society*, has gained acceptance by scholars and social activists around the world. One of the reasons for this is the presumed universality of human rights. Another has been the pervasive growth of international nongovernmental organizations (NGOs), especially in the post-Cold War global era. Yet another has been the rise of transnational social movements around such issues as economic equality, women's rights, equality of sexual orientation and environmental protection. At the same time the advent of instantaneous mass communication through cell phones and the Internet has brought individuals together in an unparalleled way on a global plane. In the twenty-first century, there is a global economy, global legal norms, global communications, and global festivals such as the Olympics and the World Cup. During the global COVID-19 pandemic people around the world were learning to connect together digitally through zoom and other online platforms.

All of these developments have led towards networks of interaction not just among national elites but also among ordinary citizens—a global civil society. Increasingly nation-state borders do not restrict whom or what we may contact, nor do they define our sense of community (as Lisa Anderson also highlights in Chapter 7 of this volume). At the same time, economic interaction on a global scale is creating another kind of global community, one that is very much focused on the transnational elites that control and profit from these flows of capital. This elite form of global economic activity is not conducive to global civil society, from Bellah's point of view. The question is whether the decentralized form of global citizenry can grow despite the attempts of a global elite to control it.

This is where Habermas' speculation about transnational governance comes into play. The emergence of a global civil society is a challenge to nationalist power and to global elite power and requires its own forms of power creation in response. Mass movements and international NGOs provide one kind of counterweight. Global public opinion as voiced over the Internet is by far the most democratic of new communications media. And other challenges to national and elite power come from newly developed transnational agencies in dealing with problems of the environment, global communications, and the worldwide diasporas of peoples and cultures. Some of these agencies are supported by the United Nations, others have been formed on their own with support from interstate or transnational social movements. Habermas is buoyed by these developments and about regional entities such as the European Union, which he regards as the first step to moving beyond narrow nationalism.

Bellah, however, is less sanguine about the efficacy of these developments in creating a sense of global citizenship on their own and returns to the idea of building a moral consensus that can provide the basis for transnational institutions of accountability. Though he appreciates Habermas' attempts to think about a sense of citizenship beyond narrow nationalism, Bellah thinks that Habermas' notion of an "abstract constitutional patriotism" is an insufficient base for creating a global civil society (Habermas 1996, 566). For that you need moral commitment. And this is where religion comes in.

Bellah admits that the passions of religious commitment do not always run towards a spirit of open tolerance and interfaith harmony. Quite the opposite is often the case. As the rise of strident nationalist religious movements around the world has demonstrated, religious fervor, as Bellah puts it, has "often been used for evil as well as good purposes." Still, Bellah believes that the potency of religious passions can be harnessed for good—by which he means a more inclusive sense of religiosity.

Moreover, global society needs this kind of religious zeal. "Only such powerful motivation could make human rights genuinely practical" on a global scale,

Bellah insists. And he goes on to point out that every religious tradition contains within it the reverence for life and the appreciation for human dignity that is at the basis of universal human rights—not only Christianity, but also Islam, Judaism, Hinduism, Buddhism and Chinese religion. The *Analects* of Confucius, Bellah reminds us, states that "all within the four seas are brothers." Buddhism regards all human life (and for that matter all animate life) as having within it the Buddha nature. Thus religious traditions are sources for a worldwide appreciation of the universality of the principles underlying human rights. So are the instincts of a new generation of global citizens whose sense of spirituality and morality know no traditionally national or culturally limited bounds.

Hence the sensibilities of the old liberal Protestants like myself and the young Millennial nones coalesce. We share a common sense of the underlying values of morality and spirituality in all religious traditions and in the vitality of a global human society that is not signified by any one religious community or name. We admire the multicultural acceptance of a global heart to humanity that makes global civil society possible. Liberal Protestants have not disappeared; we have been transformed into the citizens of a global era and the bearers of its global morality and spiritual sensibility.

We are not alone. Ours is essentially Gandhi's religion. His understanding of Hinduism was informed by Islam, Christianity and many other faiths; it was a religiosity for all people. Some of the world's leading religious spokespersons, including Gandhi, Bishop Tutu, Pope Francis, the Dalai Lama, Mother Teresa, and the Aga Khan IV, speak not just to their own religious communities but touch the spiritual pulse of the wider world. They are the saints of the global age.

In thinking about this emerging global religious community, I am reminded of the many good-hearted religious activists I have known over the years. These are people who are tirelessly working for the good of all humanity. Though inspired by their own religious backgrounds, they welcome people of all faiths and no faiths to join in their efforts at creating more just and inclusive societies. I think of Sulak Sivarksa, the Buddhist civil rights activist in Thailand, and another Buddhist leader, A.K. Ariyaratne, whose Sarvodaya movement for village uplift I visited in Sri Lanka. I think of the Gandhians I knew in India, especially my mentor, Jayaprakash Narayan, the leader of India's Sarvodaya movement and a tireless champion for social justice. I think of the women and men who have been part of the Jewish-Muslim peace movements in Israel and Palestine whom I have met, and who have worked together not just for cooperation between their religious communities but for a more just and inclusive society as a whole.

I also think of others, of Sister Maria Antonia Aranda in Mexico ministering to Central American migrants trapped at the US border, Dorothy Day who founded the Catholic Worker Movement and the Jewish-Christian philosopher and activist, Simone Weil. I think of Bishop Oscar Romero in San Salvador and Gustavo Gutiérrez in Peru and the many nuns and priests and other Catholic activists associated with liberation theology who merged the analysis of Karl Marx with the peaceful message of Jesus. And I think of Martin Luther King,

Jr. and my own teacher, Reinhold Niebuhr, whose Protestant Christianity was never an exclusive teaching, but a message of harmony for the world.

These are good people who have been speaking to the best of their religious traditions for decades. And at the same time they continue to speak to us all. They usually work side by side with those from other faiths and with the "nones" who confess no particular religious affiliation, but affirm a moral and spiritual connection with all of humanity. Their spirituality, their moral courage spans religious divides and responds to the best in everyone. Thus they are keeping religion alive, but not only for their own traditions. They may also be harbingers of the global religion of the future.

References

Bellah, Robert. 1967. "Civil Religion in America." *Daedalus*, 96(1): 1–21. Reprinted in Robert N. Bellah and Steven M. Tipton (eds.). *The Robert Bellah Reader*, 225–245. Durham, NC: Duke University Press, 2006.

Bellah, Robert. 2011. *Religion in Human Evolution: From the Paleolithic to the Axial Age*. Cambridge, MA: Belknap Press, of Harvard University Press.

Bellah, Robert. 2012. "Is Global Civil Society Possible?" Unpublished paper presented at the University of California, Santa Barbara on February 2, 2012. The paper is summarized in chap 4 of Mark The full text of the paper is available on line at: http://www.global.ucsb.edu/luceproject/papers/pdf/RobertBellah.pdf. For the video of his presentation of the paper please see: http://vimeo.com/40404248. (3 parts)

Berger, Peter and Thomas Luckmann. 1966. *The Social Construction of Reality*. New York: Penguin Random House.

Blake, Aaron. 2021, July 8. "The Rapid Decline of White Evangelical America?" *The Washington Post*. https://www.washingtonpost.com/politics/2021/07/08/rapid-decline-white-evangelical-america/

Durkheim, Émile. 1912. *Elementary Forms of Religious Life*, Translated by Karen E. Fields. New York: Free Press, 1995 [1912].

Geertz, Clifford. 1966. "Religion as a Cultural System." In Michael P. Banton (ed.). *Anthropological Approaches to the Study of Religion*, 1–46. London: Tavistock.

Habermas, Jürgen. 1989. *The Structural Transformation of the Public Sphere: An Inquiry into a Category of Bourgeois Society*. Cambridge, MA: MIT Press.

Habermas, Jürgen. 1996. *Between Facts and Norms: Contributions to a Discourse Theory of Law and Democracy*. Cambridge MA: MIT Press.

Hackett, Conrad and David McClendon. 2017. "Christians Remain World's Largest Religious Group, but They are Declining in Europe." FactTank, Pew Research Center. https://www.pewresearch.org/fact-tank/2017/04/05/christians-remain-worlds-largest-religious-group-but-they-are-declining-in-europe/

Huizinga, Johan. 1944. *Homo Ludens: A Study of the Play-Element in Culture*. London: Routledge, 1949; first published in German in Switzerland in 1944.

James, William. 1902. *The Varieties of Religious Experience*. New York: Penguin Classics, 1985 (first published in 1902).

Juergensmeyer, Mark, Dinah Griego, and John Soboslai. 2015. *God in the Tumult of the Global Square: Religion in Global Civil Society*. New York: Oxford University Press.

Juergensmeyer, Mark. 2020. *God at War: A Mediation on Religion and Warfare*. New York: Oxford University Press.

Niebuhr, Reinhold. 1932. *Moral Man and Immoral Society*. New York: Simon Schuster.

Niebuhr, Reinhold. 1939. *The Nature and Destiny of Man*. New York: Simon Schuster.

Pew Research Center. 2015. "America's Changing Religious Landscape." https://www
.pewforum.org/2015/05/12/americas-changing-religious-landscape/

Pew Research Center. 2017. "The Changing Global Religious Landscape." https://www
.pewforum.org/2017/04/05/the-changing-global-religious-landscape/

Pew Research Center. 2019. "In U.S., the Decline of Christianity Continues at a Rapid
Pace."   https://www.pewforum.org/2019/10/17/in-u-s-decline-of-christianity
-continues-at-rapid-pace/

Schütz, Alfred. 1967. *Phenomenology of the Social World*, Translated by George Walsh.
Evanston: Northwestern University Press.

Stetzer, ed. 2017, April 28. "If It Doesn't Stem Its Decline, Mainline Protestantism Has
Just 23 Easters Left," *Washington Post*. https://www.washingtonpost.com/news/acts
-of-faith/wp/2017/04/28/if-it-doesnt-stem-its-decline-mainline-protestantism-has
-just-23-easters-left/

10

HOW DO CULTURE AND LIBERTY RELATE?

Roland Bernecker and Ronald Grätz

Of chains and rocks

To connect the issues of "culture" and "liberty" is as topical as it may seem pretentious. The relevance of the questions that arise when the concepts are brought together is, however, immediately apparent. We are experiencing a crisis of liberty. And we are also witnessing a cultural crisis, which in essence is another form of the crisis of liberty. The transformation brought about by information technologies is so thorough that we are still struggling to fully capture its implications, while it increasingly goes about colonizing our minds. But which culture and which liberty are we talking about? The juxtaposition of culture and liberty leads to a critical height of abstraction. Both concepts are as demanding as they are vague, both emanate a provocative ambition.

Paradoxically, the deeper we rely on their meanings, the ever vaguer and more imprecise our terms become. But let us not underestimate the gravitational forces they exert, the incredible pull of their semantic fields. Indeed, the vagueness of the concepts of culture and liberty is nothing but the flipside of their relevance. They are of great use in our political debates due less to their (doubtless) rhetorical luster and far more because of the critical essence they provide to our self-descriptions. We draw on culture and liberty as fundamental criteria when assessing the quality of our lives and use them abundantly in the political programs we design to format our societal spaces.

"L'homme est né libre, et partout il est dans les fers"—"Man is born free and everywhere he is in chains." With this resounding sentence Jean-Jacques Rousseau begins his treatise on the *Contrat social*. Rousseau denounces a fundamental contradiction, a scandal of the highest order: liberty is the right of humans by birth, in a sense their constitutional state of being, but it is not merely sometimes withheld from them. It is systematically withheld. The absolute nature of the value of liberty corresponds to the absolute extent of its negation, and to make this clear Rousseau finds it appropriate to employ the image of *chains*.

One hundred and eighty years later, Albert Camus undertakes a re-evaluation of the problem of liberty in which the primal image of humanity's unfreedom is transformed into a more modern picture, resonating more with a contemporary feeling of life. For postmoderns, imprisoned in a permanent project mode, the hero is Sisyphus, condemned to obsessively and incessantly push a rock up a mountain—in vain, for that matter. Camus, posing the question of liberty in an existential dimension, reaches a surprising conclusion with his famous sentence: "Il faut imaginer Sisyphe heureux"—"We must imagine Sisyphus happy" (Camus 1979, 166).

The paradox has been reversed. Rousseau's political indignation is transformed into acceptance. For Rousseau, the free man is in chains. For Camus, we are forced to permanently push a rock, but in this obligation we find our freedom. Accepting the inevitable is an act of liberation. This acceptance, though, is possible only once another radical liberation has taken place: that from any kind of transcendent authorities. The acknowledgment that there are no divine or otherworldly instances (for Camus: "Cet univers désormais sans maître"—"The universe henceforth without a master") (Camus 1979, 166) that we can call upon in our unfreedom makes us the final authority. No power of cosmic proportions remains available to hear our woes or petitions. Liberty is the process of realizing this. It is a state of mind that we must willfully adopt, challenging our habitual beliefs and certainties. The struggle for the heights, Camus says, is enough to fill a man's heart.

In the sense of the Kantian *sapere aude*, one of the preconditions for liberty is the courage to bear whatever we come up against when we embrace that freedom. The emergence of the existential awareness described by Camus is a cultural process. Both the auctorial appearance of our universes and the paths to our liberation are cultural features. Culture has the dual function of providing a much-needed relief from the strains of freedom, while at the same time offering the tools that empower us to envisage liberty in the first place.

Two concepts of liberty

A highly influential and heuristically productive approach to the concept of liberty draws on a famous speech delivered by Isaiah Berlin. Berlin devoted his inaugural lecture at the University of Oxford on October 31, 1958, to thoughts on "Two Concepts of Liberty." This lecture was to have a remarkable impact in subsequent debates. Quentin Skinner (2012, 113) called Berlin's essay "the single most important discussion of these issues published in our time." Berlin calls for a cautious handling of ideal concepts such as liberty. All too often, he emphasizes, the impact of concepts is underestimated. In his eyes, ideas are "dangerous" matters, as "[w]hen ideas are neglected by those who ought to attend to them—that is to say, those who have been trained to think critically about ideas—they sometimes acquire an unchecked momentum and irresistible power over multitudes of men that may grow too violent to be affected by rational criticism" (Berlin 2002, 167). It was the real experience of totalitarian ideologies and of the excesses of human history that led Berlin (2002, 168) to address that "central question of politics—the question of obedience and freedom."

Berlin builds his entire argument on the distinction between negative and positive liberty. Negative liberty is the freedom from constraints. It is a liberty to act in the absence of obstacles imposed from the outside (for example Rousseau's chains). The principle of negative liberty denies any restriction of individual freedom, as long as this does not lead to harm to others. This concerns freedom of speech and of movement, and in particular the freedom of artistic expression. Negative liberty means that individuals are not hindered in actions they decide for themselves. It does not necessarily mean, however, that it is then possible to act according to one's wishes. Under the terms of this narrow and principled understanding of negative liberty, a lack of resources, for example, does not constitute an external restriction. Not being hindered to act is one matter; to have the resources needed to act is another. Negative liberty thus answers the question as to the extent of the private sphere (of individuals or collectives) into which no one may intervene.

The positive understanding of liberty describes the freedom to do something. What are the aims that I am able to and wish to set for myself, and which means do I wish to employ? The question here is not whether I am being hindered in doing something, but whether I myself can decide on the kind of life I wish to lead. The "positive" meaning of the concept of liberty derives from the desire not to be dependent on external forces. This dimension of freedom is the one that Camus's Sisyphus arrives at when he accepts a situation by deciding to make it his own.

This binary distinction between negative and positive liberty is a reductionist heuristic concept. It allows a clearer grasp of a fundamental and politically relevant problem. But the two perspectives are not simply complementary. Berlin (2002, 179) emphasizes that the negative and the positive understanding of liberty "historically developed in divergent directions [...] until, in the end, they came into direct conflict with one another." The positive concept of liberty can provide the justification for restrictions in negative liberty. The allegedly higher liberty of political aims can be turned against the scope of our individual spaces. For Berlin, this is a key feature of the catastrophic history of the twentieth century.

From republicanism to liberalism

Not quite a hundred and fifty years before Isaiah Berlin's inaugural lecture, one of the founders of modern liberalism, Benjamin Constant, pointed at the same conflict (see Rosenblatt 2018). Interestingly, Constant—like Berlin—presented his ideas in a speech, delivered in 1819 at the Athénée Royale in Paris. Constant's view on liberty was shaped, again not unlike that of Berlin, by his direct testimony of epochal historic constellations, in his case embracing the French Revolution, Napoléon's rise and fall, and the ensuing European restoration.

For Constant (1819, 6), the understanding of liberty encountered in the ancient world was republican and collective: "Le but des anciens était le partage du pouvoir social entre tous les citoyens d'une même patrie: c'était là ce qu'ils nommaient liberté"—"The aim of the ancients was to share social power among the citizens of a single country: that's what they called 'liberty.'" In order to maintain this liberty, the "ancients" were willing to make considerable sacrifices in the sphere of individual freedom. This collective understanding of liberty was thus compatible with "the complete subjection of the individual to the authority of the group. [...] Each one of them, feeling with pride the great value of his vote, regarded this sense of personal importance as more than making up for his sacrifices" (Constant 1819, 2).

In the "modern" times of 1819, Constant diagnosed that this form of direct political participation was no longer possible. It was no longer available as compensation for the tight social controls of the republican collective. In modern mass society, we have largely lost the sense of having our say in political life:

> Lost in the crowd, the individual can hardly ever see the influence that he exerts. His will never impresses itself on the whole; nothing confirms in his eyes his own cooperation. So the exercise of political rights offers us only a part of the benefit that the ancients found in it, while at the same time the progress of civilization, the steady increase of commerce, the communication amongst peoples, have infinitely multiplied and varied the means of personal happiness. [...] The aim of the moderns is to be secure in their private benefits; and "liberty" is their name for the guarantees accorded by institutions to these benefits.
>
> *(Constant 1819, 6)*

A main reason given by Constant for this shift in the perception of liberty was the increasing importance of trade. Whereas in the ancient world, the politically most relevant form of interaction between peoples was war, in modernity it had been replaced by trade. Constant viewed trade not only as a more peaceable, but also a more effective form of exchange and a key engine in the development of the modern individualist concept of liberty. Trade relies on the spirit of the entrepreneur and gives new relevance to the dimension of property. It is this transformed sense of property which profoundly affects the concept of liberty. For Constant, the weakening of the citizen's voice in political affairs was fully compensated by the perspective of the potential personal wealth to be gained in trade. Another important upside of trade was the emergence of a peaceful cosmopolitanism. Constant was dreaming the liberal dream of "good" globalization in which relations governed by trade and the pursuit of wealth would be more honest than those governed by power:

> Power threatens and wealth rewards; you elude power by deceiving it, but to obtain the favours of wealth you have to serve it; so wealth is bound to win.
>
> A chain of causes like that leads to the result that individual existence is less locked into political existence. Individuals carry their treasures far away; they take with them all the benefits of private life. Commerce has brought nations closer together, giving them *moeurs* and habits that are almost identical; the heads of states may be enemies, but the peoples are compatriots.
>
> *(Constant 1819, 12)*

Today, in our twenty-first century, Constant's view of a superior ethics of peaceful global trade and its clear-cut distinction from the lower, war-ridden political sphere would most likely be held by only very few people, whereas his vision of a peaceful cosmopolitan spirit embracing all of humanity is still an inspiration for many.

In the light of the increasing complexity of modernizing societies with their fervent economies, Constant concludes that political participation can only be secured through representation. However, he combines this idea of the delegation of political responsibility with a serious warning. The modern individual, so fully engaged in the pursuit of their own business, must uphold their political awareness. What is at stake now is to prevent the political authorities from interfering too much in their private affairs. In this precise point, Constant's analysis coincides with the cautioning that energizes Berlin's concept of negative liberty:

> The danger for modern liberty is that we, absorbed in the enjoyment of our private independence and the pursuit of our particular interests, might surrender too easily our right to share in political power. The holders of authority encourage us to do just that. They are so ready to spare us every sort of trouble except the trouble of obeying and paying! They will say to us: "What, basically, is the aim of your efforts, the motive of your labors, the object of all your hopes? Isn't it happiness? Well, leave this happiness to us and we'll give it to you." No, we must not leave it to them. Their tender concern to make us happy is touching, perhaps, but we should ask the authorities to stay within their limits: let them confine themselves to being just, and we'll take care of happiness.
>
> *(Constant 1819, 12–13)*

Critique of positive and negative liberty

It is said of philosopher Jacob Taubes that he asked his students to "seek in every significant work for the sentence for which it was written" (Ritter, cited in Felsch 2015, 210; authors' translation). In Berlin's "Two Concepts of Liberty" this is the idea that negative and positive liberty are not two different degrees of one concept of liberty, but are "so different indeed [...] to have led in the end to the great clash of ideologies that dominates our world" (Berlin 2002, 178).

Negative liberty comprises only a portion of what we understand by liberty today. But this is the portion that is essential for our perception of liberty. The positive concept of liberty, by contrast, bears a wider and more ambitious ideal. Both concepts can clash when positive liberty, as it too easily does, shape-shifts into the ideological prescription of how to use that liberty:

> This renders it easy for me to conceive of myself as coercing others for their own sake, in their, not my, interest. I am then claiming that I know what they truly need better than they know it themselves. What, at most, this entails is that they would not resist me if they were rational and as wise as I and understood their interests as I do. But I may go on to claim a good deal more than this. I may declare that they are actually aiming at what in their benighted state they consciously resist, because there exists within them an occult entity—their latent rational will, or their "true" purpose—and that this entity, although it is belied by all that they ought to feel and do and say, is their "real" self, of which the poor empirical self in space and time may know nothing or little [...].
>
> *(Berlin 2002, 179–180)*

Berlin clearly is drawing on Constant here. Positive liberty tends to imply an asymmetrical epistemological situation, by force of which it can easily legitimate an asymmetrical constellation of power. In the perspective of positive liberty, acknowledged authorities and politically sanctioned institutions are most likely deemed able to determine the appropriate purposes of that liberty. They have a higher and generally accepted rationality in their favor. The concept of positive liberty grants them access to a more profound source of truth than is available to the limited individual. It might then no longer be of much concern how the individual relates their own perceptions to the auctorial truth of that positive liberty. "This monstrous impersonation, which consists in equating what X would choose if he were something he is not, or at least not yet, with what X actually seeks and chooses, is at the heart of all political theories of self-realization" (Berlin 2002, 180). It is this potentially totalitarian domination of human freedoms that Berlin sees as the implicit aim of rationalist political theory since its very beginnings in the ancient world: the idea that there can be only one correct way of living.

To fully capture Berlin's critical assessment, a look at the counterposition to this concept of liberty is of use. This opposing view is again gaining in appeal today. We do not here refer to the revisions and extensions of Berlin's concept, such as Skinner's (2012) "third concept of liberty," Axel Honneth's (2004) expanded concept of "communicative freedom," and Judith N. Shklar's (1989) catchy concept of a "liberalism of fear," all of which address Berlin's famous distinction.

More important here is an understanding of the stance taken by Charles Taylor (1985) in his philosophical anthropology of self-realization. For Taylor, the difference between our pretended level of conscious self-control and our mostly deficient level of self-actualization is a crucial philosophical problem. Taylor equates liberty with true, authentic self-realization. Liberty, in his view, is not that we just do whatever we happen to want to do. How can we be sure that what we want is what we "really" want? We can be free only if we want whatever corresponds to our "real will" and our "real self": "You are not free, if you are motivated, through fear, inauthentically internalized standards, or false consciousness, to thwart your self-realization" (Taylor 1985, 215–216). In his concept of liberty, it is not sufficient to want something and to be able to do it: "It must also be that what you want does not run against the grain of your basic purposes or your self-realization" (Taylor 1985, 216).

One might call this concept of liberty therapeutic. It is in essence concerned with the diagnosis and elimination of deficits in self-realization. Here, liberty is a constant development toward ever greater authenticity. Nobody will disagree that Taylor raises a substantial point. But we have to be aware of a dangerous epistemic slope inherent to it. His ethically loaded concept of liberty becomes problematic at the precise moment when it denies to the subject authority and accountability in its own affairs. For Taylor, the description and elimination of deficits of liberty are not first and foremost matters the individual itself has the competence to deal with. There are other, better equipped instances that need to be involved, therapeutic authorities which the subject is dependent upon to find its way to its hidden authenticity:

> [T]he subject himself cannot be the final authority on the question whether he is free; for he cannot be the final authority on the question whether his desires are authentic, whether they do or do not frustrate his purposes.
>
> *(Taylor 1985, 216)*

At this juncture, one would as a matter of urgency expect an answer to the question as to who or what this final authority is. Who would occupy this position for a subject suffering a chronic deficit of authenticity and therefore in constant need of therapy? Society? Politicians? A priest or a therapist? The question is not answered. Perhaps it is the philosophers. In this constellation it must be hoped that the forces invoked for assistance are truly, authentically benevolent. Even given that, which in certain contexts might be unlikely, it is to be hoped that they make fewer mistakes in their presumptive knowledge of the true self-actualization of the subject in question than the subject itself.

Personally, we can agree with the idea proposed by Henri Laborit: "nous devrions tous être les médecins les uns des autres"—"we all should be the doctors of each other" (Laborit 1985, 30). No one being an island, our self-realization is embedded in a complex communicative space. In talking to each other, we explore what we are missing in ourselves. But in the last instance we can hardly admit that an authority other than the subject itself can responsibly guide and adopt this process. In therapy, success depends on the willingness of the subject to recognize and accept the insights on offer. To overpower or trick someone into a new perception can hardly rely on authenticity. Truly, we are all overwhelmed and struggling, not unlike Camus's Sisyphus, with the quest to become more authentic selves. But it certainly does not help to be further disillusioned by bad news from the clinical practice of moral philosophy. Especially in the perspective of freedom, what we more urgently need is a fresh boost toward the courage for freedom, advocated by Camus as the noblest human endeavor.

Taylor's critique of negative liberty corresponds with a form of conservative thinking that might somewhat imprecisely be termed a communitarian doctrine of virtues (see also Zürn, Chapter 12 in this volume). For the conservative *virtuosi*, the fundamental problem of Western societies is their fatal drive to cultural modernism. At its core, they detect a biased concept of liberty which is too much obsessed with opening up spaces for the expansion of individuality. The main tenet of a conservatism of virtuousness is that the modern individual is simply overwhelmed by the openness of spaces accorded to it and cannot responsibly cope with the choices it is forced to make. In consequence, the concept of negative liberty is seen as a mistake and a source of many troubles. Taylor spoke, precisely in this sense, of negative liberty as a "wrong" concept. Others have moved this thought to a further stage: John Milbank and Adrian Pabst (2016, 15), in their ambitious book *The Politics of Virtue*, go so far as to denounce "the tyranny of negative liberty." Now, tyranny, which was the focus of Isaiah Berlin's entire intellectual commitment, has changed sides from positive liberty, where Berlin had detected it, to negative liberty.

A conservative critique of liberalism is often linked with the assumption that today's Western societies are led by manipulative elites. This fits well with the premise of the immaturity of the human population in general. Milbank and Pabst (2016) claim to have identified oligarchical alliances as the dark forces behind the liberal ideologies of the present and their seditious effects on public morals. These would use their considerable means to perpetuate the degenerative dynamic of the wrong liberty, while making sure that their own influence remains concealed (Milbank and Pabst 2016, 379). What might seem a crude conspiracy theory is presented as an academically substantiated analysis—though upon closer inspection it suffers from an evident lack of scientific rigor. In agreement with Taylor's view of the deficient subject, Milbank and Pabst maintain that clear hierarchies are required and that elites are needed to assume leadership positions and give direction to the lesser-equipped rest of the community. Their critique of elitism, therefore, is not one of principle. In the present system, it is just the wrong elites that have placed themselves on top of history and taken over leadership. More often than not, the fiercest critics of elites simply see others in the places they themselves claim to more rightly deserve.

If we presume that our contemporary societies are in crisis and that this crisis is also a crisis of liberty, then the question arises as to an educational program that would allow us to move forward. One option, as we have seen, is a communitarian program of virtues. The individual's striving for liberty would be rather strictly limited by a coherence of values. To put it bluntly: since the individual cannot be the highest authority in knowing what its true needs are, it must be educated to let go of the idea that it might find its own path to this kind of knowledge. The other option is to define education basically as a process to increase the perception of individual liberty and to encourage the largest possible widening of spaces of freedom. Even if the best answer is somewhere in between the two, we need to opt for a direction. We have to clarify our basic assumptions about the amount of freedom we think humanity should be allowed to aspire to.

It is no coincidence and no error in the operating system of history that the strong drive for liberty and the pleasures derived from liberty are the least exhaustible motivation for human aspirations. The high-flying rhetoric of liberty in all the preambles, constitutions, and political statements is thus not false, even if reality redeems so little of it. Sisyphus cannot shed the burden of liberty onto someone else. Camus's most relevant insight from his reflection on this myth ultimately is that it is essential for our happiness that we emancipate ourselves from all the masters and mistresses, from all authorities and elites that too readily wish to relieve us of the burden of bearing the uniqueness of our own selves.

Culture and liberty

The concepts of culture and liberty are not only particularly vague and popular in elevated rhetoric. They are both situated in the critical intersection between the individual and the collective. As Constant attempted to elucidate in 1819, the concept of liberty has shifted, from the republican and collective perception of antiquity to modern individualism. Today, the focus is on the freedoms that the subject-citizen claims for itself. In the concept of culture, a similar development can be observed. The cultural, too, is constituted by two contradictory functions: to strengthen the binding forces of the collective with its shared values, norms and narratives, while also nourishing (and fomenting) the individual's resources in confirming its singularity.

UNESCO addressed this duality of the concept of culture in 1982 in a famous resolution which has since become a regularly cited reference. It was at this UNESCO World Conference on Cultural Policies in Mexico City, where a defiant Jack Lang, Minister for Culture in the then young era of the socialist French president François Mitterrand, called for international mobilization against the cultural imperialism of the United States. The Mexico City Declaration, formally endorsed by 129 states, contained a doubly expanded concept of culture, stating that

> in its widest sense, culture may now be said to be the whole complex of distinctive spiritual, material, intellectual and emotional features that characterize a society or social group. It includes not only the arts and letters,

but also modes of life, the fundamental rights of the human being, value systems, traditions and beliefs.

(UNESCO 1982, 41)

The broadening of cultural valorization to the so-called "broader notion of culture" was thus codified by the United Nations (UN). Culture was no longer the preserve of the museum-worthy peaks of cultural production, of the canonical works. Codes and tactics of everyday life, to take up the terminology of Michel de Certeau (2011), had to be considered and valued as culturally relevant. This understanding, which in 1982 was not entirely new and which was merely formally registered by UNESCO, is fully established today. The cultural turn has taught us to understand our societies as ultimately people-made and culturally codified constructs.

But there is a second part to the definition of culture in the Mexico City Declaration worth noting. In it UNESCO undertook the improbable attempt to define the key role that culture has for the individual and that the individual has for culture. In this second part, the Mexico definition targets the significance of culture for the single human being in its tireless exploration of its own fragile freedoms:

> Therefore, expressing trust in the ultimate convergence of the cultural and spiritual goals of mankind, the Conference agrees: [...] that it is culture that gives man the ability to reflect upon himself. It is culture that makes us specifically human, rational beings, endowed with a critical judgement and a sense of moral commitment. It is through culture that we discern values and make choices. It is through culture that man expresses himself, becomes aware of himself, recognizes his incompleteness, questions his own achievements, seeks untiringly for new meanings and creates works through which he transcends his limitations.
>
> *(UNESCO 1982, 38)*

This passage brought a considerable degree of subjective disquiet into an understanding of culture which in the intergovernmental arena was predominantly collectivist. The faculty to think critically, the freedom to intentionally select values, and the search for new meaning open up a distinct perspective of progress and enhancement. The individual is invited to apply its culturally acquired tools with the aim to challenge the cultural codes that define it.

The problem that this concept of cultural freedom created in the political discourse of an intergovernmental organization like UNESCO became evident in 1995, when former UN Secretary-General, Javier Pérez de Cuéllar, presented the report of the World Commission for Culture and Development. The commission had been jointly set up in 1991 by the UN and UNESCO. It was meant to promote the significance of cultural policies which had continuously failed to be recognized as a relevant issue on the international agenda. While ecological concerns increasingly gained traction and drew ever greater attention, culminating in the Rio Earth Summit in 1992, the attempt to achieve a comparable effect for cultural policies remained stuck in the narrow confines of the initiated.

Unsurprisingly, the main suggestion issued by the report of the World Commission on Culture and Development of 1995 was the organization of a cultural summit, intended to become the "Rio" for culture. This summit indeed took place in 1998 in Stockholm, but failed to create the desired global impact.

The report of 1995 is an important turning point signaling how UNESCO, as an intergovernmental arena, further dealt with the concept of culture. It took up the fundamental problem addressed in Mexico in 1982, and linked it to the question of global development. The report's title, "Our Creative Diversity," hints at the forces seen as drivers for that development: creativity, not adaptation. And diversity, not uniformity.

However, the tension between conflicting perspectives on cultural liberty around the globe becomes evident as a leitmotif in the text. For many states, respect for cultural diversity means the ability to reject any meddling from the outside with their internal affairs and with their handling of freedoms or, more likely, unfreedoms. Every nation has its own tradition in defining and eventually denying spaces for individual freedoms, the message is to be interpreted. In this reading, cultural liberty is a claim made by ruling elites, presumably on behalf of the collectives they govern. The World Commission's report concedes so much: "Cultural freedom, unlike individual freedom, is a collective freedom. It refers to the right of a group of people to follow a way of life of its choice" (World Commission on Culture and Development 1995, 15).

Cultural freedom is understood here as respect for the self-determination of the collective—with no explanation as to how this comes about and how the collective concretely proceeds to construct that self-determination. Pluralism and tolerance are seen as the quality of recognition among such collectives, referring to the respect different cultural value systems owe to each other. They are denied as a requisite quality within the system.

Pérez de Cuéllar makes a far-reaching concession to this political concept of cultural respect, when he draws upon the metaphor of a "mosaic of different cultures" in his preface to the report (World Commission on Culture and Development 1995, 22). This image of the mosaic reflects an essentialist view for which cultures have their necessary place in the grander picture of a global cultural cosmos. This cosmos is meant to represent a grand design transcending the individual cultural building blocks, which sit at their own specified places in a great ensemble. No metaphor is innocent. This one is very much the negation of what we perceive as cultural hybridity, as the blurriness of cultural borders, as the instability of our constructs in the domain of cultural identities.

But this is not the main thrust of the report. Texts of this kind operate on different levels and must cater to different political sensibilities. After the definition of cultural freedom referred to above, another definition is provided, in surprising editorial proximity to the first one. It is meant to be complementary, while destroying outright the metaphor of the mosaic: "Cultural freedom, by protecting alternative ways of living, encourages experimentation, diversity, imagination and creativity" (World Commission on Culture and Development 1995, 15).

Respect for cultural diversity here means the respect for cultural freedom and for the exploratory self-determination of the individual. In all, due to this to-and-fro between the contradictory perspectives of a deep ideological divide, the report cannot provide any sort of clear conclusion. There is, however, a prevailing perspective culminating in a passage that with striking clarity and uncompromised resolve captures the spirit of Mexico and creates the link to the pressing question of the global development agenda:

> Finally, freedom is central to culture, and in particular the freedom to decide what we have reason to value, and what lives we have reason to seek. One of the most basic needs is to be left free to define our own basic needs. This need is being threatened by a combination of global pressures and global neglect.
>
> *(World Commission on Culture and Development*
> *1995, 26)*

The classical liberal position could hardly be put more clearly and succinctly, and the confidence of this wording shows how important it was to the authors of this report. The decision as to what we value and what meaning we wish to give our own lives can only be taken in the very personal perspective of our own, individual considerations. This is a sufficiently substantial expression of cultural freedom.

This particular emphasis on the need to increase the options for action and choice of every single individual is also at the foundation of contemporary theories of development. Amartya Sen (2000) and Christian Welzel (2013), to name two important figures, reach the conclusion that development and progress are ultimately based on a transcultural dynamic. This dynamic is directed toward increasing the individual's options for action and freedoms, as well as its responsible participation in political decisionmaking processes:

> Freedom is central to the process of development for two distinct reasons. 1) The evaluative reason: assessment of progress has to be done primarily in terms of whether the freedoms that people have are enhanced; 2) The effectiveness reason: achievement of development is thoroughly dependent on the free agency of people.
>
> *(Sen 2000, 4)*

Both authors give an unequivocal answer to the question of whether the concept of individual freedom might be just a matter of a Western cultural bias. For Welzel, the phenomenon of the utility ladder of freedom is a consistent logic of every civilization. For him, the West's global monopoly will dwindle, without any doubt. But this will in no way diminish the emancipatory impetus which he sees as inherent in all world societies:

> In the era of global communications, the florescence of people-powered societies in terms of human prosperity and liberty has reached ubiquitous visibility. If the desire for emancipation was not a natural human aspiration, the heightened visibility of emancipatory achievements wouldn't garner much attention in other parts of the world. Yet, it strikes a chord with people around the world who still live in poverty and oppression but no longer in ignorance. Global communication enables these people to question their condition and join forces to mobilize for change. As this happens, human empowerment begins to detach from its original source. This does not mean the Westernization of the world but, on the contrary, its de-Westernization. For the West's monopoly over human empowerment is about to fade.
>
> *(Welzel 2013, 408)*

Crises of liberty

Is this optimistic perspective justified, even if it speaks less for a future of the West and more for the idea of a global culture of liberty? Or is this just a vain projection, reflecting deep-seated humanist aspirations? Three points come immediately to mind that indicate a crisis of liberty, rather than the inevitability of its accomplishment.

One of the attributes coined for our time is that of a postliberal age. As early as 1957, Judith N. Shklar came to the conclusion that "since the French Revolution, liberalism has become increasingly uncertain of itself, so that at present there flourishes a conservative liberalism that is just as cheerless as Christian fatalism" (1969, 219). Contradictions and inequalities in and between societies brought forth by capitalist democratic liberalism seem to confirm Shklar's verdict. It is common sense today that we face huge challenges for social cohesion. For the neoconservative stance, cultural modernism and its radical individualism are largely responsible for what is seen as a decline of established virtues and values, and in consequence the entire social setup. For this school of thought, it is individual freedom that ruins the cultural substance. Capital, commerce, and consumption, as well as an increasing commodification of human relations, are identified as the drivers of this degenerative tendency.

The political philosopher John Gray, a renegade from liberalism, draws these connections, in a column for the *New Statesman* of April 1, 2020: "With all its talk of freedom and choice, liberalism was in practice the experiment of dissolving traditional sources of social cohesion and political legitimacy and replacing them with the promise of rising material living standards."

Constant, the liberal, still saw progress in the transfer of the currency of power into the currency of money. For him, it brought about an increase in cosmopolitan humanity and contributed to the peaceful coexistence of fulfilled and coequal private spheres of life. Money is the medium that transposes cultural valorization into a general, accessible and culturally neutralizing currency. Money provides the greatest possible freedom for value-related interactions. Its all-embracing and rigorously leveling semantics allows a radical disconnect from culturally grounded allegiances. For postliberal thinking, therefore, money value is a genuine enemy of cultural values. Interestingly, it is a cultural philosopher, Boris Groys, who gave this transfer from cultural to monetary values the sharpest expression:

> Modern liberty becomes concrete in the international financial markets. Having shed all traditional cultural identities, overcome all regional restrictions, and abandoned all binding ideas, we begin to flow, to circulate freely, to become infinitely flexible and adaptable. Put another way: we become like money. The likeness of the modern soul to money has replaced its likeness to God.
>
> *(Groys 2009, 255, authors' translation)*

A strategy against the leveling force of the market is cultural self-valorization, as sociologist Andreas Reckwitz (2017) has shown in his influential study. He describes the phenomenon of cultural strategies of singularization as a general signature of our time. We live, one might conclude, in a society in which cohesion and shared points of reference have a greater unifying effect by being questioned than through the commitment they inspire.

An interesting indicator for cultural cohesion has been suggested by Peter Sloterdijk (2011). In his view, we are united across all artificially erected borders of individual self-enactment by one thing: our collective readiness for stress. Sloterdijk complements the primary category of political unfreedom with two further forms of privation of liberty, both of which have an eminently cultural character and both of which contribute to maximizing stress: the pressure exerted by the hefty burden of our everyday lives and our enslavement to false self-images. What we perceive as social cohesion is in fact often no more than the stress we cause each other, and in whose tribulations we then sense mutual recognition. Ultimately, it is the exquisite intensity of stressful emotions that connects us. Our disposition for quick social vexation is an effective regulatory mechanism for the liberties we can take without facing sanctions. This would suggest that the stress level of a society increases in direct correlation to the degree to which other binding cultural forces become weaker.

The second aspect of this crisis of liberty is geopolitical. After the end of the Cold War we entered an age in which competition for the best model of society gained renewed impetus. Political systems with a fundamentally different understanding of the relationship between state authority and civil freedoms now confidently and assertively challenge the primacy of a West, whose model of liberal modernism has evolved over long centuries and through much resistance and countless setbacks.

We need to acknowledge that we are here not merely dealing with a matter of competition between narratives. Rather, the competition is between types of political legitimation, including all the consequences for people's everyday lives and their freedoms they concretely entail. Globally rising states, even if they initially appeal only to their right to self-determination in a global prospect of cultural diversity, are making the implicit claim to serve as models. Comprehensive geopolitical strategies to expand political, economic, and cultural spheres of influence are already in full swing. Given the state of globalization and current political problems, this competition of systems is inevitably linked to hegemonic tendencies. In an interview, Peter Sloterdijk (2018) coined the succinct formula that we come from many different histories, but are heading toward one common future:

> The many cultures must understand that they look back at primarily distinct pasts and forward to primarily shared futures. [...] Local narratives are increasingly compelled to coordinate the idiochronic horizons of their constructs of history with the virtual synchronic horizon of a common world time.
>
> *(authors' translation)*

It is no longer appropriate to transfer a suitable perspective of cultural relativity to politics. When we consider culture and liberty today, we do not just critically assess the situation in our own society and the constellations in other societies. We also take into account the virtual synchronous horizon of a shared political future and ask the "central question of politics" that Isaiah Berlin has identified: the problem of coercion and liberty.

For none of the actors involved is it sufficient to appeal to their own history. In history, cultural formats shaped by unfreedom and coerced conformity constantly had to be overcome. We have no reason to recognize types of legitimation of power simply because they are ingrained in a specific culture and history. The purpose of history and of memory is not to determine what we should be thinking and how we should be behaving, but to show the options for a mainly open future that can be derived from the experiences of historical contingency. Michel Foucault (1984, 47) came up with appropriate wording for the critical ethos we should apply to ourselves and our history, as the "historico-practical test of the limits that we may go beyond, and thus as work carried out by ourselves on ourselves as free beings." This strikingly echoes the second part of the UNESCO definition of culture of Mexico City.

Irrespective of specificities of cultural history, the question arises as to whether, in light of an increasing systemic complexity, it may be necessary to restrict individual voluntarism and to yield to the higher rationality of social organization—in other words, to submit to the authority of the state. This argument is frequently used when security interests are (or are declared to be) at stake. There is no more ground for liberty when national security is put on the table.

In the fight against the COVID-19 pandemic we wondered whether authoritarian political systems had a competitive advantage in managing the crisis, as these state authorities can more directly and with less scrutiny restrict the freedoms of citizens. This view was voiced for example by John Gray (2020), who referred to the three states of Taiwan, South Korea, and Singapore: "It is hard to believe their cultural traditions, which focus on collective well-being more than personal autonomy, have not played a role in their success. They have also resisted the cult of the minimal state."

It is advisable, however, not to jump to conclusions. A key aspect of this crisis has been the trustworthiness and transparency of information. In the 2020 Reporters Without Borders Germany report, developments presently observed are characterized as follows: "Dictatorships, authoritarian and populist regimes are attempting ever more overtly to repress independent information at all costs and to enforce their illiberal worldview" (Reporter Ohne Grenzen 2020; authors' translation). The functionality of a political system must be measured by the amount of information it can generate, circulate and process—and by the quality of this information. Liberty is contingent on this information, for illusions and misinformation are just another form of dependency.

As a third aspect of the crisis of liberty, we refer to the possible effects of digital transformation. Digitization has not only made communication—a central medium of liberty—simpler and more flexible. It has also revolutionized access to information and to entertainment. This has greatly increased the range of our choices and expanded our scope for freedom. But, now that the first euphoria has faded, we are becoming aware of more and more cause for concern. Will information technology be an instrument in the service of humanity in the long term? Or will we become the inhabitants of a system that gradually imposes its own algorithmic modality on our lives? Are we assimilating the features of the tools we are using?

In their classic work of social constructivism, Berger and Luckmann (1967, 78) noted the "paradox that man is capable of producing a world that he then experiences as something other than a human product." Are we in the process of creating this world in which we will feel like strangers? Progress in the further development of artificial intelligence will open up new opportunities to delegate decisionmaking to machines, and thereby also require deliberations pertaining to human liberty. One day we will perhaps have to become accustomed to the fact that machines make better decisions. Learning algorithms generate their own procedures for acquiring knowledge, by processing enormous amounts of data at speeds that massively outdo any human capacity. This will not only be an insult to our elevated modern concept of the personal self. It will radically affect our perception of who we are and what the nature of our freedom is.

Quo vadis?

The flaw of negative liberty is that for us, as citizens, it will never be sufficient that we are left in peace. It is indispensable that we contribute to the conditions that make this peace possible. Moving on from Benjamin Constant, we must say that "admission to the public realm and participation in public affairs" (Arendt 2018, 372) is one of these conditions. Can you be free in an undemocratic society? Hannah Arendt had a clear view:

> This public freedom is a tangible worldly reality, created by men to enjoy together in public—to be seen, heard, known, and remembered by others. And this kind of freedom demands equality, it is possible only amongst peers. Institutionally speaking, it is possible only in a republic, which knows no subjects and, strictly speaking, no rulers.
>
> *(Arendt 2018, 375)*

Arendt does not neglect to warn of political ambitions that are fueled by the wrong motives, hinting at a certain type of professional politician segregated within a political caste. Political work must not be motivated by a desire to gain privileges or a "will to power." This would destroy political life.

The culture of freedom is a political culture for which the coequal assumption of shared responsibility is essential. In *Liberty before Liberalism*, Skinner (2012) reaches the exact same conclusion. He reconstructs the Roman and republican legal tradition persisting into the early modern age, according to which any dependence on the arbitrary will of a ruler is equated with slavery, even when the people living under such dominion are able to pursue their own private interests in relative peace. It is not sufficient to be able to stage a rebellion when it becomes necessary to overthrow the Leviathan you have subjugated yourself to in a social contract. True republican liberty cannot be reconciled with a situation in which participation in political self-determination is hindered, and people are at the mercy of the whims of a monarch, any party of unity, or a dominating political elite. The negative liberty of being able to shape your own life, free of arbitrary external restrictions, is only guaranteed when it is the result of true political self-determination.

This liberal republicanism fundamentally differs from the postliberal conservative republicanism that assumes an inherent immaturity of human nature. The latter republicanism sees a need for social hierarchies, the subjugation of the individual to social norms, leadership by authoritative elites, and a binding catalogue of values and virtues.

It may seem paradoxical that the structural elitism of this conservative mindset is, likewise, the central weakness of liberalism. Domenico Losurdo (2011) has pointed this out. It is one of the fundamental contradictions of liberalism that its open and cosmopolitan perspective is prone to accept so many exclusions.

It seems as if the liberal dream had already come true when the smart-enough individuals were enabled to finally escape with their treasures from the greedy state authority, leaving behind those toward whom one would prefer not to be reminded of any kind of social obligation. This is the vision set out by James Dale Davidson and William Rees-Mogg (1997) in their book *The Sovereign Individual: Mastering the Transition to the Information Age*. Cosmopolitan elites, well trained in the mechanics of a global economy, would take back control and sovereignty from the predatory welfare state, as free individuals—this is the programmatic core of Davidson and Rees-Mogg's vision. They were dreaming Constant's dream that "individual existence is less locked into political existence. Individuals carry their treasures far away, take with them all the benefits of private life" (Constant 1819, 12). The social contract would be unilaterally terminated. In the stateless space of digital information technologies, the elitist networks of sovereign individuals would join to form parallel societies. The authors were still hoping that the global digital web would allow them to evade the authoritarian grips of states. This vision of the liberation of the wealthy from the importunate demands of the less fortunate appears like the resurrection of the British Empire in a transubstantiated and somewhat ghostly form. It is, however, gravely illusory, be it only because the Internet has long ceased to be that space of freedom from governmental grasp it may have seemed in its early days.

The principle of liberty is not only threatened from outside. It is just as endangered by its own incoherence in relying on its exclusivity, or in being most generally understood as a freedom of elites. Here, we touch the real essence of the connection between culture and liberty. Only by means of an intensive and unhindered cultural exploration are we able to process our social valuations fully—emotionally, intellectually, and historically. And it is only under these terms that we are able to apply our liberty to address the contradictions and exclusions that we produce with that liberty. This cultural exploration fundamentally relates to the definition of culture in the UNESCO Mexico City Declaration of 1982. It is culture that enables us to develop critical judgment and a sense of moral obligation. We express ourselves through culture, we become aware of ourselves through culture, and through culture we acknowledge our own imperfections. It is only through culture that we recognize values and make choices concerning these values. It is inherent to culture that we can question our achievements and that we can be empowered to cross the borders that have been laid out for us.

Every culture has its demons, its repressed inhabitants. In a time of transformation, it will not suffice to draw on old certainties and mobilize a catalogue of virtues of a bygone age in order to face our challenges. We must fearlessly and precisely consider the crises that our certainties have engendered and face up to the demons that we have created with our virtues. Among these challenges, to name but three, are: diversity, which we have too long resisted with a narrow understanding of cultural uniformity; a true cosmopolitanism, such as we have failed to attain in our exclusive and colonially determined approach to the world as a whole; and a deeper grasp of sustainability, which is coming upon us as a consequence of our frenzy in exploiting the biosphere.

This is the real perspective of the civilizatory program of a culture of liberty. And this is the point where we need to think with more ambition for clarity and with a stronger passion against all contemporary excuses for intimidation and coercion. Because, as Lloyd Green (2020), former advisor to US President George Bush senior, concludes, referring to the World Freedom Index compiled by Reporters without Borders: "[O]ur freedom and trust continue to erode with no end in sight."

Acknowledgment

The authors thank Gregory Bond for his valuable assistance in redacting the English version of this text.

References

Arendt, Hannah. 2018. "The Freedom to Be Free: The Conditions and Meaning of Revolution." In Jerome Kohn (ed.). *Thinking Without a Banister: Essays in Understanding, 1953–1975*. New York: Random House.

Berger, Peter L. and Thomas Luckmann. 1967. *The Social Construction of Reality: A Treatise in the Sociology of Knowledge*. Harmondsworth: Penguin.

Berlin, Isaiah. 2002. "Two Concepts of Liberty." In Henry Hardy (ed.). *Liberty*. Oxford: Oxford University Press.

Constant, Benjamin. 1819. "The Liberty of the Ancients Compared with that of the Moderns." https://www.earlymoderntexts.com/assets/pdfs/constant1819.pdf

Davidson, Dale and William Rees-Mogg. 1997. *The Sovereign Individual: Mastering the Transition to the Information Age*. New York: Touchstone.

De Certeau, Michel. 2011. *The Practice of Everyday Life*. Berkeley and Los Angeles: University of California Press.

Felsch, Philipp. 2015. *Der lange Sommer der Theorie*. Munich: C.H. Beck.

Foucault, Michel. 1984. "What is Enlightenment?" In Paul Rabinow (ed.). *The Foucault Reader*. New York: Pantheon Books.

Gray, John. 2020, April 1. "Why this Crisis Is a Turning Point in History," *New Statesman*, https://www.newstatesman.com/international/2020/04/why-crisis-turning-point -history.

Green, Lloyd. 2020, April 26. "In Deep Review: Trump v intelligence – and Obama v the People," *The Guardian*, https://www.theguardian.com/books/2020/apr/26/in -deep-state-review-david-rohde-donald-trump-intelligence-barack-obama

Groys, Boris. 2009. *Topologie der Kunst*. Munich and Vienna: Hanser.

Honneth, Axel. 2004. "Gerechtigkeit und kommunikative Freiheit. Überlegungen im Anschluss an Hegel." In Barbara Merker, Georg Mohr, and Michael Quante (eds.). *Subjektivität und Anerkennung*, 213–227. Paderborn: Mentis.

Laborit, Henri. 1985. *Éloge de la fuite*. Paris: Gallimard.

Losurdo, Domenico. 2011. *Liberalism: A Counter-History*. Translated by Gregory Elliot. London and New York: Verso.

Milbank, John and Adrian Pabst. 2016. *The Politics of Virtue: Post-Liberalism and the Human Future*. London: Rowman and Littlefield International.

Reckwitz, Andreas. 2017. *Die Gesellschaft der Singularitäten: Zum Strukturwandel der Moderne*. Berlin: Suhrkamp.

Reporter Ohne Grenzen. 2020. "Rangliste der Pressefreiheit: Journalistinnen und Journalisten unter Druck von vielen Seiten." https://www.reporter-ohne-grenzen.de/rangliste/rangliste-2020/. Accessed July 26, 2021.

Rosenblatt, Helena. 2018. *The Lost History of Liberalism: From Ancient Rome to the Twenty-First Century*. Princeton: Princeton University Press.

Sen, Amartya. 2000. *Development as Freedom*. New York: Anchor Books.

Shklar, Judith N. 1989. "The Liberalism of Fear." In Nancy L. Rosenblum (ed.). *Liberalism and the Moral Life*. Cambridge Mass., London: Harvard University Press.

Shklar, Judith N. 1957/1969. *After Utopia: The Decline of Political Faith*. Princeton and Oxford: Princeton University Press.

Skinner, Quentin. 2012. *Liberty before Liberalism*. Cambridge: Cambridge University Press.

Sloterdijk, Peter. 2011. *Streß und Freiheit*. Berlin: Suhrkamp.

Sloterdijk, Peter. 2018. "Kulturen leiden am Gegeneinander von Tradition und Zukunft." Interview for the Global Thought Leader Index, March 7, 2018. https://www.gdi.ch/de/publikationen/trend-updates/peter-sloterdijk-kulturen-leiden-am-gegeneinander-von-tradition-und.

Taylor, Charles. 1985. "What's Wrong with Negative Liberty." In *Philosophy and the Human Science*. Philosophical Papers 2. Cambridge: Cambridge University Press.

UNESCO. 1982. *Mexico City Declaration on Cultural Policies*. World Conference on Cultural Policies, Mexico City, 26 July–6 August, final report, https://unesdoc.unesco.org/ark:/48223/pf0000052505.

Welzel, Christian. 2013. *Freedom Rising: Human Empowerment and the Quest for Emancipation*. New York: Cambridge University Press.

World Commission on Culture and Development. 1995. *Our Creative Diversity: Report of the World Commission on Culture and Development*. https://www.gcedclearinghouse.org/sites/default/files/resources/%5BENG%5D%20Notre%20diversit%C3%A9%20cr%C3%A9atrice.pdf

PART II

The international liberal order and world society

11

IS EFFECTIVE MULTILATERALISM POSSIBLE?

Inge Kaul

Introduction

As this chapter is being written, the world witnesses a rising number of unmet global challenges, ranging from climate change, cyber-insecurity, disease outbreaks such as the COVID-19 pandemic and deteriorating ocean health to international financial instability, terrorism and war, to name a few. Unsurprisingly, world-renowned scientists and technical experts' calls are multiplying, urging policymakers to make faster and scaled-up progress toward the agreed (in some cases long-agreed) global policy goals such as those outlined in the 2030 Agenda for Sustainable Development (referred to hereafter as Agenda 2030).[1] Certainly, myriad state and nonstate actors have undertaken manifold corrective actions in related policy fields and have done so with some success. Nevertheless, even scientifically and technologically well-understood high-risk challenges, including global warming, remain unresolved. This raises a critical question: Is the present system of multilateral cooperation not fit for meeting the global challenges? Many of these challenges affect us all, rich and poor, whether we live in the North or the South. They are, therefore, also known as global public goods (GPGs). However, GPGs are nothing new. International cooperation in support of their provision has worked in the past. So, why then is it failing us now? And, if cooperation failure is indeed contributing to the lengthening list of underprovided GPGs we are currently witnessing, how could its effectiveness be enhanced? What types of adjustments would be needed, and more importantly, how could they be realized?

This chapter offers possible answers to these questions for further research and debate. They can be summarized as follows. First, a proper adjustment of the conventional system of international cooperation is not only not occurring quickly enough, but in some respects, the changes that are happening are headed in the opposite direction, that is, away from more effective universal multilateralism that adequate GPG provision would require and toward more competitive and fractured multilateralism, rivalry between major powers, and even unilateralism.

Second, while several factors come into play, the two main reasons for this situation are the rising trend toward global multipolarity and the growing importance of GPGs. Owing to increasing multipolarity the conventional major powers fear that, at this time of shifting power relations, engagement in universal multilateralism entails the risk of a loss of policymaking sovereignty. In contrast, more and more developing countries have climbed up the development ladder, with some of them now being global powers themselves. They are no longer just demanding a more effective voice but are exercising strengthened agency in matters that concern them, including global matters, with a view to further secure their policymaking sovereignty. Thus, concern about sovereignty today is acting as a major constraint on adequate GPG provision because, albeit for different reasons, it makes states hesitant to accept the governance requirements of these goods, especially the interdependence and hence the compulsion they entail for states not only to cooperate but to cooperate in a universal multilateral way and with due respect to the goods' adequate provision requirements lest related problems remain unresolved.

However, and third, states' concern about sovereignty is not the main impediment. Rather, the key constraint is the lack of a persuasive change vision indicating how states could have both secure policymaking sovereignty and effective universal multilateralism (see also Zürn, Chapter 12 in this volume, who points to the lack of a compelling vision of an appropriate institutional set-up in global politics).

Fourth, as a possible way forward, this chapter suggests devising and forging a consensus on a new operating principle of multilateralism to be followed, especially when universal multilateralism is the cooperation form most "fit for purpose." The new operating principle would call on states to aim at making multilateralism sovereignty-compatible and exercising sovereignty in a way that is multilateralism-compatible, implying respect for other nations' sovereignty and the adequate provision requirements of GPGs. To achieve consensus on such a new, dual-compatibility principle may sound like a Herculean task. However, this chapter also shows that the reform steps would be quite doable and that political momentum for change is gathering strength.

Providing global public goods: the governance requirements to meet

Governance arrangements, including international cooperation processes, can be viewed as tools put in place to facilitate the attainment of certain policy purposes. Thus, they should be assessed according to the same criterion that other tools are expected to meet, namely, to be "fit for purpose." Therefore, the aim of this section is to identify the governance requirements of GPGs, with a special focus on the goods figuring prominently on today's policy agendas. They are being assessed here in terms of the pattern of state behavior that would be conducive to adequate provision of the GPGs, given the properties of the goods awaiting states' attention.[2] Accordingly, the next subsection takes a closer look at the nature of current GPG challenges; and the following subsection then distills from this analysis the demands GPGs pose in terms of state behavior. The discussion shows that more adequate GPG provision in future requires considerable rethinking and behavioral change on the part of states.

Taking a closer look at global public goods

Two main categories of GPGs can be distinguished, viz. natural GPGs, such as sunlight and moonlight or the atmosphere and the ocean, and human-made GPGs, such as global financial stability, infectious disease control, peace and security and regulation for the use of new technologies such as artificial intelligence (AI) (see Kaul et al. 2016 for an introduction to global public goods).

One reason GPGs have been thrust into the political limelight in recent decades is humanity's growing environmental footprint and the resultant over-utilization, degradation, and, in some cases, loss of natural GPGs, such as biodiversity. Slowly but steadily, these effects have made themselves felt, for example, in the form of more violent weather patterns resulting from global warming. Thereby, they have led to a growing global awareness of the fact that we cannot take the availability of natural GPGs for granted. This is because several of them belong to the group of impure GPGs, which are difficult to be made excludable but, if extensively utilized, become rival in consumption from certain thresholds onward. Hence, should we want to continue enjoying such natural GPGs, as proclaimed in numerous international resolutions, including Agenda 2030 and the Paris Agreement on climate change, this then requires global governance designed to incentivize state and nonstate actors worldwide, through financial and nonfinancial means, to use these goods sustainably. The transformations required toward this end, such as the shift towards clean energy (IRENA 2019), will not only require major investments but, in the short and medium term, produce winners and losers and, therefore, not be an easy feat to realize, although progress would need to be achieved urgently.

Another factor that has led to today's growing importance of GPGs is the rising number of human-made GPGs and the rising volume of transborder economic activity they have facilitated, including the "travel" of people, goods, services, and knowledge and information, as well as diseases, crime, and violence. As a result, national policy domains have become more interlinked so that what had previously been regional, national or local public goods became globalized and turned into GPGs as, for example, happened to financial stability, public health and law and order conditions. Moreover, owing to various technological advancements, new GPG-type phenomena have emerged that also need more multilateral, especially universal multilateral policy attention and regulation.

Examples are cybersecurity and the safe use of AI for civilian and military purposes. As Haas (2017, 226) says: "a cardinal reality" today is "little stays local."

However, many GPGs are not only global and public in consumption, in the sense that they potentially affect, for better or worse, all states and all people. Rather, they are also global and public in their provision, often requiring input from all of us, individually and collectively, to be adequately provided. Thus, GPGs tend to entail policy interdependence among countries, owing to their publicness in both consumption and provision. This implies that many of these goods cannot be self-provided through unilateral, bilateral or mini-multilateral action alone. Even the most powerful actors need the cooperation of others, often all others, if they want to enjoy goods such as climate stability, efficiently functioning international markets and supply chains or freedom from violence such as international terrorism.

Experience has shown that some GPGs "prescribe" at what scale and with what urgency corrective action must be taken for the good to generate the services expected of it. This fact is especially evident in the case of underprovided natural GPGs, such as climate change mitigation, and has led to the pronouncement that we have entered a new geological epoch, the Anthropocene. However, several of the human-made GPGs possess similar adequate provision requirements, such as international financial stability and the avoidance of ruinous global tax competition.[3]

In sum, it appears that the demand for multilateral cooperation has changed in both quantitative and qualitative terms. The agenda of unresolved GPG-type challenges is lengthening, and the urgency of tackling the long-standing underprovided goods is increasing.[4]

GPGs' demands on state behavior toward them

From the foregoing discussion it appears that GPG-related public policymaking is distinct from the conventional policy strands. It is neither just a national matter, nor just a matter of foreign affairs or development assistance. It certainly is not a matter that can simply be left to markets, civil society or the general public at large. Adequate GPG provision often needs inputs to be generated by all these other policy strands and "more." The "more" consists of the following expectations concerning the behavior of states:

- Acceptance of the interdependence that GPGs entail and the resultant need to seek the cooperation of the other concerned parties at the policysetting stage and the operational stage;
- Respect for the goods' adequate provision requirements and willingness to balance these requirements with human-centered interests, be they those of individual states or those of individual nonstate actors;
- Recognition of the fact that GPGs, like other goods including private goods, need to be assembled in a concerted and transnational manner, which calls

for willingness to support institutional innovation, notably the establishment of GPG provision as a new, added policy field sui generis and its inclusion in the governance systems at the national and international level;

- Result-orientation and preparedness to ensure full-cost budgeting of GPG projects, notably those entailing risks of potentially catastrophic proportions.

Thus, adequate GPG provision calls for new thinking and new types of behavior, notably states' acceptance of their interdependence, given that in GPG-related policy fields their interrelationships are now of a de facto universal-multilateral nature. Universal multilateralism no longer is merely a political form but also a policymaking reality, due to the global publicness of GPGs. However, the world order established in the immediate aftermath of World War II is founded on the official notion of individual, equal, and sovereign states maintaining, at their discretion, inter-nation relationships. State behavior, on which adequate GPG provision depends, clearly differs from this "official" view of states presented in the UN Charter (Article 2). Although right from the beginning, reality has tended to deviate from this notion, notably due to power asymmetry between states, the UN Charter view has nevertheless continued to shape states' self-understanding and, consequently, also the structure and functioning of the system of international cooperation at the policysetting and operational levels.

How have state actors responded to the compulsions to cooperate now posed by GPGs in ever-more unmistakable ways? Considering the melting of the Arctic ice caps, increasingly violent weather conditions, deteriorating ocean health, increasing inequality and the rising number of people on the move within and across countries in search of a decent life, which has since long been recognized as a basic human right and, hence, a GPG that by now should be available for all,[5] are there discernible signs of reinvigorated and more universal multilateralism?

States' responses to the provision requirements of global public goods

Policy pronouncements delivered by states individually or collectively since the 1980s repeatedly emphasized the world's increasing connectivity, pointed to problems of GPG underprovision and emphasized the need for more and more effective multilateral cooperation. The COVID-19 pandemic has given a further boost to such statements, with world leaders stressing the need for global solidarity because, as they tend to say, "no one is safe until all are safe." So far, however, these words have only hesitantly and partially been translated into deeds. Currently, at the global level, international cooperation is, in effect, moving in the opposite direction, becoming more competitive, fractured and shallow, as described in the next subsection. In contrast, as the following subsection shows, regional multilateralism in the Global South is on the rise, aimed at, among other things, protecting the concerned regions against negative spill-ins resulting from GPG underprovision. However, most countries, including the major powers, follow a behavioral path of "business as usual" in respect to the existing stock of multilateral agreements, complying with them as fully or as partially as in the past. Despite their varying forms, states' responses to date share a common feature: a lack of a realistic change vision about how to have both sovereignty and effective multilateralism.

Major-power rivalry at the global level

Despite all its various shortcomings, development in the developing countries has occurred and engendered a rising trend toward global multipolarity, with more and more countries of the Global South demanding and actually exercising a strengthened role in international cooperation. As a result, the conventional divide between a few major powers, notably powers from the Global North, acting as "policysetters," relegating the large "rest" of the countries to "policytakers" has been shrinking and causing "power politics" to gradually lose its teeth as the major operating principle of international cooperation. In its stead has come increasing rivalry between today's major powers, notably between China and the US and their respective allies, about access to resources, market shares, technological choices and the definition of global norms and standards (see Mahbubani, Chapter 15 in this volume, for more on the China-US rivalry). The distinction between private goods (such as rare earths) and public goods (for example, the regulation of the markets in which private goods are being traded) and, with it, clear criteria for when to compete and when to cooperate have increasingly gotten lost. Zero-sum thinking won the day; and unilateralism increased, as evident from the rising number of sanctions imposed by one state on other states, often based on allegations of unfair competition. As several analysts argue, an important source of these allegations is "innovation lethargy": a state and firms located in its jurisdiction having rested for too long on their past achievements and failing to keep up with the development of developing states, leading to important "first mover" advantages to these latecomers in several global markets (see Aghion et al. 2021; Christensen 2016; Mahbubani 2020; Roberts et al. 2019).

The fault lines in the present major-power rivalry run not only between conventional and newer powers but also between countries whose norm and value systems differ. Especially the US and members of the European Union (EU) tend to expect their allies and cooperation partners to stand for human rights and democracy. For example, the "Alliance of Multilateralism" established by the Foreign Ministers of France and Germany in 2019 espouses what could be called "conditional multilateralism." One of its objectives is to "protect, preserve and advance international law, including international humanitarian and human rights law." Accordingly, states intending to join the Alliance are expected to share these core values and norms and implement them nationally.[6] A further example of the conditional willingness to cooperate includes the US announcement that it is willing and ready once again to exercise global leadership because this will often be also the best strategy to serve US interests.[7] Similarly, the EU indicated that one of its ambitions is to pursue a multilateral approach to tackling global challenges with a view to strengthen its "strategic sovereignty" (see Anghel 2020).

In comparison to the Western pronouncements, some of China's statements on the topic of multilateralism sound different, stressing that it intends to foster multilateralism marked by openness, inclusiveness and win-win solutions, jointly bringing about a better future for humanity.[8] Often, however, China just acts on its ambitions and plans, as the Belt and Road Initiative and, more recently, its proactive COVID-19 vaccine diplomacy show. The Group of Seven (G7) and the EU critiqued both these initiatives at their 2021 Summit but decided to compete with them by promising that they, too, will donate vaccines and undertake a sort of belt and road project, maybe, in Africa.[9]

One effect of this rivalry among the major powers is that global policy statements tend to be vague. A case in point is the declaration adopted by the heads of state and government of United Nations (UN) member states in 2020, on the occasion of the organization's 75th anniversary (henceforth referred to as the UN75 Declaration), which calls for reinvigorated multilateralism but does not specify how such multilateralism would differ from the current forms of multilateralism.[10] Another effect is that agreements are of an "omnibus" style such as Agenda 2030. Its 17 major goals and 169 subgoals list something for everybody in no particular order, thus allowing those willing and capable to act to "pick" for follow-up, if any, the issues of special interest to them. Similarly, the Paris Agreement on climate change relies on states' voluntarism. Sometimes, it even seems that the slower the progress, the larger and more frequent are the meetings held on the laggard issues. Talking (the reiteration and reconfirmation of long-agreed goals) now often replaces the walking (the actual resolution of problems), lest no side gain an advantage.[11] Unsurprisingly, as repeatedly stressed in recent speeches of the UN Secretary-General and the UN's annual reports on the sustainable development goals, progress in the implementation of both these agreements is lagging.[12]

Apparently, the major powers are now realizing what has been known to developing countries for a long time, namely that sovereignty and international cooperation do not go together automatically. This is especially so now that power politics is losing its effectiveness as the main operating principle of international cooperation due to expanding multipolarity. At the same time, developing countries are increasingly demanding a more effective voice and strengthened agency in matters that concern them, including global affairs (see Lopes and Kararach 2019).

Rising regionalism in the Global South

In contrast to the major-power rivalry at the global level or, perhaps, due to the stifling effect it has on international cooperation, more and more autochthonous regional organizations (ROs) have been formed in the Global South.[13] Their purpose is to further the development of their member states through multilateral cooperation. The model of multilateralism they apply has become known as the model of the Association of South East Asian Nations (ASEAN). According to ASEAN's Charter, multilateral cooperation among the organization's member states should be based on two core principles: "seeking unity in diversity" (Article 2.1) and "mutual respect for each other's sovereignty, territorial integrity, and independence" (Article 2.2). Moreover, multilateralism should be an open process. States are encouraged to reach out to external partners, make their concerns and preferences known but also show tolerance and respect for the views of others and deliver on their international commitments. In other words, regionalism should complement not compete with globalism. That Southern ROs pursue such an open multilateralism is evident from their GPG-related cooperation initiatives. As I have shown elsewhere (Kaul 2021, 15), these initiatives range from protecting member states against negative spill-ins from various types of GPG underprovision, to facilitating members' access to such GPGs as the global knowledge stock or international markets, and supporting the region or subregion in which they operate to contribute its fair share to improving the provision status of select GPGs such as climate change mitigation or preventing open conflict situations in their neighborhood such as military skirmishes in the South China Sea. The autochthonous ROs of the Global South play an important but often overlooked role as intermediaries between the regional and the global levels of governance, filling the void that now exists between global goals and national-level implementation.

What's missing: a persuasive change vision

Lagging institutional adjustment to changing realities has been a well-known, often encountered phenomenon throughout history (North 1990). Undoubtedly, lock-in and path dependency also explain some part of change-avoiding or negating responses of states to the governance requirements of GPGs. Additionally, as van Aaken and Vasel (2019) argue, psychological factors might come into play, notably, factors related to loss aversion.

Loss aversion, in particular aversion against a loss of sovereignty, may play a role in explaining not only the major-power rivalry we are currently witnessing but also the rising regionalism in the Global South and the fact that, in respect to the huge stock of existing multilateral agreements, most states (even the major powers) follow a behavioral pattern of the "business as usual" type. They continue to comply with these agreements in the conventional way, that is, to the extent that individual state and nonstate actors' interests happen to overlap with global concerns. Many times, the overlap is partial at best. As a result, these individual efforts do not amount to what is needed for the concerned underprovided goods to achieve their respective level of adequate provision. States' commitment to the core principle of the present world order, the principle of sovereignty, clearly continues to be strong and impedes more effective multilateralism.[14]

However, states' commitment to sovereignty as such is not the problem. The main impediment is the lack of a persuasive change vision indicating the conditions under which states could freely—as sovereigns—opt for meeting the adequate provision requirements set forth earlier.

Moving forward: introducing long-postponed adjustments in the system of multilateral cooperation

A recurrent idea in Albert O. Hirschman's writings is that, at any point in time, societal systems contain both destructive and constructive forces.[15] It seems that the present policymaking realities corroborate Hirschman's insight. In light of the previous discussion, the constructive forces on which to build further change today include, for one thing, states' commitment to sovereignty and, for another, their continuing commitment to multilateralism as evident from their "business as usual"-type responses to much of the existing stock of global agreements and the rise in multilateralism at the regional level. Drawing on these findings, the next subsection outlines the core elements of what could constitute a persuasive change vision to guide future multilateral cooperation, followed by an exploration of ways to build momentum for change.

The core elements of a change vision

For states to cross the national-interest hurdle that currently limits their engagement in multilateral cooperation and to do so with the support of their various constituencies and allies, two adjustments in the system of multilateral cooperation seem to be critical: consensus on the desirability and feasibility of a new operating principle of multilateralism to guide states' interactions, notably when engaged in processes of universal multilateralism; and second, additional institutional reforms to facilitate states' compliance with this new principle.

Devising a new operating principle calling for mutual compatibility between multilateralism and sovereignty

The main driving forces behind the functioning of multilateral cooperation at present are individual state and nonstate actor interests, pursued either by actors alone or as groups or clubs in multilateral forums of different sizes ranging from mini-multilateral to universal, with no established criteria for determining which type of multilateralism best fits the issue under negotiation. As a result, many global issues are pre-negotiated in groups such as the G7, the BRICS[16] or the G20 before reaching forums of universal multilateralism. A recent case in point are negotiations on a global tax deal to reduce tax competition. In addition, non- or partial compliance with agreements is still a sort of "normal." Thus, for states to be motivated to shift policymaking gears, consensus would need to be forged on introducing a new operating principle of multilateralism, maybe, initially to be applied primarily in high-risk GPG-related policy fields.

The aim of installing such a new operating principle would be to reassure states and their various constituencies and allies that all are committed to making multilateralism sovereignty-compatible and the exercise of sovereignty compatible with multilateral cooperation, not only in a diffuse way but also in concrete ways.

For states to be interested in such a reform and do so with the support of their various constituencies and allies, they would need well-documented proof that, under well-defined conditions, multilateral cooperation is a "good thing" for the country and, with the right domestic policies in place, even a "good thing" for all, current and future generations. As more people now seem to be "mixed-motive" actors, who not only have narrow self-interests in mind but also care about other people and the planet as a whole, states would, furthermore, need reliable data and strong arguments that their country's national policy and the multilateralism they support are not only good for them but also serving global interests.[17]

Therefore, to be recognized by all concerned as being sovereignty-compatible, multilateral cooperation may be expected to meet the following criteria:

- States' engagement is self-determined;
- Cooperation is based on the principle of the sovereign equality of the inter-acting parties and other established principles, such as that of states' common but differentiated responsibilities and respective capacities, as well as respect and tolerance for diversity;
- All parties have access to all official information concerning the substance and process of their negotiations;
- All parties enter the negotiations and decisionmaking processes (at both the policysetting stage and the implementation stage) with willingness to find common ground on which to cooperate and achieve an outcome considered by all concerned as fair, generating across issue areas and over time clear and significant net benefits and, thereby, the proof that, indeed, cooperation "pays" in financial and nonfinancial terms, especially in policy fields marked by interdependence among states.

Regarding the companion commitment to an exercise of sovereignty that is compatible with multilateral cooperation, the new operating principle of multilateralism would need to call on states to abide by the following:

- To consider the "regional" and "global" when making national policy choices, including the sovereignty of other states, notably their freedom to be free from external interference, including potentially harmful but avoidable cross-border spillover effects;
- To make necessary arrangements to contribute their fair share of financial and nonfinancial resources to agreed-upon collective endeavors, which are to be undertaken collectively at the international level as complements of the

domestic corrective measures that states volunteer to implement and, to this end, to support full-cost budgeting of GPG-related projects; and

- To comply with international monitoring, evaluation and reporting requirements in the interest of global transparency, mutual accountability and trust-building among all state and nonstate cooperation partners and stakeholders.

Taken together, the two types of commitments form the core elements of what can be called the "dual-compatibility principle." Assuming states agree to adopt this principle as the new operating principle of multilateralism, it would become possible for all countries, state and nonstate actors actually to have both more secure national sovereignty and more effective multilateral cooperation and, therefore ultimately, more global sustainability.

Introducing complementary institutional reforms

To make a sound case for the adoption of this dual-compatibility principle, further research by, among others, social science, international law and international relations scholars, as well as participatory global conversations and consultations would be needed on issues such as expanding the notion of multilateralism to make it capture both the reality of the relationships among states and the governance choices they make to achieve intended policy goals; considering the legal implications, if any, of the notion of an exercise of sovereignty that considers, as suggested above, not only narrowly defined national interests but also "the regional" and "the global" and this because it is the best way of meeting national interests; and constructing a systematic theory and policy practice of global public economics, including a shared understanding of the concept of GPGs. These are feasible tasks because many relevant building blocks can already be found in the literature, waiting to be synthesized.

Progress along these lines could help policymakers and their various constituencies to see more clearly when and up to what point to engage in interstate rivalry and when in fair and effective international cooperation. Academic failure would compound the political failure, the major-power rivalry we are currently witnessing, if scholars and experts were to continue not to offer advice on how this rivalry can be averted and why universal multilateralism would be the better, more realistic and, therefore, also more effective and efficient way to meet national interests.

As regards organizational reforms that could facilitate the implementation and states' abiding by the new operational principle of multilateralism, one foundational change would be to add global issue management to the governance systems at national and international levels as a new policy field to facilitate, through appropriate platform or networking arrangements, the coming-together of the many varied inputs from numerous public and private actors that the adequate provision of GPGs often requires. Another essential reform to consider would be to systematically integrate autochthonous ROs into the system of global governance as intermediaries between the global level and the national level. This could go a long way toward avoiding risks of overstandardization and making international cooperation more sovereignty-compatible.

Thus, progress toward the suggested vision or narrative of enhanced mutual compatibility between sovereignty and cooperation may sound like a formidable task at first. However, when examined more closely, the needed reform steps appear to be quite doable from a scientific and technical viewpoint. And, as the next subsection indicates, the political demand for change is also growing.

Strengthening the momentum for change

One could consider adopting an approach that has often been used when new ideas had to be introduced into the global policy arena: the establishment of a high-level panel of eminent, internationally renowned, independent personalities to hold worldwide consultations and, based thereon, to offer advice to governments and the international community at large on how to deal with the issue at stake. Ideally, such a panel would be established under the umbrella of the UN, considering it is the UN Charter that has declared the principle of sovereign equality of all states and called on states to come together to solve the problems that no country can solve alone and given that the issue of reinvigorated multilateralism will figure in the follow-up process to the UN75 Declaration and still needs concretization. Moreover, the practice of launching global conversations on major new policy issues is by now quite well-established in the UN (United Nations Development Group 2013).

In addition, states could call for pilot projects to explore how the proposed dual-compatibility principle could work in actual practice. The pilots could be undertaken in high priority areas, such as global clean energy security or global preparedness for meeting health challenges of potentially pandemic scale, such as COVID-19.

Moreover, it seems that the notion of fostering more compatibility between multilateralism and sovereignty appears to be already gaining added policy attention, judging from recent work of the International Monetary Fund on monitoring and assisting policymakers in responding to economic and financial spillovers.[18] Mention can also be made of the collaborative effort of the OECD and the European Commission-Joint Research Centre on understanding the spillovers and the transboundary impacts of national public policies (OECD/EC-JRC 2021).

Conclusion: effective multilateralism—
possible and indispensable

In 1945, UN member states agreed on a collective approach to securing states' national borders to reduce the risk of war. Now, 75 years later, it appears to be time for UN member states to adopt a collective approach to securing national policymaking sovereignty in order to deal with growing interdependence leading to states' relationships characterized by increasing de facto universal multilateralism. The new policymaking reality requires reinvigorated multilateral governance, notably global governance arrangements marked by universal state membership and a new operating principle perhaps modeled along the lines of the dual-compatibility principle suggested in this chapter. Whatever form the new operating principle might ultimately take, it would need to achieve the twin objective of promoting multilateralism that is both sovereignty-compatible and effective in resolving global challenges.

This may sound like a Herculean task. However, as the chapter also shows, the needed reform steps are quite doable and, importantly, the political conditions for the recommended reforms appear to be ripe. These reforms would of course not solve all the risks and challenges we currently confront. However, if acted upon, they could spare us the potentially high human and financial costs of some of the crises looming already on the global policy horizon and bring us closer to the world outlined in Agenda 2030.

Acknowledgments

An earlier version of this chapter was published under the title of "Multilateralism 2.0: It Is Here—Are We Ready for It?" in *Global Perspectives*. The author would like to thank the following reviewers for their comments on this earlier version: Edward Knudsen, Carlos Lopes, Kishore Mahbubani, Michael Zürn, and an anonymous reviewer. Further comments and observations are welcome and can be sent to: contact@ingekaul.net/.

Notes

1 For the full text of Agenda 2030, see https://sustainabledevelopment.un.org/post2015/transformingourworld.

2 Under the present policymaking realities, GPG provision is, of course, a multiactor process. Nevertheless, the spotlight in this chapter is on the behavior of states. The reason is that states and their governmental entities play a special role in aggregating and acting on the interests and preferences of their various national and international constituencies. Nevertheless, the final decision on intergovernmental agreements and, thus, on many global issues is theirs. Their behavior and the thinking and attitudes underlying it are, therefore, of critical importance to issues such as the provision of GPGs and at the center of the analysis of this chapter.

3 Tanzi (1994) already argued for looking at regional and global cooperation aimed at avoiding ruinous tax competition from a public goods perspective. At present, this issue is once again at the center of the global policy debates, although still as a contested issue. See, among others, www.g20.org/third-g20-finance-ministers-and-central-bank-governors-meeting-under-the-italian-presidency.html and www.g24.org/g-24-icrict-event-how-to-get-a-global-tax-deal-that-is-fair-to-the-world/.

4 For a more detailed discussion on GPGs and their governance requirements, including a discussion on why some GPGs, such as the global transportation networks, have

been easier to provide than, for example, climate change mitigation, see Kaul et al. (2016), Barrett (2007), and Sandler (2004).

5 Global norms such as the basic human rights are GPGs that are intended to be rolled out worldwide, so to say, through global public provision, so that, ultimately, they may become global public in consumption.

6 See the Alliance's Declaration of Principles at https://multilateralism.org/.

7 See the remarks by President Biden on America's place in the world, delivered on February 4, 2021, available at www.whitehouse.gov/briefing-room/speeches-remarks/2021/02/04/remarks-by-president-biden-on-americas-place-in-the-world/.

8 See, for example, President Xi Jinping's speech at the virtual 2021 World Economic Forum at https://news.cgtn.com/news/2021-01-25/Full-text-Xi-Jinping-s-speech-at-the-virtual-Davos-Agenda-event-Xln4hwjO2Q/index.html/

9 For the final G7 Summit Communiqué, see www.consilium.europa.eu/media/50361/carbis-bay-g7-summit-communique.pdf/.

10 See, in particular, paragraph 5 of the declaration, the full text of which is available at https://undocs.org/A/RES/75/1/.

11 To illustrate, the 25th COP (Conference of the Parties to the 1992 United Nations Framework Convention on Climate Change) was attended by some 22,000 participants, including government representatives, business, civil society and other groups (https://unfccc.int/sites/default/files/resource/cp_inf4.pdf). According to some estimates, the 26th COP may involve more than 30,000 participants.

12 See, for example, the UN Secretary-General's Annual Nelson Mandela Lecture 2020 at www.nelsonmandela.org/news/entry/annual-lecture-2020-secretary-general-guterress-full-speech?fbclid=IwAR1DzPJMNFGPNnglVb-nOSqaAABr01 15IJnboSdSibhZWjZJ8Ypnm5rlcYk/ and the UN's 2021 report on the sustainable development goals (United Nations 2021).

13 The adjective "autochthonous" denotes ROs that have their roots within the particular region or regions in which they operate as opposed to regional organizations that are regional outposts of global organizations, such as, for example, the regional commissions of the UN. Examples of autochthonous ROs include the Association of South East Asian Nations (ASEAN), South Asian Association for Regional Cooperation (SAARC), the African Union (AU), and the Southern Common Market (MERCOSUR) in Latin America. For overviews of the rising trend toward regionalism in the Global South, see also Acharya (2018), Meyer et al. (2019), and Söderbaum (2016).

14 No doubt, various isolated policy innovations have happened that indicate awareness of GPGs and their governance requirements. For example, a rising number of global funds and programs have been established. Also, monitoring and evaluation of the implementation of international agreements have become a "new normal;" and this not only in the field of development but also in the areas of climate change, finance and security. However, these measures did not change the basic, country-focused, and individual interest-centered approach to international cooperation. For a more detailed discussion on this issue, see Kaul (2017, 2020).

15 See, on this point, the collection of Hirschman essays in Adelman (2015).

16 The abbreviation BRICS refers a group of emerging market economies, including Brazil, Russia, India, China, and South Africa.

17 See, on this point, among others, CIVICUS (2020).

18 See www.imf.org/en/Topics/Comprehensive-Surveillance-Review.

References

Aaken, Anne and Johann Justus Vasel. 2019. "Demultilateralization: A Cognitive Psychological Perspective." *European Law Journal*, 25: 487–493.

Acharya, Amitav. 2018. *The End of American World Order*. Cambridge, UK: Polity Press.

Adelman, Jeremy, ed. 2015. *The Essential Hirschman*. 2nd edition. Princeton, NJ: Princeton University Press.

Aghion, Philippe, Céline Antonin, and Simon Bunel. 2021. *The Power of Creative Destruction; Economic Upheaval and the Wealth of Nations*. Cambridge, MA and London: The Belknap Press of Harvard University Press.

Anghel, Suzana. 2020. "Strategic Sovereignty for Europe." European Parliamentary Research Service (EPRS) Ideas Paper. Brussels: European Parliament.

Barrett, Scott. 2007. *Why Cooperate? The Incentive to Supply Global Public Goods*. Oxford, UK: Oxford University Press.

Christensen, Clayton M. 2016. *The Innovator's Dilemma: When New Technologies Cause Great Firms to Fail*. Cambridge, MA: Harvard Business Review Press.

CIVICUS. 2020. *State of Civil Society Report 2020*. Johannesburg: CIVICUS.

Haas, Richard. 2017. *A World in Disarray*. New York: Penguin Books.

IRENA (International Renewable Energy Agency). 2019. *A New World.: The Geopolitics of the Energy Transformation*. Abu Dhabi: IRENA.

Kaul, Inge. 2017. "Providing Global Public Goods: What Role for the Multilateral Development Banks?" ODI Report. London: Overseas Development Institute.

Kaul, Inge. 2020. "Redesigning International Co-operation Finance for Global Resilience." In OECD (Ed), *Development Co-operation Report 2020: Learning from Crises, Building Resilience*. Paris: OECD Publishing.

Kaul, Inge. 2021. "Enhancing the Provision of Global Public Goods: Ready for More Realism?" Policy Brief 10. New York: UNDP Regional Bureau for Asia and the Pacific.

Kaul, Inge, Donald Blondin and Neva Nahtigal. 2016. "Understanding Global Public Goods: Where We Are and Where to Next." In Inge Kaul (ed.). *Global Public Goods. The International Library of Critical Writings in Economics*, xii–xcii. Cheltenham: Edward Elgar.

Lopes, Carlos and George Kararach. 2019. *Misperceptions, New Narratives and Development in the 21st Century*. Abingdon, Oxon and New York: Routledge.

Mahbubani, Kishore. 2020. *Has China Won?* New York: Public Affairs.

Meyer, Thomas, José Luis de Sales Marques, and Mario Telò, eds. 2019. *Regionalism and Multilateralism; Politics, Economics, Culture*. London: Routledge.

North, Douglas. 1990. *Institutions, Institutional Change and Economic Performance. Political Economy of Institutions and Decisions*. Cambridge: Cambridge University Press.

OECD/EC-JRC. (2021). *Understanding the Spillovers and Transboundary Impacts of Public Policies: Implementing the 2030 Agenda for More Resilient Societies*. Paris: OECD Publishing, https://doi.org/10.1787/862c0db7-en.

Roberts, Anthea, Henrique C. Moraes, and Victor Ferguson. 2019. "Toward a Geoeconomic Order in International Trade and Investment". *Journal of International Economic Law*, 22(4): 655–676.

Sandler, Todd. 2004. *Collective Global Action*. Cambridge: Cambridge University Press.

Söderbaum, Frederik. 2016. *Rethinking Regionalism*, 1st edition. London: Palgrave Macmillan.

Tanzi, Vito. 1994. *Taxation in an Integrating World*. Washington, DC: The Brookings Institution.

United Nations. 2021. *The Sustainable Development Goals Report 2021*. New York: United Nations.

United Nations Development Group. 2013. *The Global Conversation Begins: Emerging Views for a New Development Agenda*. New York: United Nations Development Group.

12

DO WE STILL NEED A POLITICAL VISION IN A GLOBALIZED WORLD?

Michael Zürn

The list of humanity's urgent problems is long, and it seems to get even longer every year. At the time of writing this piece, the forest fires in California make utterly clear how urgent the problem of climate change is. The spread of COVID-19 shows us all how important and challenging it is to prevent and control global pandemics. The video-sharing service TikTok exemplifies the imperative need to establish public controls for digital giants and, simultaneously, prevent trade wars. Many other problems such as global poverty, migration, and the diffusion of highly destructive technologies are currently less in focus, but they are as critical as the ones already mentioned. A book about such key or primary problems of world society and humanity is urgently needed, but it could easily become a very long one.

Political scientists are mainly concerned about institutions—about political institutions, to be more precise. Political institutions are all those that involve some element of collective decision-making on public issues and problems (Easton 1965; Hay 2007). As a political scientist, I do not want to add to the long list of primary challenges to humanity, but wish to instead shift the perspective by asking about the appropriateness of political institutions in providing satisfactory responses to these global challenges. This shift away from primary challenges brings us to second- and third-order challenges of world society.

Second-order challenges point to institutional deficits that hinder the prevention or the successful handling of urgent first-order problems. For instance, if a company does not have any research and development unit, it is hardly prepared to handle the otherwise relatively easy problem of adjusting its products to new developments. There is overwhelming evidence that the global institutional landscape is indeed not well prepared to solve global first-order problems such as climate change, pandemics, and the instability of financial markets. Moreover, the politics of global institutions is much more complicated than establishing a research and development unit within a company. Modern international institutions exist, and they often exercise political authority in their own right, partially intervening deeply in the affairs of national societies. At the same time, international institutions appear often as too weak to, for instance, regulate international financial markets or to effectively combat climate change and its impacts. The current global governance system is too weak to develop solutions with bite and too strong to create legitimacy beliefs on the side of those who favor national sovereignty. This creates a second-order problem of the lack of proper global institutions.

Even more fundamentally, in order to bring about a successful change, there is need for ideas and a vision of what an appropriate institutional order would look like and how it could be established. We know that it has to be less than a world-state but more than just a system of territorial states. This observation leads us to a third-order problem: the lack of a compelling vision of an appropriate institutional set-up in global politics. Without such a vision, a company without a research department would be lost. Executives know what a successful company with a vital research and development unit should look like—they do not have a third-order problem. The predicament of the current global governance system is that, while second-order problems point to cases of institutional defects, third-order problems point to situations in which actors are out of ideas and a vision of what problem-solving institutions should look like in order to bring about an effective and legitimate global governance system. Without such a vision, we will not find the way to a world that is doing better in solving global first-order problems such as climate change, pandemics, and the instability of financial markets.

In the remainder of the chapter, I highlight this absence of compelling visions of how political institutions can be effective *and* democratic in handling globalization problems. The emphasis here is on "compelling visions." Political institutions always were deficient in that they were hardly fully effective or democratic. Even if we know a perfect collective solution to a problem, the political process most often produces outcomes that deviate from the optimum in terms of effectiveness. For a policy to succeed in a democracy, it requires compromises that often reduce effectiveness. At the same time, even at the heyday of liberal democracy in the Western world, Robert Dahl (1971) used the term "polyarchy" to describe real-world democracies to highlight the distance to the democratic ideal. Political institutions, therefore, never have matched ideal theory. During the prime of liberal democracies, their problem-solving capacity was limited, and the process of making decisions approached democratic ideals at best. Yet the current predicament goes deeper. We lack a compelling vision of ideal political institutions for handling global problems such as climate change.

In order to develop this argument, I start by setting two criteria for a compelling vision of ideal political institutions in the first section. I then argue that the two currently most crucial institutional visions do not qualify as "compelling." I conclude by suggesting that these weaknesses on both sides of the debate contribute to pessimism and polarization, thus making the predicament worse. For these reasons, I argue that third-order problems in world society exacerbate first-order problems.

The gap

Political institutions need to be effective in terms of their problem-solving capacity, and their decisions need to be normatively justifiable. In political science speak, this means that they need to be effective and legitimate. Both effectiveness and democratic justifiability depend on a prerequisite: the congruence of social and political spaces (Held 1995). Congruence can be considered as a precondition for both effectiveness and legitimacy. In the first place, the congruence principle is based on the normative idea that those who are affected by political decisions must also be involved in the decision-making process. Both Robert Dahl (1989) and Jürgen Habermas (1996) view the right of participation of those affected as the core of democracy. According to them, one of the nation-state's historical achievements was to translate the abstract principle of being affected into the concrete principle of membership in a territorially determined community. In the second place, congruence is necessary for effectiveness. If decisions affect only part of those whose behavior causes the problem, policies will most likely be ineffective. The social space needing regulation thus should not be smaller than the relevant political space. As long as social transactions and interactions took place within nation-state borders (Deutsch 1969), the nation-state represented a potentially effective framework within which the democratic principle could be institutionalized.

However, this connection between the nation-state and the democratic principle is dissolving with globalization and digitalization. As a result of these two megatrends, social spaces become de-territorialized. To the extent that the economic and social space for action extends beyond nation-state borders and even takes place independently of space in a virtual environment, a problem arises: the subject of legitimate and effective decision-making disintegrates, or even dissolves. The effective and democratically legitimate regulation of societies thus depends on the congruence of social and political space. If economic and cultural spaces of transaction push out of the political boundaries of the nation-state, the institutional dominance of territorially limited nation-states becomes normatively deficient. The divergence of spaces must then be counteracted by either a de-territorialization of politics or a re-territorialization of society. To put it in more general terms, "[t]he more the complexity of society and the problems to be regulated politically increases, the less it seems possible to hold fast to the demanding idea of democracy, according to which the addressees of law should also be its authors" (Habermas 2013, 67).

The problem unfolds for both criteria: effectiveness and legitimacy. Today's world is so closely networked that, in view of the state of globalization and digitalization, many transnational problems can be effectively addressed only beyond the nation-state. The problem is also evident in terms of legitimacy. In a denationalized world, many decisions at the national level give rise to externalities and thus affect people regardless of whether they are involved in the state's procedures through membership. At least in areas in which transactions and their effects are largely globalized such as financial markets and climate change, national decisions blatantly violate the principle of being affected (e.g., every person that is affected by the climate policies of the US, China, and the European Union (EU)). Against this background, it seems necessary to develop new visions and blueprints for ideal political institutions; that is, for political institutions that can at least potentially be effective and legitimate. What is needed are either powerful global institutions that can provide for global collective goods, or a re-scaling of the problems so that the nation-state can become the major site of politics again.

The limits of cosmopolitanism and communitarianism[1]

Against the backdrop of de-territorialization, the debate between communitarianism and cosmopolitanism is the most relevant in searching for normative visions that fulfill the two criteria of effectiveness and legitimacy in times of globalization and digitalization.

Communitarianism, like cosmopolitanism, is a noble political philosophy in the first place. According to the communitarian conviction, a strong democracy cannot be realized in large, heterogeneous, and territorially open spaces, but is rather linked to the concrete social lives of people within a community. Such delimitation is especially necessary for the acceptance of majority decisions by minorities. The political sphere is currently dominated by an adaptation of communitarianism that places the nation and the nation-state as the bearer of popular sovereignty at the center, while sharply limiting the group that is considered to be "the people." This is the program of the authoritarian populists. They can be regarded as nationalist descendants of communitarian philosophy. They won their electoral successes because of their struggle against European integration, against globalization, against multiculturalism, and against migration. They claim that only a more homogeneous society with sufficient interpersonal trust and national identity can develop into a community based on solidarity. In such a community, it is then necessary to implement the will of the majority.

In most cases, the unconditional endorsement of majority decisions is illiberal, but it is also anti-pluralistic and anti-procedural (Schäfer und Zürn 2021). Not only does it place majority decisions above minority and individual basic rights, but it also disregards established procedures for determining the will of the majority. All those who are critical of the "silent majority" are condemned as members of an alienated and selfish elite, which is also accused of controlling the media and public opinion. Established procedures for deliberation and consensus-building are used by the "corrupt elites" as a means of political paternalism. The antidote would then be the wisdom of the leaders of new parties and movements. In extreme cases, those who know what the "average person" wants will be freed from the usual standards of political decency, as former US President Donald Trump, with his impressively stable support, has shown in large segments of the US population.

This illiberal and anti-pluralist version is by no means the only relevant political manifestation of communitarian theories. Although communitarians refer to the concrete context of concrete communities, they do not necessarily have to be illiberal. They can also take the form of a strong grassroots democracy, as portrayed in Benjamin Barber's (1994) work, or of a liberal-communitarian republicanism, as depicted in Charles Taylor's (1992) work, which combines the idea of a "right to rights" with a communitarian obligation to the common good. Calhoun (2002) complements Taylor by criticizing cosmopolitanism for underestimating the capacity of national identities and borders to promote solidarity and democracy. Taylor (1992) and Calhoun (2002) thus point to a way to reconcile liberalism and communitarianism while avoiding two pitfalls: reactionary traditionalism and chauvinist nationalism on the one hand, and deregulating global capitalism on the other.

However, all variants of communitarian theory of democracy have a common weakness. Their defense of the procedures and institutions of the democratic nation-state is based primarily on local and national communities rather than on the principle of being affected in a globalized and de-territorialized world. To the extent that the decisions of democratic nation-states in times of political and social denationalization increasingly affect people outside their borders and their effectiveness depends on decisions made elsewhere, democratic procedures within nation-states and democratic principles are no longer identical for two reasons. For one, citizens are, to a certain extent, dominated by political decisions over which they have little influence. And second, democracy presupposes the concept of effective decision-making—that is, the idea that political decisions are means by which collectives can control themselves. Yet, the effectiveness of national regulations tends to decline in times of globalization and digitalization.

This connection may also explain why the illiberal and anti-pluralist version of communitarian thought became so successful. When social and political spaces diverge, there seem to be only two possible reactions. One of them is a cosmopolitan response; the other is to close borders, reduce heterogeneity within society, and cultivate a strong nationalism. In a globalized and deeply pluralistic world, the nationalistic defense of predetermined communities seems to lead, to some extent, necessarily to anti-liberal, anti-procedural, and anti-pluralist thinking—as is already the case in contemporary Hungary and Poland. The interplay between the rejection of supranational competence beyond the nation-state, on the one hand, and closed borders (for goods, capital, and people) and the general preference of majority decisions over minority and individual fundamental rights, on the other, is not accidental. There seems to be a kind of elective affinity. Therefore, it is not surprising that authoritarian populist parties are the most visible manifestation of communitarianism that we can currently observe in Western democracies (including Eastern Europe as well as many emerging countries) and their party systems.

This elective affinity between communitarianism and authoritarian populism brings cosmopolitanism into play. Cosmopolitanism pits a global vision against nationalist political forces. Cosmopolitans are always subject to suspicions of utopianism. The core idea of cosmopolitan democracy is the democratization of international institutions. According to Archibugi, this involves the "globalization of democracy and simultaneously the democratization of globalization" (2004, 438). Cosmopolitans demand the transfer of sovereign rights to international organizations and supranational regimes even if they do not represent the vision of a democratic world government, a world parliament, or a global civil society (Archibugi 2008; Caney 2005). They plead for transfers of competence to the United Nations and the EU. They opt for free trade agreements and the International Monetary Fund, for world climate conferences and a fiscal union in the Eurozone, and for strong human rights regimes at the global level and institutions that make global redistribution possible. All of this requires the parallel democratization of these institutions.

Irrespective of the strength of the normative appearance of cosmopolitan theories of democracy, their weaknesses lie in their implementation. The concretization of their general principles into specific procedures and institutions is underdeveloped. Two objections are particularly relevant here. First, while it is true that many social, economic, and political decisions have a cross-border impact, it is also true that they are not always easy to understand. But the definition of a threshold value with respect to the extent of externalities that is necessary for having a say in the decision-making process appears mostly arbitrary (threshold question). Secondly, even if an agreement were reached on the necessary international institutions, it would appear extremely difficult to organize appropriate democratic processes at the global level (feasibility question).

To begin with the threshold question, human action and political decisions regularly generate externalities. This means that the decisions individuals make always influence other individuals, just as the decisions of a collective affect other collectives. Given this complexity, it is difficult to answer who is affected by which decision in a specific environment. It is a comparatively clear case that the inhabitants of Pacific island states, who lose their homes as a result of the climate policies of the major industrialized countries, should have had a say in climate policy—looking at it from a normative perspective. But how much does a person or a group have to be affected to be able to have a say in the many gray areas of more or less interdependence? If, for example, the Chinese government decides to invest in computer technology, this could have an impact on jobs in India or Silicon Valley. However, such externalities cannot automatically justify a right of co-decision in China's economic policy.

This raises the questions of which institutions can decide what and on what basis, who is affected by a national decision, and who is part of a cross-border community of affected persons. Should the other countries have the same voting weight in decision-making as the country deciding in the first instance? Which institutions should decide, and according to which procedures? These are unresolved normative and procedural questions that show that the "principle of affectedness" cannot easily be translated into concrete procedures for politics in world society.

Added to this is the problem of feasibility. If one takes seriously the extreme variant of the principle of being affected, one would have to conclude that the rest of the world must always be given a say in the decisions made by the US, since their decisions have far-reaching effects on the entire world. This demand may be justifiable in normative terms, but it is politically meaningless, since the most powerful states often strongly oppose the transfer of sovereign rights across national borders. The US, China, and Russia are less prepared to curtail their sovereignty than are middle powers like France, Germany, and Canada. One can even say *ceteris paribus* that the more powerful a country is, the less it wants to cede its sovereign rights to international or supranational organizations (Zürn 2018, Chapter 3).

Cosmopolitans are aware of these implementation problems. Therefore, they focus on the establishment and democratization of joint international decisions on global problems. However, here, too, democratic implementation problems arise. The larger and more complex political spaces are, the less they can be governed democratically. Processes that promote democracy—such as the equal participation of citizens, the transparency and predictability of political decisions, the control of the legislative branch, or the vertical and horizontal interlocking of power—can be implemented far less convincingly beyond the nation-state.

The cosmopolitan answer to the feasibility problem is twofold. First, it is argued that the arguments for a size limit on democracy cannot be empirically proven. Thus, Koenig-Archibugi (2012) questions the necessary preconditions for democracy and concludes that, apart from the existence of formal political structures, there are no necessary preconditions in the strict sense of the term. He thus rejects all the theses on the impossibility of global democracy and argues that political communities are constructed and that they change over time. Furthermore, the idea of national affiliation itself did not develop until the late eighteenth and nineteenth centuries. It is asked whether the feasibility of this idea might not increase over time if the current trends of communicative and economic de-territorialization continue. According to this perspective, neither individual attitudes nor patterns of political mobilization correspond to the model of the nation-state any longer.

Regardless of this debate, cosmopolitans tend to underestimate the tension between the argument in favor of global political action and the social preconditions for democracies. They stress the liberal elements of democratic self-determination, in particular, the need to protect individual rights, the rule of law, and the power of the better argument (see also Crawford Ames, Chapter 3 in this volume). In doing so, they seem to forget that majority decisions are at the core of democratic processes and that minority rights make no sense without majority decisions. They also partly overlook the fact that, in international institutions, the executive often holds an advantageous position over the legislative, thus undermining the principle of separation of powers. Thus, they seem to adhere to an understanding of democracy that devalues the role of elections, parties, and parliaments and emphasizes the position of non-majoritarian institutions. This implicit understanding of democracy confirms the tendency for liberal globalists to be biased in favor of the elitists. It is the fear of the success of this cosmopolitanism that has enabled the rise of authoritarian populists and the call for majorities. Authoritarian populism, in turn, endangers the liberal foundations of and the democratic process in political systems. As a result, both concepts appear to be deficient in shaping an effective and legitimate global governance system. The lack of compelling visions is the dilemma of democracy in the age of de-territorialization.

Need for a global vision

Instead of political visions with mobilizing potential, we seem to live in a world characterized by a cleavage between communitarian and cosmopolitan political forces. These strands of thought about effective and legitimate political institutions come across as either technocratic or backward-oriented, both displaying significant weaknesses in a de-territorialized world society. They do not provide an institutional ideal that puts us in a good position to tackle all the fundamental problems of world society discussed in this global book.

As a result, there is little hope that things will get better. The whole idea of progress depends on a vision that tells us where to go so that we can move on. In most of the consolidated democracies, huge majorities of people do not believe that their children will have a better and easier life. Without vision, there is no hope or positive scenario of the future. Without a notion of progress, the steps necessary to tackle the first-order problems of world society will not be taken. Moreover, the lack of vision does not translate into a prevalence of humility, pragmatism, or moderation. On the contrary, the weakness of the other side seems to lead to radicalization on both sides, that is, to increasing polarization. This makes the search for appropriate governance in a de-territorialized world additionally demanding. To the extent that effectiveness and legitimacy depend on and reinforce each other, we seem to be in the midst of a downward spiral. The new cleavage seems to undermine the legitimacy of policies by both cosmopolitan and communitarian institutions. This predicament in world society does not bode well for the management of first-order problems. We need to develop new visions of an ideal institutional set-up of collective decision-making in world society.

What could such a vision look like? The option of re-nationalizing societies to the extent that externalities are significantly reduced seems to be structurally impossible. A thought experiment could help here: even if it would be possible to return to the international political regulation arrangements of the 1970s, the degree of economic interdependence with new markets would still be enormous today. The development of technology would still have an incredible role in increasing externalities. Climate change would remain a global problem, so would the battle against the pandemic. It would still be necessary to regulate financial markets and digital companies. Last but not least, knowledge about the world's interdependence would still have increased. Inevitably, we would know more about global interconnectedness and its externalities, which alone makes it additionally challenging to think about a future confined within national borders. We live in a world society that cannot be brought back to independent national societies by political decisions.

The alternative of democratizing international institutions would be enormously difficult, drawn out, and the subject of strong national resistance, but it is not structurally impossible (Koenig-Archibugi 2012). The first step would require opening decision-making in international institutions to public debates. The advocates of international institutions would have to leave the political defensive and argue for a cosmopolitan world view openly, offensively, and pro-actively. The widespread tendency to agree on sensible regulations at the international level and then present them at home as having no alternative may be the simplest strategy in the short term. In the long run, however, it is harmful because it prevents genuine social debates and a public, open-ended debate on world politics. Representation thrives on justification, and democracy on open competition of ideas. Ultimately, there can be no half-baked cosmopolitanism that shifts decision-making to the global level while curbing democratic debate within the national framework.

If international institutions are to be part of public debates, a second step becomes possible: a discussion about a democratic vision of international institutions. There is no blueprint for democratic international institutions, and global experts cannot impose such a vision. It requires the participation of both communitarians and cosmopolitans to develop it.

Note

1 This section is based on Merkel and Zürn (2019).

References

Archibugi, Daniele. 2004. "Cosmopolitan Democracy and its Critics: A Review." *European Journal of International Relations*, 10(3): 437–473.

Archibugi, Daniele. 2008. *The Global Commonwealth of Citizens: Toward Cosmopolitan Democracy*. Princeton, NJ: Princeton University Press.

Barber, Benjamin. 1994. *Starke Demokratie. Über die Teilhabe am Politischen*. Hamburg: Rotbuch Verlag.

Calhoun, Craig. 2002. "The Class Consciousness of Frequent Travelers: Toward a Critique of Actually Existing Cosmopolitanism." *The South Atlantic Quarterly*, 101: 869–897.

Caney, Simon. 2005. *Justice Beyond Borders: A Global Political Theory.* Oxford: Oxford University Press.

Dahl, Robert A. 1971. *Polyarchy. Participation and Opposition.* New Haven: Yale University Press.

Dahl, Robert A. 1989. *Democracy and Its Critics.* New Haven/London: Yale University Press.

Deutsch, Karl. 1969. *Nationalism and Its Alternatives.* New York: Alfred Knopf.

Easton, David. 1965. *A Framework for Political Analysis.* Englewood Cliffs: Prentice-Hall.

Held, David. 1995. *Democracy and the Global Order. From the Modern State to Cosmopolitical Governance.* Cambridge, UK: Polity Press.

Habermas, Jürgen. 1996. *Faktizität und Geltung: Beiträge zur Diskurstheorie des Rechts und des demokratischen Rechtsstaats.* 5th edition. Frankfurt am Main: Suhrkamp.

Habermas, Jürgen. 2013. *Im Sog der Technokratie.* Berlin: Suhrkamp.

Hay, Colin. 2007. *Why We Hate Politics.* Cambridge: Polity Press.

Koenig-Archibugi, Mathias. 2012. "Global Democracy and Domestic Analogies." In Daniele Archibugi, Mathias Koenig-Archibugi und Raffaele Marchetti (eds.). *Global Democracy: Normative and Empirical Perspectives*, 160–182. Cambridge, New York: Cambridge University Press.

Merkel, Wolfgang and Michael Zürn. 2019. "Conclusion: The Defects of Cosmopolitan and Communitarian Democracy." In Pieter de Wilde et al. (eds.). *The Struggle Over Borders*, 207–238. Cambridge, UK: Cambridge University Press.

Schäfer, Armin and Michael Zürn. 2021. *Die demokratische Regression.* Berlin: Suhrkamp.

Taylor, Charles. 1992. *The Ethics of Authenticity.* Cambridge, MA: Harvard University Press.

Zürn, Michael. 2018. *A Theory of Global Governance. Authority, Legitimacy, and Contestation.* Oxford: Oxford University Press.

13

HAS COVID CHANGED THE FINANCIAL SYSTEM FOR GOOD (OR ILL)?

Howard Davies

Since 2008 almost all discussions on the future of finance have started with the Great Financial Crisis (GFC) which began in that year. In *Can financial markets be controlled?* (Davies 2015) I summarized the state of the debate at that time. Broadly, it was accepted that the reforms led by the Financial Stability Board (FSB), under the auspices of the Group of 20 (G20), had corrected some of the most obvious flaws revealed in the turmoil of 2008–2009. Banks were obliged to hold far larger capital reserves, some three or four times as big as in 2008, making them far less likely to collapse if asset prices fell and loan defaults rose. The off balance sheet vehicles which had allowed banks to hide some of their liabilities had been outlawed by regulators. Transparency rules in capital markets had been overhauled. Insurance company regulation had been tightened, with far tougher solvency rules in place. The Basel Committee and other international regulatory bodies had seen their membership expanded to cover China and other emerging markets, enhancing their legitimacy and coverage. And the FSB, reinforced with stronger political support, sat above the regulators with a remit to identify emerging threats to stability.

So far, so good. But there were also obvious weaknesses and lacunae:

- Credit creation had moved from the banking system to various forms of shadow banks. Regulators could be caricatured as playing a version of financial whack-a-mole. Whenever regulations were imposed to restrict leverage, it reappeared in a less regulated part of the forest;
- The US' regulatory system remained a balkanized mess: a complex set of bodies with overlapping responsibilities and no central coordination. One could have no confidence that the true risks in the US system were being properly addressed. A report prepared by The Volcker Alliance, which was founded by former Federal Reserve Chairman Paul Volcker, described it,

even after the extensive Dodd-Frank reforms, as "highly fragmented, out-dated and ineffective" (The Volcker Alliance 2015, 1);

- International monetary cooperation was weak. According to Eichengreen (2016, 21) it "displayed elements of order and disorder." The US Federal Reserve, whose actions are decisive in determining financial conditions across the globe, paid little attention to the impact of their decisions on financial markets elsewhere (Ogier and Rowley 2014);
- The fundamental bias in the tax systems of all major economies in favor of debt financing (interest charges may be offset against tax, while dividend payments may not be) had not been addressed (De Mooij 2011). So the conditions for a further rise in debt were in place;
- In Europe, in particular, while the introduction of the banking union had rebuilt some confidence in the regulatory oversight of the banking system, the Union was incomplete. Without a common deposit protection scheme, banks in vulnerable countries could be threatened by a bank run, and the mechanisms for lender-of-last-resort support lacked a firm legal base. As a result, the single financial market had broken down, with the European Central Bank (ECB) left to manage the interbank market itself;
- The financial system had been stabilized by massive central bank intervention: low interest rates and massive quantitative easing programs. Even so, economic recovery remained sluggish, especially in Europe, and it was not clear that the central banks had sufficient firepower in reserve to cope with a new crisis, if one emerged in the near term.

To say that this shorthand assessment represented a consensus view would be to overstate the case. There were those, in the official sector at least, who presented a more positive view of the impact of the post-crisis reforms (Carney 2019), while some "hawks" maintained that bank capital should be even stronger, with banks required to hold reserves amounting to 25% of their liabilities if not more (Admati and Hellwig 2013). Others advocated a more fundamental repositioning of the financial system to restore it to the position of a servant rather than the master of the real economy, echoing Winston Churchill's desire, expressed in 1925, that "finance should be less proud and industry more content." In *The Value of Everything*, for example, Mariana Mazzucato (2018) argues that unless the financialization of the real economy is arrested, there will be continued instability.

Through to the end of 2019 these debates ebbed and flowed. Regulators and banks declared a temporary truce on bank capital. The Basel Committee came to adopt what we might describe as an Augustinian approach. Perhaps, in an ideal world, more capital should be required—but not yet. The risk of provoking a credit crunch if banks were required to hold higher reserves was seen as potentially dangerous. The data showed that in an environment of low interest rates and depressed profitability some banks, especially in Europe, had achieved a higher capital ratio more by reducing lending than by raising new equity (Cohen

2013). Regulators reassured themselves by conducting stress tests of banks' portfolios to understand if and how they could survive a sharp downturn without breaching the minimum requirements for staying in business. Across Europe and North America banks were deemed to have passed these rigorous tests.

On the monetary side central banks maintained that they retained the ability to react to a downturn. Even though the typical monetary response to recessions since World War II has been a reduction in interest rates of some five percentage points, and rates were not above 2% in the US, and barely positive in the European Union (EU), at the end of 2019, the Fed and ECB argued that there was still more they could do, especially in terms of expanding their asset purchases, without entering into the radical territory of monetary financing of government deficits.

Such was the financial background against which the novel coronavirus made its appearance in Wuhan.

The COVID-19 crisis did not emerge in the financial sector, as its 2008 predecessor clearly did. Indeed the then head of Bafin, the German regulator, asserted that "this time banks are part of the solution, not the problem" (Frind 2020). We will never know whether those who forecast a renewed bout of financial instability arising from what they saw as the continued fragility of the banking system, or from the excesses of the shadow banking, would have been proved right or wrong in the end. But while banks cannot realistically be accused of precipitating this crisis they will inevitably be affected by it, and the state of the financial sector will influence the transmission through the economy of the massive demand and supply shocks in the COVID-19 crisis.

In the language of bank regulation we might characterize COVID-19 as an extremely severe stress test. In the last pre-crisis Bank of England stress test on UK banks, in 2019, they were required to model the impact on their lending portfolios and deposit funding of a severe recession. The main parameters of the test were that GDP would fall by 5%, unemployment would double, house and equity prices would fall by 30%, and short-term interest rates would rise 4%. (Similarly severe stresses have been used by the Federal Reserve and the European Banking Authority.) Banks argued that this extreme scenario was highly unlikely ever to appear, but the COVID-19 pandemic proved them wrong. The last feature on the list—a sharp interest rate rise—is unlikely in the foreseeable future, but the economic hit from COVID-19 was even more severe in the short term. Government loan guarantees, not built into the regulatory stress test, will partially offset the cost to the banks of bad debt, but the net impact of those support schemes on banks will still be negative over time, perhaps quite strongly so. The banks pay for the government guarantee and will incur costs trying to recover defaulted loans.

The immediate short-term impact of the crisis on the financial sector was to generate large paper losses for most banks and insurers, in part driven by the new accounting standard, IFRS9, which mandates accelerated provisioning. Not all banks were affected equally. Market volatility and the need for

businesses to find ways of protecting themselves against new types of risk created new opportunities for investment banks. But for most commercial banks
that upside will not offset the losses they will incur on corporate lending as
bankruptcies emerge and on unsecured personal lending as unemployment
rises. The prospect of continued very low or even negative interest rates rubs
salt into the wounds.

The long-term consequences remain uncertain. We do not yet know the full
economic impact of the most recent crisis. For a time, debate swirled around the
letter we might use to describe it. Would it be a V, with a sharp upturn quickly
reversing the early GDP losses? Or perhaps a W, with a second trough, but again
followed by a robust bounce back? Or a U, where we wallow for a while and then
recover, as people take time to adjust to new ways of working to accommodate
the continued prevalence of the virus? Or maybe an L, where the effect on productive capacity, and on the propensity to spend, is long-lasting and we settle at a
lower level of prosperity for a considerable time? Or even a K, in which different
parts of the economy are affected very differently: some up, some down?

But with every possible health warning about the dangers of peering through
a glass darkly, I will offer some speculative thoughts about the longer-term
impacts as I see them in mid-2021. They are in three categories: (1) certainties,
(2) probabilities, and (3) big unknowns.

Certainties

The first certainty is that there will be a huge and sustained increase in public sector debt. The governments of all the major economies have decided that
they must support the private sector during the lockdown period and beyond, in
some cases with payments directly to households, and in others through employment support or grants and guaranteed loans to employers. There have been
lively debates about the best route to take, but the financial outcomes for the
governments are similar. Debt to GDP ratios will rise, almost everywhere. The
US government forecast in February 2020 that its net borrowing in the second
quarter of 2020 would be very slightly negative. They expected a very small
general government surplus. By early May their estimate was of a borrowing
requirement of almost US$3 trillion, an astonishing turnaround (McCormick
and Mohsin 2020). The Biden administration decided in early 2021 to go even
further, with large discretionary payments to individuals, which alarmed Larry
Summers (Wolf 2021) and others and stoked inflationary fears.

These deficits, and the relative scale is similar in Europe and Japan, have
been financed at very low interest rates, so the current debt interest burden is
manageable in the near term. Much of the financing is in practice provided by
the central banks, who have become the government debt buyers of first resort.
The consequences will vary from country to country, partly depending on the
starting point. The US debt to GDP ratio has risen from 81% to well over 100%.
The UK entered the crisis period at 89% and is now also over 100%. Italy began

2020 with a government debt to GDP ratio of 135%, so has moved into territory normally only explored in the aftermath of costly wars.

Emerging markets, heavily dependent on external financing of their deficits, will be especially challenged, if their COVID-19 outbreaks are as severe and long-lasting as those in the richer countries. There are already calls for debt forgiveness. It is highly likely that a lot of forbearance will be needed. According to Eichengreen (2020), "More than $100 billion of financial capital has flowed out of these markets—three times as much as in the first two months of the 2008 financial crisis." He argues for a new Brady Plan "in which debts rendered unsustainable through no fault of the borrowers are written down and converted into new instruments."

We will discuss the longer-term consequences of this massive increase in public sector debt later.

The second certainty is that debt will rise sharply in the private sector too. Government support programs for businesses are heavily based on the provision of cheap credit. The rationale was based on the notion of a V-shaped recovery and the need to provide a bridge across the V for firms which, in the normal way, are viable. Even if the recovery is robust there will be many more heavily indebted firms in the future, and if the downturn is more prolonged there will be many companies with a debt burden they will find it hard to sustain. That in turn will result in more bankruptcies, whose impact will be most strongly felt in the banking system, unless more equity can be found to substitute for the debt. There will be opportunities for private equity firms, where they have the appetite, but governments will also come under pressure to construct equity-like investments to replace the increased debt. The penal capital treatment of equity holdings by banks make them unlikely candidates for the provision of that support, unless regulators have a change of heart. I discuss that issue further below.

A consequential certainty is that there will be many corporate debt downgrades effected by the credit rating agencies; indeed the process started in 2020. That will be a challenge for institutional investors, who will find themselves unintentionally holding non-investment grade debt and who may need to adjust their risk appetites as a result.

Another certainty is that more financial services will be provided digitally. Although most bank branches remained open through the crisis, customers were understandably reluctant to visit them. Many older customers previously resistant to online or mobile banking have become converted. The same is true in insurance and asset management. This will, quite quickly, have significant consequences for costs and employment in financial firms.

Probabilities

In the banking system the strongest, best capitalized banks seem reasonably well placed at present to survive the crisis, unless it is more severe than even the gloomiest forecasters assumed in 2020 (Beck 2020). All the large UK banks survived the 2019 stress test.

But there are banks elsewhere in Europe, in particular, whose capital is not as strong. If loan defaults rise very sharply some bank balance sheets will be put under severe pressure, and they may fall below their regulatory minimum, which would trigger recovery and resolution plans. Regulators have responded to this deteriorating outlook by using the macroprudential tools introduced after the GFC, in particular the additional buffers imposed when credit conditions are judged to be excessively loose. Those additional capital buffers have been withdrawn in the crisis, thus reducing the regulatory minimum a bank must hold.

But some banks may nonetheless find themselves close to the threshold. In those cases, I would expect to see attempts to raise more equity capital, which will be very challenging, and probably some consolidation. One key difference in this crisis is that banks have all been required to prepare recovery and resolution plans which have been submitted to their regulators and approved by them. In 2008 that was not the case, and when Lehman Brothers was allowed to fail the experience was not encouraging. The consequences for the rest of the system were severe. Lehman creditors were on average paid out only around 45% of what they were owed (Denison et al. 2019).

Will regulators therefore be less unwilling to see banks fail, on the basis that they have a resolution plan in their back pockets which, in theory, can click into action? My assumption is that regulators and governments will nonetheless be reluctant to put those plans to the test. While public support for rescuing banks is very low, this crisis, as we have seen, cannot be attributed to their excesses, and regulators will be nervous about the practicality of any resolution plans in a full-scale economic depression. Recovery plans typically depend on a combination of asset sales (where buyers will be hard to find) and equity raises, which will be extremely difficult since regulators—in Europe at least—prevented the banks from paying dividends in 2020 and have constrained payouts in 2021.

So my expectation would be that the preferred route for failing banks will be a shotgun marriage, with the shotgun held by the central bank. Shareholders may be wiped out. I doubt if there will be any appetite for a government purchase of shares which leaves private shareholders in place, even if heavily diluted.

The difficulty will be the adverse impact on competition. There are several banking markets in Europe where concentration is already high. Will competition regulators, who have tried hard to promote the entry of new competitors in recent years, be prepared to see competition further reduced? Will the European Commission's Competition Directorate be prepared to look at the EU banking system as a whole when contemplating in-country mergers? And will regulators be prepared to facilitate cross-border mergers which the ECB has long wanted to see, but which in practice have been extremely hard to deliver? There is a chance that the crisis could have the side benefit of promoting the creation of strong pan-European banks, which have often been contemplated but so far never consummated, but as yet there have been no significant moves in that direction.

The competition arguments may be made more difficult if another development I regard as probable comes to pass.

A number of new competitors have entered the banking market in Europe and the US in recent years. Some will be put under severe pressure as a result of the deep recession.

We may roughly categorize them in four groups:

- Challenger banks, offering services comparable to those of the large incumbents, perhaps with a sectoral focus or an original business model or marketing approach, but fundamentally similar to the incumbents;
- Peer-to-peer lenders;
- Fintechs, which are often private equity-backed start-ups;
- BigTech entrants, like Apple or Google, principally focused on the payment system.

Some of these competitors are agile enough, with a sufficiently persuasive customer proposition, and are so robustly funded that they will survive. And we need not worry about the finances of BigTech firms which have entered the payments business in recent years. They will stay in the financial services arena if they wish to.

Others may struggle in a credit environment which will be far more hostile than they have encountered hitherto. Some may be crushed under the wheels of an unforgiving credit cycle. There will be an element of chance in who survives and who does not. Those which had completed a funding round shortly before the crisis hit may well have the resources to ride out the storm. Others who need more capital to grow (and many are still loss-making) will find that money harder to raise except on terms which may constrain their growth ambitions. We have already seen examples of that. And there are signs among customers of a return to safety, as they fear that new bank competitors may not have the funds to support them through a difficult period. I would judge that, in the UK market at least, some of the challenger banks and the peer-to-peer lenders will struggle the most. Some failures there will be inconvenient, but probably not systemic. But the market share of the largest lenders is likely to rise, reversing the trend of the last decade.

There will also be changes in the location of financial activity in Europe. The type of Brexit chosen by the Johnson government is likely to mean that London's position as the principal European financial center diminishes over time. London will increasingly become an offshore center for EU firms (Hamre and Wright 2021). That will be a setback for London, but also for the EU.

It is possible that the crisis will, in the EU, provide the stimulus needed to energize the Capital Markets Union project, which has been languishing for some time. There will be a need for more equity to stabilize heavily indebted corporates, and deeper and more robust capital markets should be part of the solution. That will require braver action by the European Commission and the

European Parliament than has been envisaged so far. A recent Bruegel paper concludes:

> Historically, European politicians have been able to keep finance at arm's length, because of London's dominance as a financial centre. The EU now loses this shield. But the EU also has an opportunity to reshape its financial infrastructure for the better. If policymakers take up the challenge, the EU may emerge with a more unified and functional financial market, which enhances confidence in the euro area and will better serve the European economy.
>
> *(Christie and Wieser 2020, 3)*

Another probable consequence of the crisis response is that, for the foreseeable future, governments, central banks, regulators and banks (and other financial institutions) will need to work more closely together than they have done in the recent past. They did so after 2008, but in a rather different way. Politicians and central bankers saw overpaid financiers as the source of the problems which they were then obliged to resolve. There was no love lost between the two. This time banks have been seen as tools of the recovery. The dividend ban imposed by regulators in 2020 caused friction as most banks would have preferred to make some payments (and a few resisted regulatory pressure to abandon payouts). In the economic support phase there have been frustrations, as banks have sometimes been seen as too slow in delivering funds to struggling clients, but overall the commonality of interest has dominated. It seems likely that the public authorities and the banks will be condemned to work closely together for some time. Whether that results in a form of rehabilitation for the banks in the long run, or in more political coercion on them to support interventionist policies, remains to be seen.

There are some promising signs that those banks which have invested time and effort in describing their social purpose, as NatWest and Lloyds have done in the UK, have begun to be seen as more responsible citizens and as constructive "first responders" to the crisis.

I have categorized the accelerated growth of digital banking as a certainty. Alongside that, I would now judge it probable that the central banks will quite quickly launch digital currencies.

The Bank for International Settlements (BIS) reported in 2019 (Barontini and Holden 2019) that 70% of the major central banks were exploring the issue of a central bank digital currency (CBDC). That interest predated the launch by Facebook of Libra, a new asset-backed so-called stable coin, since renamed Diem. The Facebook initiative certainly accelerated those developments. Regulators were suspicious of a Facebook-promoted alternative to the traditional payments systems, which could at the limit take money creation and control of the money supply out of the hands of central banks. The Swedish Riksbank is well-advanced in its e-krona initiative. The People's Bank of China's initiative is mature, too. In April 2021, the British government launched a taskforce to investigate the introduction of a digital pound, dubbed Britcoin. It is probable that some of these CBDCs will come to fruition soon (Richemont 2020).

The crisis has given a further stimulus to the decline of cash as a payment mechanism. That is in part because of generally ill-founded concerns about the potential transmission of the virus on banknotes and coins. The BIS (Auer et al. 2020) has found little or no evidence to suggest that is true. Indeed the virus may survive longer on a plastic card than on a banknote. But the truth or otherwise is beside the point, and more and more retail outlets have decided to bias contactless card payments over cash. The trends are somewhat different from place to place. In the US the volume of cash in issue has continued to grow, and New York State has legislated, on social exclusion grounds, to prevent retail outlets from refusing cash, but in Europe cash is in decline almost everywhere.

Central banks see a further argument for a CBDC. Offering digital accounts makes it potentially easier for them to implement negative interest rates. There can be no negative interest rate on a €100 note, so while large cash holdings are possible, negative interest rates for retail customers in particular are hard to impose.

For all these reasons CBDCs are probable. They are also problematic for banks. Would they supplement bank accounts or replace them? In a zero interest rate environment why not use central bank money to settle your transactions? If they become attractive to corporates and even individuals, deposits will be drawn away from the commercial banks and into the central bank. That would be especially likely in a financial crisis and would reduce their capacity to lend. Will the central bank step in and replace their credit creation? Could a central bank sensibly manage accounts for millions of consumers? Could it develop credit appraisal expertise? Are there privacy concerns if a public authority has access to data on every transaction in the economy? These are questions which need quite urgent answers if, as I expect, we are soon faced with a CBDC (Chen and Desouza 2019).

Lastly in my probability list, I fear that the crisis will make international collaboration between regulators rather harder in the future than it has been in the recent past.

It is clear that relations between the US and China have been severely damaged, even if we can now discount some of former President Trump's more inflammatory rhetoric. Both the World Health Organization and the World Trade Organization have come in for strong criticism. So far the central banks have managed to maintain their links—albeit largely on-screen—and in spite of some criticism the Fed has continued to provide other central banks with dollar facilities through their swap lines. Chairman Bernanke was roundly abused in the US Congress for doing so in the GFC. But although the central bank network has continued to function effectively there is little sign at political level of countries coming together in the face of a common problem, which was observable after the GFC.

A hint of divergence came in the attitude to bank dividend payments at the end of March 2020. The original intention was a common statement by the Fed, the ECB, Bank of England and possibly others to the effect that banks should halt all payouts, whether in the form of share buybacks or dividends. But in the end separate statements were made, and the Fed did not support the view taken in Europe that ordinary dividends should be suspended. They concluded that, while share buybacks should be suspended, US banks were well capitalized enough to support a regular dividend and that continuing to pay would assist in future capital raising should that prove necessary (Westbrook 2020).

It is quite likely that we have passed the high water mark of international regulatory cooperation. I do not expect a Basel IV accord to come into view on any near horizon. Governments will be heavily focused on supporting credit creation in their own jurisdictions. They will be in survival mode. International agreements can wait.

There are manifest tensions in Europe, too, especially in relation to the powers of the ECB, following the German Constitutional Court ruling in May 2020 which cast serious doubt on the legality of the Bundesbank's participation in the ECB's bond-buying program (Wolf 2020). The ECB has found a way round the ruling to maintain its program, but the prospect of future challenges is undoubtedly a constraint. One longer-term answer would be the creation of a form of common bond, backed collectively by EU member states, as President Macron of France and others have proposed. Will the crisis unblock that proposal? That question goes more broadly than my focus on the future of the financial system, but there is a risk that if the ECB's ability to buy bonds where necessary to constrain spreads and maintain the integrity of the euro is restricted, that may create a debt crisis in Italy or elsewhere with incalculable consequences for the Italian and European banking system. To return to my language of probabilities, I would judge it probable that this problem will somehow be resolved, as the alternative is unpleasant to contemplate. But the route to a solution is not self-evident, and there will be painful bumps on the road.

Big unknowns

Apart from the obvious uncertainty about the depth and length of the recession, the biggest unknown is what the longer-term consequences of the debt overhang in both the public and private sectors will be.

The public debt overhang: inflation or financial repression?

Looking first at public debt it is likely that governments will emerge from the recession with debt to GDP levels unknown since the end of World War II, and an order of magnitude bigger than experienced after the GFC. Those debts will be held in a different way, as we can expect a large proportion to be on the balance sheets of the central banks, but they are nonetheless real, and large enough to threaten both financial stability and indeed political stability if they severely constrain governments' freedom of maneuver.

Economic history suggests that, generically, there are four ways in which debt to GDP levels can be reduced. A government may do so by running a primary surplus. The Greeks and Italians have done that in recent years, at great cost to their citizens. The Coalition government in the UK adopted a tight public expenditure policy after 2010, holding down public sector pay and benefits—a policy dubbed "austerity" by their opponents. The second route, the most positive one, is if the growth rate of the economy is appreciably above the nominal interest rate. That was achieved for a lengthy period in the 1950s and 1960s, on both sides of the Atlantic and in Japan, which was the principal factor behind the steady reduction in the debt to GDP ratio after World War II.

The third option, whether pursued deliberately or more often simply tolerated, is a sustained rate of inflation which reduces the real value of outstanding debt repayments. The fourth, which may have a similar effect, is some form of financial repression, where interest rates are held down to such a low rate that, even if inflation remains relatively subdued, savers are effectively penalized.

It is very hard to judge which of these routes will be followed. And they have very different consequences for the financial system.

The politics of austerity will be very difficult to handle if unemployment remains high for a lengthy period. There will be some adverse consequences for public spending in any event. The prospects for pay rises in the public sector look poor. Public sector workers have been largely insulated from the lay-offs and pay cuts which are the fate of many private sector workers, so while health service employees and other emergency services which sustained the social fabric in the lockdown will see some financial reward for their endeavors, other public sector workers may be less fortunate. But a sustained policy of spending cuts and tax rises looks unlikely on both sides of the Atlantic. It is possible that wealth and property taxes could be considered by politicians who have set their faces against them in the past. But experience in France suggests that the politically feasible yield is not very high, and Macron scrapped the tax in 2017. So large primary surpluses as a route out of excessive debt seem unlikely.

A higher growth rate would clearly be a very welcome development, but it is hard to see why we should expect that, after—perhaps—a year or two of above-trend post-crisis catch-up recovery. Productivity growth has slowed in almost all developed economies in recent years and come to halt in the UK. There are competing explanations of that new trend (Gordon 2018), but few economists forecast a sustained upturn in the near term. So it is unlikely that growth will in itself relieve governments of their newly created debt burden.

That leaves either a rise in inflation or a sustained period of financial repression, if public debt levels are to be stabilized or reduced in real terms. On that point opinion is currently very divided.

After the last crisis and the large volume of quantitative easing (QE), many monetary economists forecast a rise in inflation. For the most part, that did not happen, except in isolated cases like the UK, where the sharp decline in sterling resulted in imported inflation which the Bank of England chose not to seek to offset with interest rate rises, at a time when the economy was operating well below capacity, and the output costs of holding inflation down were deemed to be unacceptably high. In the last few years inflation-targeting central banks have struggled to lift the inflation rate up to the central target rate. The price level in the Eurozone would be around 19% higher today had the ECB met its declared objective of an inflation rate of just below 2% (Whelan 2019).

So even though the huge increases in public deficits would typically result in higher inflation after a year or two, economists are divided on the consequences. In the inflation camp we find, for example, Charles Goodhart of the London School of Economics. Goodhart and Pradhan (2020) argue that a combination of "massive fiscal and monetary expansion" on the one hand, and "a self-imposed supply shock of immense magnitude" will result in "a surge in inflation, quite likely more than 5% and even in the order of 10%...Today's policy measures are injecting cash flows that will directly raise the broader measures of money." That, combined with an increase in the bargaining power of workers as migration slows and barriers to trade are erected, will be a powerful combination. So "inflation will rise considerably above the level of nominal interest rates that our political masters can tolerate" and "the excessive debt amongst non-financial corporates and governments will get inflated away." There will be negative real interest rates, and "only when indebtedness has been restored to viable levels can an assault on inflation be mounted."

In the US, as we have seen, Larry Summers (Wolf 2021) has argued that the scale of the fiscal stimulus implemented by the Biden administration is so large that "it's a bit hard to understand why (inflation) expectations should remain anchored."

Andy Haldane (2021), as Chief Economist of the Bank of England, made a similar case in early 2021. He concluded:

> there is a tangible risk inflation proves more difficult to tame, requiring monetary policymakers to act more asserting that is currently prices into financial markets. People are right to caution about the risks of central banks acting too conservatively by tightening policy prematurely. But for me, the greater risk at present is of central bank complacency allowing the inflationary (big) cat out of the bag.

There are, however, powerful counterarguments. The supply side shock was accompanied by a demand shock of even greater magnitude. That is a difficult environment in which to raise prices, even as demand recovers. So Miles and Scott (2020) see little risk of a resurgence of inflation. A further point is that if much of the new debt ends up on the balance sheets of the central banks that may change the dynamic. Is central bank-held debt as inflationary? Miles and Scott (2020) believe that "the value of financial assets held by the private sector will be much lower after the pandemic…(and)…the total value of the wealth of the private sector is likely much more significant for consumption—and that wealth will very likely have gone down." So they consider a significant rise in inflation to be unlikely.

And is Goodhart right to assume that independent central banks would effectively suspend their inflation targets? Gertjan Vlieghe (2020), an external member of the Bank of England's monetary policy committee, takes a different view. He argues that there is "good" and "bad" monetary financing of deficits and that the current version is very different from the policies followed by the Weimar Republic or Zimbabwe.

He points out that the inflation worries after the last crisis were greatly overdone:

> Some thought that [QE] would turn out to be excessively inflationary. Instead the post-crisis recovery was generally characterized by inflation being too weak, rather than too strong. Central banks that did QE earlier ended up with inflation closer to target. Those that waited longer to act undershot their inflation target by more, some persistently so.
>
> *(Vlieghe 2020)*

(He is clearly referring to the ECB.) The key difference is that the central bank will, unless its independence is removed, continue "rigorously to frame its monetary policy actions in terms of its monetary policy remit." He explicitly rejects Goodhart's view that there may be circumstances in which it is politically impossible to raise rates to the level needed to meet the target.

The dispute is, then, as much about politics and institutional arrangements as it is about the implications of rapid growth in the monetary aggregates.

But whether or not central banks lose control of inflation, it does seem likely that a form of financial repression will be with us for some time. Central banks now actively manage the yield curve out to very long durations, with considerable skill one might add. They seem likely to continue with that policy.

How far can financial repression go? Central bankers are somewhat divided on the imposition of negative rates. Some, like the Swiss National Bank, have been content to impose them. The Fed and the Bank of England have been more reticent. Bank of England Governor Andrew Bailey (Strauss 2020) has said that negative rates are not something the Bank was planning for or contemplating at the time. But the Bank's Chief Economist, Andy Haldane, has taken a different line, saying that negative rates are "something we'll need to look at—are looking at—with greater immediacy" (Hurley and Clarence-Smith 2020).

Others believe that rates could go strongly negative, and that that would be the way out of the crisis. Rogoff (2020) argues that central banks should be bold, and push negative rates to minus 3% or lower: "negative rates would operate similarly to normal monetary policy, boosting aggregate demand and raising employment." Furthermore "a policy of deeply negative rates in advanced economies would also be a huge boon to emerging and developing economies." He believes that "central banks and governments [should] give the idea a long, hard and urgent look."

Governments will have a strong incentive to see interest rates stay lower for longer. Even a small rise in rates would have a dramatic impact on debt interest costs. In the UK the Office for Budget Responsibility has calculated that a 1% rise in rates would add £22 billion a year to interest costs. There will be governmental pressure—whether public or private—on central banks to hold rates low and tolerate an overshoot of their inflation target. Indeed the US Federal Reserve has already committed itself to "average inflation targeting" allowing inflation to overshoot for a period to compensate for past undershooting.

Even if rates do not go negative, as they have already done in some parts of the world, very low or zero rates have a significant impact on the financial system. Bank profitability will remain depressed. That will over time raise their cost of capital through ratings downgrades and a very high cost of equity, if indeed equity is available at all. That in turn will constrain bank balance sheets and make bank credit less available. The impact on banks, especially in Europe, has already been very striking. Bank share prices fell sharply in 2020. The price to book ratios became remarkably low for some very large European institutions. At the end of April 2020 BNP and NatWest, for example, were trading at around 35% of tangible net asset value and they were by no means the lowest in Europe. There was a significant recovery in 2021, as the immediate crisis receded, but a year later most European banks were still valued at well below tangible net assets. Those figures suggest that the franchise value of major banks is now negative, and even taking account of the heavy discounts to be expected on a fire sale of loan portfolios, their shareholders may be better off were they to be resolved. Such an outcome, of course, is scarcely conceivable as the consequences for the broader economy would be immensely damaging.

Insurance companies and asset managers will earn lower returns on their bond portfolios. In the general insurance market that will have the effect of raising premiums. In life insurance, returns to savers will fall, making institutional saving less attractive. These effects will take time to work through, but they will be profound. The market prices of insurers and asset managers, except those with a strong presence in growing emerging markets, have therefore also been marked down.

The position of these large institutions is, arguably, not sustainable if the prospect is for further financial repression for a long period. The US market is less badly affected. US banks have benefited from a more rapidly growing and dynamic economy. They coexist with a more flexible and receptive capital market which allows them to securitize loans to free up their balance sheets for new and more profitable opportunities. The returns on their capital market activities are structurally higher in North America than in Europe. One important consequence is that US banks have systematically gained share in EU capital markets over the last decade. From 2005 to 2015 the market share of US investment banks in European capital markets rose from 37.2% to 44.6%. The share of European banks during the same period fell from 54.7% to 46% (Goodhart and Shoenmaker 2016). The trend has continued since then and is now likely to accelerate. A number of European banks are reducing their capacity and the scale of the assets they devote to this activity, at present. Few have managed to establish a profitable presence in the US (Noonan 2020).

The combination of zero interest rates, cross-subsidized US competition in capital markets, low cost fintechs, and BigTech entry into the payments systems is a powerful set of headwinds which will reshape European banking in the next decade.

The corporate debt overhang

As I explained at the start of the chapter, the exponential growth in public sector debt as a result of the crisis is matched by ballooning private sector debt, especially in the corporate sector. How will that problem be resolved? It is hard to imagine that all the companies which borrowed heavily to carry them through the worst of the demand shortfall will be viable with a debt-laden balance sheet when some form of normality returns. Many were only marginally profitable beforehand, with more lowly geared balance sheets.

For a period, this instability will be hidden, as many of the loan support packages in place incorporate interest holidays and subsidized rates. But they will have to come to an end at some point. The early output from a review for The CityUK, a lobby group, of the potential recapitalization need in the UK corporate sector suggests that "the level of unsustainable debt held by UK Private Non-Financial Corporations (PNFCs) could be up to £90 to £105 billion" (Montague 2020). The calculation is almost certainly exaggerated, but there will be an equity gap to be filled.

One element could be the creation of some kind of "bad bank" with government backing. Currently the banks are energetically pumping funds into companies to help them to survive the deepest trough of the downturn and to avoid permanent scarring of the economy which would reduce its productive capacity in the longer term. But even if the recovery is robust, and certainly if any letter of the alphabet other than V turns out better to describe the shape, there will be unrecoverable loans at the end of the process. The banks will seek to recover, even where 100% of the loan is government guaranteed, but will not always succeed. Where the company is insolvent there will be a write-off, shared between the government and the banks, depending on the precise terms of the scheme. But there will be a category of loans, possibly quite a large one, where the companies are solvent, and trading profitably without the additional interest payments, but where they cannot afford to remunerate the additional debt, at least in the recovery phase, when the need for working capital is often the greatest. Those assets might find their way into an institution able to hold equity or quasi-equity stakes in companies, which banks currently cannot do given the heavy capital requirements. Before the GFC, banks often owned private equity arms which managed principal investments, but almost all of that activity has now been pushed off bank balance sheets by regulation, for good reasons at the time.

The type of mechanism which would help is fairly clear, but who would own and manage it, and what would its relationship be with the principal bankers to the entity in which the "bad bank" held a stake? That is still highly uncertain. But it is increasingly urgent to resolve. Becker et al. (2020) point out that "the coronavirus crisis arrives against a backdrop of private sector indebtedness... [C]orporate leverage is at an all-time high...[C]urrent policies will leave parts of the corporate sector with even larger debt burdens. These will delay a recovery." They argue for schemes which "attach options to the bailout funds in the form of stock warrants or convertibles that can ensure that the public benefits from future gains in corporate valuations." These are sensible suggestions but are more relevant to the larger corporates. They also argue for accelerated insolvency procedures, which would be of more general application.

In the EU discussions are under way on the establishment of a recovery fund which could provide needed equity support for struggling companies. There is a case for strong involvement of the banking sector, to avoid politicians deciding "unilaterally which companies to help" (Anderson et al. 2020, 3). As their Bruegel paper argues,

> The local knowledge and analytical capabilities of commercial banks is already extensively used to distribute state guarantees and subsidized loans to firms and individuals. Further partnerships will be required for equity-based instruments, especially for the more arduous assessments of the viability of smaller companies.
>
> *(Anderson et al. 2020, 3)*

But will this recapitalization exercise be so extensive as to lead to a different long-term relationship between the state, the financial sector, and nonfinancial companies? Decisions on support taken in haste may lead to very different outcomes. The central case is that there will be a range of public–private entities, certainly in Europe, which will blur the boundaries between state and private credit provision. If these entities focus on helping companies in difficulty for no fault of their own, the outcome may be a more diverse and flexible financial system. But lenders with strong state participation are always vulnerable to political pressure to sustain nonviable businesses in sensitive areas.

The global financial system

Most of the policy interventions we have discussed have been national in scope. Just as we saw in the last financial crisis, countries are thrown back on themselves when times are tough. As Mervyn King observed in relation to bank bailouts in the GFC, banks may be global in life, but they are national in death. So the major economies may be global when all goes well, but when life support mechanisms are needed the national government is the relevant actor.

But we may nonetheless ask ourselves what implications the crisis may have for the global financial system in the longer run. I have suggested that a reduction in the intensity of international collaboration is a probable consequence. Will that be a temporary phenomenon, or can we expect a prolonged return to some form of financial autarchy?

Researchers at the Institute for Advanced Sustainability Studies (IASS 2020) have developed four possible scenarios for the global financial system. They are not mutually exclusive and collectively exhaustive, but are suggestive of potential directions of change.

The US Federal Reserve still acts as the central underpinning of the global system in important ways. Just as it did in the GFC, the Fed has created and fueled swap lines with other central banks to allow the provision of dollar funding to non-US entities which need it, given the continued dominance of the dollar in international trade and finance. Though its founders hoped it would, the euro has not gained market share in the denomination of international trade in the last two decades (Papadia and Efstathiou 2018). Over the last decade the share of EU exports denominated in euros has declined from around 70% to 57%. But will the Fed, and US administrations, be prepared to continue to play this central role in the longer term? Indeed, as the IASS paper (2020) observed, "[T]he Federal Reserve's rescue efforts run counter to the policies of the Trump administration, which has probably not yet grasped the scope of these interventions."

In the longer term—they look out to 2040—the IASS team see four possible scenarios:

- A continuation of the current dollar hegemony;
- The co-existence of competing monetary blocks;
- The emergence of an international monetary federation; or
- International monetary anarchy (IASS 2020).

The implications of these scenarios are not difficult to imagine. Under the first, the Federal Reserve continues to act as the world's central bank. In the second, we see the emergence of at least two rival currency poles of attraction: the euro and the RMB. The first would require stabilization of the Eurozone through Treaty change, and almost certainly a greater degree of common fiscal policy. The Next Generation EU fund of €750 billion which will be used to promote recovery from the COVID-19 crisis is a strong move in that direction. The second scenario would be predicated on full convertibility of the RMB, which the Chinese government has not yet been prepared to accept, but in spite of that, the international role of the currency has continued to grow, with implicit official blessing. The RMB is likely to continue to play a greater role in international trade and finance in the coming decade.

The third scenario would depend on united action by the G20, at least, to introduce structured provision of liquidity on a global scale, while the fourth assumes that the Fed retreats from global dollar supply and that neither Europe nor China, nor a combination of the two, is willing or able to fill the gap.

The authors do not attempt to handicap these options today. They are all conceivable, and the odds on option four have shortened somewhat in the course of the COVID-19 crisis. It is evident that any move away from the first scenario will have immense consequences for the financial sector.

Conclusion

The terms of debate about the future of the financial system are rapidly changing. The question which seemed central as recently as February 2020—whether Basel III should be amended to increase the amount of capital in banks' trading books—seems now to belong in the history faculty rather than in finance ministries, central banks, or the boardrooms of major banks.

The new crisis will not change everything, but many previous certainties have been thrown into question, and in other areas history has been speeded up. I have tried to sketch out some probabilities and posed an incontinent number of questions. Predictions are hazardous. To adapt and update J K Galbraith's bon mot, economic and financial forecasts are designed to make epidemiologists (Galbraith chose weather forecasters) look good.

References

Admati, Anat and Martin Hellwig. 2013. *The Bankers' New Clothes: What's Wrong With Banking and What to Do About It*. Princeton and Oxford: Princeton University Press.

Anderson, Julia, Simone Tagliapietra, and Guntram B. Wolff. 2020. "Rebooting Europe: a Framework for Post-Covid Economic Recovery." Policy Brief. Issue 1: May. Brussels: Bruegel.

Auer, Raphael, Giulio Cornelli, and Jon Frost. 2020. "Covid-19, Cash, and the Future of Payments." BIS bulletin No. 3. Basel: Bank of International Settlements.

Barontini, Christian and Henry Holden. 2019. "Proceeding with Caution - a Survey on Central Bank Digital Currency." BIS Papers No. 101. Basel. Bank for International Settlements.

Beck, Thorsten. 2020. "Finance in the Times of Coronavirus." In Richard Baldwin and Beatrice Weder di Mauro (eds.). *Economics in the Time of Covid-19*, 73–76. London: CEPR Press.

Becker, Bo, Ulrich Hege, and Pierre Mella-Barral. 2020, March 21. "Corporate Debt Burdens Threaten Economic Recovery after Covid-19: Planning for Debt Restructuring Should Start Now." VOX EU. https://voxeu.org/article/corporate -debt-burdens-threaten-economic-recovery-after-covid-19. Accessed July 14, 2021.

Carney, Mark. 2019, 16 December. "Letter to Chancellor of the Exchequer, Sajid Javid." https://www.bankofengland.co.uk/-/media/boe/files/letter/2019/governor-letter -161219-prc.pdf?la=en&hash=7C988D8A5CC6AAE5945B2352AF7A1F94642 E0912. Accessed July 15, 2021.

Chen, Ye and Kevin C. Desouza. 2019, December 13. "The Current Landscape of Central Bank Digital Currencies (blog)." https://www.brookings.edu/blog/techtank/2019/12/13/the-current-landscape-of-central-bank-digital-currencies/. Accessed July 14, 2021.

Christie, Rebecca and Thomas Wieser. 2020. "The European Union's Post-Brexit Reckoning with Financial Markets." Policy Contribution Issue No. 8. Brussels: Bruegel.

Cohen, Benjamin. 2013. "How Have Banks Adjusted to Higher Capital Requirements?" *BIS Quarterly Review*, September, 25–41.

Davies, Howard. 2015. *Can Financial Markets Be Controlled?* Cambridge, UK: Polity Press.

De Mooij, Ruud A. 2011. "Tax Biases to Debt Finance: Assessing the Problem, Finding Solutions." IMF staff discussion note SDN/11/11. Washington, DC: International Monetary Fund.

Denison, Erin, Michael Fleming, and Asani Sarkar. 2019, January 19. "Creditor Recovery in Lehman's Bankruptcy." *Liberty Street Economics* (blog). https://libertystreeteconomics.newyorkfed.org/2019/01/creditor-recovery-in-lehmans-bankruptcy/. Accessed July 14, 2021.

Eichengreen, Barry. 2016. "Global Monetary Order." In *The Future of the International Monetary and Financial Architecture*. Conference Proceedings. June 27–29, 2016. (pp. 21–63). Frankfurt am Main: European Central Bank.

Eichengreen, Barry. 2020, May 13. "Managing the Coming Global Debt Crisis." *Project Syndicate.* https://www.project-syndicate.org/commentary/managiing-coming-global-debt-crisis-by-barry-eichengreen-2020-05. Accessed July 14, 2021.

Frind, Annkathrin. 2020. Coronavirus Pandemic: This Time Banks Are Part of the Solution, Interview with Felix Hufeld. 3 June. https://www.bafin.de/SharedDocs/Veroeffentlichungen/EN/Fachartikel/2020/fa_bj_2004_Corona_Hufeld_en.html

Goodhart, Charles and Manoj Pradhan. 2020, March 27. "Future Imperfect after Coronavirus." VOX EU. https://voxeu.org/article/future-imperfect-after-coronavirus. Accessed July 14, 2021.

Goodhart, Charles and Dirk Schoenmaker. 2016. "The United States Dominates Global Investment Banking: Does It Matter for Europe?" Bruegel Policy Contribution. Issue 2016/06 March. Brussels: Bruegel.

Gordon, Robert. 2018. "Why Has Economic Growth Slowed When Innovation Appears to Be Accelerating?" NBER WORKING PAPER SERIES Working Paper 24554. https://www.nber.org/papers/w24554. Accessed July 15, 2021.

Haldane, Andy. 2021. "Inflation: A Tiger by the Tail?" Speech (online), February 26. https://www.bankofengland.co.uk/-/media/boe/files/speech/2021/february/inflation-a-tiger-by-the-tail-speech-by-andy-haldane.pdf?la=en&hash=78C0DB3A631A7B9E2DF6EFBCFE9B3D138D87C449. Accessed July 14, 2021.

Hamre, Civina Friis and William Wright. 2021. *Brexit and the City: The Impact so Far.* London: New Financial. https://newfinancial.org/brexit-the-city-the-impact-so-far/. Accessed July 14, 2021.

Hurley, James and Louisa Clarence-Smith. 2020, May 18. "We're Looking at Negative Interest Rates, Bank of England's Andy Haldane Says," *The Times of London*, https://www.thetimes.co.uk/article/were-looking-at-negative-interest-rates-bank-of-englands-andy-haldane-says-6cfdprv0f. Accessed July 14, 2021.

Institute for Advanced Sustainability Studies. 2020, May 11. "How Is Covid-19 Affecting the Global Economic Order? Scenarios for the Global Monetary System." https://www.iass-potsdam.de/en/news/zukunftsvisionen-globales-finanzsystem. Accessed July 14, 2021.

Mazzucato, Mariana. 2018. *The Value of Everything: Making and Taking in the Global Economy*. London: Allen Lane.

McCormick, Liz Capo and S. Mohsin. 2020, May 4. "Mnuchin to Issue $3 Trillion in Debt After Virus Hobbles Economy." *Bloomberg Law*. https://news.bloomberglaw.com /coronavirus/mnuchin-to-issue-3-trillion-in-debt-after-virus-hobbles-economy ?context=search&index=3. Accessed July 15, 2021.

Miles, David and Andrew Scott. 2020, April 4. "Will Inflation Make a Comeback After the Crisis?" VOX EU. https://voxeu.org/article/will-inflation-make-comeback -after-crisis-ends. Accessed July 14, 2021.

Montague, Adrian. 2020, May 11. "Letter to Andrew Bailey, Governor of the Bank of England." https://www.thecityuk.com/assets/2020/ff312db314/TheCityUK -Recapitalisation-group-initial-workplan-letter-to-the-Bank-of-England.pdf. Accessed July 14, 2021.

Noonan, Laura. 2020, March 2. "The Rise and Dramatic Fall of European Investment Banks in the US," *Financial Times*, https://www.ft.com/content/68f8d7a6-56fb-11ea -a528-dd0f971febbc. Accessed July 14, 2021.

Ogier, Thierry and Anthony Rowley. 2014, October 10. "India's Rajan Warns Fed: Don't Ignore EM over Rate Rises," *GlobalCapital*, https://www.globalcapital.com/special -reports?issueid=yw0dvpttnpd6&article=yvxvct7sdn20. Accessed July 15, 2021.

Papadia, Francesco and Konstantinos Efstathiou. 2018, December. "The Euro as an International Currency." Policy Contribution No. 25. Brussels: Bruegel.

Richemont, Sabrina. 2020, May 13. "Are Retail Central Bank Digital Currencies (CBDCs) in the Fast Lane?" *Institute and Faculty of Actuaries* (blog). https://www .actuaries.org.uk/news-and-insights/news/2020-are-retail-central-bank-digital -currencies-cbdc-last-lane. Accessed July 14, 2021.

Rogoff, Kenneth. 2020, May 4. "The Case for Deeply Negative Interest Rates." *Project Syndicate*. https://www.project-syndicate.org/commentary/advanced-economies -need-deeply-negative-interest-rates-by-kenneth-rogoff-2020-05. Accessed July 14, 2021.

Strauss, Dephine. 2020, May 14. "BoE Is Financing UK's Coronavirus Measures, Bailey Acknowledges," *Financial Times*, https://www.ft.com/content/ad63e45c-ad55-41a2 -ae2e-8d550ff0ac92. Accessed July 14, 2021.

The Volcker Alliance. 2015. *Reshaping the Financial Regulatory System*. New York: The Volcker Alliance.

Vlieghe, Gertjan. 2020, April 23. "Monetary Policy and the Bank of England's Balance Sheet." Speech (online). https://www.bankofengland.co.uk/speech/2020/gertjan -vlieghe-speech-monetary-policy-and-the-boes-balance-sheet. Accessed July 14, 2021.

Westbrook, Jesse. 2020, April 9. "Powell Says Banks Well-capitalized, No Need to Halt Dividends," *Bloomberg*. https://www.bloomberg.com/news/articles/2020-04-09/ powell-says-banks-well-capitalized-no-need-to-halt-dividends. Accessed July 14, 2021.

Whelan, Karl. 2019. "Recommendations for the European Central Bank's Monetary Policy Strategy Review." Monetary dialogue papers. Brussels: European Parliament.

Wolf, Martin. 2020, May 15. "German Court Decides to Take Back Control with ECB Ruling," *Financial Times*, https://www.ft.com/content/37825304-9428-11ea-af4b -499244625ac4. Accessed July 14, 2021.

Wolf, Martin. 2021, April 12. "Larry Summers: 'I'm Concerned that What Is Being Done Is Substantially Excessive'," *Financial Times*. https://www.ft.com/content /380ea811-e927-4fe1-aa5b-d213816e9073. Accessed July 14, 2021.

14

DO WE NEED A COLLECTIVE SOCIAL CONSCIENCE?

Nabil Fahmy

As the public orders in the global community, in particular being liberal or illiberal, have lost their "social conscience," we build on lessons learned to create better circumstances, rather than simply making historic judgments—all while striving to reinvigorate the "social conscience" with a greater sense of collectiveness to provide a more comprehensive order for a new global culture. The goal here is to determine how best to regenerate a wider understanding of the "common good" amongst our societies and how to ensure that we as "peoples" appreciate and embrace collectiveness and determine that our decisions will increasingly have a greater "social conscience" collectively. In a world of globalization, it is important to understand the interconnectedness of people and systems alike. Decisions built on an understanding of the "common good" and "social conscience" will ultimately have a wider influence on a potential global culture willing to reap the benefits of individual assets and achievements.

Changing from "balance of power and authority"-driven systems to ones driven by a different kind of system in an attempt to achieve a "balance of interest" is due. A paradigm shift should be in force, whereby marginalization and inequality will be reduced, yet not erased.

With this critical juncture in the twenty-first century, it is imperative to rethink the common good as well as reinvigorate the "social conscience" and collective sense which are essential to facing the ever-changing global order.

Correctly determining as well as addressing "the great question of our time" is more precisely and wisely done in retrospect, with the luxury of hindsight. Time provides context for comparison and for factoring in relativism, thus providing a better basis for determining what was really great in comparison to other questions or decisions. If rigorous contextual criteria are applied, time also allows us to properly assess the immediate and long-term consequences of these questions and decisions. Needless to say, a paramount factor in this kind of judgment and determination is to clearly define what is meant by the phrase "our time." Are we looking at generational perspectives, which tend to be a quarter of a century; longer than one generation; or even further than that if the question is placed in the "nation" context (my country, Egypt, considers hundreds of years to be contemporary)?

Regrettably, however, embracing this cautious approach in many respects defeats the very purpose of the exercise because the pressing objective is to build on lessons learned to create better circumstances rather than simply to make historic judgments. This is particularly true given that it requires being reflective and applying critical thinking to achieve better outcomes, especially in handling and dealing with common goods and services for the general public. Needless to say, this is the essence and foundation of a stable and fulfilled public order.

Another point that warrants retrospect and reflection is that the intellectual public seems to have crudely defined the choices in public order to being exclusively either "liberal" or "illiberal." The general public, as well as some pundits, push this artificial, imprecise divide even further as simply being between "democratic" and "autocratic" systems of government.

All of these assumptions are, in my opinion, imperfect if not blatantly wrong. Democratic orders are not necessarily perfectly liberal or, in fact, always consistent with liberal values in respecting and objectively applying common values. Equally true is that autocratic orders or systems are not necessarily agnostic to value systems or immune to critical thinking or concepts of the common good in dealing with public order. Neither of the systems is exclusively liberal or illiberal. The basic difference between the two is the width and intensity of the shades of gray in their application.

Recent examples of domestic disturbances in the US because of racial tensions, as well as populist trends with clear isolationist and often racist tendencies in democratic states in Europe, are cases in point. And even in normal, less turbulent times, the interpretation of the term "liberal" differs even in democratic societies because values and value systems differ even among democracies. The US, most of what was considered to be Western Europe in the past, and India— all established democracies, even if imperfect—have different values and concepts of liberalism and thus are very relevant cases in point here.

Equally true is that autocratic systems, often lauded as symbols of stability, have also had a stream of instability and revolutions over the contemporary history of nations. Thus, they cannot claim to be perfect islands of sustained stability if the context of time is wider. And if that is the objective, they are not an option one should be satisfied with. Nor can they completely project themselves as being agnostic to values of societies or aspirations of their constituents. This is self-evident in that given globalization, connectivity, and expanding transparency, even authoritarian systems have increasingly couched and justified their actions through what are normally considered to be the tools and expressions of democratic liberal systems. These include elections as expressions of public support, as well as legislative actions to legitimize rules and procedures.

My salient conclusions from all of this are that the great questions of our time are not about the success or failure of the liberal world order, or the efficacy of a liberal versus an illiberal order. Rather, I would strongly argue that all systems of public order are being challenged domestically, regionally, and globally and that a paramount challenge of our time is to determine the reason for this simultaneous onslaught on societal and governance systems. That challenge may actually constitute one of the great—if not the greatest—questions of our time.

Given that these challenges have not been restricted to particular political systems or even specific geographical theaters, without unnecessary obfuscation or over analysis, my conclusion is that our public order systems have been challenged because they have been unable to respond in a satisfactory manner to the needs and aspirations of their own constituencies. Public systems and those in the relevant executive positions in politics, the marketplace, and even the social sphere, where ideas and norms are generated, have increasingly become elitist among those in a position of power, ignoring and even being disrespectful toward a large segment of their societies, which feel increasingly marginalized.

In order to settle these challenges or deal with them in an orderly fashion, national, regional, and global orders need reconsideration and recalibration. However, I would even go further to argue that the public orders in the global community in particular, be they liberal or illiberal, have lost their "social conscience." Consequently, they have increasingly failed in establishing and managing global and regional priorities, besides being a catalyst in fueling domestic disparity and dysfunction. The systems need revamping, but even more importantly, we need to find more—even if not complete—common ground on common values. Reinvigorating the social challenge is, I believe, the greatest challenge we all face today.

However, I would like to underline here that I am not suggesting or, in fact, associating myself with the argument that the choices we face are between democratic liberal and authoritarian illiberal values. The issue in my opinion far exceeds this artificial dichotomy and goes much deeper. In essence, we should recognize from our practices over the last half century and some that we have lost our "social conscience" in our societies—whether our systems are democratic, autocratic, or somewhere in between, with pragmatic, realpolitik balance of power and influence considerations making social values determined and subservient to objectives and aspirations of those in positions of power, be that in government, the marketplace, or other domains.

Testimony to the absence of a "social conscience" is that we strive to find security and justify the need to provide extremely substantial resources to ensure the capacity to destroy each other many times over through absurd but highly proclaimed Cold War concepts like "mutually assured destruction." By doing so, we are hedging our future and very coexistence not only on the sustained, infallible, and indefinite rationality of others but also on the naive assumption that individuals, as well as systems, are indefinitely fault- and error-free.

To fuel and feed these erroneous assumptions, military expenditures have increased by 75% over the past 20 years, reaching astronomical levels of US $1.822 trillion, according to the most recent Stockholm International Peace Research Institute report (SIPRI 2020). This increase has occurred at a time when even affluent countries are suffering from a shortage of strategic resources to deal with pandemics such as COVID-19 or even, in many countries, for basic health services. Security is, of course, important. However, excessive zeal in its pursuit or subjugation to the military-industrial complexes at the expense of basic and fundamental needs of our constituents is fuel for discontent and instability in our political systems. This choice of priorities raises questions about our "social conscience" in the political sense, besides shedding a dark shadow on our moral standards.

Another citation from our present-day reality that raises questions about the "social conscience" of our world order is the abhorrent concentration of wealth, where in the wealthiest countries, such as the US, the wealthiest 1% have acquired more wealth than the bottom 90%. Meanwhile, 10% of the world community was living below the poverty line of US $1.90 a day in 2015. This remains true even after globalization had brought vast numbers above the poverty line and reduced this percentage from 36% of the global population. That being said, according to World Bank group estimates (World Bank 2020), the ramifications of COVID-19 were estimated to cause 40 to 60 million to fall back under US $1.90 a day in 2020.

It would be significant to highlight a distinction between two often inter-related terms, ones that can be used interchangeably, but for current purposes should be outlined as meaning different things. The meaning of the process of globalization is different from international cooperation. Yes, international cooperation is facilitated by the circumstances that globalization puts forth, but they are two different phenomena. Globalization is a process of unauthorized integration and interaction among constituencies globally. Therefore, one of its main characteristics is a growing interdependence of the global economy, cultures, and populations. The increased interaction on a global scale, especially with increased movement and exchanges of products, ideas, investment, technology, information, and even people, has created a global process within which the international community operates.

International cooperation is not a predetermined process, but a choice. It is the voluntary acceptance of global interaction for the benefit of the international community as a whole. To clarify, international cooperation is essential if we are to establish a collective "social conscience." States realize that they cannot solve problems on their own, and therefore, they need treaties, conventions, international organizations, and the like. These institutions and agreements can organize a situation where all states are better off than if they were to tackle issues alone. More so, it is up to the international community to decide that we need to cooperate to enhance our "social conscience" because of the rollbacks of the twenty-first century public orders and the inevitable negative effects of globalization.

Again, as a point of emphasis, my arguments here are not moralistic; nor are they necessarily in support of socialism or big government versus market economics. Neither are they a pushback against globalization stages and phases that are inevitable and beneficial in bringing vast numbers out of poverty. The shallowness, if not absence, of "social conscience" is, in fact, not exclusive to economic or political systems, nor is it solely a function of wealth or poverty of nations or individuals. There are wonderful philanthropic examples, but they are the exception. Nor is this a moralist, naive call for reawakening from an idealist. Regrettably, decades of public service have fueled cynicism at the expense of idealism in my mindset. However, I am proud that this cynicism has not clouded my vision of what is right and wrong, and I am determined not to allow time to weaken my concern for the common good. Individual and occasionally exclusive needs of particular constituencies have increasingly overwhelmed and dimmed calls for societal or collective interests, whether in culture, economics, and the marketplace, or in politics and security issues and practices. Was this always the case, and can the situation be redressed?

It is noteworthy that the United Nations (UN), the core intergovernmental organization of the post-World War II order, was established to safeguard the world from the scourge, devastation, and ravages of a third world war. Its tenets were reached with realpolitik and global social context in play. The preamble of the UN Charter uses the phrase "We the people" to give context and texture to the pursuant charter goals and provisions. While respecting sovereignty and noninterference in internal affairs of states, the charter is replete with references to "collective action." And it is the collectiveness of the "social conscience" of the international community that was the springboard for all the subsequent international legislation developing norms and standards for international practices that have emerged over the last seven decades.

Ironically, while death, destruction, and devastation drove and energized our "social conscience" in the middle of the last century, progress and material fulfillment seem to have driven us off course, numbing the senses and clouding the memory of the nation-state founders of the UN with respect to their noble goals and wise collective outlook—hopefully only temporarily so.

In short, the greatest question of our time is: why did the international community lose its social conscience as a community of nations globally, in our immediate regional domains as well as within our respective national systems? In essence, the loss was an unintended consequence and ramification of glorious successes of individualism and singular goals and objectives. Without the drive, determination, ingenuity, and creativity that is characteristic of high-achieving individuals and nation-states, much of the progress of the last century would not have occurred. However, this progress has frequently come at the expense of the call for collectivity. The rebalancing between the genius and productivity of singular ambitions and that of collective interests is our greatest contemporary challenge. And that will require societal changes.

With globalization, our collectivity is virtually much tighter and closer. That is, in my view, a positive aspect of globalization. Closeness and interdependence remove barriers, increasing the pace as well as the scope of interaction. With the increased collectivity comes a much more naked level of transparency, with both its constructive and potentially challenging implications. That requires a greater capacity to find collective but not necessarily equal interests, in order for our diversity to remain a source of wealth and richness rather than of discord and adversity.

With respect to the world order, I believe it is imperative to regain our sense of "collectiveness" if we are to continue to reap the benefits of our individual assets and achievements. A more acceptable balance between individual and collective pursuits and applications needs to be developed. The choice is not between individualism or collectiveness but rather a balance between the two, because in a globally networked, transparent global village, the paradigm is one where borders are sovereign but not boundaries or obstacles.

This is essentially a call for a paradigm shift from systems driven by "balance of power and authority" to ones driven by different systems attempting to achieve a "balance of interest." This by no means implies that all will get equal shares of the pie, or, in fact, that all will remain fulfilled. However, it would be correct to assume that one of the goals of this paradigm shift would be to reduce the sense of marginalization and futility that exists in many parts of the world.

To achieve this objective and develop complementary rules and procedures for the world as we move forward, it is time to invite great minds to merge with experienced former practitioners in order to think outside the box—but practically so. I very much encourage different disciplines, professions, and stakeholders in society to organize processes of creative thinking on how they best see us moving forward. While such thought processes would be useful, the objective here is not essentially to search for technical solutions to problems of security, development, the environment, equal rights, and the like. In fact, numerous Sustainable Development Goals (SDGs) adopted by the United Nations exist as agreed targets of global aspirations, albeit many of them remain unfulfilled. Consequently, a series of action-oriented measures have been suggested, if belatedly so. To achieve these goals and, furthermore, to provide a more comprehensive order, a new global culture with an invigorated "social conscience" factor needs to be developed.

The goal here is to determine how best to regenerate a wider understanding of the "common good" among our societies, how to ensure that we as "peoples" appreciate and embrace collectiveness and determine that our decisions will increasingly have a greater "social conscience," be that in relation to other communities, different strata in societies, or, in fact, future generations. This is a larger goal, extending well into the future beyond envisaged priorities of the day, but I believe it would also greatly facilitate the fulfillment of the SDGs' objectives.

For this to become a truly global endeavor, I recommend that the UN Secretary General also organize a set of discussions under the organization's auspices. These discussions should start at the outset with groups of individuals in their personal capacity, in order to not get entangled in governmental competition or bureaucracies. The level, composition of participation, and format should extend well beyond the traditional weekend brainstorming sessions held previously, truly allowing for perspectives that relate to future challenges without ignoring present realities, with a special emphasis on collectiveness and common interests. Here the objective should be to raise the debate to a higher level both in posture and in recognition as well as in substance, in a way that obliges our leaders and our societies to respond and engage on the discussions, without their becoming hypothetical or theoretical.

Once a set of principles, goals, and measures are developed about how best to revive our "social conscience" with a greater sense of collectiveness, the UN Secretary General should then undertake an intensive effort of quiet diplomacy, both with governmental bodies and opinion-makers, to create a societal discussion and debate about these issues.

And, subsequently, as a third step, these ideas and principles should be put up for adoption collectively before the community of nations at the UN General Assembly or its Security Council, with concrete topical issues discussed further and in depth in the respective international and regional bodies. I understand that the politics of the nation-state system today is not conducive to creatively thinking outside the box, free from the constraints of the immediate and pressing needs of our constituencies. However, I believe that we cannot shy away from taking on substantive and ambitious efforts to reestablish our national, legal, and global order. And, to safeguard against falling back into the trap of accommodation based on the prevailing balance of power, which changes over time, these principles and ideas should be formally adopted and thus legislated nationally, regionally, and globally. This is a cumbersome but logical imperative. Rule of law has to be the prevailing practice to ensure the interests of all.

In essence, we are at important junctures and thresholds once again. In the middle of the last century, devastating losses caused by world wars created a collective awareness that we had to work together to ensure that these tragic situations did not reoccur. In the twenty-first century, it is time now to raise our achievements to ever higher levels and to prevent the arrogance of power or greed for unlimited fulfillment from being the reasons for dramatic self-destruction or the infamy of inhumanity. Reinvigorating the social conscience and elevating collective perspectives are paramount for the success of these efforts.

References

SIPRI. 2020. *SIPRI Yearbook 2020: Armaments, Disarmament and International Security*. Oxford: Oxford University Press.

World Bank. 2020. *Poverty and Shared Prosperity 2020: Reversals of Fortune*. Washington, DC: World Bank.

15

CAN A PLANET IN PERIL CONTAIN GEOPOLITICAL RIVALRIES?

Kishore Mahbubani

There is no doubt about what is the biggest question of our time: can the human species, all 7.8 billion of us, prevent one of the stupidest events in human history from breaking out in our time—namely, a major geopolitical contest between America and China? Why stupid? Our planet is in peril from multiple challenges, from global warming to deforestation and overfishing, and possibly the most important health crisis in this generation: COVID-19.[1]

Most scholars agree that our planet is in peril on many counts. Professor Benjamin Horton of Nanyang Technological University (NTU) of Singapore makes this point clearly and succinctly:

> For millennia, the forces of nature kept everything in balance, with death by viral disease playing a part, affecting all species, plants and animals, including humans. But in the 20th and 21st centuries, things have changed dramatically. Earth's ecosystems have been subject to unprecedented levels of global change stemming from human activities, a period referred to as the Great Acceleration, including climate change, land use intensification, atmospheric pollution, and species extinctions and invasions.
>
> *(Horton 2020)*

COVID-19 should have provided humanity a badly needed wake-up call. Its rapid spread to all corners of the world, killing human beings of diverse ethnic groups, should have made it clear that the human species now lives on a virus-infected cruise ship. There is no point in taking care of our cabin only. We need to take care of the global ship as a whole. An even greater moral imperative is for all nations (read "countries") to cooperate, rather than fight each other, when all of humanity faces many common perils.

Against this backdrop, we can see clearly the folly of America and China plunging into a major geopolitical contest at this point in history. As I say in *Has China Won?*:

> Humans would look pityingly at two tribes of apes that continued fighting over territory while the forest around them was burning. But this is how America and China will appear to future generations if they continue to focus on their differences while the earth is facing an extended moment of great peril.
>
> *(Mahbubani 2020, 281–282)*

The goal of this essay is twofold: to explain how this great act of human folly is appearing during our time and to also suggest how humanity can work together to prevent it from imperiling planet earth, including the six billion people who live outside America and China. Indeed, there is also now a clear moral imperative for these six billion people to speak out loudly and clearly to both America and China. However, we can do so only if we understand clearly the origins and driving forces behind their massive geopolitical contest. In trying to explain and understand this contest, we must be clinical, neutral, and objective in our analysis. Given the highly charged political environment between America and China, this may be a tall order. Yet, if we base our analysis on facts, not suppositions, we can see clearly how unnecessary this geopolitical contest is. The essay also proposes how China and the US could work together in spite of their geopolitical rivalries in tackling the most pressing concerns of humanity, including the COVID-19 challenge.

So what triggered this contest in the first place? As social scientists, we can say that the trigger came from China. After having experienced a century of humiliation (1842 to 1949) at the hands of Western powers and Japan and some travails from the 1950s to the 1970s (from the Great Leap Forward to the Cultural Revolution), China finally found its way forward after Deng Xiaoping launched the "Four Modernizations" in 1979. What followed was completely unprecedented in human history: the fastest ever economic growth that any major nation-state has seen in human history. The statistics describe what happened. In purchasing power parity (PPP) terms, China's GNP was one-tenth that of America in 1980. By 2014 it had become bigger.

Clearly, the "mistake" China made was to grow so big and so fast. Yet China could not have rescued 800 million out of poverty and delivered middle-class living standards to hundreds of millions of Chinese without this rapid economic growth. Curiously, China has no intention of replacing America's global leadership or to undermine or weaken it. China knows well that the 1945 rules-based order was a gift from America to the world. China has emerged as the biggest beneficiary of it since it is now the world's number one trading power. This is why I argue strongly in *Has China Won?* that there is no necessary reason for a geopolitical contest to break out.

Yet it has! Unfortunately, a series of events and decisions have triggered it. The first and most important fact to know is that it was America's decision to launch this contest. Sadly, America unwisely decided to launch it without first working out a comprehensive long-term strategy. The man who alerted me to this was one of America's greatest strategic thinkers, Henry Kissinger. That was the message he conveyed to me over a one-on-one lunch at his private club in New York in March 2018. This is also the big message of his book *On China* (Kissinger 2011).

This decision by America to plunge into a geopolitical contest with China without working out a strategy is strange for many reasons. It did the opposite when it plunged into a contest with the Soviet Union, a far less formidable rival when compared to China. The great American strategic thinker of that time was George Kennan. He was the author of the famous "X" essay that appeared in 1947 in *Foreign Affairs*. Indeed, he gave many valuable pieces of advice to his fellow Americans. When America embarked on its great geopolitical contest against the Soviet Union, Kennan said the final outcome would be determined as follows:

> It is rather a question of the degree to which the United States can create among the peoples of the world generally the impression of a country which knows what it wants, which is coping successfully with the problem of its internal life and with the responsibilities of a World Power, and which has a spiritual vitality capable of holding its own among the major ideological currents of the time.

He added that with this "spiritual vitality," America should cultivate more "friends and allies." He also counseled "humility" and bravely said America should avoid "insulting" the Soviet Union, as America would still have to deal with it (see Mahbubani 2020, 6).

Fortunately, Kennan's strategic advice was heeded. America won the geopolitical contest against the Soviet Union handsomely. Curiously, America has not attempted to work out a comprehensive long-term strategy to deal with China. This is even though China will be a more formidable superpower competitor for America. It has four times the population of America and a political resilience that is at least 4,000 years old. Despite this, America didn't just fail to work out a comprehensive long-term strategy. It has also ignored all four pieces of advice that Kennan provided. For example, if Kennan is right and the contest will be determined by domestic "spiritual vitality," China is winning. America is the only major developed society where the average income of the bottom 50% declined over a 30-year period. Even more shockingly, 40% of American families don't have US $400 in emergency cash. By contrast, the 1.4 billion Chinese people have experienced the greatest improvement ever in their standard of living. The past 40 years are the best the Chinese have experienced in 4,000 years. As a result, as Stanford University professor Jean Fan (2019) has documented,

"In contrast to America's stagnation, China's culture, self-concept and morale are being transformed at a rapid pace—mostly for the better." China has spiritual vitality. America doesn't.

There is no shortage of strategic mistakes America is making in its management of the China challenge. For example, can America make U-turns and focus on domestic economic and social development instead of wasteful external adventures? In theory, yes. In practice, as I demonstrate in *Has China Won?*, it will be difficult to do so. America has had many brilliant defense secretaries. None could reduce defense expenses. Why not? Defense spending is not decided as a result of a comprehensive, rational strategy. Instead, weapons systems are purchased as a result of a complex lobbying system.

Now comes the really shocking part. Even though the Trump administration (2017–2021) clearly made strategic mistakes in its management of the Sino-American relationship, the only policy that the administration got solid bipartisan support for was its policy toward China. Indeed, despite the deep political polarization in America today, there is a convergence of views on China. A Pew Research Center survey (2020) shows that nine in ten Americans believe China is a threat. The "deep state" has also turned against China. Hank Paulson says, "You have Homeland Security, the FBI, CIA, Defense Department, treating China as the enemy and members of Congress competing to see who can be the most belligerent China hawk. No one is leaning against the wind, providing balance" (Ip 2019).

Why are so many Americans, including thoughtful Americans, supporting a clearly flawed strategy toward China? Many Americans feel very angry toward China. Indeed, many feel betrayed by China. The depth of the anger toward China in the American body politic was demonstrated by the American reactions to the COVID-19 challenge. One of the most basic rules of geopolitics is that the enemy of your enemy is your friend. COVID-19 is the enemy of America. China is also an enemy of COVID-19. Basic common sense would suggest that America should have pressed the pause button on the strategic contest with China and worked with China to fight a common enemy. This is what leaders like Churchill and Franklin Delano Roosevelt would have advised America to do. Indeed, they defeated Hitler by allying with Stalin, a truly brutal dictator. Yet the political environment toward China has become so toxic that not one major American figure dared to make this commonsense suggestion.

Why has the political environment in America become so toxic toward China? This is a very difficult question to answer because both rational and nonrational factors are at play here. Some of the "nonrational" dimensions are "taboo" for political discussions in the politically correct environment of America, even though they are clearly at play. For example, the "yellow peril" dimension, a subconscious impulse, is alive and at play in this contest.

It may be easier to list out the "rational" factors that have caused the major deterioration in the relationship. This list would include the following: China's mistreatment and alienation of the American business community in China (and this was an unnecessary mistake by China); the failure of China to politically liberalize and become a democracy like America (an almost universal expectation in America, as documented by Kurt Campbell, a former assistant secretary of state, in his *Foreign Affairs* essay co-authored with Ely Ratner; see Campbell and Ratner 2018); China's military adventurism in the South China Sea (including a widely believed but false story that President Xi Jinping had promised to demilitarize the islands there); China's launch of the Asian Infrastructure Investment Bank (AIIB) and Belt and Road Initiative (which were seen as threats to America's globally dominant position); and, perhaps most dangerously, China's ability to move ahead of America in critical areas of advanced technology, such as 5G technology (which explains the ferocious campaign against Huawei) and artificial intelligence. In this last area, one initiative by China really hit a raw nerve in America. As Campbell and Ratner (2018, 62) said,

> rather than opening the country up to greater competition, the Chinese Communist Party (CCP), intent on maintaining control of the economy, is instead consolidating state-owned enterprises and pursuing industrial policies (notably its "Made in China 2025" plan) that aim to promote national technology champions in critical sectors, including aerospace, biomedicine, and robotics

by 2025.

Each one of the dimensions listed above is a complex subject. Yet it is also clear that one main driving force in the united American campaign against China is a widely held belief among influential Americans that America cannot and should never allow any other power to replace America as the "number one" power in the world. This same American impulse to thwart potential geopolitical rivals was also shown when the Soviet Union (in its famous Sputnik moment) and Japan (in its "Japan is number one" moment) threatened to overtake America. Fortunately for America, neither the Soviet Union nor Japan came close. Unfortunately for America, it is a very likely possibility that America will become number two to China in economic weight within a decade or two. Clearly, this fear of the loss of American primacy is probably the main driving force in the American campaign to somehow diminish or undermine China.

It is important to emphasize that this addiction to "American primacy" is deeply rooted. There is a strong consensus within the American body politic, especially among the American elite, that America should remain number one. Americans also feel an obligation to lead the world. Madeleine Albright expressed this well in 1998: "If we have to use force, it is because we are America; we are the indispensable nation. We stand tall and we see further than other countries into the future, and we see the danger here to all of us" (Zenko 2014). Americans also want America to be the "shining city on the hill," inspiring the rest of the world.

Indeed, the rest of the world would be happy to see a strong, self-confident America inspiring the world. However, its "shine" comes from its domestic record, not its military adventures. Clearly, the "sea of despair" among the working classes, the rise of American populism, and the election of Donald Trump have dented America's standing in the world. Any objective empirical study would show that while America's global geopolitical influence has been receding, China's has been gradually expanding.

The incompetent response by many Western countries to COVID-19, particularly when compared to the strong responses of China and other East Asian countries, has led to further decline in the West's standing in the eyes of the world, even as China and East Asia have risen in esteem.

This may also explain the strong consensus among the "deep state" members of the American establishment that this is the moment for America to stop China's rise, before it is too late. This goal may be understandable since this is an impulse that all great powers have when faced with rising rivals, as documented by Graham Allison (2017) in his book *Destined for War*. Yet, if the strategic establishment of America has decided to plunge into a geopolitical contest with China, should it not work out a strategy first? Fareed Zakaria, like Henry Kissinger, has confirmed this lack of strategy:

> The US had a comprehensive bipartisan strategy towards China from the opening in 1972 until recently—to integrate China into the world, politically, economically and culturally. But in recent years, that strategy produced complications and complexities—helped usher in a new, more powerful China that did not conform to Western expectations. In the wake of this transformation, the US has been frozen. It has not been able to conceive of a new comprehensive strategy toward the Middle Kingdom.
> *(Mahbubani 2020, 50)*

Since it is unwise for any great power, even one as powerful as America, to plunge into a geopolitical contest without first working out a strategy, the time has come for friends of America, especially scholars all around the world (including in Europe), to speak out and advise America to take a wiser course of action in dealing with China. A wiser course of action can only be based on an objective and clear-headed analysis of contemporary geopolitical realities and not on the wishful thinking that has characterized much American analysis and understanding of China. This wishful thinking has resulted in a flawed consensus that is a result of three grand illusions that have bedeviled American thinking on China.

The first grand illusion is the belief that, as China's economy grew and prospered as a result of economic liberalization, political liberalization would naturally follow, and China would become, like America, a liberal democracy. As indicated earlier, Kurt Campbell captured well this expectation of the entire American establishment. He said that:

ever since [rapprochement began under Nixon], the assumption that deepening commercial, diplomatic, and cultural ties would transform China's internal development and external behaviour has been a bedrock of U.S. strategy. Even those in U.S. policy circles who were skeptical of China's intentions still shared the underlying belief that U.S. power and hegemony could readily mold China to the United States' liking.

(see Mahbubani 2020, 135)

Hillary Clinton said that the Chinese "are trying to stop history, which is a fool's errand. They cannot do it. But they're going to hold it off as long as possible" (Luttwak 2012, 233).

It's revealing that Hillary Clinton used the word *history*. Historians are accustomed to taking a long view of human events. With this perspective, it is clear that the American republic has enjoyed a history of less than 250 years since its founding in 1776. By contrast, the Chinese state has had a long, continuous history, whose beginnings can be traced to the first unification of China by Emperor Qin Shi Huang in 221 BCE. China's political culture and traditions go back almost ten times as long as America's political history. Future historians will undoubtedly be puzzled by the strong conviction of American policymakers that a smaller and younger republic could decisively influence the political evolution of a state that was four times larger in population and had a history almost ten times longer.

The Chinese see their history through their own lenses. Over the course of the past 2,200 years, China has been divided and broken up more often than it has been united and cohesive. Each time, central political control from the capital breaks down, disorder results, and the Chinese people suffer a host of deprivations, from starvation and famine to civil war and rampant violence. In Chinese political culture, the biggest fear is of chaos. The Chinese have a word for it: luàn (乱). Given these many long periods of suffering from chaos—including one as recent as the century of humiliation from the Opium War of 1842 to the creation of the People's Republic of China in 1949—when the Chinese people are given a choice between strong central control and the chaos of political competition, they have a reflexive tendency to choose strong central control.

There is therefore one simple but painful hard truth that American policymakers and pundits must accept: China will behave like China, not America. At the end of the day, the government of China will rest or fall on one key issue: does it or doesn't it enjoy the support of the 1.4 billion Chinese people. No Chinese government, no matter how powerful, can suppress 1.4 billion people. A long Chinese political tradition allows the Chinese people to rise up against the government when it is perceived to have lost "the mandate of heaven." In this area, there is one other painful hard truth Americans must learn to accept. The current Chinese government enjoys enormous support among the Chinese people. All the surveys show this. In a Pew survey in 2013 (Pew Research Center 2013), 85% of Chinese people indicated that they were satisfied with the direction the country was heading. According to the Edelman Trust Barometer (2020), 90% of Chinese people indicated that they trust the Chinese government.

Paradoxically, the strong attacks on China by American policymakers and pundits have only strengthened the legitimacy of and the public support for the Chinese government. It is truly unfortunate that the Trump administration launched a torrent of abuse on the Chinese government (ignoring the wise advice of George Kennan to not "insult" adversaries) because of COVID-19. In response to this torrent of abuse, the Chinese people compared the competent response of the Chinese government and the incompetent response of the Trump administration. Over time, respect for America (called "the beautiful country" by the Chinese people) has gone down among the Chinese. Even before Trump became president, a Pew survey in 2016 had found that 50% of Chinese polled had a favorable view of the US, down from 58% in 2010, while 45% saw the US as a major threat to China, up from 39% in 2013 (Pew Research Center 2016).

Getting rid of the grand illusions of Americans will also help Americans to accept a new historical reality. For the past 200 years, we have been living in a monocivilizational world dominated by one civilization, the Western civilization. Now we are moving toward a multicivilizational world with many successful civilizations. The new successful civilizations, like the Indian and Chinese civilizations, will not become replicas of Western civilizations. Instead, they will enjoy a rich cultural renaissance of their own deep and vibrant civilizational traditions. A multicivilizational world should be a joy to behold, not a threat to fear.

The second grand illusion that Americans must get rid of is the black-and-white view they have of the Sino-American relationship. Many Americans, including thoughtful Americans, believe that in both its domestic and its international behavior, America is "virtuous." By contrast, China is seen as a malevolent actor, both domestically and internationally. This claim is not an exaggeration. Here is a sample of what senior American figures say about China. US Senator Marco Rubio (2019) said that "the Chinese Communist party's ideological commitment to totalitarianism has become mobilized into regular, brutal action, intended to forcibly assimilate anyone who dares question the Communist party's political and cultural control." US Senator Tom Cotton (2019) has said that

> Today the Chinese government is purging every vestige of its subjects' freedoms at home to pave the way for its economic, military, and political expansion abroad. China has a plan for the world, and it's as concrete as the prison cells where it keeps dissenters.

As I document in my book, this "assumption of virtue" is deeply rooted in the American mind. Other scholars have also noted this. Professor Stephen Walt (2011) of Harvard University has noted that "over the last two centuries, prominent Americans have described the US as an 'empire of liberty,' a 'shining city on a hill,' the 'last best hope of Earth,' the 'leader of the free world,' and the 'indispensable nation.'" He also explains why many Americans believe that America is the best country in the world:

> Most statements of 'American exceptionalism' presume that America's values, political system, and history are unique and worthy of universal admiration. They also imply that the US is both destined and entitled to play a distinct and positive role on the world stage.
>
> *(Walt 2011)*

He then goes on to make a claim that most Americans would reject: "The only thing wrong with this self-congratulatory portrait of America's global role is that it is mostly a myth" (Walt 2011).

The simple truth therefore is that America is not inherently virtuous. Nor is China inherently malevolent. Both are normal countries. All "normal" countries of the world have their shares of virtues and vices. It is unwise for any country in the world, including America, to proclaim that it is morally superior to other countries. This is why it was wise for Kennan to advise his fellow Americans to be "humble" and allow for America's "spiritual vitality" to speak for itself.

The explosive improvements in the living standards of the American middle-class population were a source of joy and inspiration to the world. America's other achievements also inspired the world. It is still the only country to send a man to the moon. At the end of the day, performance matters.

Sadly, America has been underperforming on many counts in recent decades. Two Princeton University economists, Anne Case and Angus Deaton, have documented this. The white working classes of America used to carry the American dream of getting a better life in their hearts and souls. Today, as Case and Deaton say, there is a "sea of despair" among them. They conclude: "Ultimately, we see our story as about the collapse of the white, high-school-educated working class after its heyday in the early 1970s, and the pathologies that accompany that decline" (Case and Deaton 2017, 438). Their detailed study documents how the fact of poor economic prospects "compounds over time through family dysfunction, social isolation, addiction, obesity and other pathologies" (Achenbach and Keating 2017).

One of America's greatest political philosophers of recent times was John Rawls. If he were alive today, he would be shocked to see how badly off the least advantaged Americans have become. In his book *Oligarchy*, American political scientist Jeffrey Winters (2011) provides a stunning illustration of just how dire US inequality has become: the average wealth of the richest 100 American households relative to that of the bottom 90% approximates the wealth disparity between a Roman senator and a slave at the height of the Roman Empire.

Given America's enormous and rising socioeconomic problems at home and given China's remarkable success in uplifting the living conditions of Chinese people, it would be wiser for America to drop the grand illusion that there is a black-and-white difference between the performance of American and Chinese societies. Here there is one fundamental ideological obstacle that American minds will have to overcome: the belief that a "democratic" society is inherently morally superior to a "communist" society.

The third grand illusion that America will have to abandon is that the vast majority of the six billion people of the world who live outside America and China will naturally gravitate to support America in its geopolitical contest against China because America is an inherently superior and more attractive country than China, just as many more nations supported America in its Cold War against the Soviet Union. Many Americans, even thoughtful Americans, believe this. Yet the world of 2020 is very different from the world of 1950 when the Cold War began. In 1950 most nations of the world, including many European nations, lay prostrate and weak. Much of the Third World remained colonized. By contrast, in 2020 the world is full of many strong and self-confident nations. Most believe that they are capable of making independent judgments on which nation is right or wrong.

A test case of the relative global credibility of America and China was provided during the COVID-19 crisis. On May 3, 2020, US Secretary of State Mike Pompeo said that "there is a significant amount of evidence that this came from that laboratory in Wuhan" (ABC News 2020). This was, of course, a serious allegation by one of the most powerful persons in the global community. In the past, if the US secretary of state made such a strong claim, it would have been both taken seriously and immediately supported by the allies of the US. In this case, not one country in the world supported this claim. This is a clear bellwether of how much the world has changed.

Most countries around the world prefer to listen to trusted scientists and scholars on the subject of COVID-19. Hence, even in response to the lesser US charge that China has "hidden" from the world information on COVID-19, the world gave greater credibility to the points made by Dr. Richard Horton, the editor-in-chief of *The Lancet*, one of the most prestigious journals in the medical field. He said:

> The reason why I've been very critical of the UK government, the US Administration and many European countries is because the Lancet published 5 papers in the last week of January. Those papers tell the story of what has unfolded in the Western world in the recent months. Those 5 papers described a new virus. They showed that this virus was deadly, that it was related to SARS, that it was killing people and that the number of deaths was rising. The patients were being admitted to ICUs and required ventilation. Those papers showed that there was no treatment for the virus. They showed that there was person to person transmission. They explained the importance of personal protective equipment. They explained why testing and tracing contacts and isolating people was absolutely key to controlling the pandemic. And they indeed also warned of the pandemic potential of this virus. We knew all of this in the last week of

January. Most Western countries and the US wasted the whole of February and early March before they acted. That is the human tragedy of COVID-19. Thanks to the work of the Chinese doctors and scientists working in international collaborations, all of this information was known in January. But for reasons that are still difficult to understand, the world did not pay attention.

(CGTN 2020)

Equally significantly, on May 4, 2020, at the initiative of the World Health Organization (WHO), several world leaders joined a conference to show global support for the development of a vaccine. Germany's Prime Minister Angela Merkel and France's President Emmanuel Macron participated in the conference. China sent a representative, Mr. Zhang Ming, Beijing's ambassador to the EU, who stood in for China's Premier Li Keqiang. The US refused to attend. However, an important qualification needs to be inserted here. This strong and violent antipathy to multilateralism may be peculiar to the Trump administration. Since Joe Biden became president in January 2021, relations between the US and multilateral organizations have improved.

However, even after Joe Biden has been elected, America still continues to use its power to persuade or pressure other countries to fall in line. In the coming, inevitable geopolitical contest between America and China, each will be tempted to use its sturdy geopolitical muscles to cajole, bribe, pressure, and arm-twist other countries to join its side. This is normal superpower behavior.

Except the world has moved on since the Cold War. America's relative economic power and cultural influence have diminished since its heyday. China's relative economic power is far greater than that of the former Soviet Union. The most important ratio is that between the relative combined weight of America and China and that of the rest of the world. Many countries and regions have become big enough to walk away from both America and China. Most countries have also become shrewder at weighing and acting in their own geopolitical interests. Chan Heng Chee (2019), who served as Singapore's ambassador in Washington, DC, from 1996 to 2012, observed that many Asian countries "are carefully defining their own positions, pushing back against pressure to choose sides between the US and China." Hence, both America and China will have to get used to dealing with other countries that have become more confident and less compliant over time.

In short, if America were to proceed full steam ahead with its geopolitical contest against China and expect the rest of the world, especially its friends and allies, to fall in line in this campaign, it may find itself standing alone or joined by very few allies. Similarly, very few will support China outright. The vast majority of the world's countries would counsel both America and China to think twice before initiating such a geopolitical contest.

Equally importantly, if both America and China were to do a rational cost-benefit analysis of such a major geopolitical contest, they would find that both may be better off avoiding it. If we could marshal the forces of reason to develop an understanding of the real national interests of both America and China, we would come to the conclusion that there should be no fundamental contradiction between the two powers. Indeed, there are actually five noncontradictions between America and China. If wise heads could prevail in both capitals, they should reflect on and highlight these five fundamental noncontradictions.

China and the US have not been able to work together effectively in tackling the COVID-19 crisis. Geopolitics has gotten in the way, with both countries trading accusations and counter-accusations against each other. Several American leaders, led by President Trump, have made insulting remarks about China. Secretary of State Pompeo said,

> Remember, this is the Wuhan coronavirus that's caused this, and the information that we got at the front end of this thing wasn't perfect and has led us now to a place where much of the challenge we face today has put us behind the curve.
>
> *(Stankiewicz 2020)*

These noncontradictions show a way forward in overcoming, or at least sidestepping, the geopolitical competition between China and the US when dealing with a common catastrophe afflicting humanity, such as COVID-19.

First, there is a noncontradiction between the fundamental national interests of both countries. The fundamental national interest of both societies is to improve the well-being of their people. In March 1809, Thomas Jefferson (1809) wrote, on his departure from the US presidency, "the care of human life and happiness, and not their destruction, is the first and only legitimate object of good government."

America is a much richer country than China. Its nominal per capita income of US $62,641 is at least six times larger than that of China's at US $9,771. Yet even though America is richer, the well-being of its people, especially the bottom 50% of the population, has deteriorated in recent decades. One fact cannot be denied: America has wasted more than US $6 trillion on wars in the Middle East since 9/11. Brown University's Watson Institute (2021) reported: "Through Fiscal Year 2020, the United States federal government has spent or obligated $6.4 trillion dollars on the post-9/11 wars in Afghanistan, Pakistan, Iraq, and elsewhere." If these $6 trillion had been shared among the bottom 50% of the American population, each American citizen would have received about US $39,000. If this amount is laid alongside the statistic that two-thirds of American households do not have access to emergency cash of $500, it shows clearly why it is in America's national interest to put the well-being of its people first. Heidi Garrett-Peltier wrote in a 2017 paper for Brown University's Watson Institute:

> Since 2001, because the federal government has spent trillions of dollars on the wars in Iraq, Afghanistan, Syria, and Pakistan, we have lost

opportunities to create millions of jobs in the domestic economy, and we have lost opportunities to improve educational, health, and environmental outcomes for the American public. [...] Education and healthcare create more than twice as many jobs as defense for the same level of spending, while clean energy and infrastructure create over 40 percent more jobs. In fact, over the past 16 years, by spending money on war rather than in these other areas of the domestic economy, the US lost the opportunity to create between one million and three million additional jobs.

(Garrett-Peltier 2017, 1–2)

In short, the American people would be far better off if America stopped fighting unnecessary foreign wars and used its resources to improve the well-being of its people. Since China's per capita income is much lower than America's, it is also in China's national interest to improve the well-being of its people. The argument that both America and China should make improving the well-being of their people their primary national interest should be incontestable. Yet the fact that the strategic thinkers cannot see this fundamental point demonstrates just how distorted their perspectives have become. It is the good fortune of both America and China that the vast Pacific Ocean separates them. If they can both focus on the well-being of their people and allow the Pacific Ocean to protect their respective homelands, both societies will be better off.

They could also find areas to cooperate in. America is suffering from a serious infrastructure deficit. China has emerged as an infrastructure superpower. It can build high-speed train networks faster than any other country. In 2012 Keith Bradsher of the *New York Times* reported that "China began service ... on the world's longest high-speed rail line, covering a distance in eight hours that is about equal to that from New York to Key West, FL, Amtrak trains from New York to Miami, a shorter distance, still take nearly 30 hours" (Bradsher 2012). Common sense would dictate that both countries should cooperate in infrastructure. Yet, given the poisonous political attitudes toward each other, common sense cannot operate. This is why a major strategic reboot is needed in the relationship between the two powers. If the two powers first try to define what their core national interests are—especially their core interests in improving the livelihoods of their people—they would come to the logical conclusion that there is fundamentally a noncontradiction between their national interests.

Second, there is also a fundamental noncontradiction between America and China in slowing the forces of climate change. If climate change makes the planet progressively uninhabitable, both American and Chinese citizens will be fellow passengers on a sinking ship. It has become a cliche to say that it is foolish to rearrange the deck chairs on the *Titanic*. Yet this is precisely what the leaders of America and China are doing when they argue over their geopolitical differences instead of focusing on their common interest in protecting our planet.

Some wise soul has remarked that the best thing that could happen for humanity would be for astronomers to detect a distant comet on a collision path with the earth, with no certainty which continent it would land on. Only such a common threat would make the 7.5 billion people on the planet (including 1.4 billion in China and 330 million in America) aware that their common interests as earth citizens are far greater than their national interests. Unfortunately, even though COVID-19 has been such a common threat, it has not brought the global population together. The simple truth is that, as Yuval Noah Harari writes in *Sapiens*:

> Today almost all humans share the same geopolitical system ... the same economic system ... the same legal system ... and the same scientific system. The single global culture is not homogeneous. Yet they are all closely connected and they influence one another in myriad ways. They still argue and fight, but they argue using the same concepts and fight using the same weapons. [ ] Today when Iran and the United States rattle swords at one another, they both speak the language of nation states, capitalist economies, international rights and nuclear physics.
>
> *(see Mahbubani 2020, 266)*

As our only habitable planet faces a great peril, should we focus on our differences or our similarities? The human species is supposed to be the most intelligent species on earth. This is the apparent reason why we have become the world's dominant species. Yet the most intelligent species is now acting in a suicidal fashion by allowing climate change to gain traction without acting in common to reverse it. Instead, we are arguing about which countries are to blame. Robert Blackwill (2019, 18), the distinguished former American ambassador, is right to highlight that China today "generates approximately 28 percent of global carbon emissions and the United States is responsible for only about 15 percent." Yet it is also a fact that global warming is happening not only because of current flows of greenhouse gas emissions but also because of the stock of greenhouse gases, especially CO_2, emitted by Western countries, including America, since the coal-fired Industrial Revolution. In terms of cumulative CO_2 emissions by the major powers, China has contributed far less than America and the European Union. All industrialized nations need to take responsibility for their actions and work together to limit further environmental damage.

China and India have been remarkably responsible in not walking away from the Paris climate accords when the Trump administration decided to do so in 2017. It is a truly strange world we live in when the relatively poor countries like China and India (per capita income US $2,016) respect their global obligations, while a relatively rich country like America walks away from them. As Blackwill (2019, 18–19) states:

> the U.S. withdrawal from the Paris Agreement has made China an informal global leader on climate change, as the signatories of the agreement proceed without U.S. involvement. This contributes to a widespread

international view that the United States, reflected in the policies of the Trump administration, is withdrawing from the world.

Global warming is not the only "global commons" challenge that humanity faces. There are equally pressing challenges in many other areas. The United Nations has identified 17 Sustainable Development Goals to "meet the urgent environmental, political and economic challenges facing our world." These are what the 17 goals aim to accomplish:

1. End extreme poverty in all forms by 2030;
2. End hunger, achieve food security and improved nutrition, and promote sustainable agriculture;
3. Ensure healthy lives and promote well-being for all at all ages;
4. Ensure inclusive and equitable quality education and promote lifelong learning opportunities for all;
5. Achieve gender equality and empower all women and girls;
6. Ensure availability and sustainable management of water and sanitation for all;
7. Ensure access to affordable, reliable, sustainable, and modern energy for all;
8. Promote sustained, inclusive, and sustainable economic growth, full and productive employment, and decent work for all;
9. Build resilient infrastructure, promote inclusive and sustainable industrialization, and foster innovation;
10. Reduce inequality within and among countries;
11. Make cities and human settlements inclusive, safe, resilient, and sustainable;
12. Ensure sustainable consumption and production patterns;
13. Take urgent action to combat climate change and its impacts;
14. Conserve and sustainably use the oceans, seas, and marine resources for sustainable development;
15. Protect, restore, and promote sustainable use of terrestrial ecosystems, sustainably manage forests, combat desertification, halt and reverse land degradation, and halt biodiversity loss;
16. Promote peaceful and inclusive societies for sustainable development, provide access to justice for all, and build effective, accountable, and inclusive institutions at all levels;
17. Strengthen the means of implementation and revitalize the global partnership for sustainable development.

This noncontradiction assumes particular seriousness in today's world, which probably faces the biggest crisis of this generation: how to deal with COVID-19 and other future pandemics. The COVID-19 pandemic has already claimed hundreds of thousands of lives around the world, including more than 100,000 deaths in the US. China, by employing measures that were seen as "draconian" by Western standards, was able to stem the impact of COVID-19 within its own population. It recorded fewer than 5,000 deaths. However, instead of looking for ways to collaborate with each other and gaining knowledge of best practices, the US and China exchanged barbs over which country ought to be assigned greater blame for the pandemic's spread.

One fact is undeniable: if the world's two biggest powers cooperate on these common challenges, we are more likely to find solutions. The actions of either one of them can have a major impact. Here is one example. When China made the bold decision to lock down Wuhan in January 2020, right before its Chinese New Year holiday, it also stemmed an even more fatal spread of COVID-19. Likewise, research for an effective medicine and eventually a vaccine for COVID-19 is taking place all over the world, through sustained collaboration among the scientific communities in several countries.

The third noncontradiction between America and China lies in the ideological sphere. This statement may come as a surprise. It is commonly believed that a key driving force in the Sino-American geopolitical contest is a deep and profound ideological divide. There was indeed a time when China promoted communism. However, it has now been more than 40 years since the CCP stopped promoting communism globally.

The noncommunist countries of Southeast Asia and indeed most countries of the world therefore do not feel threatened in any way by Chinese ideology. Many thoughtful Americans may deem this naive. Many Americans have become convinced (almost as a matter of religious belief) that the success of Chinese communism inherently poses a threat to democracies. For example, in *The Hundred-Year Marathon*, Michael Pillsbury (2016) has written:

> Chinese officials prefer a world with more autocracies and fewer democracies. [...] As China's power continues to grow, its ability to protect dictatorial, pro-China governments and to undermine representative governments will likely grow dramatically as well. [...] [S]uch efforts have begun with the manipulation of news and information. Part of its $6.58 billion "overseas propaganda" project expressly advocates autocratic forms of government.
>
> *(Pillsbury 2016, 177–196)*

If Chinese communism is an inherent threat to democracies, it should be perceived as a threat by many other democracies. The three largest democracies in the world, in terms of population size, are India (1.3 billion), the US (330 million), and Indonesia (250 million). If Chinese communism is a threat to democracies, all three should feel threatened. Some American policymakers feel threatened. Yet, if one were to ask either Prime Minister Modi of India or President Jokowi of Indonesia (or any of their senior colleagues) whether Indian democracy or Indonesian democracy feels threatened by Chinese communism, they would be puzzled by this question. Since both India and Indonesia are geographically much closer to China and have many more links with China, they understand China well. Certainly, the rise of Chinese power is a matter of concern to them. But Chinese communist ideology is of no concern to them. They see no desire or effort on the part of Chinese leaders to export or promote communism. In this respect, the attitude and behavior of the Chinese Communist Party is the exact opposite of the Soviet Communist Party.

Unfortunately, many American thinkers have unthinkingly transferred their previous assumptions about Soviet behavior to the CCP. There is a danger in doing this. The Chinese Communist Party is far more capable and adaptable than the Soviet Communist Party. Unlike the Soviet Communist Party, it is in no danger of disappearing anytime soon. At the 2019 Shangri-La Dialogue, Singapore's Prime Minister Lee Hsien Loong remarked:

> The Cold War ended with the total collapse of the sclerotic planned economies of the Soviet Union and the Eastern European countries, under the pressure of enormous defense spending. Even then, it took 40 years. It is highly improbable that the vigorous Chinese economy will collapse in the same way.
>
> *(quoted in Mahbubani 2020, 271)*

Why is it more resilient? Unlike the Soviet Communist Party, it is not riding on an ideological wave; it is riding the wave of a resurgent civilization, and that civilization has proven itself to be one of the strongest and most resilient in history.

American strategic minds are making a mistake when they focus on the fact that China is a communist country. Chinese communism is not a threat to American democracy. Instead, the success and competitiveness of the Chinese economy and society are the real challenge. To meet this challenge, American thinkers should focus on ensuring the success and competitiveness of the American economy and society. Interestingly, George Kennan, in his famous Mr. X essay, also emphasized the importance of a strong domestic American society. He used two key phrases that Americans should take note of. The outcome of the forthcoming contest, like the Cold War, will depend on the "spiritual vitality" of America and on America's success in avoiding "exhibitions of indecision, disunity and internal disintegration." In short, it will be domestic factors, not external threats, that will determine how well America does. Sadly, America today is suffering both from a lack of spiritual vitality and from disunity and internal disintegration. Instead of wasting precious resources on a nonexistent ideological threat from China, America should use the same resources to revitalize its own society. There is fundamentally a noncontradiction between American and Chinese ideology, as counterintuitive as this may seem.

Even more surprisingly, there is a noncontradiction between American and Chinese civilizations. Despite Samuel P. Huntington's warning in 1993, there is no imminent danger of a clash of civilizations between the West and China. Here, too, if reason could be the driving force in relations between countries, we would not need to fear the impact of civilizational difference. The arguments of reason and logic, as the great philosophers have taught us, have universal applicability in all cultures and civilizations. There is no reason why different civilizations cannot interact rationally with each other.

Yet just as human beings are heavily influenced by emotions in their personal decisions, they are equally influenced by emotions in their geopolitical judgments. To make matters worse, these emotions are quite often buried in the subconscious. While they may not appear on the surface, they are very much alive.

Emotions are also affecting Sino-American relations. It would have been easier for America to accept the rise of another power if China had been a fellow Western democratic power, especially a fellow Anglo-Saxon power. This explains why the power transition from the United Kingdom to the US went relatively smoothly: one Anglo-Saxon power was giving way to another. No dark emotional overtones accompanied this transition. By contrast, China is a very different culture and has always been perceived to be different in the Western imagination. Between America and China, there is a natural and legitimate concern: will they understand us, our interests and values? Will we understand them?

To make matters worse, there has been buried deep in the unconscious of the Western psyche an inchoate but real fear of the "yellow peril." Since it is buried deep in the unconscious, it seldom surfaces.

When senior American policymakers make their decisions on China, they can say with all sincerity that they are driven by rational, not emotional, considerations. Yet, to an external observer, it is manifestly clear that America's reactions to China's rise are influenced by deep emotional reactions too. Just as individual human beings have difficulty unearthing the unconscious motives that drive our behavior, countries and civilizations also have difficulty unearthing their unconscious impulses.

There is no doubt that, over the past 200 to 300 years, fears of the yellow peril have resulted in various acts of discrimination against "yellow-skinned" people, from the Chinese Exclusion Act at the end of the nineteenth century to the internment of Japanese Americans during World War II. The strong anti-China mood that has swept through Washington, DC, may in part be the result of rational dissatisfaction with some of China's policies, probably as a result of the fear of China's unfamiliar culture, but also in part from deeper emotional undercurrents. As the former US ambassador Chas Freeman Jr. (2019) has observed,

> in their views of China, many Americans now appear subconsciously to have combined images of the insidious Dr. Fu Manchu, Japan's unnerving 1980s challenge to US industrial and financial primacy, and a sense of existential threat analogous to the Sino-phobia that inspired the Anti-Coolie and Chinese Exclusion Acts.

Given the psychological reality of this "yellow peril" undercurrent, the American people need to question how much of their reaction to China's rise results from hard-headed, rational analysis and how much is a result of deep discomfort with the success of a non-Caucasian civilization. We may never know the real answer, as these struggles between reason and emotion are playing out in subconscious terrain. Still, we should thank Kiron Skinner for alluding to the fact that such subconscious dimensions are at play here (Ward 2019). The time has come for an honest discussion of the "yellow peril" dimension in US-China relations. The best way to deal with our subconscious fears is to surface them and deal with them.

Fortunately, we can overcome our irrational impulses. In our modern era, civilizations are not separated from one another like distinct billiard balls. Instead, we have developed into an interdependent human community in a small global village, and our civilizations are deeply connected and integrated with one another. In an article titled "The Fusion of Civilizations," Lawrence Summers and I pointed out the following:

> The great world civilizations, which used to have detached and separate identities, now have increasingly overlapping areas of commonality. Most people around the world now have the same aspirations as the Western middle classes: they want their children to get good educations, land good jobs, and live happy, productive lives as members of stable, peaceful communities. Instead of feeling depressed, the West should be celebrating its phenomenal success at injecting the key elements of its worldview into other great civilizations.
>
> *(Mahbubani and Summers 2016, 126)*

Instead of fearing a clash of civilizations, American policymakers should be cheered by our observation that "the march of reason, triggered in the West by the Enlightenment, is spreading globally, leading to the emergence of pragmatic problem-solving cultures in every region and making it possible to envisage the emergence of a stable and sustainable rules-based order" (Mahbubani and Summers 2016).

We also observed that the overriding dynamic of the fusion of civilizations is also taking place between the West and China. As we wrote:

> The second great challenge many worry about is the rise of China. China's success, however, can also be seen as the ultimate triumph of the West. The emperor Qianlong famously wrote to Great Britain's King George III in 1793 saying, "Our Celestial Empire possesses all things in prolific abundance and lacks no product within its own borders. There [is] therefore no need to import the manufactures of outside barbarians in exchange for our own produce." Two centuries later, the Chinese understand that absorbing Western modernity into their society has been crucial to their country's re-emergence. It has led to rapid economic growth, new and gleaming infrastructure, triumphs in space exploration, the spectacular 2008 Olympic Games in Beijing, and much more.
>
> *(Mahbubani and Summers 2016, 130)*

Even as Chinese society has accepted modernity with great enthusiasm, however, it has not abandoned its Chinese cultural roots. The Chinese look at their modern Chinese civilization and emphasize its Chineseness, seeing no contradiction.

Chinese leaders have also emphasized that despite China's cultural differences with the West, there need not be a clash of civilizations. Speaking at the opening of the Conference on Dialogue of Asian Civilizations in Beijing in May 2019, President Xi Jinping said:

> Civilizations don't have to clash with each other; what is needed are eyes to see the beauty in all civilizations. We should keep our own civilizations dynamic and create conditions for other civilizations to flourish. Together we can make the garden of world civilizations colorful and vibrant.

One curious aspect of our times is that in the past, it was Western leaders, not Chinese leaders, who espoused the values of embracing diversity. The one American president who lived through the nightmare of facing a realistic possibility of a nuclear war was John F. Kennedy. He was severely chastened by the experience, and on reflecting on this experience, he provided his fellow Americans with some valuable advice. In his commencement address at American University in 1963, he said:

> So, let us not be blind to our differences—but let us also direct attention to our common interests and to the means by which those differences can be resolved. And if we cannot end now our differences, at least we can help make the world safe for diversity. For, in the final analysis, our most basic common link is that we all inhabit this small planet. We all breathe the same air. We all cherish our children's future. And we are all mortal.
>
> *(Kennedy 1963)*

The key words in his statement are: make the world safe for diversity.

In short, foresighted American leaders of the past have arrived at the logical conclusion that even though humanity lives in different cultures and civilizations, there need not be a clash of civilizations. If we listen to them, then even in this dimension, where there could be a dangerous divide between America and China, there is a noncontradiction.

Finally, the one area where there appears to be a fundamental contradiction between America and China would be in the area of values, especially political values. Americans hold sacrosanct the ideals of freedom of speech, the press, assembly, and religion and also believe that every human being is entitled to the same fundamental human rights. The Chinese believe that social needs and social harmony are more important than individual needs and rights and that the prevention of chaos and turbulence is the main goal of governance. In short, America and China clearly believe in two different sets of political values.

Yet a fundamental contradiction would only arise in this area if China tries to export its values to America, and America tries to export its values to China. Some Americans, who have become obsessed with the threat from China, have begun to suggest that China is trying to undermine the values of American society. This was implied in the famous remark by FBI director Christopher Wray, who said that there was now a "whole-of-society" threat from China. Sadly, the report put out by a group of American scholars entitled "Chinese Influence and American Interests" also said that China was trying to undermine American freedoms. The report said: "Openness and freedom are fundamental elements of American democracy and intrinsic strengths of the United States and its way of life. These values must be protected against corrosive actions by China and other countries" (Working Group 2018). Yet, although China, like America and every other country in the world, engages in espionage, and there may be some objectionable activities by some Chinese agencies in America, it is possible to assert with great confidence that the Chinese government has no desire or plan to undermine or overthrow American democracy. Why not? The simple answer is that Chinese leaders are political realists. They would not waste their time or resources on a mission impossible.

Sadly, the same is not true in the American political system. Many Americans believe that they have a moral obligation to support efforts to overthrow a tyrannical communist party system and help liberate the Chinese people from political oppression—that since America succeeded in liberating so many people from the Soviet yoke, it could and should do the same with China. As documented several times in this essay, many Americans believe that China is "on the wrong side of history" and that America should try to help move China to the right side. They also believe that since America is a "shining city on the hill," it has an obligation to promote human rights in China.

Many Americans have expressed outrage over the treatment of innocent Muslim civilians by the Chinese government. Americans believe that they have the right to express outrage because they believe that America treats innocent Muslim civilians better.

But which country treats innocent Muslim civilians better, America or China? If the reports are true, the Chinese government has incarcerated hundreds of thousands of innocent Muslim civilians in reeducation camps. If the reports are true, the American government has tortured or killed thousands of innocent Muslim civilians since September 11, 2001. Unfortunately, in both cases, the facts seem to be true. The Chinese government has incarcerated hundreds of thousands of Muslim civilians. Enough media reports have confirmed this. Similarly, the American government has tortured thousands of Muslims. Since 9/11, America has been dropping thousands of bombs on Islamic countries, killing many innocent civilians as a result.

Since the records of both the American and the Chinese governments in respecting the human rights of innocent Muslim civilians has been less than perfect, it would be unwise for either government to preach to the other the importance of respecting fundamental human rights. A wiser approach for both governments to take is to look at the big picture and acknowledge that both governments face a common challenge of dealing with the threats posed by terrorists recruited by radical Islamic groups.

If America and China were to focus on their core interests of improving the livelihood and well-being of their citizens, they would come to realize that there are no fundamental contradictions in their long-term national interests. In 2010 then Indian Prime Minister Manmohan Singh and Chinese Premier Wen Jiabao captured the positive spirit of Sino-Indian relations in a joint statement: "There is enough space in the world for the development of both India and China and indeed, enough areas for India and China to cooperate." Similarly, there is enough space in the world for both America and China to thrive.

Equally important, in the face of the unprecedented health crisis of COVID-19, the US and China have a responsibility to steer the world toward a safer paradigm. COVID-19 will certainly not be the last pandemic affecting humanity. It is important that we come up with a stronger response to common health crises at a global, institutional level. Likewise, the overriding challenge of global warming: America and China have a fundamental common interest in keeping the planet habitable for the 1.7 billion people of America and China and the remaining 6 billion people of the world. These pressing and grave challenges to humanity should take precedence over all other challenges.

Moral philosophers and religious sages throughout the ages have reminded us that we will never succeed in creating perfection. Nor will we have simple black-and-white options to choose from. At the end of the day, we always have to make trade-offs, including moral ones; to figure out what our overriding imperatives are; and to learn how to focus on them. At the end of the day, this is what the six billion people of the rest of the world expect America and China to do: to focus on saving the planet and improving the living conditions of humanity, including those of their own people.

In short, it is in the interest of humanity as a whole to see America and China work together to "contain" their geopolitical rivalry rather than to allow that rivalry to explode in the coming decades.

Note

1 This essay includes several excerpts from Mahbubani (2020).

References

ABC News. 2020. "'This Week' Transcript 5-3-20: Mike Pompeo, Gov. Mike DeWine, Ronna McDaniel, Tom Perez." https://abcnews.go.com/Politics/week-transcript-20-mike-pompeo-gov-mike-dewine/story?id=70478442. Accessed July 12, 2021.

Achenbach, Joel and Dan Keating. 2017, March 23. "New Research Identifies a 'Sea of Despair' Among White Working-Class Americans," *Washington Post*, https://www

.washingtonpost.com/national/health-science/new-research-identifies-a-sea-of
-despair-among-white-working-class-americans/2017/03/22/c777ab6e-0da6-11e7
-9b0d-d27c98455440_story.html. Accessed July 12, 2021.

Allison, Graham. 2017. *Destined for War: Can America and China Escape Thucydides's Trap?*
New York: Houghton Mifflin Harcourt.

Blackwill, Robert D. 2019. *Trump's Foreign Policies Are Better Than They Seem*. New York:
Council on Foreign Relations.

Bradsher, Keith. 2012, December 26. "China Opens Longest High-Speed Rail Line,"
New York Times, https://www.nytimes.com/2012/12/27/business/global/worlds
-longest-high-speed-rail-line-opens-in-china.html. Accessed July 12, 2021.

Campbell, Kurt and Ely Ratner. 2018. "The China Reckoning: How Beijing Defied
American Expectations." *Foreign Affairs*, 97(2): 60–70.

Case, Anne and Angus Deaton. 2017. "Mortality and Morbidity in the 21st
Century." Brookings Papers on Economic Activity, Spring: 397–476.

CGTN. 2020. "The Lancet Editor-in-Chief: The US Has Wasted Time." https://www
.youtube.com/watch?v=J5d SUG3gYk8. Accessed July 12, 2021.

Chan, Heng Chee. 2019, June 18. "Resisting the Polarising Pull of US-China Rivalry,"
Straits Times (Singapore). https://www.straitstimes.com/opinion/resisting-the
-polarising-pull-of-us-china-rivalry. Accessed July 12, 2021.

Cotton, Tom. 2019. "Cotton Addresses Hudson Institute on Xinjiang Province, China,"
Speech delivered February 6, 2019. https://www.cotton.senate.gov/news/speeches
/cotton-addresses-hudson-institute-on-xinjiang-province-china. Accessed July 12,
2021.

Edelman Data & Intelligence. 2020. *Edelman Trust Barometer*. New York: Edelman Data
& Intelligence.

Fan, Jean. 2019, October 11. "The American Dream Is Alive in China," *Palladium
Magazine*. https://palladiummag.com/2019/10/11/the-american-dream-is-alive-in
-china/. Accessed July 12, 2021.

Freeman, Chas W., Jr. 2019, May 3. "On Hostile Coexistence with China." Remarks to
the Freeman Spogli Institute for International Studies China Program. California:
Stanford. https://chasfreeman.net/on-hostile-coexistence-with-china/. Accessed
July 12, 2021.

Garrett-Peltier, Heidi. 2017. "Job Opportunity Cost of War." Providence: Watson
Institute, International & Public Affairs, Brown University. https://watson.brown
.edu/costsofwar/files/cow/imce/papers/2017/Job%20Opportunity%20Cost%20of
%20War%20-%20HGP%20-%20FINAL.pdf. Accessed July 8, 2021.

Horton, Benjamin. 2020, May 2. "Coronavirus: Chance of a Lifetime to Transform
Way We Live for Sustainable Future," *Straits Times*, https://www.straitstimes.com
/singapore/health/lessons-for-climate-change-chance-of-a-lifetime-to-transform
-way-we-live-for. Accessed July 12, 2021.

Ip, Greg. 2019, August 28. "Has America's China Backlash Gone Too Far?" *Wall Street
Journal*. https://www.wsj.com/articles/has-americas-china-backlash-gone-too-far
-11566990232?mod=rsswn. Accessed July 12, 2021.

Jefferson, Thomas. 1809. "Thomas Jefferson to the Republicans of Washington County,
Maryland, 31 March 1809." Founders Online. https://founders.archives.gov/
documents/Jefferson/03-01-02-0088

Kennedy, John F. 1963, June 10. "Commencement Address at American
University."Washington, DC. https://www.jfklibrary.org/archives/other-resources
/john-f-kennedy-speeches/american-university-19630610. Accessed July 12, 2021.

Kissinger, Henry. 2011. *On China*. New York: Penguin.

Luttwak, Edward N. 2012. *The Rise of China vs. the Logic of Strategy.* Cambridge, MA: Belknap Press.

Mahbubani, Kishore. 2020. *Has China Won?: The Chinese Challenge to American Primacy.* New York: Public Affairs.

Mahbubani, Kishore, and Lawrence H. Summers. 2016. "The Fusion of Civilizations: The Case for Global Optimism." *Foreign Affairs,* 95(3): 126–135.

Pillsbury, Michael. 2016. *The Hundred-Year Marathon.* New York: Harry Holt and Company.

Pew Research Center. 2013. *Economies of Emerging Markets Better Rated During Difficult Times: Global Downturn Takes Heavy Toll; Inequality Seen as Rising.* Washington, DC: Pew Research Center.

Pew Research Center. 2016. *Chinese Public Sees More Powerful Role in World, Names U.S. as Top Threat.* Washington, DC: Pew Research Center.

Pew Research Center. 2020. *U.S. Views of China Increasingly Negative Amid Coronavirus Outbreak.* Washington, DC: Pew Research Center.

Rubio, Marco. 2019, October 31. "We Must Stand Up to China's Abuse of Its Muslim Minorities," *The Guardian,* https://www.theguardian.com/commentisfree/2019/oct/31/china-uighurs-muslims-religious-minorities-marco-rubio. Accessed July 12, 2021.

Stankiewicz, Kevin. 2020, March 6. "Secretary of State Mike Pompeo Accuses China of Setting Back Coronavirus Prevention Efforts," *CNBC,* https://www.cnbc.com/2020/03/06/secretary-of-state-mike-pompeo-says-china-not-forthcoming-initially-on-coronavirus-setting-prevention-efforts-back.html. Accessed July 12, 2021.

Walt, Stephen M. 2011, October 11. "The Myth of American Exceptionalism," *Foreign Policy,* https://foreignpolicy.com/2011/10/11/the-myth-of-american-exceptionalism/. Accessed July 12, 2021.

Ward, Steven. 2019, May 4. "Because China Isn't 'Caucasian,' the U.S. Is Planning for a 'Clash of Civilizations.' That Could Be Dangerous," *Washington Post,* https://www.washingtonpost.com/politics/2019/05/04/because-china-isnt-caucasian-us-is-planning-clash-civilizations-that-could-be-dangerous/. Accessed July 12, 2021.

Watson Institute. 2021. "Costs of War." https://watson.brown.edu/costsofwar/costs/economic/budget. Accessed July 12, 2021.

Winters, Jeffrey. 2011. *Oligarchy.* New York: Cambridge University Press.

Working Group on Chinese Influence Activities in the United States. 2018. *Chinese Influence and American Interests: Promoting Constructive Vigilance.* Stanford, CA: Hoover Institution Press.

Zenko, Micah. 2014, November 6. "The Myth of the Indispensable Nation." *Foreign Policy.* https://foreignpolicy.com/2014/11/06/the-myth-of-the-indispensable-nation/. Accessed July 12, 2021.

16

CONCLUSION

The future of the liberal order

Helmut K. Anheier

One is easily tempted by cyclical interpretations when looking at the rise and fall of civilizations and empires, as many historians and social scientists have been in the past, Ferguson (2012, 296) reminds us. Imperial overstretch (Kennedy 1987) leading to internal problems of state capacity is a frequently identified reason why empires decline. This line of thinking is close to work that identifies a crucial weakness that over time triggers others, leading to general deterioration. Max Weber's (1950) analysis of the decline of the Roman Empire is perhaps the best exemplar of this approach when he identified the dependency on a sufficient supply of slaves as the Achilles heel of the Roman economy and state capacity. When Roman conquests could no longer supply the number of slaves needed to sustain its economy and society, stagnation set in, followed by a prolonged period of gradual decline and ultimately the emergence of early feudalism.

However, one should be careful applying cyclical approaches to the Western liberal order today, let alone resort to Marxist thinking of the kind that contends that modern societies ultimately develop toward some teleological end point. Instead, Ikenberry (2018, 22) argues that "the liberal international project has travelled from the eighteenth century to our own time through repeated crises, upheavals, disasters and breakdown—almost all of them worse than those appearing today" and suggests that "it is not a blueprint for an ideal world order; it is a methodology or machinery for responding to the opportunities and dangers of modernity."

For Ikenberry (2018), linking the various domestic approaches to reform the liberal order (e.g., Chapter 2 by Filip and me, or Chapter 3 by Crawford Ames, in this volume) with an international reform agenda (e.g., Chapter 11 by Kaul and Chapter 14 by Fahmy) seems essential. This policy link happened forcefully in the early twentieth century when in the United States liberal internationalism was closely tied to progressive agendas at home. By contrast, the market liberalization in the latter parts of the twentieth century were not accompanied by an international reform agenda to help manage globalization. How, then, can the liberal order be re-branded and cut its ideological affinity to late twentieth-century neoliberalism? And, recalling the Atlantic Charter signed by American President Franklin D. Roosevelt and British Prime Minister Winston Churchill in 1941 (see Chapter 1 in this volume), can the core social justice agenda be restored, even modernized?

Levitsky and Ziblatt (2018, 212) write that

> when American democracy has worked it has relied upon two norms that we often take for granted—mutual tolerance and institutional forbearance. Treating rivals as legitimate contenders for power and underutilizing one's institutional prerogatives in the spirit of fair play are not written in the American Constitution. Yet without them, our institutional checks and balances will not operate as we expect them to.

Put differently, for checks and balances to work over time, innovations are necessary for the liberal order to adjust to changing circumstances.

Indeed, the liberal order as a blueprint has repeatedly responded to shortcomings and crisis as well as opportunities. In the past, the institutionalization of political parties in the electoral process was one such innovation, as were universal suffrage and equal opportunity policies, among many others. Indeed, one is reminded of Ferguson (2012, 305–306) who emphasizes competition as the first of the six "killer apps" that gave the West a competitive advantage. As Elias (1969) reminds us, politically, economically, and socially fragmented into multiple power centers with competing institutions creating greater interdependencies over time, competition meant frequent innovations that ultimately helped shape Western civilization and ultimately also its ascendency.

Prominently, over time, economic competition extended into the political system (competitive elections) and society (social mobility and status competition), in which the rule of law and representative government first emerged in the English-speaking world to spread to more and more countries in the nineteenth and twentieth century, yielding the various forms of democracies we have today. Yet democracies as part of the liberal order are living systems and like societies and economies are rarely stable but subject to gradual changes and unforeseen discontinuities, even jolts. Plattner (2010) suggests that liberal democracies today owe much of their resilience to an ongoing balancing of two leading sources of internal opposition: populism, or in Offe's (2017) terms, popular sovereignty, on the one hand and radical pluralism, i.e., minority rights and preferences, on the other. These sources are inherently in tension with each other, and both are at work to different degrees across liberal orders, especially today. To some extent, they can cancel each other out or neutralize potentially negative outcomes that might arise, but sometimes one becomes more dominant, triggering in turn reactions by the other.

The elements of democratic malaise in many liberal orders today are closely related to the imbalances that Plattner and Offe identify, as do Crawford Ames (Chapter 3), Anderson (Chapter 7), and others in this volume. Such imbalances may well be signs of deep-seated changes occurring in societies—changes that seek answers within, and through, democratic systems that are not yet established or ready for such tasks. In this respect, Merkel (2017) argues that the tension-ridden nature of democracy and the many challenges today's democracies face should not be mistaken for the breakdown and disintegration of the liberal order generally. A search for resilience requires recalibration and innovation. Indeed, as the Hertie School's *Governance Report 2017* suggests, the democratic malaise that many countries within the liberal order experience implies attempts at change and a search for remedies.

Democratic innovations[1]

Innovations in liberal orders arise out of tensions and frictions and are a main reason for the liberal order's resilience. Such innovations often emerge, as Smilov (2017) argues, from certain myths, for example, the unquestioned dominance of a noble fiction of the citizen eager to contribute time, resources, and efforts for the advancement of the public interest (see also Anderson, Chapter 7 in this volume). While this myth has an empowering effect for some groups, motivates the building of democratic institutions and processes, and adds to the resilience of democracies, it falls short of a reality characterized by deficiencies that include disinterested and self-serving individuals, semi-loyal elite, entrenched power structures, and malfunctioning, even corrupt, institutions (see Seibel, Chapter 8 in this volume). Thus, democratic innovations can emerge as the result of contradictions between ideals and reality, a point that also emerges from Crawford Ames' essay (Chapter 3 in this volume).

What are some of the main goals and types of democratic innovations in liberal orders? As Offe (2017) points out, there are two sets of issues innovations could address: "by-the-people" issues and "for-the-people" issues. Specifically:

- Increasing active involvement in the democratic project in places where citizens are dissatisfied or disillusioned with current politicians in office or the political system in place and are disinclined to participate through voting, taking part in political parties or associations, or even presenting themselves as candidates for elected office;
- Enhancing the voice of citizens through not only formal democratic processes such as elections but also other opportunities to make substantive contributions to decision-making and to make their opinions heard on a subject;
- Bolstering legitimacy and trust in the democratic process where skepticism of traditional democratic institutions and mechanisms is on the rise, accountability and authority are in question, or political leadership seems to ignore citizens;

- Safeguarding institutions and ensuring the rule of law to maintain a balance between security and liberty, majority and minority rule, and other tensions that are innate to democracies while preventing or at least limiting backsliding and hollowing out of democratic principles.

The main categories of types of intervention include:

- Government-initiated direct democratic innovations, such as referendums and deliberative forums, that are introduced by the government of the day, often to gain or consolidate power but also often in response to ideas or experiments started by social movements or civil society groups;
- Citizen engagement approaches, most often emerging from civil society or social movement efforts to develop new ways for citizens to make their voices heard;
- Electoral reforms that seek to expand or improve opportunities for citizens to vote in elections and for those votes to have impact;
- Institutional provisions that either strengthen the polity's capacity to monitor and manage democratic processes or create openings for new types of institutional actors.

Obviously, all these innovations seek to address at least one symptom or cause of the perceived democratic malaise in liberal orders, contribute to the resilience of new and consolidated democracies, or assist the expansion of democracy generally. None by itself is the answer to rising illiberalism, populism, or citizens' apparent distrust, disinterest, and disengagement. They rarely involve fundamental reversal and profound discontinuities. Instead, as Smilov (2017) notes on Eastern Europe, they are typically of a more incremental and gradual nature, trying to fix and improve rather than displace. And, as witnessed in Hungary and Poland over the last decade, the reverse is also possible.

Innovations that seem to be taking place on the margins of democratic systems can still have significant consequences. At first glance, automatic voter registration may seem a rather insignificant change, but it could have a strong impact on political inclusion and hence participation, as a higher number of registered voters is likely to result in increased voter turnout, thereby influencing election results. Other seemingly marginal changes include absentee voting and early voting, which increase the potential pool of voters and, like automatic voter registration, might well impact the outcome of important elections.

Challenges to, and innovations in, democratic systems are significantly path dependent and context bound. Strict voter identification requirements may be commonplace in many countries but raise issues of access in the US due to historical precedent (Kuo 2017). Media-based political parties can be considered an innovation in Eastern Europe given the historical and regional context, but did they foster democracy in places such as Italy under Berlusconi? New online forms of political activism (Hall 2017) and social movements (Della Porta and

Felicetti 2017) can broaden access and provide voice, but what if they replicate or even reinforce political fault lines and leave a divided polity and civil society?

In other words, even those types of innovations that could indeed be considered best practices cannot necessarily be translated seamlessly into other contexts, as has been the case for participatory budgeting. Developed in Porto Alegre, Brazil as a political strategy that combined social justice aims with a set of administrative reforms, related projects have been undertaken successfully in Brazil and elsewhere in Latin America. As a best practice that has become a politically neutral device to improve governance, its application in Europe has marginalized the social justice principle and the administrative reform goal and has thus had little impact, if any (Pogrebinschi 2017; Ganuza and Baiocchi 2012). The translation process could, of course, lead to further innovation, as in Latin America, or it could result in disillusionment, as seems to be the case in some parts of Eastern Europe.

Thus, innovations in democratic systems, as in the liberal order generally, are highly context bound and path dependent, which makes their generation and adoption very conditional and riddled with externalities and dilemmas as well as opportunities and risks. Managing and caring for democracy within a liberal order require constant questioning and monitoring, a kind of general stewardship to maintain political checks and balances, test the actions of leaders to ensure responsibility and accountability, pay attention to socioeconomic issues such as equity and inequality, and create awareness that sovereignty is limited. Such stewardship has been, and continues to be, in short supply.

Culture of innovations and change

Yet the future of the liberal order depends on more than innovations of the core democratic system alone. Many others are necessary for adjusting the liberal order to today's changed and changing circumstances. Indeed, for realizing Ikenberry's (2018, 22) notion that "it is a methodology or machinery for responding to the opportunities and dangers of modernity" a culture of innovation is needed. That culture can ensure that state and society, or in other words, democracy and civil society, are mutually re-enforcing. Acemoglu and Robinson (2019) use the image of Lewis Carroll's "Red Queen's race," in which state and society must run at about equal speeds if they are to maintain their position, let alone advance.

In other words, the Western liberal order cannot stand still, and even to survive, it must innovate and adjust in the case of its many internal contradictions and external challenges. The chapters in this volume offer deep insights into what these contradictions and challenges are. Many also present recommendations and suggestions as to how the liberal order could react, what needs changing and what adjustments in the "Red Queen's race" might be necessary for state and society to remain strong, democratic, and open. These include:

- Creating social policy buffers for population groups threatened by economic globalization;
- Revisiting the notion of individual freedom of speech in the context of changes in communication technologies;
- Modernize the notion of citizenship;
- Initiating a participatory process towards a new economic consensus to move beyond the limitations of the neoliberal economic model;
- Revitalizing the concept of public service and ethos;
- Considering the importance of sense-making, meaning, and identity in increasingly secular Western societies;
- Making multilateralism sovereignty-compatible and sovereignty multilateralism-compatible;
- Anticipating the likely challenges to the global financial system;
- Engaging in a proactive approach towards a new global consciousness or responsibility;
- Reframing the changing geopolitical dynamics to avoid the traps international relations experts anticipate.

The domestic liberal order and fundamental issues

In our chapter "How to square the circle between economic globalization, social cohesion, and liberal democracy?," Alexandru Filip and I provide an empirical formulation and operationalization of two theorems of increasing relevance in the currently tumultuous international political economy: Dani Rodrik's Globalization Trilemma (2011) and Ralf Dahrendorf's Quandary (1995). Both theorems in essence posit that democracy, national sovereignty, and global economic integration are mutually incompatible. Our findings, however, show considerable nuance, as individual country performance is too different to support the broad assertions Rodrik and Dahrendorf make in their respective writings. One interpretation of the findings suggests that countries rarely escape the tensions implied in the Trilemma/Quandary, but they can generally manage them, evoking a pattern of push-and-pull among drivers and stressors. The drivers of economic globalization find at least some correction in policy action to better deal with stressors and thereby reduce governance problems. Countries that manage to create a "buffer" between the forces of globalization on the one hand and the socioeconomic position of population groups threatened by economic stressors on the other fared better than those which did not. The insights from our chapter point to the importance a proactive, forward-looking social policy in managing the inherent tensions the Trilemma and Quandary highlight (see also Garrett 1998).

Beverly Crawford Ames' chapter "Why the future of the liberal order is in danger and what we can do to safeguard it" argues that to rely on liberal principles as a foundation for social order is to lean on a weak reed. That reed can bend and break in the face of entrenched inequality and precarity, weakened communities, and threats to rational discourse via new communication technologies that facilitate the spread of disinformation. She suggests that liberal principles must be drastically reformed to include a redefinition of the principle of individual freedom to include a strong repudiation of hate speech and intolerance, and strict regulation of digital technologies; a reversal of the growth of economic inequality and precarity (concretely, through a tax on wealth); and respect for community and a way to incorporate "the other" into communities without threatening their boundaries (concretely, through institutions like public schools). Without such reforms, liberal communities will not have the ability to oppose antiliberal forces.

"What future for politics?" asks Jan Zielonka. He fears that the political interventions undertaken by governments to fight COVID-19 harmed a democratic system already challenged. The measures were taken amidst growing doubts about both the willingness and the capacity of governments to undertake major reforms to reduce inequalities, curb racism, or protect the natural environment. Therefore, he suggests, we must try to build democracy on pillars other than representation alone: inclusive deliberation, fair ways of contestation, greater transparency, and most crucially, broader participation are essential components of reformed democracy. In addition, we need to rebuild public administration systems that have been weakened by neoliberal policies, new public management approaches and lacking investments. Across all levels of government and administration, this reform includes the rediscovery of the meaning of public ethos as expressed in the noble term "civil servants."

Linda Yueh addresses the possibility of coming to a new consensus about how to govern market economies. Consensus about economic governance has broken down before, last after the Great Recession that followed the global financial crisis of 2008–2009. In a very different set of circumstances, the COVID-19 pandemic has led governments to take extraordinary measures in all areas of citizens' lives. This has further fueled the need to discuss how to rebuild the consensus about the most appropriate economic system. Is there a twenty-first-century equivalent to the transformation of the nineteenth-century capitalist system into twentieth-century welfare state capitalism? Building such a consensus will take a long time and involve a battle for hearts as well as minds. The process may be as important as the outcomes and requires a robust debate that involves many voices, and not just economic experts.

What polarization means for democracy is the topic of Rudolf Stichweh's chapter. The desirable type of democratic society is a non-divided society based on universal formal equality, personal freedom and an inclusive system of solidarity. This, obviously, is not the society we live in, he argues, as the basic value preferences and promises of modernity remain unrealized for many. However, inequalities by themselves do not bring about divided societies. As long as inequalities produce continuous gradations of life chances, there will be hope of upward social mobility and status change. Once discontinuities develop, social divisions and asymmetrical dependencies arise which soon transform into cultural polarization. Stichweh does not venture to propose solutions, but rather highlights aspects that must be understood to come to solutions that might overcome these deficiencies.

Lisa Anderson examines the dilemmas of citizenship in the twenty-first century and wonders whether the Middle East holds lessons for the West. Citizenship has two fundamental dimensions linked to the two faces of the modern state: sovereignty based on Westphalian criteria (the world was organized into independent and equal state units) and that based on Weberian criteria (the state was meant to be the only legitimate holder of physical force). Citizenship reflects a formal, abstract, legal relationship between the individual and the state, outlining the mutual rights and responsibilities of these modern individuals and the public authorities. In theory, citizenship was to supersede other sources of political identity and authority. In the Middle East, however, effective citizenship has long eroded, and in the absence of reliable access to rights-based government services, people turned to alternative identities and communities (family, ethnicity/sect, "shareholder," Facebook "friends"). There, the rights we cavalierly call "universal" are privileges accorded to certain social groups and rewards for good behavior. The lesson then is that, at the very least, a common understanding of the notion of citizenship for the twenty-first century is required. At its core are three levels of rights: belonging to a community (or nation) with which one has a genuine connection and in which one can effectively exercise civil rights. Difficult as it might be to imagine, we need to acknowledge that there is no other mechanism beyond the state designed to establish a formal community and to guarantee the realization of these rights.

Functioning impartial public administration systems are essential for the liberal order. Yet can we trust them, asks Wolfgang Seibel. Trust is the basis of delegated power, especially where government is entrusted with the protection of human security. Given the increased complexity and interdependence of public administration in an age of new public management, identifying structural risk zones of public administration and normative appeals insisting on mindfulness remain insufficient as long as predictable counterincentives to recognize risk zones and to take measures to contain their harmful effects are not systematically addressed. Insisting on personal responsibility for the sake of maintaining professional and institutional integrity is, from that normative perspective, a crucial ingredient of making public authorities high reliability organizations in the real world of a democratic polity. As in Zielonka's chapter (Chapter 4), the notion of a public service ethos becomes central.

Religion has been one of the underestimated forces of the early twenty-first century. So Mark Juergensmeyer's question "Is religion dead?" is not whether religion will survive, but in what way. Thinking about religion as alternative reality providing moral commitment is a fundamental part of the creative imagination, a constituent of culture as certain as art or music. Religious traditions can be a future source for a worldwide appreciation of the universality of the principles underlying human rights. So are the instincts of a new generation of global citizens whose sense of spirituality and morality know no traditionally national or culturally limited bounds. And like Max Weber saw a close affinity between the Protestant ethic and the spirit of capitalism, the generation of global citizens can be the forebearers of broader human spirituality that transcends the chasms between traditional religions.

Culture is one of the most complex words of the English language, Williams (1975, 87) famously stated in his book *Keywords*. The concept of liberty may well be a close contender. "How do culture and liberty relate?" is the topic of Roland Bernecker and Ronald Grätz's chapter. For them, culture has the dual function of providing a much-needed relief from the strains of freedom, while at the same time offering the tools that empower us to envisage liberty in the first place. The cultural is constituted by two contradictory functions: to strengthen the binding forces of the collective with its shared values, norms, and narratives, while also nourishing the individual's resources in confirming its singularity. The balance between culture and freedom now depends on the ability to come to terms with growing diversity (long resisted with a narrow understanding of cultural uniformity at the level of the nation state), the exclusive notion of Western cosmopolitanism (to overcome the lingering effects of coloniality), and environmental sustainability.

The international liberal order and world society

In her chapter, Inge Kaul wonders why international cooperation in support of global public goods is failing. And, if cooperation failure is indeed contributing to the lengthening list of underprovided global public goods, how could its effectiveness be enhanced? The two main drivers behind flailing multilateralism are the rising trend toward global multipolarity and the fear of losing sovereignty on the one hand and the growing demand for global public goods on the other. New operating principles are called for which would both make multilateralism sovereignty-compatible and make a multilateralism-compatible exercise of sovereignty possible. States would consider the regional and global when making national policy choices, including the sovereignty of other states, while being mindful of external interference and cross-border spillover effects. States would make necessary arrangements to contribute their fair share of financial and nonfinancial resources to agreed-upon collective endeavors, which are to be undertaken collectively at the international level as complements of the domestic corrective measures. Finally, states would comply with international monitoring, evaluation and reporting requirements in the interest of global transparency, mutual accountability, and trust-building.

Michael Zürn questions the need for a political vision in a globalized world, and sees a world characterized by a cleavage between communitarian and cosmopolitan political forces. The option of re-nationalizing societies to the extent that externalities are significantly reduced seems to be structurally impossible: we live in a world society that cannot be brought back to independent national societies by sheer political decisions. The alternative of democratizing international institutions would be enormously difficult, drawn out, and the subject of strong national resistance, but it is not structurally impossible. The first step would require opening decision-making in international institutions to public debates. If international institutions are to be part of public debates, a second step becomes possible: a discussion about a democratic vision of international institutions. There is no blueprint for democratic international institutions, and global experts cannot impose such a vision. Developing it requires the participation of both communitarians and cosmopolitans.

Focusing on the financial system, Howard Davies explores the impact of the COVID-19 pandemic as of mid-2021 and foresees certainties, probabilities, and unknowns as to future developments. Certainties at the time include a huge and sustained increase in public debt, a sharp debt increase in the private sector, and more financial services provided digitally. Likely outcomes are more banks in financial difficulties, closer cooperation between banks and governments, the establishment of central bank digital currencies, the continued decline of cash, and more conflicts between national and international regulators. Unknowns stem mostly from debt overhang, such as inflation or investments, and the global financial system, for example the continuation of dollar hegemony, the co-existence of competing monetary blocs, the emergence of international monetary federations, or the spread of international monetary anarchy.

Nabil Fahmy addresses the need for a collective social conscience. For him, the great questions of our time are not about the success or failure of the liberal world order, or the efficacy of a liberal versus an illiberal order. Rather, all systems of public order are being challenged domestically, regionally, and globally, and a paramount challenge of our time is to determine the reason for this simultaneous onslaught on societal and governance systems. International cooperation is not a predetermined process, but a choice. It is the voluntary acceptance of global interaction for the benefit of the international community as a whole. Such cooperation is essential if we are to establish a collective social conscience. He recommends that the United Nations Secretary General organize a broad process of debate and consultations involving many voices and stakeholders, followed by an intensive effort of quiet diplomacy, both with governmental bodies and opinion-makers. As a third step, the ideas and principles resulting from the process should be put up for adoption by the community of nations at the UN General Assembly, with concrete topical issues discussed further and in depth in the respective international and regional bodies.

Examining geopolitical rivalries, Kishore Mahbubani argues that the origins of the contest lie in China's rapid growth since the Deng era, the relative socio-economic decline of the US, and the failure of the US to work out a rational, comprehensive strategy for managing China's rise. He points to what he calls grand illusions: that, as China's economy grew and prospered as a result of economic liberalization, political liberalization would naturally follow, and China would become, like America, a liberal democracy; the assumption of American virtue and Chinese malevolence; and that the vast majority of the six billion people of the world who live outside America and China will naturally gravitate to support America. Instead, he argues that it is not Chinese communism that is a threat to American democracy but China's economic success. Furthermore, there is no imminent danger of a clash of civilizations between the West and China: a fundamental contradiction would only arise if China tries to export its values to America, and America tries to export its values to China. In the end, in his view, it is in the interest of humanity to see America and China work together to contain their geopolitical rivalry.

In summary, and despite their critical assessments, the chapters in this volume are also encouraging in that they point to a simple message: the current challenges can be managed within the liberal order, and the negative consequences of globalization, open markets or climate change, among many other problems, can be offset by forward-looking policies that seek to avoid regional disparities, deskilling of the labor force, environmental degradation, loss of trust, social exclusion or falling in either the Thucydides's Trap (Allison 2017) or the Kindleberger Trap (Nye 2017). To make progress and to nurture the culture of innovations and reforms that is needed, it is crucial to reinvigorate social mobility, reduce widespread inequalities, and stop viewing the social as separate from the economic. In the words of economists Katharina Lima de Miranda and Dennis J. Snower (2020), we must recouple the economic and the social to advance on the political. The very future of the liberal order and liberal democracy may well depend on our willingness to take up the call and our success in doing so.

Concluding thoughts: the question of will and leadership

Collectively, the chapters in this volume express an essential feature of Western liberal societies. While the liberal order provides a machinery for responding to the opportunities and dangers of modernity (Ikenberry 2018), it does so based on competing economic, political and social models that generate tensions and conflicts of many kinds. These can trigger innovations and reforms, or at least a greater awareness of the issues involved, be they increasing inequality, climate change or deficiencies in democracy. Unlike other orders, and despite a most tragic record of wars and upheavals, as Dahrendorf forcefully argued when considering the relationship between conflict and liberty (1988), it is the capacity to innovate and to self-correct, to manage conflicts in a positive way rather than through widespread violence, suppression or revolutions that has contributed to the resilience of the West.

Yet are these largely institutional and structural characteristics enough? Ferguson (2012, 325) is doubtful and asks whether it might be that "the real threat is posed not by China, Islam or CO2 emissions, but by our own loss of faith in the civilization we inherited from our ancestors." The calls for a renewal of public ethos and stewardship (see Chapter 4 by Zielonka and Chapter 8 by

Seibel, in this volume) and a reform of basic liberal principles (see Chapter 3 by Crawford Ames) as well as the development of a global ethic (see Chapter 9 by Juergensmeyer and Chapter 14 by Fahmy) address this issue.

At the same time, there is no new vision and anti-thesis, no real attractive alternative. The governance orders of China and Islam have limited global potential and appeal, the former a version of the Despotic Leviathan in Acemoglu and Robertson's (2019) terms, and the latter their Paper Leviathan based on authoritarian tendencies with weak state capacity. They write:

> Human progress depends on the expansion of the state's capacity to meet new challenges and combat all dominances, old and new, but that won't happen unless society demands it and mobilizes to defend everybody's right. There is nothing easy or automatic about that, but it can and does happen.
>
> *(Acemoglu and Robinson 2019, 496)*

This brings us to the issue of leadership and its exercise to mobilize and express popular will to compensate for the loss of faith Ferguson (2012) and, in this volume, Fahmy (Chapter 14) and Juergensmeyer (Chapter 9) hint at. More than any other event since the global financial crisis of 2008–2009, the COVID-19 pandemic has revealed the importance of leadership. At the same time, leadership in many countries has been poor, with even longstanding democracies displaying autocratic temptations toward a "strongman" leader (Walker 2021). Max Weber famously argued that quality leadership requires a balance of "an ethics of personal conviction" and "an ethics of responsibility" (Robin 2020). During the pandemic, failure to achieve such a balance was clearly visible, and detached, self-serving or cynical leadership styles all too common. In the context of lower trust and increased polarization, leadership can become a brutal power play, leaving little room for balancing personal conviction and responsibility.

There is a clear dual causality in leadership: leadership emerges from strong, open institutions and good leaders foster an effective democratic system. Indeed, democratic leadership recruitment and formation need open systems: inequality of opportunity, as Crawford Ames reminds us in Chapter 3 of this volume, prevents the search for and rise of such leadership based on talent rather than connections, with elite closure posing a serious problem. At the same time, democratic leadership can mobilize liberal democratic sentiments and practices for building trust, healing polarization, and being accountable to the public.

We can therefore say that leadership is the most "active" ingredient, as it dynamically shapes all other aspects of the governance of liberal orders. Leadership creates and nurtures that culture of innovation the resilience of the liberal order needs; it encourages innovations that will revitalize and reset the "machinery" of the liberal order so that it can resolve the tensions and conflicts that have arisen and will invariably arise.

Note

1 This section draws on Anheier, Kaufmann and List (2017).

References

Acemoglu, Daron and James A. Robinson. 2019. *The Narrow Corridor: States, Societies and the Fate of Liberty.* New York: Penguin.

Allison, Graham T. 2017. *Destined for War: Can America and China Escape Thucydides's Trap?* New York: Houghton Mifflin Harcourt.

Anheier, Helmut K., Sonja Kaufmann, and Regina A. List. 2017. "Innovations at a Glance." In Hertie School of Governance. *The Governance Report 2017,* 165–175. Oxford: Oxford University Press.

Dahrendorf, Ralf. 1988. *The Modern Social Conflict: The Politics of Liberty.* London: Routledge.

Dahrendorf, Ralf. 1995. *Economic Opportunity, Civil Society and Political Liberty.* UNRISD Discussion Paper 58. Geneva: United Nations Research Institute for Social Development.

Della Porta, Donatella and Andrea Felicetti. 2017. "Democratic Innovations and Social Movements." In Hertie School of Governance. *The Governance Report 2017,* 127–142. Oxford: Oxford University Press.

Elias, Norbert. 1969. *The Civilizing Process, Vol. I. The History of Manners.* Oxford: Blackwell.

Ferguson, Niall. 2012. *Civilization: The West and the Rest.* New York: Penguin.

Ganuza, Ernesto and Gianpaolo Baiocchi. 2012. "The Power of Ambiguity: How Participatory Budgeting Travels the Globe." *Journal of Public Deliberation,* 8(2). https://doi.org/10.16997/jdd.142.

Garrett, Geoffrey. 1998. "Global Markets and National Politics: Collision Course or Virtuous Circle?" *International Organization,* 52(4): 149–176.

Hall, Nina. 2017. "Innovations in Activism in the Digital Era: Campaigning for Refugee Rights 2015-16." In Hertie School of Governance. *The Governance Report 2017,* 143–156. Oxford: Oxford University Press.

Lima de Miranda, Katharina and Dennis J. Snower. 2020. "Recoupling Economic and Social Prosperity." *Global Perspectives,* 1(1): 11867. https://doi.org/10.1525/001c.11867

Ikenberry, G. John. 2018. "The End of the Liberal International Order?" *International Affairs,* 94(1): 7–23. https://doi.org/10.1093/ia/iix241

Kennedy, Paul. 1987. *The Rise and Fall of Great Powers: Economic Changes and Military Conflict from 1500 to 2000.* New York: Random House.

Kuo, Didi. 2017. "The Contradictions of Democratic Innovation in the United States." In Hertie School of Governance. *The Governance Report 2017,* 43–56. Oxford: Oxford University Press.

Levitsky, Steven and Daniel Ziblatt. 2018. *How Democracies Die.* New York: Crown.

Merkel, Wolfgang. 2017. "The Limits of Democratic Innovations in Established Democracies." In Hertie School of Governance. *The Governance Report 2017,* 111–126. Oxford: Oxford University Press.

Nye, Joseph S. 2017, January 9. "The Kindleberger Trap." Project Syndicate. https://www.project-syndicate.org/commentary/trump-china-kindleberger-trap-by-joseph-s--nye-2017-01?barrier=accesspaylog. Accessed September 22, 2021.

Offe, Claus. 2017. "On Democratic Innovations." In Hertie School of Governance. *The Governance Report 2017,* 21–24. Oxford: Oxford University Press.

Plattner, Marc F. 2010. "Populism, Pluralism, and Liberal Democracy." *Journal of Democracy*, 21(1): 81–92.

Pogrebinschi, Thamy. 2017. "Democratic Innovations: Lessons from Beyond the West." In Hertie School of Governance. *The Governance Report 2017*, 57–72. Oxford: Oxford University Press.

Robin, Corey. 2020, November 12. "The Professor and the Politician," *The New Yorker*, https://www.newyorker.com/books/under-review/max-weber-the-professor-and -the-politician. Accessed September 22, 2021.

Rodrik, Dani. 2011. *The Globalization Paradox: Why Global Markets, States, and Democracy Can't Coexist*. New York: W. W. Norton & Company.

Smilov, Daniel. 2017. "Democratic Innovation and the Politics of Fear: Lessons from Eastern Europe." In Hertie School of Governance. *The Governance Report 2017*, 25–42. Oxford: Oxford University Press.

Walker, Tony. 2021, July 7. "Why the World Should Be Worried about the Rise of Strongman Politics," *The Conversation*, https://theconversation.com/why-the -world-should-be-worried-about-the-rise-of-strongman-politics-100165. Accessed September 22, 2021.

Weber, Max. 1950. "The Social Causes of the Decay of Ancient Civilization." *The Journal of General Education*, 5(1): 75–88.

Williams, Raymond. 1975. *Keywords: A Vocabulary of Culture and Society*. London: Fontana.

INDEX

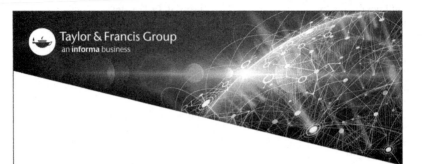

Printed in the United States
by Baker & Taylor Publisher Services